Norfolk and Suffolk Churches

Copyright © David Butcher

First published 2019 by Poppyland Publishing, Lowestoft, NR32 3BB

www.poppyland.co.uk

ISBN 978 1 909796 61 4

Designed and typeset in 12 on 14 pt Caslon Pro

Picture credits:

Author – plates 2 to 10.
Hallam-Jones D. under Creative Commons Licence – plate 1.
Page M. – front cover top, (Heckingham), bottom (Mutford)
Palmer J. J. N. , Slater G., and opendomesday.org under Creative Commons Licence – front cover (background).

Norfolk and Suffolk Churches

The Domesday Record

A Handbook for Reference and Use

David Butcher

POPPYLAND PUBLISHING

Contents

Illustrations

Acknowledgements

A work of this nature would not have been possible without the assistance of other agencies and people. In the first instance, the Phillimore double-volume sets of the Domesday text and translation made possible convenient, direct access to the recorded data of 1086. The whole series of publications has had its criticism over the years, which it is unnecessary to rehearse here, but it nevertheless constitutes a most useful resource for anyone wishing to study the nature of English communities at the time that William I's national survey was carried out and the documentation compiled. While perhaps having deficiencies for specialist Domesday-text scholars, the Phillimore books remain for the majority of people interested the most accessible and reasonably priced means of studying the late Anglo-Saxon world in terms of socio-economic and demographic structure, of topographical features, and of ecclesiastical provision.

Much closer in connection to the writer in personal terms is the creator of the maps used to illustrate geographical and statistical aspects of the text and, as in previous publications, a debt of gratitude is owed to Ivan Bunn for his cartographical skills and attention to detail. His expertise in graphics has enhanced the overall effect of the work by producing images that are able to give visual expression to both tabulated data and topographical commentary. An expression of thanks is also due to my wife, Ann, who took and processed the images of the local churches used in Chapter 3, and to Leslie Parfitt of the Lowestoft Heritage Workshop Centre who produced print-offs of the text for the necessary tasks of proof-reading and editing. Finally, Gareth Davies of Poppyland Publishing has been sufficiently supportive of the work to bring it to the attention of anyone who feels that such a book has a useful part to play in the study of East Anglian history.

Introduction

Much has been speculated and written about the churches of the counties of Norfolk and Suffolk, partly in terms of their having far more places of Christian worship than any of the other English shires (Lincolnshire excepted) and partly in response to the considerable disparity in numbers between them. Attempts have also been made to place their origins and location within what may be termed the "minster and satellites model", identified particularly by John Blair as forming the basic structure of ecclesiastical provision during the Anglo-Saxon period. This work aims simply at presenting the Domesday data relating to the churches of both counties, as an aid to anyone interested in their existence at whatever level that interest functions: specialist or otherwise. It is meant to serve as a handbook, assisting investigation on an individual level (or as a group activity) into the location and distribution of the churches recorded in William I's great survey. Certain factors in their founding seem to be suggested in, or by, the material, but no didactic statement is intended regarding it – and should not be assumed to be present. At the same time, part of the intention of this book is to encourage some degree of re-appraisal of church origins and their pattern of distribution in the two counties under scrutiny.

The information contained in the various tables derives from the double-volume set for each county, published by Phillimore in 1984 and 1986 under the general editorship of John Morris (part of a 35-volume series produced between 1973 and 1986). Philippa Brown was dedicated editor for the Norfolk volumes and Alex Rumble for their Suffolk counterparts. Each pair of books has the original Latin text on the left-hand page, faced by a translation to the right. Detailed notes and copious indexing facilitate the reader's use of the material, though inevitably (given the huge complexity of the task) minor anomalies and errors are to be found. Overall, for the local historian, at all levels of activity whether it be in-depth or more cursory, the Phillimore sets are a valuable resource in assisting research of all kinds into the presence of churches in the counties of Norfolk and Suffolk – and no doubt in other counties as well. They are, furthermore, an essential aid towards understanding the economic and social structure of both shires, as well as their topography and governance.

In the matter of providing a peripheral context for the data relating to ecclesiastical provision during the Anglo-Saxon and (possibly) immediate post-Conquest periods, use has been made of other works. Tom Williamson's *The Origins of Norfolk* (Manchester, 1993) and Peter Warner's *The Origins of Suffolk* (Manchester, 1996) provide a number of points of comparison and contrast regarding the possible origins of parish churches, as do Norman Scarfe's *The Suffolk Landscape* (London, 1972), his *Suffolk in the Middle Ages* (1986) and David Dymond's *The Norfolk Landscape* (London, 1985). Further information relating to both counties is to be found in H. C. Darby, *The Domesday Geography of Eastern England*, 3rd ed. (Cambridge, 1971), David Dymond and Edward Martin (eds.), *An Historical Atlas of Suffolk*, 2nd ed. (Ipswich, 1989) and Trevor Ashwin and Alan Davison (eds.), *An Historical Atlas of Norfolk*, 3rd ed. (Chichester, 2005). Relating to Norfolk alone is Matthew Godfrey's PhD thesis (University of Leicester, 2007), 'The Churches, Settlements and Archaeology of Early Medieval Norfolk'.

These particular studies, taken collectively, have a positive contribution to make in the matter of theories concerning the founding of churches, but all very much by way of overview. *Landscapes of Monastic Foundation* (Woodbridge, 2004), Tim Pestell's authoritative study of the establishment of religious houses in East Anglia during Anglo-Saxon and post-Conquest times (with its pronounced archaeological and topographical base), sits outside the remit here, but is recommended reading concerning the establishment of Christianity in the region. The same applies to Richard Hoggett's most interesting paper, 'The Early Christian Landscape of East Anglia' (deriving from his University of East Anglia PhD thesis of 2007), which raises the possibility of a widespread 7th century evangelisation of Norfolk and Suffolk – with a consequent number of churches to match. And Peter Warner's doctoral discourse, 'Blything Hundred: a Study in the Development of Settlement, AD 400-1400' (University of Leicester, 1982), has much to commend it in terms of specialist attention to both subject matter and chosen location.

What is lacking, in the very nature of the texts specifically named above, is focus on all the individual churches recorded in Domesday and on their various associated endowments of land – a specific aspect which is a major feature of this book. The work centres its attention on each and every foundation mentioned, hundred by hundred, and on the different land-holders on whose estates the buildings stood – both pre-1066 and in 1086. Following each table, explanations of the conventions adopted are given, together with statistical analysis of the data. The only aspect which sits outside presentation of the Domesday material is an indication of those churches which have round towers – mainly relating to buildings which are still to be seen intact, but with reference also to a minority which are ruins of one kind or another. The decision was taken to identify round-tower churches, not only because a good deal of attention has been devoted to their origins in terms of architectural style and building methods, but also because they are such a distinctive feature of East Norfolk and North-east Suffolk particularly. The writer has no intention of being drawn into specialist discussion (sometimes controversial) of the nature of their construction, but is happy for their geographical location(s) to be indicated in the cause of making their presence even better known than it already is. Given the interest in them, and in the work of the Round Tower Churches Society itself, it is to be hoped that this book may add something to the extant body of knowledge concerning them.

In order to place both Norfolk and Suffolk in a national context, a statement of some preliminary statistical work regarding the Domesday Survey is necessary. The overall number of churches recorded in England has been put at 2,061 in 1,796 communities, with a further 491 settlements having a priest attributed to them but with no church building referred to – this, out of a total number of 13,400 places in all.[1] H.C. Darby, in *The Domesday Geography of Eastern England* (cited two paragraphs above and simply referred to hereafter, in Chapters 1 and 2, as Darby), pp. 138 and 190, does not provide specific numbers of churches for either Norfolk or Suffolk. Instead, he gives 217 communities in the former county as having places of worship (not including the towns of Norwich, Thetford and Yarmouth) and 345 in the latter (exclusive of the towns of Beccles, Bury, Clare, Dunwich, Eye, Ipswich and Sudbury). The writer of this book has not included Norwich in his Norfolk data because of the size and complexity of the township, as well as the uncertainty surrounding just how many churches it had, but he has included Yarmouth and given alternative numbers for the presence or omission of Thetford. Similarly, in Suffolk, Bury and Ipswich have been omitted for reasons similar to those adduced for Norwich, but the other five places included.

After much counting and recounting, and allowing for slight ambiguity of text in places, the Domesday figure for Norfolk is a total of 226-7 communities (out of 714 in the county, as a whole) having 270-2 churches between them, with Thetford included, and 256-8 without it. For Suffolk, 357 communities (out of 634) were found to have had 448+ churches – the latter number (as with Norfolk) being in excess of that of the total of "churched" settlements and resulting from some places having more than one building. Darby mentions this characteristic in connection with both counties, but does not attempt to work out a specific, finalised figure for either of them. His reference to the 491 English communities with no churches recorded, but with the presence of a priest, is mirrored in both Norfolk and Suffolk – but only minimally (probably because of the large number of churches present). Norfolk has seven "priest only" references, Suffolk ten – and three of the latter refer to the same man in one particular local area. If national numbers of places with churches and of the churches themselves are taken, Norfolk and Suffolk combined had 33% of the former and 35% of the latter. Individually, as counties, Norfolk had 13% and 13%, Suffolk 20% and 22%. Darby's overall figures in the matter of communities with churches must therefore be approached with a certain degree of caution, which is perhaps no surprise in view of the sheer extent and scope of his work.[2]

Earlier estimates of the number of churches in each county may be usefully referred to at this point, rather than later on in the text. Sir Henry Ellis, in his *A General Introduction to Domesday Book*, vol. 1 (London, 1833), p. 287, records 243 for Norfolk and 364 for Suffolk – the latter figure repeated by B.A. Lees in her 'Introduction to the Suffolk Domesday', in *The Victoria County History of Suffolk*, vol. 1 (London, 1911), fn. 367, p. 402. She also cites, in the same foot-note, the total of 398 arrived at by the Revd. J. Cox in his 'Ecclesiastical History', in volume 2 of the *VCH* (London, 1907), p. 9 – an essay in which he also notes the presence of chapels in Thorney and Wissett. The single figure available for Norfolk is closer to the one established by the writer of this work, while the two produced for Suffolk (though falling further short) do at least maintain the differential between the two counties.

As a supplement to the main mass of material, what may be termed two corollaries have been appended in different forms. The first (presented as Chapter 3) is a study of the half-hundreds of Lothingland and Mutford as a possible model for areas that were comparatively lacking in churches according to the Domesday record, but had all their parishes fully operational by the end of the twelfth century. This is followed by a series of tables, set out as Appendices 1-4, showing a) the valuation of church land-endowments for which such data is available and parishes with existing round-tower buildings, and b) the presence of freewomen as land-holders and the possible role some of them may have had either as founders of churches or as encouragers of other people to establish them. Their importance in Suffolk seems to have been much more notable than in Norfolk, and the former county also had a much more significant number of high-born women who appear to have been influential in communities where churches were in existence. A fifth appendix provides analysis of the place-names of Lothingland and Mutford half-hundreds as back-up to, and extension of, the material presented in Chapter 3, while a sixth one records the number of dedications to Margaret of Antioch and King Edmund of East Anglia, looking at the former's possible connection with Roger Bigot (al. Bigod), Sheriff of Norfolk and Suffolk in the post-Conquest period, and at the latter's comparatively small number of dedications in his former realm.

A number of conventions have been adopted, in order to make the material more accessible to the reader, most of which are explained *in situ* below the tables. However, there are a few which can be usefully referred to here. The first is a stylistic matter: instead of writing numbers up to ninety-nine as words, Arabic numerals have mainly been used instead – this, in order to enable information have an immediate impact and make it easy to discern. Next, is what may be termed a concentrating mechanism in the summaries of land-holding patterns for all the individual hundreds, whereby a tenant-name such as Ranulph brother of Ilger has the comma of apposition following the first element omitted – this, to avoid any possible ambiguity caused by using it. Frequent use of semi-colons and dashes has been made in places, in tables and commentary, in the interests of clarity and also to avoid misunderstanding of the data presented. Likewise, use of the multiplication-symbol x (e.g. x 5) serves to indicate the number of times a person is referred to in the data recorded, while the Latin preposition *sub* (appearing as sub, in text) shows a tenant being under the patronage or jurisdiction of a social superior. Finally, an attempt has been made (wherever possible and within the writer's capabilities) to render Anglo-Saxon names in Old English form rather than the Latinised versions used by the Domesday commissioners themselves. The only exceptions are monarchs and their spouses – relating chiefly to Edward (Eadweard) the Confessor and Queen Edith (Ealdgyth) – which appear in their commonly used modern forms.

The use of extended (and extensive) tables, with vertical layout of the data, is the easiest way of imparting the information relating to the churches of Norfolk and Suffolk, in order to make it accessible to the reader. In fact, tabular structure is the best way of revealing what Domesday has to say when dealing with any of its material – particularly when there is a large amount of it. Much attention has been given to the matter of accuracy in the overall process of presentation, but such is the complexity of the material at times that no guarantee of totally faultless information can be given. There are also times when the Domesday text appears to be ambiguous or contradictory, which calls for personal interpretation to be applied, and this has been done wherever felt to be necessary. Both conventional brackets and square have been used, either to question the textual information given or to add to it in the cause of elucidation, and it is hoped that reinforcement of this kind will be found to be useful. There is also periodic, deliberate repetition of textual explanation in the notes following the tables, to aid targeted investigation of particular areas of Norfolk and Suffolk, and even of individual churches alone. The whole purpose of this book is to reveal the body of extant material relating to the churches of the two counties, as it was found to be in the year 1086, and to allow it to be used as widely and flexibly as required. As much care as possible has been taken (within the writer's capabilities) to achieve accuracy and consistency in its presentation – with a number of periodic cross-checks carried out – and an apology is offered in advance for any errors which might be detected.

In both Chapter 1 and Chapter 2 there are sections which summarise the details of tenancy in 1066 and 1086 (revealed in Tables 2, 4, 8 and 10), hundred by hundred. These parts of the text are presented in prose form and are meant to give an overview of the pattern of land-holding connected with those estates which had churches recorded in the Domesday Survey. It proved challenging to devise a set of conventions which provide an accessible, but straightforward, account of who held what – but, hopefully, this has been achieved. As part of this summative process, those hundreds which are known to have had early centres of Christian activity have had these agencies not only referred to, but consideration given to any possible, discernible influence they may have had regarding the establishment of churches in their various localities. The overall judgement reached is that it appears to have been minimal at best where Domesday churches are concerned, but that it is not possible to make informed comment regarding the situation three or four hundred years earlier, prior to the major, severely disruptive Danish invasions.

In conclusion, it needs to be said that the writer is not an Anglo-Saxon specialist, but has had a long-standing interest in the period because of the influence it exercised on the formation of England itself. Many commentators always appear eager to pronounce on the profound changes in the country caused by the Norman Conquest – though their judgements often seem to consist mainly of comments on the visual legacy of architectural developments, whereby stone-built castles, cathedrals and abbeys came to dominate the landscape and declare the authority of the invaders in establishing a new order. There were profound social and economic shifts, of course – not least, in the near-total removal of the Anglo-Saxon governing élite (both secular and ecclesiastical) and in the downgrading of the position held by women – but it should never be forgotten that the Normans inherited what was arguably the most efficient administrative mechanism in Europe at the time and re-shaped it for their own use and advantage. With the passage of time, the legacy of the Anglo-Saxon world (including a notable Danish influence) ultimately proved more significant than that of the invaders. The native language eventually became the national one; place-names retained their time-honoured identity; the configuration of shire, hundred and parish defined both landscape and local government; the common law of the land developed from ancient custom and practice; and both invaders and their conquered subjects progressively merged their separate identities to form one people.

Notes

1 H.C. Darby, *Domesday England* (Cambridge, 1977), p. 53. Any reference to a priest would seem to suggest some kind of ministry being exercised, without there necessarily having been a building in which to carry out acts of worship. In Christian belief, the Church consists of its people, not a structure raised to stage observance and ritual.

2 One other cautionary note to be made regarding Darby, *Domesday Geography*, p. 138, concerns the five Norfolk hundreds cited as having one recorded church only: Earsham, Forehoe, North Greenhoe, Grimshoe and Smethdon. Earsham, in fact, had three or four churches and Grimshoe three.

SNITT
ERLEY

There is / berew
ick comprising
/ carucate of
land always 7
villans & /
bordar always
/ plough bel-
onging to the
men then worth
£20, / night's
honey & 100s
in customary
dues now worth
£50

Plate 1. The Snitterley Stone is one of three Welsh slate stones (the Holt slate and the Cley stone being the other two) erected in north Norfolk with words from the Domesday book. Snitterley was the name for Blakeney in 1086. (Note: the valuations of £20 and £50 refer to the whole of the Holt estate not the 'berwick' as suggested by the inscription.)

Photograph © Copyright David Hallam-Jones and licensed for reuse under Creative Commons Licence.

Norfolk Churches

West Norfolk

Map 1. West Norfolk hundreds (overall percentages of communities with recorded churches)

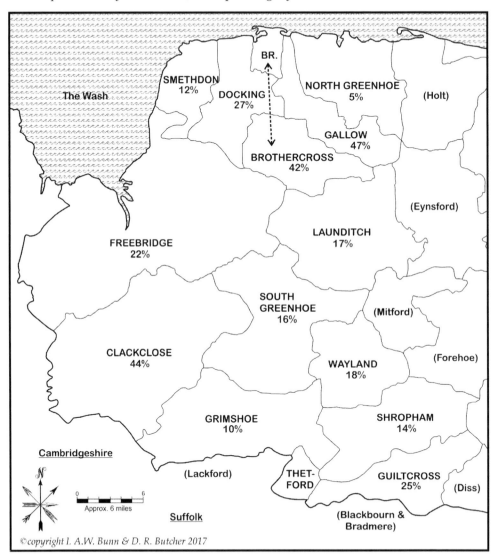

Map details

- This illustration (as well as those of East Norfolk and West & East Suffolk) was created using various sources: the maps present at the end of Part Two of each Phillimore set, those featuring in the Norfolk and Suffolk Historic Atlases (pp. 97 & 19), and various representations of the two counties available on the Internet.

- The West Norfolk-East Norfolk demarcation chooses itself in the northern half, with a simple, well-defined boundary abutting Holt and Eynsford hundreds, but becomes more irregular thereafter, with Shropham and Guiltcross protruding noticeably eastwards. Mitford, with its irregular eastern demarcation might arguably have been included in West Norfolk, but a decision was made to make it part of the eastern sector of the county.

- Delineation of the thirteen hundreds (Thetford not included, in its own right, as part of the data) was partly the result of geological and topgraphical features and partly that of the layout of ancient, post-Roman estates.

- Two adjacent West Suffolk hundreds are shown bracketed, as well as four East Norfolk ones.

Table 1. Norfolk communities and churches (western half)

Hundred	Community	Church	Land (acres)	Reference
Brothercross	1. **Barmer (rt)** – (outlier to Rudham?).	½ [1]	?	8.108
	2. Colkirk	1	40	10.6
	3. Hempton	1	1	8.114
	4. *(Hel)Houghton* – outlier to Rudham.	1	0	8.108
	5. (Pudding) Norton – outlier to Fakenham.	1	8	1.16
	6. (East & West) Rudham	2	60	8.107
	7. **Shereford (rt)**	1	12	8.112
	8. Tatterset	2	40 (combined)	8.110
		(10)		
	1. Bagthorpe			
	2. Broomsthorpe			
	3. **(Burnham) Deepdale (rt)**			
	4. **Burnham** (Norton, Sutton, Ulph, Westgate) **(rt)**			
	5. Dunton			
	6. Helhoughton			
	7. (East & West) Raynham			
	8. South Raynham			
	9. **(Great) Ryburgh (rt)**			
	10. **Syderstone (rt)**			
	11. Toftrees			

Clackclose			
1. Barton (Bendish)	2	12 & 24	13.3 & 31.21
2. **Beechamwell (rt)**	1	30	9.233
3. **Bexwell (rt)**	1	24	66.9
4. Boughton	¼ [1]	20	31.25
5. Fincham	1	?	13.2
6. Marham	1	6	15.1
7. Shouldham (All Saints & St. Margaret)	2	73 (combined)	31.22
8. Stoke (Ferry)	¼ & 1 [2]	5 & 27	31.26
9. Stow (Bardolph) [TW 147]	1	53	13.7
10. Stradsett – possibly same church referred to in separate statements.	2	30 & 30	13.10
11. (Shouldham) Thorpe	½ [1]	16	66.14
12. Thorpland	1	6	13.6
13. Wallington	1	26	66.16
14. West Briggs	1	5	13.5
15. Wormegay [TW 147]	1	?	13.4
	(19)		
1. Crimplesham			
2. Denver			
3. **(West) Dereham (rt) [TW 147]**			
4. Downham (Market)			
5. Fodderstone			
6. Fordham			
7. Hilgay			

*Mildenhall [Lackford H. – Suffolk]			
8. Outwell			
9. Roxham			
10. Runcton (Holme & South)			
11. Ryston			
12. Shingham			
13. Snore			
14. Southery			
15. Toombers			
16. Tottenhill			
17. Upwell			
18. Wereham			
19. Wimbotsham			
Docking			
1. Barwick	½ [1]	10	8.33
2. (Great) Bircham	1	4	19.9
3. (Bircham) Newton	1	20	20.1
1. Brancaster	(3)		
2. Docking			
3. Fring			
4. Shernborne			
5. Southmere			
6. Stanhoe			
7. **Titchwell (rt)**			

8. (Bircham) Tofts			
Freebridge			
1. (Castle & West) Acre	1	30	8.22
2. **Appleton (rt)***	1	12	9.7
3. Congham	1	120	8.27
4. Flitcham	1	8	9.4
5. Islington	1	2	13.13
6. Pentney	1	30	9.2
7. (North) Runcton	1	30	13.14
8. **(Gayton) Thorpe (rt)**	½ [1]	30	66.22
9. (West) Walton	1 (½ + ½)	7 (free) & 15	15.29n & 66.21
	(9)		
1. Anmer			
2. (Ash) Wicken			
3. Babingley [TW 143]			
4. Bawsey [TW 147]			
5. (West) Bilney			
6. Clenchwarton			
7. Dersingham			
8. East Winch			
9. Gayton			
10. Gaywood			
11. Glosthorpe			
12. Grimston			
13. Harpley			

14. Hillington				
15. Leziate				
16. (King's, North, South & West) Lynn				
17. (Great & Little) Massingham				
18. Middleton – priest referred to.	?			4.45
19. Mintlyn				
20. (West) Newton				
21. (Castle) Rising				
22. Roydon				
23. Sandringham				
24. Snettisham [TW 154]				
25. Terrington (St. Clement & St. John)				
26. Walpole				
27. Walsoken				
28. (East) Walton (rt)				
29. West Winch.				
30. Wiggenhall (St. Germans, St. Mary Magdalen, St. Mary the Virgin & St. Peter)				
31. (North & South) Wootton				
Gallow				
1. (East & West) Barsham	3	100, 12 & 8		8.99 & 100
2. Burnham Thorpe	1	80		8.105
3. (North & South) Creake	1	5		8.102
4. *Croxton* (rt)	1	0		8.104

5. *Fulmodeston*	1	0	8.103
6. Saxlingham – outlier to Thornage (10.8) [Located in North Greenhoe and, later on, in Holt]	1	12	10.7
7. Sculthorpe	1	60	8.98
8. **(Little) Snoring (rt)**	1	8	8.101
9. Stibbard	½ [1]	3	8.106
1. Alethorpe	(11)		
2. (North) Barsham			
3. Burnham (Overy) [TW 154]			
4. Clipstone			
5. Fakenham			
6. Kettlestone			
7. Pensthorpe			
8. (Little) Ryburgh			
9. Thorpland			
10. Waterden			
N. Greenhoe 1. Stiffkey	1	30	21.25
1. Barney	(1)		
2. Binham			
3. (Cock)Thorpe			
4. Egemere (+ *Murlai*)			
5. (Field) Dalling			

Place			
6. Hindringham			
7. Holkham [TW 147]			
8. Houghton			
9. Quarles			
10. (Great) Snoring			
11. Thursford			
12. (Great) Walsingham			
13. (Little) Walsingham			
14. Warham (All Saints)			
15. Warham (St. Mary)			
16. Wells (next-the Sea)			
17. Wighton			
S. Greenhoe			
1. (East & West) Bradenham	1	15	31.34
2. (Great) Cressingham – outlier to Necton (22.4).	2	20 & 15	10.1 & 22.4
3. Necton	1	36	22.1
4. (North & **South**) **Pickenham (rt)** – outlier to Necton.	1	17	22.3
	(5)		
1. (South) Acre			
2. Bodney			
3. Caldecote			
4. Cleythorpe			
5. **(Cockley) Cley (rt)**			
6. (Little) Cressingham – outlier to Necton (22.5).			

7. Didlington			
8. Foulden			
9. Gooderstone			
10. Hilborough			
11. Holme (Hale)			
12. Houghton (on the Hill)			
13. Langford			
14. Narborough			
15. Narford			
16. Newton			
17. Oxborough			
18. Palgrave			
19. Sporle			
20. Swaffham [TW 153]			
Grimshoe			
1. **Feltwell (rt)** – possibly, 1 church referred to in different sources.	2	? & 30 (free)	8.37 & 15.29n
2. Northwold	1	12 (free)	15.29n
1. Buckenham (Tofts)	(3)		
2. Colveston			
3. **Cranwich (rt)**			
4. Croxton			
5. Hockwold			
6. Ickburgh			

7. Lynford			
8. Methwold			
9. Mundford			
10. Ottering Hithe			
11. Rising			
12. Santon			
13. **Stanford (rt)**			
14. Sturston			
15. (West) Tofts			
16. **Weeting (rt)**			
17. Wilton			
Guiltcross			
1. Banham	1	30	19.13
2. (Blo) Norton	1	5	14.8
3. (East & West) Harling	1	4	19.15
1. Garboldisham	(3)		
2. Kenninghall			
3. (North & South) Lopham			
4. **Quidenham (rt)**			
5. Riddlesworth			
6. Rushford			
7. (Great) Snarehill			
8. (Little) Snarehill			
9. Wick			

Launditch			
1. (North) Elmham [TW 143]	1	60 & 1 plough	10.5
2. (East & West) Lexham (rt)	1	30	20.8
3. Litcham	½ [1]	4	13.16
4. Swanton (Morley)	1	1½	20.7
5. Tittleshall	1	6	31.38
	(5)		
1. Bentley			
2. Bittering			
3. (Great & Little) Dunham – Reynold the Priest referred to as holding 480 acres with previous tenant's daughter.	?		46.1
4. (Great & Little) Fransham			
5. Gately			
6. Godwick			
7. Gressenhall			
8. Hoe			
9. Horningtoft			
10. Kempston			
11. Kipton			
12. Kirtling			
13. Longham			
14. Mileham			
15. Oxwick			
16. Pattesley			
17. Rougham			

18. Scarning			
19. Stanfield			
20. Sutton			
21. Weasenham (All Saints & St. Margaret)			
22. Wellingham			
23. Wendling			
24. Wereham			
Shropham			
1. Bridgham – a priest was attached to the manor (15.10).	1	12 (free)	15.29n
2. (Great) Ellingham	1	20	13.15
3. Wilby	1	10	19.11
	(3)		
1. Ashby			
2. Attleborough (& Attleborough Minor)			
3. Baconsthorpe			
4. Besthorpe			
5. Brettenham			
6. Buckenham			
7. Eccles (rt) [TW 147]			
8. Hargham			
9. Hockham			
10. Illington			
11. **Kilverstone (rt)**			
12. Larling			
13. Little Hockham			

Name			
14. Rockland (All Saints & St. Andrew)			
15. Roudham			
16. Shropham			
17. Snetterton (East & West)			
18. (East & West) Wretham			
Smethdon			
1. *Hunstanton*	49.2	0	1
			(1)
1. Gnatingdon			
2. Heacham			
3. Holme (next-the-Sea)			
4. Ingoldisthorpe			
5. **Ringstead (rt)***			
6. **Sedgeford (rt)**			
7. Thornham			
Thetford [TW 151]			
1. Church of St. Mary (those of St. Peter, St. John, St. Martin & St. Margaret attached) – minster set-up.	1.69	710	5
2. Bury Abbey (1 church), Ely Abbey (3 churches)	1.70	?	4
3. Bishop of Thetford	1.70	?	½ [1]
4. Abbey, held by Roger Bigot [St. George's – cell to Bury]	1.70	?	1
5. 1 church & church of St. Helen	1.210	120 (St. Helen)	2
6. Church (unnamed)	9.1	?	1
			(14)
Wayland			
1. (West) Carbrooke	49.5	20	1

	2	10 & 24	8.71 & 49.4
2. Griston – outlier to Carbrooke			
3. Watton (rt)	1	20	9.11
	(4)		
1. Ashill			
2. (Stow) Bedon [TW 147]			
3. Breccles (rt)			
4. Carbrooke			
5. Caston			
6. (Little) Ellingham			
7. Merton (rt)			
8. Panworth			
9. Rockland (St. Peter) (rt)			
10. Saham (Toney) [TW 144]			
11. Scoulton			
12. Thompson			
13. Threxton (rt)			
14. Tottington			

Table details

- A total of 77 churches (66 communities), plus 2 communities with the stated presence of a priest. It is possible that Feltwell and Stradsett had 1 church each, not 2, producing 75 in all.

- A total of 91 churches and 67 communities, with Thetford included.

- A total of 272 communities in all (273, Thetford included).

- It has been said that churches were recorded in Domesday only if they had an endowment of land. The 4 examples in the table of buildings described as being without land (in Brothercross, Gallow and Smethdon) show that this was not so. A further 7 references – in Brothercross, Clackclose (2), Grimshoe and Thetford (3) – have no mention whatsoever of land. Williamson, p. 157, says that 220 Norfolk churches had endowments of land; the overall number arrived at in this study is <u>242</u>.

- The endowments of arable land made to each church, varying considerably in size (and therefore in value), probably had a dual function: to maintain a priest – and his family, if he were married – and to create income (if leased) for the work of Christian ministry. In the former case, the land would have formed what later became known as *glebe* (from L. *glæba* = land, or soil).

- Ploughing capacity is recorded in only one case: North Elmham (Launditch), which was centre of the East Anglian diocese from the mid-late tenth century until 1075. The presence of a plough-team may have been part of the original endowment to the church, or a later supplement.

- The 4 references to free land (West Walton in Freebridge, Feltwell & Northwold in Grimshoe, and Bridgham in Shropham) all feature in the later *Inquisitio Eliensis*, not in original Domesday Survey and represent only 5% of the total number of churches. Freely held land meant that the priest – and/or, perhaps the donors also – could (in theory, at least) dispose of it without encumbrance. R. Welldon Finn, *Domesday Studies: the Eastern Counties* (London, 1967), p. 109, says that it is not known whether or not such land was exempt from geld assessment.

- 9 communities are shown as having 2 churches: Barton Bendish, Great Cressingham, Feltwell, Griston, East/West Rudham, Shouldham, Stoke Ferry, Stradsett and Tattersett, and East/West Barsham was recorded with 3. Thus, 16% of "churched" settlements had more than one foundation. As indicated in the table, it is possible that Feltwell and

Stradsett had only 1 church each.

- Communities shown in bold font, with **(rt)** appended, are those with round-tower churches. An asterisk following indicates the remains or ruins of a round tower.

- Use of bold italic font shows communities where 4 recorded churches had no endowment of land.

- The recorded presence of clergy is indicated by underlining. The communities thus noted (2 in number) may possibly have had churches.

- Use of italic font in a recorded community's name indicates one which either disappeared during the period following the Survey or was subsumed in a neighbour and became part of it.

- The use of brackets in place-names show added elements which produce the names in use today.

- Bold font, square-bracketed initials TW, with number, are page-references in T. Williamson, *The Origins of Norfolk*, indicating early Christian sites of monastic or minster status.

Table 2. *Norfolk (western half) – tenancy details: communities with churches*

Hundred	Community	Land-holder (1066)	Tenant-in-chief (1086)	Reference
Brothercross	**Barmer (rt)** – outlier to Rudham.	4 sokemen [under Toki?]	William of Warenne (Ralph – 4 sokemen)	8.108
	Colkirk	Bishop of Thetford	Bishop of Thetford	10.6
	(Hel)Houghton – outlier to Rudham.	1 sokeman [sub Toki?]	William of Warenne (Ralph – 1 sokeman)	8.108
	Hempton	[4 freemen?]	William of Warenne (4 freemen)	8.114
	(Pudding) Norton – outlier to Fakenham.	[Harold Godwineson?]	The King	1.16
	(E. & W.) Rudham	Toki, freeman	William of Warenne (Ralph)	8.107
	Shereford (rt)	6 freemen	William of Warenne [6 freemen?]	8.112
	Tatterset	Toki, freeman	William of Warenne (Rainer)	8.110
Clackclose	Barton (Bendish)	Thorketel, freeman, & Æthelgyth, freewoman	Hermer of Ferrers (William) & Ralph Baynard	13.3 & 31.21
	Beechamwell (rt)	Ælfheah, freeman	Roger Bigot (Robert of Vaux)	9.233
	Bexwell (rt)	[7 freemen?]	Hermer of Ferrers - annexation	66.9
	Boughton	Æthelgyth, freewoman	Ralph Baynard	31.25

Hundred	Place	Predecessor	Landholder	Ref.
	Fincham	[Thorketel?]	Hermer of Ferrers	13.2
	Marham	Ely Abbey	Ely Abbey	15.1
	Shouldham (All Saints & St. Margaret)	Æthelgyth, freewoman	Ralph Baynard	31.22
	Stoke (Ferry)	13 freemen (sub Æthelgyth)	Ralph Baynard	31.26
	Stow (Bardolph)	Thorketel [freeman]	Hermer of Ferrers	13.7
	Stradsett	Swarting, freeman	Hermer of Ferrers (Fulbert)	13.10
	(Shouldham) Thorpe	[11½ freemen?]	Hermer of Ferrers – annexation	66.14
	Thorpland	Thorketel [freeman]	Hermer of Ferrers (Bordin)	13.6
	Wallington	Thurstan, freeman	Hermer of Ferrers – annexation	66.16
	West Briggs	Thorketel [freeman]	Hermer of Ferrers	13.5
	Wormegay	Thorketel [freeman]	Hermer of Ferrers	13.4
Docking	Barwick	2 freemen (sub Harold Godwineson & Frederic's predecessor)	William of Warenne (Frederic) – Simon, sub-tenant	8.33
	(Great) Bircham	Bernard (sub King Edward)	William of Ecouis (Roger of Evreux)	19.9
	(Bircham) Newton	Tovi, freeman	Ralph of Beaufour	20.1
Freebridge	(Castle & West) Acre	Toki, freeman	William of Warenne	8.22
	Appleton (rt)*	Abba (sub Stigand)	Roger Bigot	9.7
	Congham	1 freeman [sub Ælfgifu, freewoman?]	William of Warenne	8.27

Hundred	Place	Pre-Conquest holder	Tenant-in-chief	Reference
	Flitcham	[1 freeman?]	Roger Bigot (Robert of Vaux?)	9.4
	Islington	Thorketel [freeman] (sub Stigand)	Hermer of Ferrers	13.13
	[Middleton?]	Ralph Wader [following Ralph the Constable, his father]	Count Alan of Brittany (Ribald)	4.45
	Pentney	Hagni	Roger Bigot (Robert of Vaux)	9.2
	(North) Runcton	Thorketel, freeman	Hermer of Ferrers	13.14
	(Gayton) Thorpe (rt)	Thork[et]el, freeman	Hermer of Ferrers (Bordin) – annexation	66.22
	(West) Walton	[Ely Abbey? + 3 freemen?]	Ely Abbey & Hermer of Ferrers (Bordin) – annexation	15.29n & 66.21
Gallow	(East & West) Barsham	Toki & 1 other freeman – 8.99; Toki – 8.100	William of Warenne (Hugh & Rainer)	8.99 & 100
	Burnham Thorpe	Toki, freeman	William of Warenne (Walter)	8.105
	(North & South) Creake	1 freeman (sub another freeman)	William of Warenne [Lambert?]	8.102
	Croxton (rt)	Toki, freeman	William of Warenne	8.104
	Fulmodeston	Toki, freeman	William of Warenne (Walter)	8.103
	Saxlingham – outlier to Thornage. [Located in North Greenhoe]	Bishop of Thetford	Bishop of Thetford	10.7
	Sculthorpe	Toki, freeman	William of Warenne (Frederic)	8.98
	(Little) Snoring (rt)	2 sokemen [sub Toki?]	William of Warenne	8.101

Hundred	Place			
	Stibbard	1 sokeman [sub.Toki?]	William of Warenne (Peter of Valognes)	8.106
N. Greenhoe	Stiffkey	Ketel, freeman	Reynold, son of Ivo (Ranulf)	21.25
S. Greenhoe	(East & West) Bradenham	Æthelgyth (freewoman) & 8 attached sokemen	Ralph Baynard	31.34
	(Great) Cressingham – outlier to Necton.	Bishop of Thetford & Harold Godwineson	Bishop of Thetford & Ralph of Tosny	10.1 & 22.4
	Necton	Harold Godwineson	Ralph of Tosny	22.1
	(North & **South**) Pickenham (rt) – outlier to Necton.	Harold Godwineson	Ralph of Tosny	22.3
Grimshoe	Feltwell (rt)	40 sokemen [sub Ely Abbey?] – 8.37	William of Warenne & Ely Abbey	8.37 & 15.29n
	Northwold	[Ely Abbey?]	Ely Abbey	15.29n
Guiltcross	Banham	Fathir, freeman	William of Ecouis	19.13
	(Blo) Norton	1 sokeman (sub Bury Abbey)	Bury Abbey	14.8
	(E. & W.) Harling	Ketel, freeman	William of Ecouis (Ingulf)	19.15
Launditch	[(Great & Little) Dunham?]	Payne	Edmund, son of Payne (Reynold the Priest & the daughter of Payne)	46.1
	(North) Elmham	Bishop of Thetford	Bishop of Thetford	10.5

(East & West) Lexham (rt)	Fathir, freeman	Ralph of Beaufour (Richard)	20.8
Litcham	Thorketel, freeman	Hermer of Ferrers (William)	13.16
Swanton (Morley)	Godwine, freeman	Ralph of Beaufour	20.7
Tittleshall	Norman, freeman	Ralph Baynard (Ralph Sturmy)	31.38
Shropham			
Bridgham	[Ely Abbey?]	Ely Abbey	15.29n
Great Ellingham	Thorketel, freeman	Hermer of Ferrers (Warenbold)	13.15
Wilby	Fathir, freeman	William of Ecouis	19.11
Smethdon			
Hunstanton	Bovi	John, nephew of Waleran	49.2
Thetford			
Thetford	Stigand – 1.69; Bury Abbey & Ely Abbey – 1.70; Stigand – 1.210; [King Edward?] – 9.1	The King – 1.69; The King – 1.70; the King – 1.210; Roger Bigot – 9.1	1.69, 70 & 210, & 9.1
Wayland			
(West) Carbrooke	Ælfheah, freeman	John, nephew of Waleran (Osbert)	49.5
Griston – outlier to Carbrooke	[Ralph the Constable? – 8.71?]; Ælfheah, freeman (49.4)	William of Warenne & John, nephew of Waleran (Osbert)	8.71 & 49.4
Watton (rt)	Ældreda, freewoman	Roger Bigot (Ranulf, son of Walter)	9.11

Table details

- Communities shown in bold font, with **(rt)** appended, are those with round-tower churches. An asterisk following indicates the remains or ruins of a round tower.

- Use of bold italic font shows communities where recorded churches had no endowment of land.

- Communities which have a question mark appended within square brackets are those which have a priest referred to and which, therefore, might possibly have had a place of worship of some kind.

- The names in brackets in the third column indicate the land-holders' patrons (an adoption acceptable to both parties, by process of *commendation*) or exercisers of jurisdiction – in those cases where patronage or jurisdiction is stated or implied. Sometimes the connection is specifically referred to, sometimes not, and because of the element of uncertainty caused thereby no attempt has been made to differentiate between patronage and jurisdiction.

- The names in brackets in the fourth column are those of sub-tenants of the tenants-in-chief, in cases where this information is given.

- No distinction is made between freemen (*libi hoes*) and sokemen (*soc*) in the translation of the text, all such tenants being classed as the former. Identification has been made in the table, as freemen usually held their land independently, whereas sokemen were bound by customary services of some kind. The latter were probably also unable to *commend* themselves to the patronage of a social superior (see D. Roffe, *Decoding Domesday*, p. 223).

West Norfolk Summary (proportion of communities with churches)

Brothercross – 42%.

Clackclose – 44% (3 early Christian foundations noted).

Docking – 27%. Later, absorbed Smethdon Hundred.

Freebridge – 22% (3 early Christian foundations noted). Later, split into Freebridge Lynn and Freebridge Marshland hundreds.

Gallow – 47% (1 early Christian foundation noted).

North Greenhoe – 5% (1 early Christian foundation noted).

South Greenhoe – 16% (1 early Christian foundation noted).

Grimshoe – 10%.

Guiltcross – 25%.

Launditch – 17% (1 early Christian foundatrion noted).

Shropham – 14% (1 early Christian foundation noted).

Smethdon – 12%. Later, incorporated into Docking Hundred.

Thetford – not assessable (1 early Christian foundation noted).

Wayland – 18% (2 early Christian foundations noted).

- West Norfolk: 67 communities with churches, out of 273 in all = 24% (Thetford included).

- 2 other possible churches, on 2 recorded presences of a priest.

- County as a whole: 226/227 (excluding or including Thetford) communities with churches, out of a total of 714 recorded = 32%.

- Number of churches in county: 270/272 (including Thetford & excluding Norwich); 256/258 (excluding Thetford also).

East Norfolk

Map 2. East Norfolk hundreds (overall percentages of communities with recorded churches)

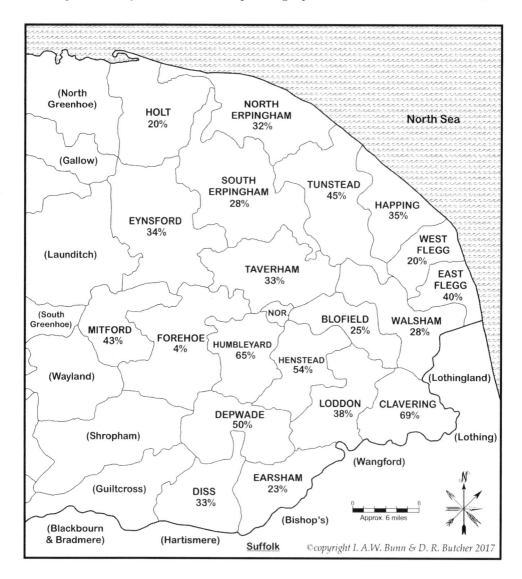

(North Greenhoe)

HOLT 20%

NORTH ERPINGHAM 32%

North Sea

(Gallow)

SOUTH ERPINGHAM 28%

TUNSTEAD 45%

HAPPING 35%

EYNSFORD 34%

WEST FLEGG 20%

(Launditch)

TAVERHAM 33%

EAST FLEGG 40%

(South Greenhoe)

MITFORD 43%

FOREHOE 4%

NOR.

BLOFIELD 25%

WALSHAM 28%

HUMBLEYARD 65%

HENSTEAD 54%

(Wayland)

(Lothingland)

LODDON 38%

CLAVERING 69%

DEPWADE 50%

(Shropham)

(Lothing)

(Wangford)

(Guiltcross)

EARSHAM 23%

DISS 33%

(Blackbourn & Bradmere)

(Hartismere)

(Bishop's)

Suffolk

Approx. 6 miles

0   6

©copyright I. A.W. Bunn & D. R. Butcher 2017

Map details

- East Norfolk's twenty hundreds (Norwich not counted, in its own right, and not included in the data) represent the effect of geological and topographical factors in their configuration and in the boundaries formed, together with the residual legacy of ancient estates.

- A generally denser pattern of settlement than that of West Norfolk prevailed, partly as a result of superior soil-quality overall and the opportunities this offered to incomers (including late-9th century Danish ones).

- Six adjacent Suffolk hundreds (five East Suffolk and one West) are shown bracketed.

Table 3. Norfolk communities and churches (eastern half)

Hundred	Community	Church	Land (acres)	Reference
Blofield				
	1. Bradeston	1	10	10.76
	2. **(North) Burlingham (rt)***	2/3	10 (free); 30; 40 & 10	1.99, 10.68 & 73
	3. South Burlingham	½ [1]	15	10.74
	4. *Letha*	1	5	10.72
	5. Postwick	1	20	24.6
		(6/7)		
	1. Blofield			
	2. Brundall			
	3. Buckenham			
	4. Cantley			
	5. Catton			
	6. **Freethorpe (rt)**			
	7. **Hassingham (rt)**			
	8. Limpenhoe			
	9. Moor			
	10. (Great) Plumstead			
	11. **(Little) Plumstead (rt)**			
	12. Southwood			
	13. Strumpshaw			
	14. Thorpe (St. Andrew)			
	15. Witton			

Clavering	1. Aldeby	1	12	20.36
	2. Ellingham	1	24	1.239
	3. Gillingham	1	30 (free)	1.239
	4. **Hales (rt)**	1	20 (free)	14.42
	5. **Heckingham (rt)**	1	8	12.42
	6. **Kirby (Cane) (rt)**	1 & $^2/_3$ [2]	20 (in alms) & 14	14.41
	7. **Raveningham (rt)**	1	60	50.12
	8. **Stockton (rt)** – outlier to Earsham Hundred.	1	65	1.239
	9. *Thurketeliart* (nr. Aldeby)	1	20	20.36
	10. Thurlton	½ [1]	12	19.40
	11. Wheatacre	2	60 (in alms – combined)	31.17
		(13)		
	1. **Haddiscoe (rt)**			
	2. *Iarpestuna/Ierpestuna*			
	3. *Naruestuna*			
	4. **Norton (Subcourse) (rt)** – also recorded in Loddon.			
	5. Toft (Monks)			
Depwade	1. Carleton (Rode)	2	30 (combined)	9.209
	2. **Forncett (St. Peter & St. Mary) (rt)**	1	15	9.98
	3. **Fritton (rt)**	1	40	9.208
	4. Fundenhall	1	24 (free)	6.6
	5. Hapton	1	15	6.6
	6. Hempnall – priest referred to (31.6).	2	120 (combined)	31.6

7. Hudeston	1	30, 2 meadow & ½ plough	9.100
8. Moulton (St. Michael) – Aski the Priest referred to as holding 2 freemen & 2½ acres (65.13).	1	15	9.212
9. Shelton	1	16	9.216
10. Swanton – land described as "the alms of very many men".	1	60 (free)	9.221
11. Tharston	1	40	9.99
12. (Morning)Thorpe (rt)	1	12	14.40
	(14)		
1. Aslacton (rt)			
2. Boyland			
3. Halas			
4. Hardwick (rt)			
5. Kettleton			
6. Middleton			
7. Schieteshagg (in Hempnall)			
8. Stratton (St. Michael & St. Mary) [al. Long Stratton] (rt)			
9. Tacolneston			
10. Tasburgh (rt)			
11. (Ashwell)Thorpe			
12. Tibenham			
Diss 1. Bressingham	1	15	14.24
2. Dickleburgh – 2 priests referred to as holding 240 acres [TW 147].	1	30	14.29

	3. Diss	1	24	ESf 1
	4. Shelfanger	1	16	14.32
	5. **Shimpling (rt)**	1	10	9.46
	6. Tivetshall (St, Margaret & St. Mary)	2	40 (combined)	14.23
		(7)		
	1. Burston			
	2. Fersfield			
	3. Frenze			
	4. **Gissing (rt)**			
	5. Osmondiston			
	6. **Roydon (rt)**			
	7. Thelveton			
	8. **Thorpe (Parva) (rt)***			
	9. **Wacton (rt)**			
	10. *Watlingseta* (lost in Diss)			
	11. Winfarthing			
Earsham	1. Pulham (St. Mary Magdalene & St. Mary the Virgin)	2	2 (combined)	15.29n
	2. Starston – ref. to 15 Bury Abbey sokemen holding 60 acres "entirely in the church".	1?	60	1.223
	3. **Thorpe (Abbots) (rt)**	1	12	14.18
		(4?)		
	1. Alburgh			
	2. Billingford			
	3. Brockdish			

Hundred	Place	Churches	Acres	Ref.
	4. Denton (rt)			
	5. Earsham			
	6. Harleston			
	*Mendham [Bishop's H., Suffolk] – Ælfgar the Priest held 43 acres of ecclesiastical land under William of Noyers			10.32
	7. Redenhall			
	*Rumburgh [Blything H., Suffolk] – 12 acres in Alburgh.			4.48
	8. Rushall (rt)			
	9. Semere			
	10. Shotford			
North Erpingham	1. Aylmerton (rt)	½ [1]	10	8.132
	2. (East) Beckham – outlier to Thornage (10.8) & later added to Blickling (10.65).	1	2½	10.65
	3. Gimingham	1	28	8.119
	4. Mundesley	1	12	8.123
	5. (North) Repps	1	18	8.126
	6. (South) Repps (+ North Repps)	1	12	8.128
	7. (East & West) Runton	1	6	19.22
	8. Sheringham	1	15	19.18
	9. Thorpe (Market)	1	10	8.122
	10. Trunch	1	10	8.124
		(10)		
	1. Aldborough			
	2. Antingham			

3. (North) Barningham			
4. Beeston (Regis)			
5. **Bessingham (rt)**			
6. Felbrigg			
7. **Gresham (rt)**			
8. Gunton			
9. Hanworth			
10. *Hottune*			
11. Knapton			
12. Metton			
13. Overstrand			
14. Plumstead			
15. **Roughton (rt)**			
16. Salthouse			
17. Shipden [lost]			
18. **Sidestrand (rt)**			
19, Suffield			
20. **Sustead (rt)**			
21. Thurgarton			
South Erpingham			
1. (Little) Barningham	1	9	8.8
2. Belaugh	½ [1]	3	17.33
3. Buxton	1	30 (in alms)	20.29
4. *Calthorpe*	1	0	17.26
5. Coltishall	1	10	8.8

6. Corpusty	$^3/_4$ [1]	9	19.34
7. Erpingham	1	6	30.6
8. Oxnead	1	24	61.2
9. Scottow	1	14	17.23
10. Swanton (Abbot)	1	7	17.25
11. Thwaite (rt)	1	6	17.27
12. Wolterton (rt)*	½ [1]	4	17.32
	(12)		
1. Alby			
2. Aylsham			
3. Banningham			
4. (West) Beckham			
5. Blickling			
6. Booton			
7. Brampton (rt)			
8. Burgh (next Aylsham)			
9. Cawston			
10. Colby			
11. Crackford			
12. Custhorpe [Located in South Greenhoe]			
13. Easton			
14. (Great & Little) Hautbois (rt)			
15. Hevingham – freeman priest held 40 acres in alms & sang 3 masses a week.	[1]		1.195
16. Ingworth (rt)			

17. Irmingland			
18. Itteringham			
19. Lamas			
20. Mannington			
21. Marsham			
22. **Matlaske (rt)**			
23. Mortoft			
24. Oulton			
25. Rippon			
26. Saxthorpe			
27. Skeyton			
28. Stratton (Strawless)			
29. (Bacons)Thorpe			
30. **Tuttington (rt)**			
31. **Wickmere (rt)**			
Eynsford			
1. Elsing	1	18 & 1 meadow	8.6
2. Foulsham	2	16 & 22	1.52
3. **Haveringland (rt)**	1	10	21.29
4. Helmingham	2	10 (combined)	10.16
5. Hindolveston	1	26	10.15
6. Kerdiston – ½ priest also referred to, holding 7 acres.	½ [1]	7	8.2
7. (Wood) Norton – outlier to Hindolveston.	⅓ [1]	2½	10.15
8. Sparham	1	40	12.27
9. Stinton	1	14	8.1

10. Weston (Longville) – outlier to (Great & Little) Witchingham.		1	12	19.32
11. *(Great & Little) Witchingham*	(13)	1	0	19.32
1. Bawdeswell				
2. Beck				
3. Billingford				
4. Bintree				
5. **Brandiston (rt)**				
6. **Bylaugh (rt)**				
7. (Wood) Dalling				
8. Foxley				
9. Guestwick				
10. Guist				
11. Guton				
12. Hackford				
13. Lyng				
14. Reepham				
15. Ringland				
16. Salle				
17. Swannington				
18. Thurning				
19. Thurton				
20. Tyby				
21. Whitwell				

East Flegg				
1. Scratby	1	36		10.43
2. Stokesby	1	23 & 3 meadow		19.36
3. Thrigby	1	5		19.37
4. (Great) Yarmouth – held by Bishop of Thetford.	1	?		1.68
	(4)			
1. Caister				
2. Filby				
3. Herringby				
4. **Mautby (rt)**				
5. Ormesby (St. Margaret & St. Michael)				
6. Runham				
West Flegg				
1. Billockby	2/3 [1]	7		10.90
2. Hemsby	1	20		10.30
3. Martham	1	50		10.86
	(3)			
1. Ashby				
2. Bastwick				
3. Burgh (St. Margaret)				
4. **Clippesby (rt)**				
5. Ness				
6. Oby				
7. **Repps (rt)**				
8. **Rollesby (rt)**				

9. Sco				
10. (East & West) **Somerton (rt)**				
11. Thurne				
12. Winterton				
1. Dykebeck	¼ [1] (1)	5	31.42	
Forehoe				
1. Barford				
2. Barnham (Broom)				
3. **Bawburgh (rt)**				
4. Bickerston				
5. Bowthorpe				
6. Brandon (Parva)				
7. Carleton (Forehoe)				
8. Colton				
9. Costessey				
10. Crownthorpe				
11. Deopham				
12. Easton				
13. Hackford				
14. Hingham				
15. Honingham				
16. Honingham (Thorpe)				
17. Kimberley				

Entry				
18. Marlingford – noted as having a church belonging to free-woman, Silfled, during 10th/11th century – will ref. (Dymond, *Norfolk Landscape*, p. 85).	?			[4.13]
19. Morley (St. Botolph & St. Peter) – <u>priest</u> referred to, holding 120 acres pre-1066.	?			8.78
20. **Runhall (rt)**				
21. *Tockestorp/Toke(s)torp* [in/near Wramplingham]				
22. **Welborne (rt)**				
23. Wicklewood				
24. **Wramplingham (rt)**				
25. Wymondham				
Happing				
1. Brumstead – outlier to Sutton.	1	9	9.88	
2. Catfield – outlier to Sutton.	1	20	9.88	
3. Hickling	1	20	4.38	
4. Sutton	1	10	9.88	
5. Walcott	1	20	36.5	
6. Waxham	2	20 & 18	4.40 & 42	
	(7)			
1. **Eccles (rt)** [destroyed by sea erosion]				
2. Happisburgh				
3. **(Potter) Heigham (rt)**				
4. Hempstead				
45 **Horsey (rt)**				
6. Ingham				
7. Lessingham				

8. (Sea) Palling			
9. (East) Ruston			
10, Stalham			
11. Whimpwell			
Henstead			
1. Bixley	1	24	9.32
2. Bramerton	1	24	9.28
3. Caistor (St. Edmunds)	1	11	14.15
4. Framingham (Earl & Pigot) (rt)	1	30	9.30
5. Howe (rt)	1	15	14.16
6. Kirby (Bedon) (rt)*	1	10	9.29
7. Poringland (rt)	1	12	9.37
8. Rockland (St. Mary)	1	12	9.27
9. Saxlingham (Nethergate)	1	10	49.7
10. Shotesham (All Saints & St. Mary)	½ & ¼ [1/2]	15 & ?	9.24 & 14.16
11. Whitlingham (rt)*	1	10	9.31
12. Yelverton	1	20	9.36
	(12/13)		
1. Alpington			
2. Arminghall			
3. Bergh (Apton)			
4. Brooke (rt)			
5. Grensvill			
6. Holverston			

	7. Newton			
	8. **Surlingham (rt)**			
	9. Trowse			
	10. Washingford			
Holt				
	1. Blakeney (al. Snitterley)	1	30	10.56
	2. Briningham (2 identical references – probably to the same church)	1	12	10.57 & 10.59
	3. Langham	2	16 (combined)	10.22
	4. Melton (Constable)	1	6	10.58
	5. Thornage	1	32	10.8
		(6)		
	1. Bale			
	2. Bayfield			
	3. Bodham			
	4. Brinton			
	5. Briston			
	6. Cley (next-the-Sea)			
	7. Edgefield			
	8. Glandford			
	9. Hempstead			
	10. Holt			
	11. Hunworth			
	12. Kelling			
	13. **Letheringsett (rt)**			

	14. Morston			
	15. *Neutuna* (lost, near Holt)			
	16. Sharrington			
	17. **Stody (rt)**			
	18. Swanton (Novers)			
	19. Weybourne			
	20. Wiveton			
Humbleyard	1. Bracon Ash – St. Nicholas, built by Colbeorn the Priest, with King's assent; mass & psalms sung each week for the monarch.	1	20	45.1
	2. (East) Carleton	2	38 (combined)	9.96
	3. Earlham	1	14 & ½ meadow	1.206
	4. Eaton	1	14	1.205
	5. Hethel	1	30	9.94
	6. Hethersett	2	60 & 8	4.52
	7. **Intwood (rt)**	1	14 & 1½ meadow	24.7
	8. Ketteringham	1	40	9.95
	9. Lakenham – outlier to Thorpe (St. Andrew).	1	13 (in alms)	1.236
	10. Markshall	1	6	20.35
	11. (Great) Melton	1	3	32.4
	12. Mulbarton	1	15	20.34
	13. Stoke (Holy Cross)	1½ [2]	23 (combined)	48.3
	14. **Swainsthorpe (rt)**	1	23	48.4
	15. Walsingham	1	60	32.2
	16. Wreningham	1	10	13.24

	1. **Colney (rt)**	(19)		
	2. Cringleford – Ælfred the priest had held 120 acres pre-1066.	?		2.12
	3. Dunston			
	4. Flordon			
	5. Heigham			
	6. Kenningham			
	7. **Keswick (rt)**			
	8. Mangreen			
	9. (Little) Melton			
	10 Nayland			
	11. Newton (Flotman)			
	12. Rainthorpe			
	13. Swardeston			
Loddon	1. Carleton (St. Peter)	1	80 (free)	21.26
	2. Chedgrave	1	50 & 1 meadow	31.44
	3. Claxton	1	30	9.56
	4. Kirstead [or Langhale]	1	12	14.38
	5. Langley – one whole priest and two halves referred to, in connection with St. Andrew's Church [**TW 152**].	1	100	10.33
	6. Loddon [**TW 144**]	1	60 & 4 meadow	14.35
	7. Mundham	½ [1]	10	1.183
	8. **Seething (rt)** – a poor nun claimed 4 acres, held under Ralph Wader prior to his forfeiture (47.7) – holding 9.25 was an outlier to Stoke Holy Cross & 9.51 to Framingham (Earl & Pigot).	3	18 & 16 (latter, 2 churches combined)	9.25 & 51

9. *Torp* [in/near Sisland, or the Thorpe in Mitford Hundred – 15.17?]	1	12 (free)	15.29n
10. **Woodton (rt)**	1	12	9.54
1. *Alcmuntona/Algamundestuna* [near Sisland?]	(12)		
2. *Appletona/tuna*			
3. Ashby (St. Mary)			
4. **Bedingham (rt)**			
5. *Brant*			
6. Broome			
7. Ditchingham			
*Gorleston [Lothingland H., Suffolk] – ref. 35 acres in Gillingham (1.60) & full manor details (ESf etc.)			1.60 & ESf 2,5 & 6
8. **Hardley (rt)**			
9. Hedenham			
10. **Hellington (rt)**			
11. Ingloss			
12. Langhale [in Kirstead]			
13. Pirnhow			
*Rumburgh [Blything H., Suffolk] – ref. 30 acres in Mundham.			ENf 4
14. Sisland			
15. Thurton			
16. **Topcroft (rt)** – 2 priests had held 240 acres pre-1066.	?		14.37
1. (South)Burgh	1	12	8.82
Mitford			

		30 (free) & 1 plough	
2. (East) Dereham [TW 145]	1	30 (free) & 1 plough	15.29n
3. Garveston – outlier to Whinburgh	1	7	13.19
4. Letton	1	12	8.83
5. Mattishall	1	20	20.16
6. Shipdam	½ [1]	8	8.84
7. *Thurestuna* [Thuxton?]	1	16	9.134
8. (East) Tuddenham	1	20	13.23
9. (North) Tuddenham	2	20 (combined)	20.15
10. Whinburgh	1	6	13.19
	(11)		
1. *Baskenea*			
2. Calvely			
3. Cranworth			
4. Flockthorpe			
5. Hockering			
6. Manson			
7. *Oscelea* [in/near Wood Rising?]			
8. Reymerston			
9. Swathing			
10. Thorpe (in Shipdam)	?		See 15.29n
11. Thuxton			
12. Westfield			
13. **Yaxham (rt)** – freeman priest Aldwy had held 30 acres pre-1066.	?		9.82

Norwich	1. Norwich	2 & ⅙ [3]	1 dwelling & 6 acres meadow (one church only)	1.61
	2. Norwich	15	181 land & meadow (in alms)	1.61
	3. Norwich (All Saints, St. Martin, St. Michael, Holy Trinity, St. Laurence and St. Simon & St. Jude named – part of, or separate from, the 15 above?)	6	2 meadow – 12 – 112, 6 meadow & 1 plough – 180? – ? – ¾ mill, ½ meadow & 1 dwelling	1.61
	4. Norwich (burgess chapels)	[43]	?	1.61
	5. Norwich (St. Sepulchre referred to)	1	2 meadow	1.64
	6. Norwich (in the new borough – founded by Ralph Waher and held by Wala the Priest).	1	?	1.66
		(26)		
Taverham	1. Attlebridge	1	6	10.37
	2. Beeston (St. Andrew)	½ [1]	?	20.25
	3. Drayton	1	8	20.26
	4. *Hellesdon*	1	0	61.1
	5. Taverham (rt)	¼ & ¼ [1]	3 & 15	8.7 & 20.27
	6. Wroxham	2	33 (combined)	20.24
		(7)		
	1. **(Old) Catton (rt)**			
	2. Crostwick			
	3. Felthorpe			
	4. Frettenham			
	5. Hainford			

6. Horsford			
7. Horsham (St. Faith)			
8. Mayton			
9. Rackheath – monk referred to as illegally holding 30 acres after a post-1066 forfeiture (17.22).			
10. Spixworth			
11. Sprowston			
12. Stanninghall			
Tunstead			
1. Barton Turf	2	33 (combined)	17.50
2. Felmingham	1	2	17.39
3. Hoveton (St. John & St. Peter)	2	16 (combined)	17.37
4. Neatished	1	10	17.36
5. Paston	1	1	8.11
6. Sloley	1	1	20.33
7. Swafield	1	28	10.18
8. (North) Walsham [TW 152]	1	30	17.38
9. **Witton (rt)** – priest holding 30 acres in alms, in return for singing 3 masses for the King & Queen (1.196).	1	10	8.12
10. Worstead	2	28 (combined)	17.43
	(13)		
1. Bacton			
2. **Beeston (St. Lawrence) (rt)**			
3. *Clareia*			
4. Crostwight			

5. **Dilham (rt)**			
6. Honing			
7. Horning [**TW 147**] – ref. St. Benet's Abbey.			
8. Ridlington			
9. (Sco) Ruston			
10. Smallburgh			
11. Tunstead			
12. Westwick			
Walsham			
1. Beighton	1	7	10.25
2. Panxworth	1	8	19.25
3. Reedham [**TW 144**]	1	40	19.24
4. Tunstall	1	8	24.5
	(4)		
1. **Acle (rt)**			
2. **Fishley (rt)**			
3. Halvergate			
4. **Hemblington (rt)**			
5. **Moulton (St. Mary) (rt)**			
6. Ranworth			
7. Upton			
8. (South) Walsham			
9. Wickhampton			
10. Westwick			

Table details

- A total of 179/181 churches in all (excluding Norwich); 139 communities. In addition, 5 communities have the stated presence of a priest, with 1 other featuring in a late Anglo-Saxon probate reference. Starston (Earsham Hundred) is queried bcause of ambiguity in the statement regarding land held "entirely in the church". Did this relate to a local church, or to land held by Bury Abbey? The former possibility has been the one accepted.

- Therefore, 6 other possibilities, on the recorded presence of a priest and on the probate reference. Hevingham is almost certain to have had a church, based on the evidence of an endowment of land and a description of priestly duties.

- There are 3 examples (one each in South Erpingham, Eynsford and Taverham) of churches recorded as being without an endowment of land and a further 5 (1 each in East Flegg, Henstead and Taverham, 2 in Norwich) where no mention of land is made.

- A total of 442 communities in all. Williamson, p. 157, says that, 220 Norfolk churches had endowments of land; the overall number arrived at in this study is <u>242</u>.

- Ploughing capacity is recorded in three cases: Hudeston (Depwade), East Dereham (Mitford) and St. Michael's church, Norwich. Again, as with North Elmham (Launditch), the presence of plough-teams may have resulted from the original endowments or from later gifts.

- The 5 references to land being *in alms* (Kirby Cane & Wheatacre in Clavering, Buxton in South Erpingham, Lakenham in Humbleyard, and 15 Norwich churches) shows that the endowments were the gift of a donor for the maintenance of a priest and ministry to his flock. There is no information as to whether or not the land was able to be disposed of. Welldon Finn, pp. 77 & 110, says that such land (described as *in elemosina*, in Domesday)) seems to have been exempt from paying geld.

- As is the case in West Norfolk (4 examples), the 7 references to freely held land (Gillingham & Hales in Clavering, Fundenhall & Swanton in Depwade, Carleton St. Peter & *Torp* in Loddon, and East Dereham in Mitford) represent a very small proportion (4%) of the total number of churches.

- 18 communities are shown as having 2 churches: Barton Turf, Carleton Rode, East Carleton, Foulsham, Helmingham, Hempnall, Hethersett,

Hoveton, Kirby Cane, Langham, North Tuddenham, Pulham, Stoke Holy Cross, Tivetshall, Waxham, Wheatacre, Worstead and Wroxham. Of a further 2, North Burlingham may have had 3 and Seething did have that number. Thus, 12% of "churched" settlements had more than one foundation.

- As has been noted earlier, there were 10 examples of "multi-church" presence recorded in West Norfolk (p. 33), in addition to the 20 in the Eastern sector indicated immediately above.

- Communities shown in bold font, with **(rt)** appended, are those with round-tower churches. An asterisk following indicates the ruins or remains of a round tower.

- Bold italic font shows settlements where recorded churches had no endowment of land (3 examples).

- The presence of clergy is recorded by underlining. The communities thus noted (6 in number) might well have had churches (Hevingham almost certainly did).

- Use of italic font in a recorded community's name indicates one which either disappeared during the period following the Survey or was subsumed in a neighbour and became part of it.

- The use of brackets in place-names show added elements which produce the names in use today.

- The bold font, square-bracketed initials TW, followed by a number, are page-references in T. Williamson, *The Origins of Norfolk*, indicating early Christian sites of monastic or minster status (both definite and conjectured).

Table 4. Norfolk (eastern half) – tenancy details: communities with churches

Hundred	Community	Land-holder (1066)	Tenant-in-chief (1086)	Reference
Blofield	Bradeston	Eadric, royal steersman (under King Edward)	Bishop of Thetford	10.76
	(North) Burlingham [ruined church of St. Peter] **(rt)***	1 freeman (sub Ralph the Constable) – 1.99; 15 freemen (sub Bishop of Thetford) – 10.68; 1 freeman (sub Bishop of Thetford) – 10.73	The King Bishop of Thetford (William of Noyers – 10.68; Eli – 10.73)	1.99 10.68 & 73
	South Burlingham	8 freemen (sub Bishop of Thetford)	Bishop of Thetford (William of Noyers)	10.74
	Letha	7 freemen (sub Bishop of Thetford)	Bishop of Thetford (Reynold)	10.72
	Postwick	Skuli, freeman	Eudo the Steward	24.6
Clavering	Aldeby	1 freeman (sub Stigand)	Ralph of Beaufour	20.36
	Ellingham	5 sokemen (sub Stigand)	The King [5 sokemen?]	1.239
	Gillingham	12 freemen (mixed patronage)	The King [12 freemen?]	1.239
	Hales **(rt)**	2 sokemen (sub the Abbey) & 7 sokemen (commendation only)	Bury Abbey (Frodo)	14.42
	Heckingham **(rt)**	Hagni (sub Stigand)	Godric the Steward	12.42
	Kirby (Cane) **(rt)**	Bury Abbey	Bury Abbey (Radfrid)	14.41
	Raveningham **(rt)**	Osbeorn, thegn	Roger son of Rainard	50.12
	Stockton (rt) – outlier to Earsham Hundred.	Stigand	The King	1.239
	Thurketeliart (nr. Aldeby)	1 freeman (sub Stigand)	Ralph of Beaufour	20.36

	Thurlton	7½ freemen (sub Ralph of Beaufour)	William of Ecouis (Oder)	19.40
	Wheatacre	1 freeman (sub Harold Godwineson) & Thored, thegn	Ralph Baynard (Geoffrey)	31.17
Depwade	Carleton (Rode)	16½ freemen [sub Stigand?]	Roger Bigot (16½ freemen?)	9.209
	Forncett (St. Mary & **St. Peter**) **(rt)**	Coleman, freeman (sub Stigand)	Roger Bigot [1 freeman?]	9.98
	Fritton (rt)	3½ freemen [sub Stigand?]	Roger Bigot (3½ freemen?)	9.208
	Fundenhall	Burgheard, thegn	Earl Hugh (Roger Bigot)	6.6
	Hapton	1 freeman (sub Stigand) & 1 (sub Gyrth Godwineson)	Earl Hugh (Roger Bigot))	6.6
	Hempnall	Thorn	Ralph Baynard	31.6
	Hudeston	Ælfwine of Thetford	Roger Bigot (Robert of Courson)	9.100
	Moulton (St. Michael)	1 freeman [sub Stigand?]	Roger Bigot (1 freeman)	9.212
	Shelton	9½ freemen [sub Stigand?]	Roger Bigot (Durand)	9.216
	Swanton	Oslac [sub Stigand?]	Roger Bigot (Oslac)	9.221
	Tharston	Wulfric (sub Stigand)	Roger Bigot (Robert of Vaux)	9.99
	(Morning)Thorpe (rt)	Bury Abbey	Bury Abbey (Robert of Vaux)	14.40
Diss	Bressingham	Bury Abbey	Bury Abbey	14.24
	Dickleburgh	Bury Abbey	Bury Abbey (2 priests)	14.29
	Diss	King Edward	The King	ESf 1
	Shelfanger	Bury Abbey (1 freeman)	Bury Abbey (1 freeman)	14.32

Hundred	Vill	1066 holder	1086 holder	Ref.
	Shimpling (rt)	Thorbert, freeman (sub Stigand)	Roger Bigot (Robert of Vaux)	9.46
	Tivetshall (St. Margaret & Mary)	Bury Abbey	Bury Abbey	14.23
Earsham	Pulham (St. Mary Magdalene & St. Mary the Virgin)	[Ely Abbey?]	Ely Abbey	15.29n
	Starston?	15 sokemen sub Bury Abbey	The King (15 sokemen)	1.223
	Thorpe (Abbots) (rt)	Bury Abbey	Bury Abbey	14.18
North Erpingham	**Aylmerton (rt)**	Wigulf, freeman (sub Eadric – of Laxfield?)	William of Warenne (Frederic)	8.132
	(East) Beckham – outlier to Thornage and, later, to Blickling	1 freeman (sub Bishop of Thetford)	Bishop of Thetford [1 freeman?]	10.65
	Gimingham	[Stigand?]	William of Warenne (Rathi, freeman)	8.119
	Mundesley	[Grimketel, freeman?]	William of Warenne (Grimketel, freeman)	8.123
	(North) Repps	[1 freeman (sub Ketel)?]	William of Warenne (1 freeman, under Ketel)	8.126
	(South) Repps + (North) Repps	[Stigand?]	William of Warenne (8 freemen: 2 of Abbot Alfwold, 5 of Rathi of Gimingham & 1 of Osbert)	8.128
	(East & West) Runton	Thorkell Hako	William of Écouis (Ingulf)	19.22
	Sheringham	Siward Bairn	William of Ecouis	19.18
	Thorpe (Market)	1 freeman (sub Stigand)	William of Warenne (Ralph)	8.122

Hundred	Place	1066	1086	Ref
	Trunch	3 freemen (sub Harold Godwineson, Ralph the Constable & Ketel)	William of Warenne [3 freemen?]	8.124
South Erpingham	(Little) Barningham	2 freemen (sub Harold Godwineson)	William of Warenne (2 freemen of Harold's)	8.8
	Belaugh	1 sokeman (sub ?), 10½ sokemen (sub Ralph the Constable), 1 sokeman (sub St. Benet's Abbey)	St. Benet's Abbey (1 sokeman) & 1 other (under ?)	17.33
	Buxton (sub Ralph the Constable)	5 freemen – brothers	Ralph of Beaufour (5 freemen, brothers)	20.29
	Caltborpe	St. Benet's Abbey	St. Benet's Abbey	17.26
	Coltishall	16 sokemen (sub Stigand & Ralph the Constable)	William of Warenne (Thorold)	8.8
	Corpusty	Hardwine, freeman	William of Ecouis	19.34
	Erpingham	1 freeman	Drogo of Beuvrière	30.6
	[Hevingham?]	Freeman priest (sub Leofstan)	The King (freeman priest)	1.195
	Oxnead	Aildag, freeman (sub Gyrth Godwineson)	Godwine Haldane	61.2
	Scottow	St. Benet's Abbey	St. Benet's Abbey	17.23
	Swanton (Abbot)	St. Benet's Abbey	St. Benet's Abbey	17.25
	Thwaite (rt)	St. Benet's Abbey	St. Benet's Abbey	17.27
	Wolterton (rt)*	St. Benet's Abbey	St. Benet's Abbey	17.32
Eynsford	Elsing	Lokki, freeman	William of Warenne (Frederic) – Wymer, sub-tenant	8.6
	Foulsham	King Edward	The King	1.52
	Haveringland (rt)	Godwine, freeman	Reynold, son of Ivo	21.29

	Helmingham	Bishop of Thetford	Bishop of Thetford (Gunfrid the Archdeacon)	10.16
	Hindolveston	Bishop of Thetford	Bishop of Thetford	10.15
	Kerdiston	Godwine, freeman	William of Warenne (Randolph)	8.2
	(Wood) Norton – outlier to Hindolveston	Bishop of Thetford	Bishop of Thetford	10.15
	Sparham	Eadwine, freeman	Godric the Steward	12.27
	Stinton	Wither, freeman	William of Warenne (Randolph)	8.1
	Weston (Longville)	Hardwine, freeman	William of Ecouis	19.32
	(Great & Little) Witchingham	Hardwine, freeman	William of Ecouis	19.32
East Flegg	Scratby	Bishop of Thetford [7 sokemen?]	Bishop of Thetford (7 sokemen)	10.43
	Stokesby	Eadwine, freeman (sub Gyrth Godwineson)	William of Ecouis	19.36
	Thrigby	[10 freemen?]	William of Ecouis (Hugh)	19.37
	(Great) Yarmouth	Bishop of Thetford (sub St. Benet's Abbey)	Bishop of Thetford	1.68
West Flegg	Billockby	St. Benet's Abbey [later annexed by Bishop Herfast]	Bishop of Thetford (Bernard)	10.90
	Hemsby	Earl Ælfgar; then Ælfwine, by purchase; then Bishop of Thetford, by grant of Stigand	Bishop of Thetford	10.30
	Martham	36 freemen (sub Bishop of Thetford)	Bishop of Thetford [36 freemen?]	10.86

Forehoe	Dykebeck	Norman, freeman	Ralph Baynard	31.42
	[Marlingford?]	[2 sokemen, sub ?]	Count Alan of Brittany (2 sokemen)	[4.13]
	[Morley (St. Botolph & St. Peter)?]	1 priest & 5 freemen	William of Warenne	8.78
Happing	Brumstead – outlier to Sutton	Eadric of Laxfield	Roger Bigot (Robert)	9.88
	Catfield – outlier to Sutton	Eadric of Laxfield	Roger Bigot	9.88
	Hickling	Godwine, freeman (sub Eadric of Laxfield)	Count Alan of Brittany (Wymarc)	4.38
	Sutton	Eadric of Laxfield	Roger Bigot	9.88
	Walcott	Eadric, thegn [of Laxfield?]	Ranulf, brother of Ilger	36.5
	Waxham	2 freemen (1 sub Eadric of Laxfield & 1 sub him & St. Benet's Abbey) – 4.40; Eadric, freeman (sub Eadric of Laxfield) – 4.42	Count Alan of Brittany (2 freemen) – 4.40; Count Alan (1 freeman) – 4.42	4.40 & 4.42
Henstead	Bixley	Genred, freeman (sub Stigand)	Roger Bigot (Ranulf, son of Walter)	9.32
	Bramerton	12 freemen (9 sub Ulfketel, 1 sub Bury Abbey & 2 sub Stigand)	Roger Bigot (Ulfketel)	9.28
	Caistor (St. Edmund)	Bury Abbey	Bury Abbey	14.15
	Framingham (Earl & Pigot) (rt)	1 freeman (sub Eadwine, then Godric the Steward)	Roger Bigot	9.30
	Howe (rt)	1 freeman (sub Gyrth Godwineson)	Bury Abbey (Berenger)	14.16
	Kirby (Bedon) (rt)*	6 freemen (3 sub Ulfketel, 1 sub Ælfwine of Thetford, 1 sub Genred & 1 sub Ælfred)	Roger Bigot (Robert of Courson)	9.29

	Place	1066	1086	Ref
Poringland (rt)	7 freemen (sub Ulfketel)	Roger Bigot (Ulfketel)	9.37
	Rockland (St. Mary)	14 freemen & 6 half-freemen (sub Ulfketel)	Roger Bigot (Ulfketel)	9.27
	Saxlingham (Nethergate)	Stergar, royal guard (sub King Edward)	John, nephew of Waleran	49.7
	Shotesham (All Saints & St. Mary)	1 freeman (sub Stigand) & 16 (sub Gyrth Godwineson)	Roger Bigot (Ranulf, son of Walter) & Bury Abbey	9.24 & 14.16
Whitlingham (rt)*	Wulflet, freewoman (sub Stigand)	Roger Bigot (Robert of Courson)	9.31
	Yelverton	3 freemen (sub Ulfketel)	Roger Bigot (Ulfketel)	9.36
Holt	Blakeney (al. Snitterley)	Eadric [of Laxfield?] (sub Harold Godwineson)	Bishop of Thetford (William of Noyers)	10.56
	Briningham	4 freemen (sub Harold Godwineson) – 10.57; Ralph the Constable – 10.59	Bishop of Thetford (both Roger Longsword)	10.57 & 59
	Langham	Gyrth Godwineson	Bishop of Thetford (Peter of Valognes)	10.22
	Melton (Constable)	4 freemen (sub Harold Godwineson)	Bishop of Thetford (Roger Longsword & Ansketel the Reeve)	10.58
	Thornage	Bishop of Thetford	Bishop of Thetford	10.8
Humbleyard	Bracon Ash	[5 freemen – 9.189]	Colbeorn the Priest	45.1
	(East) Carleton	Ulf, thegn	Roger Bigot (Walter)	9.96
	[Cringleford?]	Ælfred the Priest (under Stigand)	Bishop of Bayeux (Roger Bigot)	2.12
	Earlham	3 freemen [sub Wulfgeat?]	The King (Wulfgeat)	1.206
	Eaton	10 freemen (sub Eadric of Laxfield)	The King	1.205
	Hethel	Ulf, thegn	Roger Bigot	9.94

Hundred	Place	TRE holder	1086 holder	Ref.
	Hethersett	Ulf, thegn	Count Alan of Brittany (Ribald)	4.52
	Intwood (rt)	Coleman, freeman (sub Stigand)	Eudo the Steward (Ralph)	24.7
	Ketteringham	Ulf, thegn	Roger Bigot (Ranulf, son of Walter)	9.95
	Lakenham – outlier to Thorpe (St. Andrew)	Stigand	The King	1.236
	Markshall	Godwine, freeman (sub Stigand)	Ralph of Beaufour	20.35
	(Great) Melton	Ketel, thegn (sub Stigand)	Ranulf Peverel (Warin)	32.4
	Mulbarton	Ording, thegn	Ralph of Beaufour (Richard)	20.34
	Stoke (Holy Cross)	Ingold, thegn	Tovi	48.3
	Swainsthorpe (rt)	15 freemen (11½ sub Ralph the Constable, 3 sub Stigand & ½ sub predecessor of Godric the Steward)	Tovi (15 freemen)	48.4
	Walsingham	Ketel, thegn (sub Stigand)	Ranulf Peverel (Warin)	32.2
	Wreningham	Leofwald, thegn	Hermer of Ferrers (Wagen)	13.24
Loddon	Carleton (St. Peter)	Ælfric, freeman (sub King Edward)	Reynold, son of Ivo	21.26
	Chedgrave	Leofric, freeman (sub Harold Godwineson)	Ralph Baynard (Geoffrey)	31.44
	Claxton	Sweetman, freeman (sub Stigand)	Roger Bigot (Robert of Vaux)	9.56
	Kirstead-with-Langhale	27 sokemen (sub Bury Abbey)	Bury Abbey (27 sokemen)	14.38
	Langley	Anand, freeman (sub King Edward), + 1 priest and 2 half-priests	Bishop of Thetford	10.33

	Loddon	Bury Abbey	Bury Abbey (Frodo)	14.35
	Mundham	[Ketel, freeman (sub Eadwine)?]	The King	1.183
	Seething (rt) – outlier to Stoke Holy Cross (9.25); outlier to Framingham (Earl & Pigot) – 9.51	Ælfwine of Thetford – 9.25; Ælfric, freeman (sub Stigand) – 9.51;	Roger Bigot (William Petch) – 9.25: Roger Bigot – 9.51 (5 smallholders)	9.25 & 51
	[Topcroft?]	2 priests (sub Bury Abbey)	Bury Abbey (Berenger)	14.37
	Torp	[Ely Abbey?]	Ely Abbey	15.29n
	Woodton (rt)	1 freeman (sub Ulfketel, after Ælfric's outlawry)	Roger Bigot (Ulfketel, King's reeve)	9.54
Mitford	(South)Burgh	[7 freemen?]	William of Warenne (7 freemen)	8.82
	(East) Dereham	[Ely Abbey?]	Ely Abbey	15.29n
	Garveston – outlier to Whinburgh	Thorketel, freeman	Hermer of Ferrers	13.19
	Letton	9 freemen	William of Warenne [9 freemen?]	8.83
	Mattishall	[14 freemen?]	Ralph of Beaufour (14 freemen)	20.16
	Shipdam	[11 freemen?]	William of Warenne (11 freemen)	8.84
	Thurestuna [Thruxton?]	1 freeman [sub?]	Roger Bigot (1 freeman under Robert of Vaux)	9.134
	(East) Tuddenham	Thorketel, freeman	Hermer of Ferrers	13.23
	(North) Tuddenham	[Sigar, freeman?]	Ralph of Beaufour (Richard)	20.15
	Whinburgh	Thorketel, freeman	Hermer of Ferrers	13.19
	[**Yaxham?**] (rt)	Freeman priest, Aldwine	Roger Bigot (Ranulf, son of Walter)	9.82

Hundred	Place	1066 holder	1086 holder	Ref
Norwich	Norwich	The burgesses (sub King Edward, the Earl of East Anglia, Stigand & Harold Godwineson)	The King	1.61
Taverham	Attlebridge	[1 freeman?]	Bishop of Thetford (Geoffrey, freeman)	10.37
	Beeston (St. Andrew)	1 freeman [sub Ralph the Constable?]	Ralph of Beaufour (1 freeman)	20.25
	Drayton	Aldwulf, freeman	Ralph of Beaufour (Oder)	20.26
	Hellesdon	Stigand	Godwine Haldane	61.1
	Taverham (rt)	Toki; freeman – 8.7; Ulf – 20.27	William of Warenne (Frederic) / Ralph of Beaufour (Oder)	8.7 / 20.27
	Wroxham	Stigand	Ralph of Beaufour	20.24
Tunstead	Barton Turf	1 sokeman (sub St. Benet's Abbey & Ralph the Constable)	St. Benet's Abbey	17.50
	Felmingham	St. Benet's Abbey	St. Benet's Abbey	17.39
	Hoveton (St.John & St. Peter)	Ralph the Constable	St. Benet's Abbey	17.37
	Neatishead	St. Benet's Abbey	St. Benet's Abbey	17.36
	(North) Walsham	St. Benet's Abbey	St. Benet's Abbey	17.38
	Paston	[St. Benet's Abbey?]	William of Warenne (Thorold)	8.11
	Sloley	1 sokeman (sub St. Benet's Abbey) & 3 other sokemen (sub ?)	Ralph of Beaufour (1 sokeman of St. Benet's Abbey)	20.33

Swafield	[1 sokeman (sub Bishop of Thetford)?]	Bishop of Thetford (1 sokeman under Gunfrid)	10.18
Witton (rt) – <u>priest</u> ref. in 1.196	1 freeman (sub St. Benet's Abbey)	William of Warenne (1 freeman)	8.12
Worstead	St. Benet's Abbey	St. Benet's Abbey	17.43
Walsham Beighton	Bishop of Thetford (acquired from Earl Ælfgar)	Bishop of Thetford	10.25
Panxworth	Godwine, freeman	William of Ecouis (Hugh)	19.25
Reedham	Brictric, freeman	William of Ecouis (Richard)	19.24
Tunstall	Skuli, freeman (sub Harold Godwineson)	Eudo the Steward	24.5

Table details

- Communities shown in bold font, with **(rt)** appended, are those with round-tower churches. An asterisk following indicates the ruins or remains of a round tower.

- Use of bold italic font shows communities where recorded churches had no endowment of land.

- Communities which have a question mark appended within square brackets are those which have a priest referred to and which, therefore, might possibly have had a place of worship of some kind.

- The names in brackets in the third column indicate the land-holders' patrons (an adoption acceptable to both parties, by process of *commendation*) or exercisers of jurisdiction – in those cases where patronage or jurisdiction is stated or implied. Sometimes the connection is specifically referred to, sometimes not, and because of the element of uncertainty caused thereby no attempt has been made to differentiate between patronage and jurisdiction.

- The names in brackets in the fourth column are those of sub-tenants of the tenants-in-chief, in cases where this information is given.

- No distinction is made between freemen (*libi hoes*) and sokemen (*soc*) in the translation of the text, all such tenants being classed as the former. Necessary adjustment has been made in the table, as freemen usually held their land independently, whereas sokemen were tied to an estate by customary services of some kind. The latter were probably also unable to attach themselves to the patronage of a social superior by the process of *commendation* (see Roffe, p. 223).

- The half-freemen occasionally referred to were probably commended to more than one lord (Welldon Finn, p. 125).

East Norfolk Summary (proportion of communities with churches)

Blofield – 25%.

Clavering – 69%.

Depwade – 50%.

Diss – 33% (1 early Christian foundation noted).

Earsham – 23%.

North Erpingham – 32%.

South Erpingham – 28%.

Eynsford – 34%.

East Flegg – 40%.

West Flegg – 20%.

Forehoe – 4%.

Happing – 35% (1 early Christian foundation noted).

Henstead – 54%.

Holt – 20%.

Humbleyard – 65%.

Loddon – 38% (2 early Christian foundations noted).

Mitford – 43% (1 early Christian foundation noted).

Norwich – not assessable.

Taverham – 33%.

Tunstead – 45% (2 early Christian foundations noted).

Walsham – 28% (1early Christian foundation noted).

- East Norfolk: 157/158 communities with churches, out of 442 in all = 35%.
- 6 other possible churches, on 5 recorded presences of a priest and on 1 other reference.
- County as a whole: 226/227 (excluding or including Thetford) communities with churches out of a total of 714 recorded = 32%.
- Number of churches in county: 270/272 (including Thetford & excluding Norwich); 256/258 (excluding Thetford also).

Table 5. Norfolk primary title-holders and church location (whole county)

Tenant-in-chief (1086)	Land-holder (1066)	Community	Sector	Reference
The King	[Harold Godwineson?]	(Pudding) Norton	West	1.16 (u)
	Stigand, Bury Abbey & Ely Abbey, Stigand	Thetford	West	1.69 (u), 1.70 (u) & 1.210 (m?)
	1 freeman (sub Ralph the Constable)	**(North) Burlingham (rt)***	East	1.99 (f)
	King Edward	Diss	East	1.8 Suffolk (m)
	3 freemen [sub Wulfgeat?]	Earlham	East	1.206 (f)
	10 freemen (sub Eadric of Laxfield)	Eaton	East	1.205 (f)
	5 sokemen [sub Stigand?]	Ellingham	East	1.239 (f)
	King Edward	Foulsham	East	1.52 (2m)
	12 freemen (mixed patronage)	Gillingham	East	1.239 (f)
	Freeman priest (sub Leofstan)	[Hevingham?]	East	1.195 (f?)
	Stigand – outlier to Thorpe St. Andrew	Lakenham	East	1.236 (o)
	[Ketel, freeman (sub Eadwine)?]	Mundham	East	1.183 (u)
	The burgesses (sub King Edward, the Earl of East Anglia, Stigand and Harold Godwineson)	Norwich	East	1.61 (u)
	15 sokemen (sub Bury Abbey)	Starston?	East	1.223
	Stigand – outlier to Earsham Hundred	**Stockton (rt)**	East	1.239 (o)
	Bishop of Thetford (sub St. Benet's Abbey)	(Great) Yarmouth	East	1.68 (u)
Bishop of Bayeux	Ælfred the Priest (sub Stigand)	[Cringleford?]	East	2.12 (m)
Count Alan of Britanny	Ralph Wader [following Ralph the Constable, his father]	[Middleton?]	West	4.45 (m)

	Ulf, thegn	Hethersett	East	4.52 (m)
	Godwine, freeman (sub Eadric of Laxfield)	Hickling	East	4.38 (m)
	[2 sokemen sub ?]	[Marlingford?]	East	[4.13] (f)
	2 freemen (1 sub Eadric of Laxfield & 1 sub him & St. Benet's Abbey) – 4.40; Eadric, freeman (sub Eadric of Laxfield) – 4.42	Waxham	East	4.40 (f) & 4.42 (m)
Earl Hugh	Burgheard, thegn	Fundenhall	East	6.6 (m)
	1 freeman (sub Stigand) & 1 other (sub Gyrth Godwineson) – see Roger Bigot 9.218	Hapton	East	6.6 (m)
William of Warenne	Toki, freeman	(Castle & West) Acre	West	8.22 (m)
	4 freemen [subToki?]	**Barmer (rt)**	West	8.108 (f)
	Toki, freeman, & 1 other freeman – 8.99; Toki – 8.100	(East & West) Barsham	West	8.99 (m & f) & 100 (m)
(Frederic)	2 freemen (sub Harold Godwineson & Frederic's predecessor)	Barwick	West	8.33 (m)
	Toki, freeman	Burnham Thorpe	West	8.105 (m)
	[Ælfgifu, freewoman?]	Congham	West	8.27 (m)
	1 freeman (sub another freeman)	(North & South) Creake	West	8.102 (f)
	Toki, freeman	*Croxton (rt)*	West	8.104 (f)
	40 sokemen [sub Ely Abbey?]	*Feltwell (rt)*	West	8.37 (f)
	Toki, freeman	*Fulmodeston*	West	8.103 (m)
	[Ralph the Constable?]	Griston	West	8.71 (u)
	[4 freemen?]	Hempton	West	8.114 (f)
	1 sokeman [sub Toki?]	*(Hel)Houghton*	West	8.108 (o)

(Frederic)	Toki, freeman	(East & West) Rudham	West	8.107 (2m)
	Toki, freeman	Sculthorpe	West	8.98 (m)
	6 freemen	Shereford (rt)	West	8.112 (f)
	2 sokemen [sub Toki?]	(Little) Snoring (rt)	West	8.101 (f)
	1 sokeman [sub Toki?]	Stibbard	West	8.106 (f)
	Toki, freeman	Tatterset	West	8.110 (m)
(Frederic)	Wigulf, freeman (sub Eadric – of Laxfield?)	Aylmerton (rt)	East	8.132 (m)
	2 freemen (sub Harold Godwineson)	(Little) Barningham	East	8.8 (f)
	16 sokemen (sub Stigand & Ralph the Constable)	Coltishall	East	8.8 (f)
(Frederic)	Lokki, freeman	Elsing	East	8.6 (m)
	[Stigand?]	Gimingham	East	8.119 (m)
	Godwine, freeman	Kerdiston	East	8.2 (m)
	9 freemen	Letton	East	8.83 (f)
	1 priest & 5 freemen	[Morley (St. Botolph & St. Peter)?]	East	8.78 (f)
	[Grimketel, freeman?]	Mundesley	East	8.123 (f)
	[St. Benet's Abbey?]	Paston	East	8.11 (f)
	[1 freeman (sub Ketel)?]	(North) Repps	East	8.126 (f)
	[Stigand?]	(South) Repps	East	8.128 (f)
	[11 freemen?]	Shipdam	East	8.84 (f)
	[7 freemen?]	(South)Burgh	East	8.82 (f)
	Wither, freeman	Stinton	East	8.1 (m)
(Frederic)	Toki, freeman	Taverham (rt)	East	8.7 (m)
	1 freeman (sub Stigand)	Thorpe (Market)	East	8.122 (m)

3 freemen (sub Harold Godwineson, Ralph the Constable & Ketel)	Trunch	East	8.124 (f)
1 freeman (sub St.Benet's Abbey)	Witton (rt)	East	8.12 (f)
Roger Bigot			
Abba (sub Stigand)	Appleton (rt)*	West	9.7 (m)
Ælfeah, freeman	Beechamwell (rt)	West	9.233 (m)
[1 freeman?]	Flitcham	West	9.4 (f)
Hagni	Pentney	West	9.2 (m)
[King Edward?]	Thetford	West	9.1 (m)
Ældreda, freewoman	Watton (rt)	West	9.11 (m)
Genred, freeman (sub Stigand)	Bixley	East	9.32 (m)
12 freemen (9 sub Ulfketel, 1 sub Bury Abbey & 2 sub Stigand)	Bramerton	East	9.28 (f)
Eadric of Laxfield	Brumstead	East	9.88 (o)
Ulf, thegn	(East) Carleton	East	9.96 (2m)
16½ freemen? [sub Stigand?]	Carleton (Rode)	East	9.209 (2f)
Eadric of Laxfield	Catfield	East	9.88 (o)
Sweetman, freeman (sub Stigand)	Claxton	East	9.56 (m)
Coleman, freeman (sub Stigand)	Forncett (St. Mary & **St. Peter**) (rt)	East	9.98 (m)
1 freeman (sub Eadwine, then Godric the Steward)	Framingham (**Earl** & Pigot) (rt)	East	9.30 (f)
3½ freemen? [sub Stigand?]	Fritton (rt)	East	9.208 (f)
Ulf, thegn	Hethel	East	9.94 (m)
Ælfwine of Thetford	Hudeston	East	9.100 (m)
Ulf, thegn	Ketteringham	East	9.95 (m)

6 freemen (3 sub Ulfketel, 1 sub Ælfwine of Thetford, 1 sub Genred & 1 sub Ælfred)	Kirby (Bedon) (rt)*	East	9.29 (f)
1 freeman? [sub Stigand?]	Moulton (St. Michael)	East	9.212 (f)
7 freemen (sub Ulfketel)	Poringland (rt)	East	9.37 (f)
14 freemen & 6 half-freemen (sub Ulfketel)	Rockland (St. Mary)	East	9.27 (f)
1 villan belonging in Stoke Holy Cross (sub Ælfwine of Thetford) – 9.25; 5 smallholders belonging in Framingham – 9.51	Seething (rt)	East	9.25 (m) & 9.51 (2m)
9½ freemen? [sub Stigand?]	Shelton	East	9.216 (f)
Thorbert, freeman (sub Stigand)	Shimpling (rt)	East	9.46 (m)
1 freeman (sub Stigand)	Shotesham (All Saints & St. Mary)	East	9.24 (m)
Eadric of Laxfield	Sutton	East	9.88 (m)
Oslac, freeman [sub Stigand?]	Swanton	East	9.221 (f)
Wulfric (sub Stigand)	Tharston	East	9.99 (m)
1 freeman [sub ?]	*Thurestuna*	East	9.134 (f)
Wulflet, freewoman (sub Stigand)	Whitlingham (rt)*	East	9.31 (m)
1 freeman (sub a freeman of Ælfric, Stigand's man – later, sub Ulfketel)	Woodton (rt)	East	9.54 (f)
Aldwine, freeman priest	[Yaxham?]	East	9.82 (f)
3 freemen (sub Ulfketel)	Yelverton	East	9.36 (f)
Bishop of Thetford (diocesan)			
Bishop	Colkirk	West	10.6 (m)
Bishop	(Great) Cressingham	West	10.1 (m)
Bishop	(North) Elmham	West	10.5 (m)
Bishop	Saxlingham	West	10.7 (m)

Bishop	Helmingham	East	10.16 (2m)
Bishop	Hindolveston	East	10.15 (m)
Bishop	(Wood) Norton	East	10.15 (o)
[1 sokeman (sub Bishop of Thetford)?]	Swafield	East	10.18 (f)
Bishop	Thornage	East	10.8 (m)
Bishop of Thetford (acquired)			
[1 freeman?]	Attlebridge	East	10.37 (f)
Bishop (acquired from Earl Ælfgar)	Beighton	East	10.25 (m)
St. Benet's Abbey [later annexed by Bishop Herfast]	Billockby	East	10.90 (m)
Eadric [of Laxfield?] (sub Harold Godwineson)	Blakeney (al. Snitterley)	East	10.56 (m)
1 freeman (sub Bishop)	(East) Beckham	East	10.65 (o)
Eadric, royal steersman (sub King Edward)	Bradeston	East	10.76 (m)
4 freemen (sub Harold Godwineson) – 10.57; Ralph the Constable – 10.59	Briningham	East	10.57 & 10.59 (m)
15 freemen (sub Bishop) -10.68; 1 freeman (sub Bishop) – 10.73	(North) Burlingham (rt)*	East	10.68 (f) & 10.73 (f)
8 freemen (sub Bishop)	South Burlingham	East	10.74 (f)
Earl Ælfgar; then Ælfwine, by purchase; then Bishop by grant of Stigand	Hemsby	East	10.30 (m)
Gyrth Godwineson	Langham	East	10.22 (2m)
Anand, freeman (sub King Edward), + 1 priest & 2 half-priests	Langley	East	10.33 (m)
7 freemen (sub Bishop)	*Letha*	East	10.72 (f)
36 freemen (sub Bishop)	Martham	East	10.86 (f)
4 freemen (sub Harold Godwineson)	Melton (Constable)	East	10.58 (f)

Tenant	Holder	Place	Location	Reference
?		Mendham [E. Suffolk] – priest Ælfgar held 43 acres of church land		10.32
	[7 sokemen, attached to Hemsby?]	Scratby	East	10.43 (f)
Godric the Steward	Hagni (sub Stigand)	**Heckingham (rt)**	East	12.42 (m)
	Eadwine, freeman	Sparham	East	12.27 (m)
Hermer of Ferrers	Thorketel, freeman	Barton (Bendish)	West	13.3 (m)
	Thorketel, freeman	(Great) Ellingham	West	13.15 (m)
	[Thorketel?]	Fincham	West	13.2 (m)
	Thorketel (sub Stigand)	Islington	West	13.13 (m)
	Thorketel, freeman	Litcham	West	13.16 (m)
	Thorketel, freeman	(North) Runcton	West	13.14 (m)
	Thorketel [freeman]	Stow (Bardolph)	West	13.7 (m)
	Swarting, freeman	Stradsett	West	13.10 (m & f)
	Thorketel [freeman]	Thorpland	West	13.6 (m)
	Thorketel [freeman]	West Briggs	West	13.5 (m)
	Thorketel [freeman]	Wormegay	West	13.4 (m)
	Thorketel, freeman	Garveston	East	13.19 (o)
	Thorketel, freeman	(East) Tuddenham	East	13.23 (m)
	Thorketel, freeman	Whinburgh	East	13.19 (m)
	Leofwald, thegn	Wreningham	East	13.24 (m)
Annexation	[7 freemen?]	**Bexwell (rt)**	West	66.9 (f)
Annexation	Thork[et]el, freeman	**(Gayton) Thorpe (rt)**	West	66.22 (m)
Annexation	[11½ freemen?]	(Shouldham) Thorpe	West	66.14 (f)

Annexation	Thurstan, freeman	Wallington	West	66.16 (f)
Annexation	[3 freemen?]	(West) Walton	West	66.21 (f)
Bury Abbey				
	1 sokeman (sub Abbey)	(Blo) Norton	West	14.8 (m)
	Abbey	Bressingham	East	14.24 (m)
	Abbey	Caistor (St. Edmund)	East	14.15 (m)
	Abbey	Dickleburgh	East	14.29 (m)
	2 sokemen (sub Abbey) & 7 sokemen (patronage only)	Hales (rt)	East	14.42 (f)
	1 freeman (sub Gyrth Godwineson)	Howe (rt)	East	14.16 (m)
	Abbey	Kirby (Cane) (rt)	East	14.41 (2m)
	27 sokemen (sub Abbey)	Kirstead-with-Langhale	East	14.38 (f)
	Abbey	Loddon	East	14.35 (m)
	1 freeman (sub Abbey)	Shelfanger	East	14.32 (f)
	16 freemen (sub Gyrth Godwineson)	Shotesham (All Saints & St. Mary)	East	14.16 (f)
	Abbey	Thorpe (Abbots) (rt)	East	14.18 (m)
	Abbey	(Morning)Thorpe (rt)	East	14.40 (m)
	Abbey	Tivetshall (St. Margaret & St. Mary)	East	14.23 (2m)
	2 priests (sub Abbey)	[Topcroft?]	East	14.37 (m)
Ely Abbey				
	Abbey	Bridgham	West	15.29n (u)
	Abbey	Feltwell	West	15.29n (u)
	Abbey	Marham	West	15.1 (m)
	Abbey	Northwold	West	15.29n (u)
	Abbey	(West) Walton	West	15.29n (u)

	Abbey	(East) Dereham	East	15.29n (u)
	Abbey	Pulham (St. Mary Magdalene & St. Mary the Virgin)	East	15.29n (u)
	Abbey	*Torp*	East	15.29n (u)
St. Benet's Abbey	1 sokeman (sub the Abbey & Ralph the Constable)	Barton (Turf)	East	17.50 (2f)
	12½ sokeman (1 sub ?, 10½ sub Ralph the Constable & 1 sub the Abbey)	Belaugh	East	17.33 (f)
	Abbey	*Calthorpe*	East	17.26 (m)
	Abbey	Felmingham	East	17.39 (m)
	Ralph the Constable	Hoveton (St. John)	East	17.37 (m & f)
	Abbey	Neatishead	East	17.36 (m)
	Abbey	Scottow	East	17.23 (m)
	Abbey	Swanton (Abbot)	East	17.25 (m)
	Abbey	**Thwaite (rt)**	East	17.27 (m)
	Abbey	(North) Walsham	East	17.38 (m)
	Abbey	**Wolterton (rt)***	East	17.32 (m?)
	Abbey	Worstead	East	17.43 (2m)
William of Ecouis	Fathir, freeman	Banham	West	19.13 (m)
	Bernard (sub King Edward)	(Great) Bircham	West	19.9 (m)
	Ketel, freeman	(East & West) Harling	West	19.15 (m)
	Fathir, freeman	Wilby	West	19.11 (m)
	Hardwine, freeman	Corpusty	East	19.34 (u)
	Godwine, freeman	Panxworth	East	19.25 (m)
	Brictric, freeman	Reedham	East	19.24 (m)

	Thorkell Hako	(East & West) Runton	East	19.22 (m)
	Siward Bairn	Sheringham	East	19.18 (m)
	Eadwine, freeman (sub Gyrth Godwineson)	Stokesby	East	19.36 (m)
	[10 freemen?]	Thrigby	East	19.37 (f)
	7½ freemen (sub Ralph of Beaufour)	Thurlton	East	19.40 (f)
	Hardwine, freeman	Weston (Longville)	East	19.32 (o)
	Hardwine, freeman	*(Great & Little) Witchingham*	East	19.32 (m)
Ralph of Beaufour	Fathir, freeman	**(East & West) Lexham (rt)**	West	20.8 (m)
	Tovi, freeman	(Bircham) Newton	West	20.1 (m)
	Godwine, freeman	Swanton (Morley)	West	20.7 (m)
	1 freeman (sub Stigand)	Aldeby	East	20.36 (m)
	1 freeman [sub Ralph the Constable?]	Beeston (St. Andrew)	East	20.25 (f)
	5 freemen – brothers	Buxton	East	20.29 (m)
	Aldwulf, freeman	Drayton	East	20.26 (m)
	Godwine, freeman (sub Stigand)	Markshall	East	20.35 (m)
	[14 freemen?]	Mattishall	East	20.16 (f)
	Ording, thegn	Mulbarton	East	20.34 (m)
	1 sokeman (sub St. Benet's Abbey) & 3 other sokemen (sub ?)	Sloley	East	20.33 (f)
	Ulf	**Taverham (rt)**	East	20.27 (m)
	1 freeman (sub Stigand)	*Thurketeliart*	East	20.36 (m)
	[Sigar, freeman?]	(North) Tuddenham	East	20.15 (2m)
	Stigand	Wroxham	East	20.24 (m & f)

Reynold, son of Ivo	Ketel, freeman	Stiffkey	West	21.25 (m)
	Ælfric, freeman (sub King Edward)	Carleton (St. Peter)	East	21.26 (m)
	Godwine, freeman	Haveringland (rt)	East	21.29 (m)
Ralph of Tosny	Harold Godwineson	(Great) Cressingham	West	22.4 (o)
	Harold Godwineson	Necton	West	22.1 (m)
	Harold Godwineson	(North & South) Pickenham	West	22.3 (o)
Eudo the Steward	Coleman, freeman (sub Stigand)	Intwood (rt)	East	24.7 (m)
	Skuli, freeman [same man as below?]	Postwick	East	24.6 (m)
	Skuli, freeman (sub Harold Godwineson)	Tunstall	East	24.5 (m)
Drogo of Beuvrière	1 freeman	Erpingham	East	30.6 (f)
Ralph Baynard	Æthelgyth, freewoman	Barton (Bendish)	West	31.21 (m)
	Æthelgyth, freewoman	Boughton	West	31.25 (m)
	Æthelgyth, freewoman, & 8 attached sokemen	(East & West) Bradenham	West	31.34 (m)
	Æthelgyth, freewoman	Shouldham (All Saints & St. Margaret)	West	31.22 (2m)
	13 freemen (sub Æthelgyth)	Stoke (Ferry)	West	31.26 (2f)
	Norman, freeman	Tittleshall	West	31.38 (m)
	Leofric, freeman (sub Harold Godwineson)	Chedgrave	East	31.44 (m)
	Norman, freeman	Dykebeck	East	31.42 (m)
	Thorn	Hempnall	East	31.6 (2m)
	1 freeman (sub Harold Godwineson) & Thored, thegn	Wheatacre	East	31.17 (2m)

Ranulf Peverel	Ketel, thegn (sub Stigand)	(Great) Melton	East	32.4 (m)
	Ketel, thegn (sub Stigand)	Walsingham	East	32.2 (m)
Ranulf, brother of Ilger	Eadric, thegn [of Laxfield?]	Walcott	East	36.5 (m)
Colbeorn the Priest	[5 freemen – 9.189]	Bracon Ash	East	45.1 (u)
Edmund, son of Payne	Payne	[(Great & Little) Dunham?]	West	46.1 (m)
Tovi	Ingold, thegn, & Ketel, freeman, & 1 other freeman (both sub Stigand)	Stoke (Holy Cross)	East	48.3 (m & f)
	15 freemen (11½ sub Ralph the Constable, 3 (sub Stigand) & ½ (sub Godric the Steward's predecessor)	Swainsthorpe (rt)	East	48.4 (f)
John, nephew of Waleran	Ælfheah, freeman	Griston	West	49.4 (o)
	Bovi	*Hunstanton*	West	49.2 (m)
	Ælfheah, freeman	West Carbrooke	West	49.5 (m)
	Stergar, royal guard (sub King Edward)	Saxlingham (Nethergate)	East	49.7 (m)
Roger, son of Rainard	Osbern, thegn	*Raveningham (rt)*	East	50.12 (m)
Godwine Haldane	Stigand	*Hellesdon*	East	61.1 (m)
	Aildag, freeman (sub Gyrth Godwineson)	Oxnead	East	61.2 (m)

Table details

- Communities shown in bold font, with **(rt)** appended, are those with round-tower churches. An asterisk following indicates the ruins or remains of a round tower.

- Use of bold italic font shows communities where recorded churches had no endowment of land.

- The fifth and last column indicates, wherever possible (from the information given), the type of estate to which a church or churches was/were attached. The symbols used are as follows: (f) = freeholding, (m) = manor, (o) = outlier and (u) = uncertain. Uncertainty occurs either when the Domesday scribe places a church at the very end of a series of entries, making it difficult to attach it to any particular estate (when two or more of these are listed), or when an entry stands in isolation from any supporting information (e.g. the seven churches recorded for Ely Abbey in the note to 15.29). Given the generally larger size of manors relative to that of freemen's estates, it would seem that the church was mainly a manorial asset and this has usually been the categorisation adopted.

- Estate summary, as follows: 155 manor and 12 outlier (64%), 75 freeholding (30%), 1 manor and freeholding combined (Shotesham), and 15 uncertain (6%) – Norwich & Thetford excluded because of urban complexity and the large number of churches recorded there.

- Only 3 Norfolk churches (Shotesham, Taverham and West Walton) had the shared interest of 2 different tenants-in-chief, compared with 23 in Suffolk. They are shown <u>underlined</u>.

- Note, also, 8 possible other churches, based on 7 references to the presence of a priest and one late Anglo-Saxon will reference (Marlingford) – whereas H.C. Darby, *Domesday England* (Cambridge, 1986), Fig.17, p. 54, cites 5 "priest-only" cases for Norfolk. Priests are recorded in connection weith the following communities: Cringleford, (Great & Little) Dunham, Hevingham, Middleton, Morley (St. Botolph & St. Peter), Topcroft and Yaxham. They are square-bracketed in the table.

- The first category of Bishop of Thetford holdings represents those estates which were an established part of the diocese; the second consists of ones acquired by Æthelmær.

- Note that Frederic [of St. Omer] was William of Warenne's brother-in-law. Estates connected with him, by use made of the Latin present tense (*est* = is), would suggest sub-tenancy under his relative. Welldon Finn, p. 210, however, says that Warenne had acquired the lands from Frederic.

Table 6. Incomplete shared church interest (1086)

Community	Hundred	Proportion	Reference
Barmer	Brothercross	½	8.108
Fincham	Clackclose	¼	13.2
Stoke (Ferry)		¼	31.26
(Shouldham) Thorpe		½	66.14
Barwick	Docking	½	8.33
(Gayton) Thorpe	Freebridge	½	66.22
Stibbard	Gallow	½	8.106
Litcham	Launditch	½	13.16
South Burlingham	Blofield	½	10.74
Kirby (Cane)	Clavering	$2/_3$	14.41
Thurlton		½	19.40
Aylmerton	North Erpingham	½	8.132
Belaugh	South Erpingham	½	17.33
Corpusty		¾	19.34
Wolterton		½	17.32
Kerdiston	Eynsford	½	8.2
(Wood) Norton		$1/_3$	10.15
Billockby	West Flegg	$2/_3$	10.90
Dykebeck	Forehoe	¼	31.42
Shotesham (All Saints & St. Mary)	Henstead	½ & ¼	9.24 & 14.16
Stoke (Holy Cross)	Humbleyard	½	48.3
Mundham	Loddon	½	1.183
Shipdam	Mitford	½	8.84
Beeston (St. Andrew)	Taverham	½	20.25
Taverham		¼ & ¼	8.7 & 20.27

Table details

- The "two parts" description for Kirby Cane and Billockby has been interpreted as two-thirds.

- Complete shared interest is found once (West Walton), on a half-and-half basis (15.29n. & 66.21).

- The first word in the table's title may be misleading, since it is likely that there was no other party, or parties, with an interest in each church (given the level of detail present in Domesday, it is hard to believe that as many as twenty-five foundations would have been inaccurately recorded). The different fractions given probably refer to the nature of the various founding endowments made, though there is no means of working out what these were.

Summative comments for the county of Norfolk

The number of churches recorded

Taking the tabulated data above, a total of 256/258 churches has been arrived at, excluding two main urban centres: Norwich, with 26 foundations (seven of them named) and 43 private, burgess chapels, and Thetford, with its 14 (6 of them named). The third, Yarmouth (not given the epithet "Great" until the thirteenth century, to distinguish it from the community of Little Yarmouth, or Southtown, which had grown up on the Suffolk side of the River Yare) has been included because of one single church being recorded – with the minimal effect this gives on the overall figures and percentages. Even with the 40 Norwich and Thetford churches added to the county total, the figure falls short of the Domesday number of 330 given by Neil Batcock, 'Medieval Churches in Use and in Ruins', in *Norfolk Atlas*, p. 58. Williamson (p. 154) gives a total of 250, exclusive of Norwich, while Dymond (p. 81) cites a figure of 217 rural foundations – possibly drawing upon Darby, p. 138 – and this is repeated in Godfrey (pp. 2 & 27), who later in his work gives a total of 231 (p. 132).[1]

So much for what may be termed church "head-counts", with their degrees of variance. The one thing that all five commentators are agreed upon is that the number of churches recorded in Norfolk, at Domesday, fell far short of the true total. Broadly summarised, the assumption seems to be that the county, with its high level of population (compared with other parts of the country) and its measurable degree of wealth, must of necessity have had more churches than the record shows – particularly when the number of foundations known to have been in existence by the mid-thirteenth century (some 800 or so) is taken in to account. Various other reasons are offered regarding the assumed deficiency, which can now be considered following the sequence of publications cited in the previous paragraph and referred to in full in the Introduction.

Batcock, p. 58, refers to the disparity in numbers of churches between the South Norfolk hundreds of Clavering (thirteen) and Earsham (three), thereby implying inconsistency of recording on the part of the clerical staff gathering the Domesday information, while Williamson, p. 154, cites churches referred to in late Anglo-Saxon wills and charters which do not feature in the Survey (but which might, for one reason or another, have gone out of existence in the interim). Dymond, p. 81, finds it inconceivable that Norfolk should have had a significantly lower proportion of early churches than Suffolk, with the similarity of settlement patterns evident in each county, and attributes the disparity to differing priorties of local assessors. Darby, p. 138, simply says that it cannot be supposed for one moment that the churches recorded were the only ones in the county, adding that "the weight of probability is against such an idea", while Godfrey in his summing-up (pp. 249 & 250) remarks that it is clear from a comparison of Domesday and architectural evidence that there must have been far more churches than those listed in 1086 – adding that the Survey does not record any of the county's foundations in a systematic way and that reasons for inclusions or omissions remain obscure. The first piece of this concluding statement requires comment. Domesday is extremely systematic in the way that the information was collected and (for the most part) presented; and just because the results are not always easy for the present-day scholar to access and perhaps disapppointing in what he or she hopes to find, their formation and survival is a miracle of its kind.

Accuracy or inaccuracy?

According to a much-cited quotation, taken from *The Anglo-Saxon Chronicle*, "there was no single hide nor virgate of land, nor indeed (it is a shame to relate but it seemed for him [i.e. William I] no shame to do) one ox nor one cow nor one pig which was there left out, and not put down in his record." If this was the case, why should the number of churches have been so singularly misrepresented in the county of Norfolk? With arable land and livestock (and all other demesne assets) being so carefully recorded, why should churches have been omitted – especially when their physical presence and spiritual function are taken in to account? It seems arguable that they were.

It may well be that commentators have looked at the Domesday record and, in the light of the late medieval, rural parish structure (which is effectively that seen today), have then assumed that a similar network of parochial units was in existence in 1086. Undoubtedly, many parishes had reached their final physical definition by then, but there were also probably a large number where boundaries had not been finalised. Even as late as 1256, in Suffolk, the demarcation between Southwold to the south and Easton [Bavents] to the north had not been fixed, and an order in council of 8 March that year was given to the county Sheriff, at the request of the Abbot of Bury (Southwold's lord) and Hubert de Bavent (Easton's lord), to ensure that it was done.[2] Furthermore, given the way that a substantial number of Domesday settlements did not always achieve permanency (being incorporated in adjacent ones, as in Mutford and Lothingland half-hundreds, and also the manner in which new parishes were formed from existing ones during the post-Domesday period, as in Lothingland), it is perhaps best not to assume the existence of a fully developed parish system in 1086.

In any case, it would take decades of dedicated field-walking by a large number of experienced, enthusiastic volunteers (such as the late Alan Davison carried out in Breckland and South Norfolk), in tandem with exhaustive archaeological investigation on a multitude of sites, before anything like a comprehensive picture of church location and distribution in relation to defined boundaries could be achieved. And, to put it bluntly, this will never happen. It is simply too demanding in terms of human effort and financial cost. Moreover, the notion that Norfolk must have had as many churches as Suffolk (whereas, in fact, 190 fewer were recorded) is founded on the premise that its assessors had different priorities from their Suffolk counterparts. But why should they have done? Their task was to record what they found in each and every community on their circuit(s) – and if indeed Suffolk was far more heavily "churched" than Norfolk, there must have been good reasons for it. The next chapter will provide some possible explanations.

A final point to be considered is the type of ministry exercised by the priesthood of the time and, more importantly perhaps, patterns of community practice. There is little statistical information with which to provide a firm basis for analysis of clergy numbers and function, but it should always be borne in mind that in both essence and doctrine the Christian Church is the *people*, not the buildings where they congregate! The latter are simply meeting-places for worship and other activities and it is known that, at different times in history and in different parts of the world, Christians have assembled in varying numbers in all kinds of places to follow and express their beliefs.

In the absence of the fully developed parish-structure, which everyone has come to accept as the norm in England because it has been in existence for so long, it is likely that at least some Christian worship and witness during the mid Anglo-Saxon period was carried out in the open air – probably at key land-marks with former pagan associations or current significance as meeting-places. This, in turn, would seem to imply itinerant priests operating from monasteries or minsters within a locality and a pattern of worship that was occasional rather than regular. Where churches did exist, with a priest attached, it is likely that people from surrounding communities would gravitate there for Sunday worship, be it regularly or occasionally. Having to walk distances that might seem challenging today would not have posed serious problems for people at the time and a scrutiny of Domesday church distribution in Norfolk shows that most communities by then, without buildings of their own, were within walking-distance of a church. By the late Anglo-Saxon period, few places (if any) were more than five to six miles from a place of worship – even in West Norfolk, with a more widely dispersed pattern of settlement than its eastern counterpart and with significantly fewer churches – and, in many locations, they were a good deal closer.

It may well have been the case that, during the middle Anglo-Saxon period, minsters and monasteries did exercise an influence on the founding and location of local churches. However, a century or so of Danish conquest and occupation from the mid-ninth century onwards (which is believed to have been more disruptive in Norfolk than it was in Suffolk) would have resulted in the decline and disappearance of these established centres, as well as most of the churches themselves. The major cultural change which must have occurred during the period of Danelaw would have had a profound effect on the practice of Christianity by its adherents and it is highly likely that, without the presence and support of centres of organised religion, any proto-parochial structure would have fallen apart. The churches themselves, such as they were, being in most cases constructed of timber, would either have been abandoned and left to decay or undergone dismantlement and had their materials re-used. And, so, the pattern of church location as recorded and presented in Domesday is likely to have been the result of tenth and eleventh century "re-Christianisation" (if such a term is permissible) following the lengthy period of Danish influence and eventual unification of England under Æthelstan. It is difficult to see it as being connected with the earlier phase of evangelisation during the seventh and eight centuries. Finally, in the matter of the comparatively small number of churches referred to in pre-1066 documentation which do not appear in the Domesday Survey, they could easily have fallen out of use for a number of reasons and (in the case of timber-framed buildings) even been dismantled. One only has to think of the number of places of Christian worship (of all denominations) which became redundant for one reason or another during the twentieth century, especially in the larger urban areas, and were either converted to other uses or demolished.

Possible influences on the existence and location of Norfolk churches

In Williamson, pp.143-54, there is information relating to early, mid-Saxon centres of organised Christian religion or places which may possibly have had such function in the county.[3] An attempt will be made to ascertain if there was any noticeable effect that these institutions had, or may have had, on the founding and presence of local churches recorded in Domesday. All of them will be identified according to type (monastery, minster, hub-parish etc.) and placed in the various hundreds where they were located.[4] The number of settlements with churches will be appended for each hundred, together with the percentage of settlements which this represents, and some kind of opinion offered as to any possible correlation between the named centres and the presence of churches within their localities. All thirty-three hundreds will feature, as a means of demonstrating the overall county picture, and each will have a summary of the major tenancy influence (with regard to those communities having churches) revealed by the Domesday data for 1086 and by the occupants specified for the pre-Conquest era. The presence of Anglo-Saxon freewomen is indicated by underlining.

WEST NORFOLK

Brothercross (8 – 42%) – no early Christian centre identified – **1086**, 3 tenants-in-chief: William of Warenne x 7; Bishop of Thetford; the King. **Pre-1066**, Toki x 4: 2 direct and 4 sokemen and 1 sokeman (possibly under him); Bishop of Thetford; 4 freemen?; Harold Godwineson?; 6 freemen.

Clackclose (15 – 44%) – Stow Bardolph (possible minster), West Dereham (possible monastery) and Wormegay (possible monastery) – **1086**, 4 tenants-in-chief: Hermer of Ferrers x 10; Ralph Baynard x 4; Roger Bigot; Ely Abbey. **Pre-1066**, Thorketel x 6 (1shared with Æthelgyth); freewoman Æthelgyth x 4 (1 shared with Thorketel); freeman Ælfheah; 7 freemen; Ely Abbey; freeman Swarting; 11½ freemen; freeman Thurstan.

Docking (3 – 27%) – no early Christian centre identified – **1086**, 3 tenants-in-chief: William of Warenne; William of Écouis; Ralph of Beaufour. **Pre-1066**, 2 freemen; Bernard; freeman Tovi.

Freebridge (9 – 22%) – Babingley (monastery), Bawsey (possible monastery) and Snettisham (royal estate, with cruciform church – possibly evidential of a former minster) – **1086**, 4 tenants-in-chief: Hermer of Ferrers x 4; Roger Bigot x 3; William of Warenne x 2; Ely Abbey. **Pre-1066**, Thorketel x 3; freeman Toki; Abba; Hagni; 2 freemen; Ely Abbey.

Gallow (9 – 47%) – Burnham Overy (royal estate, with cruciform church – possibly evidential of a former minster) – **1086**, 2 tenants-in-chief: William of Warenne x 9; Bishop of Thetford. **Pre-1066**, freeman Toki x 6: all direct (1 shared with another freeman); Toki x 2 possible: 2 sokemen and 1 sokeman (under him); 1 freeman (sub 1 other freeman); Bishop of Theford.

North Greenhoe (1 – 5%) – Holkham (possible monastery) – **1086,** 1 tenant-in-chief: Reynold, son of Ivo. **Pre-1066,** freeman Ketel.

South Greenhoe (4 – 16%) – Swaffham (hub parish-possible minster) – **1066,** 3 tenants-in-chief: Ralph Tosny x 3; Bishop of Thetford; Ralph Baynard. **Pre-1066,** Harold Godwineson x 3; freewoman Æthelgyth and 8 sokemen (under her); Bishop of Thetford (shared with Harold Godwineson).[5]

Grimshoe (2 – 10%) – no early Christian centre identified – **1086,** 2 tenants-in-chief: Ely Abbey x 2; William of Warenne. **Pre-1066,** Ely Abbey x 2: 1 direct and 40 sokemen (under it).

Guiltcross (3 – 25%) – no early Christian centre identified – **1086,** 2 tenants-in-chief: William of Écouis x 2; Bury Abbey. **Pre-1066,** freeman Ketel; freeman Fathir; 1 sokeman (sub Bury Abbey).

Launditch (5 – 17%) – North Elmham (monastery-minster-diocesan centre) – **1086,** 4 tenants-in-chief: Ralph of Beaufour x 2; Hermer of Ferrers; Ralph Baynard; Bishop of Thetford. **Pre-1066,** Payne; Bishop of Thetford; freeman Fathir; freeman Thorketel; freeman Godwine; freeman Norman.

Shropham (3 – 14%) – Eccles (possible monastery) – **1086,** 3 tenants-in-chief: Ely Abbey; Hermer of Ferrers; William of Écouis. **Pre-1066,** Ely Abbey; freeman Thorketel; freeman Fathir._

Smethdon (1 – 12%) – no early Chrisitian centre identified – **1086:** 1 tenant-in-chief: John, nephew of Waleran. **Pre-1066,** Bovi.

Thetford (14 recorded churches in **1086;** minster-diocesan centre) – no further analysis.

Wayland (3 – 18%) – Saham Toney (possible monastery) and Stow Bedon (possible monastery) – **1086,** 3 tenants-in-chief: John, nephew of Waleran x 2; William of Warenne; Roger Bigot. **Pre-1066,** freeman Ælfheah x 2; freewoman Ældreda; Ralph the Constable (?).

The first thing to be said is that five of the thirteen hundreds have no recorded evidence of early Christian centres of any kind and that one of them (Brothercross) has one of the highest percentages of communities with churches (42%). Significantly, perhaps, it adjoined Gallow Hundred, which had the highest percentage of all (47%). If there was a possible influence in each jurisdiction being well churched, it might have been an earlier minster foundation at Burnham Overy, suggested as a possibility by Williamson p. 154. Regarding the remaining eight hundreds, it would seem from the generally low percentages that the presence of monasteries or minsters in mid Anglo-Saxon times seems to have had limited impact on the founding of churches, and any possible residual influence is hard to assess. Clackclose (44%) is the one hundred where a connection seems feasible, given the possible presence at one time or another of three foundations: West Dereham and Stow Bardolph in the middle of the hundred and Wormegay in its northern sector, close to the boundary with Freebridge.

Another possible influence regarding the presence of churches in the south-eastern part of West Norfolk – particularly regarding the nearby hundreds of Grimshoe, Shropham, Wayland and South Greenhoe – is the important urban centre of Thetford. It had fourteen churches recorded in 1086, one of which (St. Mary) may have been a minster on the evidence of four satellite churches referred to (Williamson, pp. 151-2). It also served as the cathedral of the East Anglian diocese for a short time (1075-95) after control of the see had been moved from North Elmham and before it became established at Norwich. In addition to a minster foundation, there was also a monastery recorded in the town, under the patronage of Roger Bigot (dedicated to St. George), which had been planted early in the eleventh century as a cell to the great house at Bury St. Edmunds, a mere twelve miles or so to the south. Such a pedigree in terms of ecclesiastical establishment should perhaps have served as a stimulus to the creation of local churches – but if it did, the effect seems to have been minimal. Grimshoe shows only 10% of its communities with churches, Shropham with 14%, Wayland 18% and South Greenhoe 16% – and the last three hundreds are accredited with possible monastic (Eccles, Saham Toney and Stow Bedon) and minster (Swaffham) sites of their own. Even Guiltcross, immediately to the east of Thetford, had no more than 25% of its settlements with churches, but it had no sites of Christian mission accredited to it.

Three hundreds with such identification attached remain to be mentioned: Freebridge, North Greenhoe and Launditch. At 22%, the effect of two possible monastic sites (Babingley and Bawsey) and one minster (Snettisham) in the first named would seem to be unimpressive – while the second jurisdiction, with the possibility of a monastery once located at Holkham, has the second lowest percentage (5%) in the whole of the county, exceeded only by Forehoe (4%) in East Norfolk. Finally, there is Launditch (17%), which contained North Elmham (centre of the East Anglian diocese from c. 950 until 1075).[6] Again, especially given its role as the seat of the bishop and therefore the pastoral hub of two counties, it seems to have had limited influence at best on the founding of churches in its immediate locality. Furthermore, the presence of markets at Great/Little Dunham (1.212) and nearby Litcham (13.16) – the former having a priest recorded as holding a large estate and the latter with a church – does not seem to have had much effect either.

If, then, it is the case that the existence of West Norfolk's Anglo-Saxon monasteries or minsters seems to have had a relatively small effect on the founding of rural churches, is it possible that other contributing agencies are detectable in the data? In information relating to the pre-Conquest era, in every hundred except Grimshoe, it is noticeable that freemen (and two freewomen) are a strong feature, with the thegns Thorketel and Toki being dominant presences in Clackclose, Freebridge and Gallow particularly (and Toki also in Brothercross) – along with the freewoman Aethelgyth, also in Clackclose. All three of them appear in other hundreds as well, along with quite a number of other named individuals who were probably not of thegnly status, but important enough to have their names recorded – a privilege not accorded to their lesser counterparts, who remain anonymous but who nevertheless are to be observed in Brothercross, Clackclose, Docking, Freebridge and Gallow. Institutionally, the outside abbeys of Ely and Bury St. Edmunds appear from time to time (five times and once, respectively), as does the Bishop of Thetford (four times).[7] However, far from being direct founding agencies, it is likely that all three of them were more interested in acquiring benefices to boost their influence and material wealth than in starting them off. Having said that, it is also conceivable that they might have encouraged the establishment of churches where the will to build them was apparent.

What of the twenty years between the Conquest and Domesday? If freemen seem to have been possible factor in the founding of churches during the final years of Anglo-Saxon England, is there anything to be seen in the years of upheaval and establishment of a new order? Both William of Warenne (Brothercross and Gallow) and Hermer of Ferrers (Clackclose and Freebridge) were notable presences in these hundreds and might just have had a hand in encouraging, and perhaps even helping to fund, the founding of churches among their tenants as a means of establishing and reinforcing their authority on local populations. Having earned their reward by military might, it would not have seemed unusual at the time among the ruling élite for tenants-in-chief to express thanks for their good fortune in supporting a programme of church-building. The invading Normans had shown a strong sense of the moral (even divine) justice of their cause in their forcible acquisition of the kingdom of England and houses of God would therefore have sat well with a deserved victory.

EAST NORFOLK

<u>Blofield</u> (5 – 25%) – no early Christian centre identified – **1086**, 5 tenants-in-chief: Bishop of Thetford x 2; the King; William of Noyers; Reynold; Eudo the Steward. **Pre-1066**, Bishop of Thetford x 4: 15 freemen, 1 freeman, 8 freemen and 7 freemen (all under him); Eadric the Steersman; freeman Skuli.

<u>Clavering</u> (11 – 69%) – no early Christian centre identified – **1066**, 7 tenants-in-chief: the King x 3; Ralph of Beaufour x 2; Bury Abbey x 2; Godric the Steward; Roger son of Rainard; William of Écouis; Ralph Baynard. **Pre-1066**, Stigand x 5: 1 direct and 1 freeman, 5 sokemen, Hagni and 1 freeman (under him); Bury Abbey x 2: 1 direct and 1 sokemen (under it); thegn Osbeorn; thegn Thored; 7½ freemen (sub Ralph of Beaufour).[8]

<u>Depwade</u> (12 – 50%) – no early Christian centre identified – **1086**, 4 tenants-in-chief: Roger Bigot x 8; Earl Hugh x 2; Ralph Baynard; Bury Abbey. **Pre-1066**, Stigand x 8: freeman Coleman and 1 freeman (under him), and 16½ freemen, 3½ freemen, 1 freeman, 9½ freemen, Oslac and Wulfric (all probably under him); thegn Burgheard; 1 freeman (sub Gyrth Godwineson); Thorn; Ælfwine of Thetford; Bury Abbey.[9]

<u>Diss</u> (6 – 33%) – Dickleburgh (possible minster) – **1066**, 3 tenants-in-chief: Bury Abbey x 4; the King; Roger Bigot. **Pre-1066**, Bury Abbey x 4: 3 direct and 1 freeman (under it); King Edward; freeman Thorbert (sub Stigand).

<u>Earsham</u> (3 – 23%) – no early Christian centre identified – **1086**, 3 tenants-in-chief: Ely Abbey; the King; Bury Abbey. **Pre-1066**, Bury Abbey x 2: 1 direct and 15 sokemen (under it); Ely Abbey.

<u>North Erpingham</u> (10 – 32%) – no early Christian centre identified – **1086**, 3 tenants-in-chief: William of Warenne x 7; William of Écouis; Bishop of Thetford. **Pre-1066**, Stigand x 3: 2 probable direct & 1 freeman (under him); freeman Wigulf (sub Eadric of Laxfield?); 1 freeman (sub Bishop of Thetford); freeman Grimketel?; 1 freeman (sub Ketel?); Thorkell Hako; Siward Bairn; 3 freemen (sub Harold Godwineson, Ralph the Constable & Ketel).

<u>South Erpingham</u> (12 – 28%) – no early Christian centre identified – **1086**, 6 tenants-in-chief: St. Benet Holm x 5; William of Warenne x 2; Ralph of Beaufour; William of Écouis; Drogo of Beuvrière; Godwine Haldane. **Pre-1066**, St. Benet's Abbey x 5; 2 freemen (sub Harold Godwineson); 1 sokeman (sub ?), 10½ sokemen (sub Ralph the Constable) & 1 sokeman (sub St. Benet's Abbey); 16 sokemen (sub Stigand & Ralph the Constable); freeman Hardwine; 1 freeman; freeman Leofson; freeman Aildag (sub Gyrth Godwineson).

Eynsford (11 – 34%) – no early Christian centre identified – **1086**, 6 tenants-in-chief: William of Warenne x 3; Bishop of Thetford x 2; William of Écouis x 2; the King; Reynold son of Ivo; Godric the Steward. **Pre-1066**, Bishop of Thetford x 3; freeman Hardwine x 2; freeman Godwine x 2; freeman Lokki (sub Frederic); King Edward; freeman Eadwine; freeman Wither.

East Flegg (4 – 40%) – no early Christian centre identified – **1086**, 2 tenants-in-chief: Bishop of Thetford x 2; William of Ecouis x 2. **Pre-1066**, 7 sokemen? (sub Bishop of Thetford); freeman Eadwine (sub Gyrth Godwineson), 10 freemen?; Bishop of Thetford (sub St. Benet's Abbey).

West Flegg (3 – 20%) – no early Christian centre identified – **1086**, 1 tenant-in-chief: Bishop of Thetford x 3. **Pre-1066**, Bishop of Thetford x 3: 2 direct (1 formerly held by St. Benet's Abbey and 1 by grant of Stigand) and 36 freemen (under him).

Forehoe (1 – 4%) – no early Christian centre identified – **1086**, 2 tenants-in-chief: Ralph Baynard & William Warenne. **Pre-1066**, freeman Norman; 1 priest & 5 freemen.[10]

Happing (6 – 35%) – no early Christian centre identified – **1086**, 4 tenants-in-chief: Roger Bigot x 3; Count Alan of Britanny x 2; Earl Hugh; Ranulf brother of Ilger. **Pre-1066**, Eadric of Laxfield x 6: 4 direct and freeman Godwine and freeman Eadric (under him); 2 freemen (1 sub Eadric of Laxfield and 1 sub St. Benet's Abbey); 2 freemen (1 sub Stigand & 1 sub Gyrth Godwineson).[11]

Henstead (12 – 54%) – no early Christian centre identified – **1086**, 3 tenants-in-chief: Roger Bigot x 9; Bury Abbey x 2; John nephew of Waleran. **Pre-1066**, Ulfketel x 5: 9 freemen, 3 freemen, 7 freemen, 14 freemen & 6 half-freemen, and 3 freemen (all under him); Stigand x 4: freeman Genred, 2 freemen, 1 freeman and freewoman Wulflet (all under him); Bury Abbey x 2: 1 direct & 1 freeman (under it); Gyrth Godwineson x 2: 1 freeman and 16 freemen (under him); 1 freeman (sub Eadwine, then Godric the Steward); 1 freeman (sub Ælfwine of Thetford);1 freeman (sub Genred); 1 freeman (sub Alfred); Stergar, royal guard (sub King Edward).

Holt (5 – 20%) – no early Christian centre identified – **1086**, 1 tenant-in-chief: Bishop of Thetford x 5. **Pre-1066**, Harold Godwineson x 3: Eadric, 4 freemen (with Ralph the Constable) and 4 other freemen (all under him); Gyrth Godwineson; Bishop of Thetford.

Humbleyard (16 – 65%) – no early Christian centre identified – **1086**, 9 tenants-in-chief: Roger Bigot x 3; the King x 3; Ralph of Beaufour x 2; Tovi x 2; Ranulf Peverel x 2; Colbern the Priest; Count Alan of Brittany; Eudo the Steward; Hermer of Ferrers. **Pre-1066**, Stigand x 6: 1 direct and Ælfred the Priest, freeman Coleman, freeman Godwine and thegn Ketel x 2 (all under him); thegn Ulf x 4; 15 freemen; 3 freemen; 10 freemen (sub Eadric of Laxfield); thegn Ording; thegn Ingold; 15 freemen (11½ sub Ralph the Constable, 3 sub Stigand & ½ sub Godric the Steward's predecessor) and thegn Leofwold.

Loddon (10 – 38%) – Langley (possible minster), Loddon (hub parish-monastery-minster) – **1086**, 7 tenants-in-chief: Roger Bigot x 3; Bury Abbey x 2; the King; Ely Abbey; Reynold son of Ivo; Ralph Baynard; Bishop of Thetford. **Pre-1066**: Bury Abbey x 3: 1 direct and 22 sokemen and 2 priests (under it); King Edward x 2: freeman Ælfric and freeman Anand; Stigand x 2: freeman Sweetman and freeman Ælfric (under him); freeman Leofric (sub Harold Godwineson); freeman Ketel (sub Eadwine?); Ælfwine of Thetford; Ely Abbey?; 1 freeman (sub Ulfketel, King's reeve).

Mitford (10 – 43%) – East Dereham (monastery) – **1086**, 5 tenants-in-chief: William of Warenne x 3; Hermer of Ferrers x 3; Ely Abbey; Ralph of Beaufour & Ely Abbey; Roger Bigot. **Pre-1066**, freeman Thorketel x 3; 7 freemen?; Ely Abbey?; 9 freemen; 14 freemen?; 11 freemen?; 1 freeman (sub ?); 1 freeman?; freeman Sigar?

Taverham (6 – 33%) – no early Christian centre identified – **1086**, 4 tenants-in-chief: Ralph of Beaufour x 4; Bishop of Thetford; Godwine Haldane; William Warenne. **Pre-1066**, Stigand x 2; 1 freeman?; 1 freeman (sub Ralph the Constable?); freeman Aldwulf; freeman Toki; freeman Ulf.

Tunstead (10 – 45%) – North Walsham (hub parish-possible minster) and St. Benet at Holm (monastery) – **1086**, 4 tenants-in-chief: St. Benet's Abbey x 6; William of Warenne x 2; Ralph of Beaufour; Bishop of Thetford. **Pre-1066**, St. Benet's Abbey x 8: 5 direct (4 definite and 1 likely) and 1 sokeman (shared with Ralph the Constable), 1 other sokeman and 1 freeman (under it); Ralph the Constable x 2: 1 direct and 1 sokeman (shared with St, Benet's Abbey); 3 sokemen (sub ?); 1 sokeman (sub Bishop of Thetford).[12]

Walsham (4 – 28%) – Reedham (monastery-minster) – **1086**, 3 tenants-in-chief: William of Écouis x 2; Bishop of Thetford; Eudo the Steward. **Pre-1066**, Bishop of Thetford; freeman Godwine; freeman Brictric; freeman Skuli (sub Harold Godwineson).

Owing to a greater number of hundreds and communities, East Norfolk is more difficult to analyse succinctly than its western counterpart. Fifteen of its twenty hundreds do not have references to early Christian centres accorded them and yet four have the highest percentages of communities with churches: Clavering (69%), Humbleyard (65%), Henstead (54%) and Depwade (50%). Of the hundreds with proven or possible monastic-minster antecedents, only Tunstead (45%) and Mitford (43%) begin to approach them. The remaining three, Loddon (38%), Diss (33%) and Walsham (28%) are further adrift.

All four of the highest-percentage hundreds had one thing in common, pre-Conquest: notable concentrations of freemen, and this may well have been a factor in the founding of churches given the comparative autonomy such tenants had. The proximity of Humbleyard and Henstead to Norwich (particularly the former, with its noticeably high number of thegns) may also have had an effect from both jurisdictions being exposed to urban influences and attitudes, and this in turn may have been transferred to Depwade, which lay immediately to the south of them.[13] The high-ranking cleric, Stigand, seems also to have been an important background presence in Depwade, as overlord, and it is possible that he may have been an encourager of church building – especially if any revenues could then be diverted to him. He was also a presence in Clavering – perhaps the most interesting of the four high-percentage hundreds. It is difficult to see this area as having been particularly influenced by adjacent Loddon Hundred's two posssible monastic-minster foundations, in view of the latter jurisdiction having only 38% of its own communities with churches, but another explanation offers itself: proximity to Beccles, with its market facility. It would only have been a comparatively short step away, over the Gillingham marshes, to Suffolk's most northerly urban settlement and regular contact with it and its church could possibly have been influential.

Of the remaining eleven hundreds which were without known pre-Conquest ecclesiastical hubs of one kind or another, Earsham shows a single link with sokemen (its four churches, overall, seemingly connected with the abbeys at Bury and Ely).[14] The other ten (Blofield, North Erpingham, South Erpingham, Eynsford, East Flegg, West Flegg, Forehore, Happing, Holt and Taverham) all show more marked associations with freemen and sokemen – a number of them under the patronage of religious houses or prelates (Stigand and the Bishop of Thetford, in the latter case) and of Eadric of Laxfield. Scrutiny of their churched community percentages reveals figures ranging from 20% to 40% – with the exception of Forehoe, which is only 4% (one church, at Dykebeck). No explanation readily offers itself for such a strikingly low figure and, if defective recording of churches is mooted, why should just one hundred have been so under-represented? Scrutiny of its twenty-seven vills shows the presence of freemen in nearly all of them, sometimes in appreciable numbers, but with no apparent effect on the presence of churches. Regarding possible clerical influence, Stigand is detectable in Barford, Crownthorpe, Morley and Wymondham, and St. Benet's Abbey in Barford and Carleton Forehoe – but again there is no recorded church presence.

Having made reference to the possible effect of local urban centres in the matter of their being a possible positive factor in the founding of churches, in the preceding paragraph but one, it was noted earlier in the summative comments on West Norfolk that heavily churched Thetford, with its fourteen foundations (including an abbey), seems to have had little effect on the hundreds of Grimshoe, Guiltcross, Shropham, South Greenhoe and Wayland.[15] It would seem, on the face of it, that Thetford should have exercised a noticeable influence on nearby jurisdictions – but it doesn't seem to have done. Exactly why this was the case is not able to be assessed and, as in so many other areas, Domesday raises as many questions as answers – perhaps even more!

One thing which is detectable in the five jurisdictions with possible monastic-minster antecedents (in common with the ones which didn't) is the pronounced presence of freemen and sokemen. The one exception is Diss, which seems to have been more under the influence of Bury Abbey than any other agency – being only twenty miles or so in distance from it. As for the rest, they too all exhibit an ecclesiastical presence of some kind, in addition to the freemen – often in association with these very people who worked the land or who supervised the ones who did. Bury Abbey and Stigand both appear in Loddon, while Ely Abbey is observed in Mitford. The Bishop of Thetford is recorded in Tunstead and Walsham, while Happing had a clerical connection with Stigand (in conjunction with Earl Gyrth Godwineson) and a less marked association with St. Benet's Abbey via one freeman under that abbey's patronage.[16] St. Benet's most marked presence was in Tunstead and, to a lesser degree, in South Erpingham. Its dedicated section in Domesday, after the opening *Terra Sci benedicti*, is followed with *ad victū monachorum* – "for the sustenance, or supply, of the monks" – leaving the reader in no doubt as to the primary function of the different estates recorded.

Regarding the remaining seven hundreds without apparent monastic-minster antecedents, which have not yet been commented on specifically, Blofield, North Erpingham, Eynsford, East Flegg, West Flegg, Holt and Taverham all have a detectable freemen element, to one degree or another, with both independence and patronage in evidence. All of them, apart from Taverham, show connections with the Bishop of Thetford, but Stigand features in Taverham – as well as in North Erpingham. The remaining ecclesiastical connection is that of St. Benet's Abbey in Tunstead. Moving to the very top of secular authority and control, a royal connection is noticeable in Eynsford, with Edward the Confessor holding a large and important manor there (in Foulsham), while a Godwineson family presence is detectable in Holt, with Harold himself being overlord of three churched estates (in Blakeney, Briningham and Melton Constable) and his brother Gyrth of one (Langham). This may possibly show a vestigial link with a former ancient estate in the hundred (Williamson, p. 153), though the vill of Holt itself (which served as the hub) is not recorded in Domesday as having a church. Nor does its staging of a market (1.19) seem to have generated the presence of one.

As for possible post-Conquest influences in the matter of church founding, The Bishop of Thetford and Bury Abbey are noticeable presences in a number of hundreds, as they were prior to 1066, but it is hard to assess any role each may have had. Direct creation of churches is unlikely; it was probably more a matter of encouraging the many freemen under patronage to build and endow their own. The diocese or abbey, as the case was, would then benefit from revenues which might come to it – as well as having an interest in the appointment of clergy. As far as secular influence is concerned, a considerable number of Norman overlords is apparent and it is unncecessary to name them here. Suffice it to say that the two dominant county presences, Roger Bigot (Sheriff of Norfolk and Suffolk) and William of Warenne (Earl of Surrey), feature prominently in Depwade and Henstead in the former case and in North Erpingham in the latter. If the founding of rural churches in the immediate post-Conquest period was ever a means of reinforcing the authority of the new, foreign, ruling élite, then both of these tenants-in-chief would have been well placed to impose their presence on the native Anglo-Saxon population.

With analysis of both halves of the county now having been carried out, in terms of the churches recorded in 1086, it is worth returning briefly to the matter of whether or not their number is seriously deficient. At the beginning of this summative section (pp. 94-8), various caveats – objections being too strong a term – were discussed by way of suggesting that this may not be the case. At the same time, the matter of inaccurate recording (for whatever reason) has to be considered as a possibility. Experienced and well accredited commentators have argued for it, and it cannot therefore be dismissed out of hand. Nor should it be. Historical evaluation is a process whereby available evidence is interpreted in a particular way by the individual researcher involved – and this can vary from person to person. The writer of this particular work does not believe that Norfolk's total number of churches is as seriously under-enumerated as sometimes maintained, but nor would he claim that the Domesday count is one hundred per cent accurate! The problem with what may be termed "missing churches" (such as the seven referred to in *Inquisitio*

Eliensis) is that there is simply no way of knowing just how many, or how few, there were!

A further problem remains with a matter alluded to earlier on pp. 95-8 – that of parish structure and numbers. There is no doubt that the evangelising and reformative work carried out by Theodore of Canterbury and Wilfrid of York (also of Selsey, Leicester and Hexham) during the second half of the seventh century – and the beginning of the eighth, in the case of Wilfrid – was instrumental in developing a proto-parochial system of ministry. But to what degree is not able to be assessed because of a lack of relevant, documentary evidence. In the interests of brevity, and without becoming side-tracked from the main emphasis of this particular study, suffice it to say that various commentators remark upon the importance of the seventh and eighth centuries in the development of parishes, without being any more specific than that. J.R.H. Moorman, for instance, in his study of the English Church, refers to the parochial system "struggling into existence", as well as acknowledging the importance of local land-holders as founding influences (a factor which sits well with what the late Anglo-Saxon times also seem to suggest), before moving on two hundred years later to the tenth century.[17]

Even as eminent a commentator on the Anglo-Saxon period as Frank Stenton is relatively unforthcoming on the matter of parish formation and function, limiting himself largely to commentary on the influence of monasteries and minsters, the role of lay nobility as founders of local churches, the use of standing-crosses to mark places of worship where there was no church building as such and the matter of how income to support priests was created.[18] He does, however, perhaps significantly, say that "at the end of the eighth century many Christian communities of long standing were still unprovided with any form of church". He then goes on to comment later that, although "the development of a parochial system is the central thread of English ecclesiastical history in the generations following Theodore, it is virtually ignored by contemporary writers".[19] This he attributes to the fact that such commentators (including Bede himself, presumably) ignored the establishment of parish churches because they regarded it as part of episcopal duties and saw nothing remarkable about it. Their interest and emphasis lay very much on the monastic life and its proponents – a case, perhaps, of St. Benedict taking precedence over local benediction its broadest sense.

Notes

1 Darby does not say that Norfolk had 217 rural churches, but that "churches are mentioned in connection with 217 villages, apart from those of Norwich, Thetford and Yarmouth". This would include those places (28 in number) which had more than one church. The writer's estimate is 256-258 churches in 226 communities.

2 *Calendar of Close Rolls, Henry III*, vol. 9, p. 402.

3 A serious geographical error is in evidence on the map of monastic sites on p. 147. Burgh Castle (*or Cnobheresburh*, as it had been previously named) only became part of Norfolk in 1974, with the annexation of five of Lothingland's northern parishes under the Local Government Act of 1972. The seventh century Celtic monastery, built within the walls of the Roman shore-fort of *Gariannonum*, was part of Suffolk!

4 *Hub-parish* is a term conveniently used to describe one which has a number of (usually) smaller neighbours, eight or more in number, surrounding it (Williamson, pp. 152-3). Such units may have been the centres of archaic large estates, with certain of them having had minsters founded at some point in their history.

5 Harold II, the last English Anglo-Saxon king, is never referred to as a monarch in the Domesday Survey. As far as the Normans were concerned, he was an oath-breaker and usurper and is simply referred to as Harold. His family name has been used to make clear his identity.

6 The see's history is a complex one, having been originally founded by St. Felix in c. 630, probably at Dunwich. Forty years later, in 672-3, another centre of influence was established at Elmham (either South Elmham, in Suffolk, or North Elmham, in Norfolk – opinions vary). Dunwich continued its role until c. 870, when Danish incursions and the death of King Edmund caused a lengthy period of religious dislocation. The diocese was eventually re-established during the early tenth century, with North Elmham becoming its hub.

7 This diocesan title was of comparatively recent pedigree, the see having been based at North Elmham until 1075.

8 Stigand had become Bishop of Elmham in 1043 and, on being translated to Winchester in 1047, was succeeded by his brother, Æthelmær (al. Aelmer). In 1052, he was elevated to Canterbury, continuing to hold Winchester and being excommunicated for pluralism. Managing to stay in post after the Conquest, he was finally deposed by papal legates in 1070.

9 Burgheard may well have been the thegn who features in Hartismere, Lothing, and Wangford (East Suffolk) – sometimes found referred to as Burghard of Mendlesham. Gyrth Godwineson was the younger brother of Harold – killed with him at Hastings and, up until then, Earl of East Anglia.

10 T. Pestell, 'Monasteries', in *Norfolk Atlas*, pp. 66-7, postulates a minster church at Wymondham, but it is not referred to in any way in Williamson's *Origins of Norfolk*.

11 Eadric of Laxfield was the most important, individual, late Anglo-Saxon landholder in Suffolk. Following the Conquest, the great majority of his estates were taken over by the Malet family.

12 The Benedictine abbey of St. Benet at Holm, in Horning, had been originally established c. 800, but had not survived the Danish incursions. It was re-founded in 1019. Ralph the Constable (al. de Gaël), referred to here and previously, served in a military capacity under Edward the Confessor. His son and successor, Ralph de Gaël (al. Wader/Waher or de Guader), became Earl of East Anglia – the Earl Ralph of some Domesday entries.

13 According to a pronouncement of King Æthelstan (927-39), it was a thegnly duty to found churches.

14 Williamson, p. 155, cites one church only.

15 The demarcation between the western and eastern sectors of Norfolk is not as easily and neatly defined as that applying to Suffolk, owing to the hundreds of Mitford, Shropham and Guiltcross extending prominently eastwards. Mitford might therefore have been included in West Norfolk, but the decision was made to place it in the East (see Map 1 notes, p. 19).

16 As has been noted earlier, Happing's main connection, or influence, was the largest secular landholder in Suffolk: Eadric of Laxfield.

17 J.R.H. Moorman, *A History of the Church in England*, 3rd ed. (London, 1973), pp. 28-9 & 50.

18 F.W. Stenton, *Anglo-Saxon England*, 3rd ed. (Oxford, 1971), pp. 148-52.

19 Stenton, p. 157.

Suffolk Churches

West Suffolk

Map 3. West Suffolk hundreds (overall percentages of communities with recorded churches)

(Grimshoe)

Norfolk

(Thetford)

(Guiltcross)

LACKFORD
94%

BLACKBOURN & BRADMERE
80%

(Hartismere)

BURY

THINGOE
94%

THEDWESTRY
90%

(Stow)

Cambridgeshire

RISBRIDGE
62%

(Bosmere)

COSFORD
54%

BABERGH
53%

Essex

(Samford)

0   5
Approx. 5 miles

©copyright I. A.W. Bunn & D. R. Butcher 2017

Map details

- Delineation of the seven hundreds, in terms of their boundaries, was the result of geological and topographical factors and the residual influence of ancient estates.

- Poorer soil-quality overall led to a more dispersed pattern of settlement than is evident in the easten sector of the county.

- Bury does not feature as a hundred, in its own right, and does not contribute to the data.

- What may be termed the Exning "island" (which later became part of Lackford Hundred) formed part of Cambridgeshire at the time of Domesday and is therefore not shown.

- Two adjacent West Norfolk hundreds and the borough of Thetford are shown bracketed.

Table 7. Suffolk communities and churches (western half)

Hundred	Community	Church	Land (acres)	Reference
Babergh				
	1. Acton	1	30 (free)	34.2
	2. Assington	1	30 (free)	34.3
	3. Bures	1	18 (free)	25.42
	4. Cavendish	1	30 (free)	43.2
	5. Chilton	1	5 (free)	6.2
	6. Coddenham – outlier to Cavendish.	1	20 (free)	43.2
	7. *(Great & Little) Cornard*	2	0 & 15 (free)	1.98 & 76.4
	8. Edwardstone	1	30 (free)	6.1
	9. (Brent & Monks) Eleigh	1	22½	15.5
	10. Glemsford	1	30 (free)	21.10
	11. Hartest	1	80 (free)	21.11
	12. Lawshall	1	30 (free)	17.1
	13. (Long) Melford	1	240 & 2 ploughs	14.23
	14. Milden – Walter the Deacon was lord (240 acres).	1	15 (free)	41.10
	15. Newton	1½ [2]	30 (free) & 8 (free)	43.3
	16. Preston	1	7	14.26
	17. Shimpling	2	60 (free) & 30	33.13 & 46.1
	18. Stanstead	1	25 (free)	31.41
	19. Stoke (by Nayland)	1	60 (free)	27.3
	20. (Great & Little) Waldingfield	1⅓ [2]	30 & 10 (free)	8.48 & 25.46
		(24)		

1. Aveley			
2. Boxted			
3. Brandeston			
4. Chadacre			
5. Cockfield			
6. *Coresfella*			
7. Fenstead			
8. Groton			
9. *Hanilega*			
10. Houghton			
11. Kentwell			
12. Lavenham			
13. *Linbou*			
14. Nayland			
15. Polstead			
16. *Saibamus*			
17. Somerton			
18. Withermarsh			
*°Blackbourn & °Bradmere			
1. *°(Great) Ashfield	2	12 (free) & 8/9	14.93 & 66.3 (+14.92n)
2. * Bardwell	1	8 (free)	14.82
3. *°Barnham	½ [1]	8	14.89
4. *°Barningham	1	15 (free, in alms)	14.81
5. *Coney Weston	1	8 (free, in alms)	14.76

6. *Elmswell	1	20 (free, in alms)	14.73
7. *°(Great) Fakenham	2	40 (combined) & ½ meadow + 1 plough	37.1
8. *°Hepworth	1	15 (free, in alms)	14.78
9. *Hinderclay	1	1 (free, in alms)	14.74
10. *Honington	1	20 (free)	14.85
11. *Hopton	1	13 (free, in alms)	14.80
12. *Hunston	½ [1]	15 (free)	14.95
13. °Ingham	1	24 (free, in alms)	14.69
14. *°Ixworth	1	80 (free) & 1 meadow + 1 plough	66.1
15. *Knettishall	1	12	14.99
16. *°Langham	1	20 (free)	14.94
17. *Little Livermere – Walter, nephew of Peter the Cleric held 3 freemen (14.87n).	1	12 (free)	14.87
18. *Norton	1	30	1.88
19. **Rickinghall (Inferior) (rt)**	1	24 (free, in alms)	14.75
20. *°Sapiston	⅔ [1]	6 (free, in alms)	14.83
21. *Stanton	2¼ [3]	4, 28 & 7	6.301 & 14.72
22. °(West) Stow	1	12 (free, in alms)	14.71
23. *Stow(langtoft)	1	40 (free)	14.77
24. *Thelnetham	1	20	12.1
25. *°Walsham (le Willows)	½ [1]	10 & 1 meadow	66.2
26. *°Wattisfield	1	12 (free, in alms)	14.79

27. *(Market) Weston	2		9.2 & 60.1
28. *Wordwell	1	1 (free)	14.88
	(33)		
1. °Culford			
2. *Euston			
3. *Little Fakenham			
4. °Rushford			
5. *°(Ixworth) Thorpe			
6. *Troston			
7. °Wyken			
*Places assigned to Blackbourn only; °places assigned to Bradmere only; *° places assigned to both hundreds.			
Bury St. Edmunds			
1. Bury St. Edmunds – 30 priests, deacons & clerics, + 28 nuns [PW 110]	?		14.167
Cosford			
1. **Aldham (rt)**	2	2 & 7	14.112 & 35.6
2. Bildeston – Walter the Deacon was lord (720 acres).	1	40 & 1 meadow + 1 plough	41.1
3. Brettenham	1	24	2.13
4. Chelsworth	1	30 & 1 meadow	14.109
5. Elmsett	1	15 + ½ plough	29.12
6. Hadleigh	1	120 (free) + 1 plough & a mill	15.2
7. Hitcham	1	2	21.42
8. Kersey	1	3	24.1

9. Layham	1	40, 1 meadow + 1 plough	28.7
10. Lindsey	1	10	14.113
11. Nedging	1	7	21.43
12. Semer	1	30, 1 meadow + 1 plough	14.108
13. Thorpe (Morieux)	1	50, 2 meadow + ¼ plough	8.35
	(14)		
1. Ash (Street)			
2. *Kalletuna*			
3. Kettlebaston			
4. Loose			
5. Manton			
6. *Redles*			
7. Rushbrooke			
8. Stone Street			
9. Toppesfield			
10. Wattisham			
11. Whatfield			
Lackford			
1. Brandon [PW 123]	1	30	21.5
2. Cavenham – outlier to Desning.	1	60 (free)	25.35
3. Chamberlain's Hall – outlier to Eriswell.	1	60	28.1b
4. (Santon) Downham	1	20	14.21

5. Elveden (church mentioned in all four entries – shared interest, therefore)	1	15 (free) [x4 = 60]	5.3, 14.20, 25.34 & 26.3
6. Eriswell	1	60	28.1a
7. Freckenham	1	20	20.1
8. Herringswell	1	30 (free)	14.18
9. Icklingham – outlier to Mildenhall.	1	24	1.115
10. Lakenheath	1	60	21.6
11. Mildenhall	1	40	1.115
12. Tuddenham	1	30	28.3
13. *Undley*	1	0	21.7
14. Wangford	1	15 (free)	14.19
15. *Worlington*	1	0	12.3
	(15)		
1. Barton (Mills)			
Risbridge			
1. Badmondisfield	1	10 (free)	1.121
2. (Great & **Little**) **Bradley** (rt)	1	15 (free)	44.1
3. Clare – manor of 2880 acres gifted to St. John's church, pre-1066, by Ælfric, father of Wihtgar.	1	?	25.1
4. Cowlinge	1	50 + ½ plough	3.1
5. Dalham	1	40 (free) + ½ plough	25.6
6. *Denham*	1	0	25.7
7. Depden	1	24 (free)	26.9
8. Desning	2	180 (combined) + 1½ ploughs	25.3

9. Haverhill	1	5	42.2
10. Hawkedon	½ [1]	15 (free)	8.34
11. Hundon	2	60 acres & 4½ acres + 1 plough	25.2
12. Kedington	1	40 (free) & 1½ meadow	33.1
13. Ousden	1	30 (free) + ½ plough	5.1
14. Poslingford	1	40 (free)	33.2
15. Stansfield	1	15 (free)	25.78
16. Stoke (by Clare)	1	60	25.97
17. Stradishall	1	30	25.100
18. (Great & Little) Thurlow	2	32 (free) + ½ plough & 29	1.90 & 25.93
19. Thurston	½ [1]	15 (free)	8.33
20. Wixoe	1	5	33.3
21. (Great & Little) Wratting	2	32 (free) & 13	25.10 & 85
	(25)		
1. Boyton			
2. Brockley			
3. Chedburgh			
4. Chilbourne			
5. Clopton			
6. Farley			
7. Hanchet			
8. *Lafham*			

	9. Lidgate			
	10. Moulton			
	11. Wickhambrook			
	12. *Wimundestuna*			
	13. Withersfield			
Thedwestry	1. Ampton	1	8 (free, as alms)	14.64
	2. (Great) Barton	1	50 (free, as alms)	14.48
	3. Bradfield (Combust, St. Clare & St. George)	1	10½ (free, as alms)	14.52
	4. Drinkstone	1	12	21.3
	5. Felsham	1	10 (free, in alms)	14.58
	6. Fornham St. Genevieve – outlier to Bury Abbey.	1	14 (free, as alms)	14.53
	7. Fornham (St. Martin)	1	16 (free, in alms)	14.50
	8. Gedding	1	6 (free, in alms)	14.60
	9. Hessett	1	12	14.57
	10. (Great) Livermere	1	12	14.68
	11. Pakenham	1	30 (free, in alms)	14.49
	12. Rattlesden	1	24	21.1
	13. Rougham	1	40 (free, in alms)	14.51
	14. Stanningfield	1	16 (free, in alms)	14.66
	15. Thurston	1	30 (free, in alms)	14.54
	16 Timworth	1	30 (free, in alms)	14.63
	17. Tostock	1	12 (free, in alms)	14.65

	Entry	No.	Holding	Ref.
	18. (Great & Little) Welnetham (rt)*	2		14.62
	19. Woolpit – outlier to Bury Abbey.	1	15 (in alms)	14.55
	1. **Beyton (rt)**	(20)		
	2. Rushbrooke			
Thingoe	1. Barrow	1	17 (free)	1.120
	2. Brockley – Theobald the Cleric held jointly with Robert (3 freemen & 240 acres).	1	6 (free)	14.14
	3. Chevington	1	30 (free)	14.5
	4. Flempton	1	8 (free)	14.12
	5. Fornham (All Saints)	1	30 (free)	14.9
	6. Hargrave	1	12 (free)	54.2
	7. Hawstead – 2 clerics, Albold & Peter, held 240 acres (14.13).	1	30 (free)	14.13
	8. **Hengrave (rt)**	1	30 (free)	14.8
	9. Horringer	1	6 (free)	14.2
	10. Ickworth	1	½	14.10
	11. Lackford	1	20 (free)	14.7
	12. Nowton	1	8 (free)	14.4
	13. Rede	1	12 (free)	25.32
	14. **Risby (rt)**	1	24 (free)	14.1
	15. (Great & Little) **Saxham (rt)**	²/₃ [1]	6	14.11
	16. Sudbury (St. Gregory's) [PW 142] [Located in Babergh]	1	50 (free)	1.97
	17. Westley	¹/₃ & 1 [1]	4 & 8	14.17 & 25.27

			14.3
	1	30 (free)	
18. Whepstead	(18)		
1. Manston			

Table details

- A total of 149 churches – excluding Bury St. Edmunds (134 communities).

- A total of 187 communities in all.

- There are 4 examples (in Babergh, Lackford and Risbridge) of churches without endowment of land.

- References to land held freely or in alms (*in elemosina*) have been made in the previous chapter, in the notes following Table 3 (p. 65).

- West Suffolk has many more examples of both than either Norfolk sector. Out of the 149 recorded churches, 83 had freehold land (53%) – and 26 of these have the endowments identified as alms-gifts: 11 in Blackbourn & Bradmere and 15 in Thedwestry (Woolpit, in the latter hundred, has 15 acres "in alms" without any reference to freehold). All of them relate directly to Bury Abbey estates.

- The freehold endowments vary considerably from hundred to hundred (Babergh 75% of its churches, Blackbourn & Bradmere 61%, Cosford 7%, Lackford 27%, Risbridge 40%, Thedwestry 75% and Thingoe 83%) and do not always correspond harmoniously with the overall percentages of churches per community. The one exception is Cosford, which comes last in the league table in both instances.

- Ploughing capacity is referred to in three hundreds: Blackbourn & Bradmere (3 examples), Cosford (6 examples) and Risbridge (6 examples). It was either part of the original endowments or a later supplement to these.

- 11 communities are shown as having 2 churches: Aldham, Great Ashfield, Desning, Great Fakenham, Hundon, Market Weston, Newton, Great/ Little Thurlow, Great/Little Waldingfield, Great/Little Welnetham, Great/Little Wratting, and Stanton was recorded with 3. Thus, 9% of "churched" settlements had more than one foundation.

- Communities shown in bold font, with **(rt)** appended, are those with round-tower churches. An asterisk following indicates the ruins or remains of a round tower.

- Use of bold italic font shows communities where recorded churches had no endowment of land (4 examples).

- There is no recorded clergy presence in communities without churches, as there is in East Suffolk.

- Use of italic font in a recorded community's name indicates one which either disappeared during the period following the Survey or was subsumed in a neighbour and became part of it.

- The use of brackets in place-names show added elements which produce the names in use today.

- The bold font, square-bracketed initials PW, followed by a number, are page-references in P. Warner, *The Origins of Suffolk*, indicating early Christian sites of monastic or minster status (both definite and conjectured). Apart from Brandon, Bury and Sudbury, all the other communities referred to are in East Suffolk.

Table 8. Suffolk (western half) – tenancy details: communities with churches

Hundred	Community	Land-holder (1066)	Tenant-in-chief (1086)	Reference
Babergh				
	Acton	Siward of Maldon, thegn	Ranulf Peverel	34.2
	Assington	Siward of Maldon, thegn	Ranulf Peverel	34.3
	Bures	22 freemen (sub Whtgar)	Richard, son of Count Gilbert	25.42
	Cavendish	Norman (sub King Edward)	Ralph of Limésy	43.2
	Chilton	Godwine, son of Ælfhere (sub King Edward)	Robert Malet (Hubert)	6.2
	Coddenham – outlier to Caven-dish	Norman (sub King Edward)	Ralph of Limésy	43.2
	(Great & Little) Cornard	Earl Morcar's mother, Ælfeva – 1.98; 2 freemen (sub Ælfric Kemp) – 76.4	The King – 1.98; Richard, son of Count Gilbert (annexation) – 76.4	1.98 & 76.4
	Edwardstone	Godwine, son of Ælfhere (sub King Edward)	Robert Malet (Walter, son of Aubrey)	6.1
	(Brent & Monks) Eleigh	Canterbury Cathedral	Canterbury Cathedral (Arch-bishop Lanfranc)	15.5
	Glemsford	Ely Abbey	Ely Abbey	21.10
	Hartest	Ely Abbey	Ely Abbey	21.11
	Lawshall	Ramsey Abbey	Ramsey Abbey	17.1
	(Long) Melford	Bury Abbey & 2 sokemen (sub Abbey)	Bury Abbey (& 2 sokemen)	14.23
	Milden	Leofwine of Bacton, thegn (sub King Edward)	Walter the Deacon	41.10
	Newton	Uhtred (sub Harold Godwineson)	Ralph of Limésy	43.3
	Preston	Arnulf, freeman, & 3 sokemen (sub Bury Abbey)	Bury Abbey (Arnulf, freeman)	14.26

Shimpling	Æthelgyth, freewoman (sub King Edward) – 33.13; Wulfric, thegn (sub King Edward) – 46.1	Ralph Baynard – 33.13; Countess of Aumâle – 46.1	33.13 & 46.1
Stanstead	Guthmund, thegn	Hugh de Montfort	31.41
Stoke (by Nayland)	Robert son of Wymarc – father of Sweyn	Sweyn of Essex	27.3
(Great & Little) Waldingfield	Wulfmær, thegn (sub Harold Godwineson) – 8.48; 3 freemen (sub Wihtgar) – 25.46	Roger of Poitou – 8.48; Richard, son of Count Gilbert – 25.6	8.48 & 25.46
Blackbourn & °Bradmere			
*° Great Ashfield	21 freemen or 1 sokeman (sub Bury Abbey) – 14.93; Aki, or Ketel, or other freemen – 66.3	Bury Abbey (freemen and sokeman, as before) – 14.93; Robert Blunt – 66.3 (freemen, as before)	14.93 & 66.3 (+14.92n)
*Bardwell	8 freemen (sub Bury Abbey)	Bury Abbey (Burcard & 8 freemen)	14.82
*Barnham	3 freemen (sub Bury Abbey)	Bury Abbey (3 freemen)	14.89
*°Barningham	19 freemen (sub Bury Abbey)	Bury Abbey (19 freemen – 3 sub Burcard & 6 sub Peter of Valognes)	14.81
*Coney Weston	Bury Abbey & 12 sokemen (sub Abbey)	Bury Abbey (12 sokemen)	14.76
*Elmswell	Bury Abbey & 5 sokemen (sub Abbey)	Bury Abbey (5 sokemen)	14.73
*°(Great) Fakenham	Alstane, thegn	Peter of Valognes	37.1
*°Hepworth	20 freemen (sub Bury Abbey)	Bury Abbey (20 freemen)	14.78
*Hinderclay	Bury Abbey & 7 sokemen (sub Abbey)	Bury Abbey (7 sokemen)	14.74
*Honington	16 freemen (sub Bury Abbey)	Bury Abbey (16 freemen)	14.85
*Hopton	23 freemen (sub Bury Abbey)	Bury Abbey (23 freemen)	14.80

*Hunston	9 freemen (sub Bury Abbey)	Bury Abbey (9 freemen – 6 sub Burcard)	14.95
°Ingham	Wulfwy, man-at-arms (sub Bury Abbey) & 21 sokemen (sub Abbey)	Bury Abbey (21 sokemen)	14.69
*°Ixworth	Aki, or 30 freemen (sub Aki)	Robert Blunt [30 freemen?]	66.1
*Knettishall	4 freemen (sub Bury Abbey)	Bury Abbey (4 freemen sub Fulcher)	14.99
*°Langham	7 freemen (sub Bury Abbey)	Bury Abbey (7 freemen)	14.94
*Little Livermere	7 freemen (sub Bury Abbey)	Bury Abbey (7 freemen – 3 under Walter of Caen?)	14.87
*Norton	Ealdgyth (sub Bury Abbey, on lease until death) or 34 sokemen	The King [34 sokemen?]	1.88
Rickinghall (Inferior) (rt)	22 sokemen & 2 freemen (sub Bury Abbey)	Bury Abbey (22 sokemen & 2 freemen)	14.75
*°Sapiston	11 freemen (sub Bury Abbey)	Bury Abbey (11 freemen – 4 sub Peter of Valognes)	14.83
*Stanton	1 freeman (sub Eadric of Laxfield & Bury Abbey) – 6.301; Bury Abbey; + 60 sokemen & 7 freemen (sub Abbey) – 14.72	Robert Malet (Walter of Caen, + 2 freemen under him) – 6.301; Bury Abbey (with sokemen & freemen attached) – 14.72	6.301 & 14.72
°(West) Stow	22 freemen (sub Bury Abbey)	Bury Abbey (22 freemen)	14.71
*Stow(langtoft)	2 freemen & 14 others (sub Bury Abbey)	Bury Abbey (Durand & 14 freemen)	14.77
*Thelnetham	Acwulf, thegn, & 15 freemen under him	Frodo, brother of Abbot of Bury (15 freemen under him)	12.1
*°Walsham (le Willows)	Aki, or 23½ freemen (under him)	Robert Blunt [23½ freemen?]	66.2
*Wattisfield	20 freemen (sub Bury Abbey)	Bury Abbey (Roric & ? freemen)	14.79

	Place	1066	1086	Ref.
	*(Market) Weston	Ælfric, freeman (9.2) & Alsi, freeman (60.1)	William of Ecouis (Huard of Vernon) – 9.2; Robert of Verly – 60.1	9.2 & 60.1
	*Wordwell	11 freemen (sub Bury Abbey)	Bury Abbey (11 freemen)	14.88
	*o As in Table 7			
Bury St. Edmunds	Bury St. Edmunds	Bury Abbey	Bury Abbey	14.167
Cosford	Aldham (rt)	6 freemen (sub Bury Abbey) – 14.112; Wulfwine – 35.6	Bury Abbey (6 freemen) – 14.112; Aubrey de Vere – 35.6	14.112 & 35.6
	Bildeston	Queen Edith	Walter the Deacon	41.1
	Brettenham	Wulfnoth	Robert, Count of Mortain	2.13
	Chelsworth	Bury Abbey	Bury Abbey	14.109
	Elmsett	Tovi, thegn	Roger of Auberville	29.12
	Hadleigh	Canterbury Cathedral	Canterbury Cathedral (Archbishop Lanfranc)	15.2
	Hitcham	Ely Abbey	Ely Abbey	21.42
	Kersey	Chatteris Abbey	Chatteris Abbey	24.1
	Layham	Ælfric Kemp	Eudo the Steward	28.7
	Lindsey	20 freemen (sub Bury Abbey)	Bury Abbey (20 freemen)	14.113
	Nedging	Ely Abbey	Ely Abbey	21.43
	Semer	Bury Abbey	Bury Abbey	14.108
	Thorpe (Morieux)	1 freeman, + 7 added by Norman, son of Tancred	Roger of Poitou [1 freeman + 7?]	8.35
Lackford	Brandon	Ely Abbey	Ely Abbey	21.5
	Cavenham – outlier to Desning	Wihtgar	Richard, son of Count Gilbert	25.35

	Place	TRE holder	TRW holder	Ref
	Chamberlain's Hall – outlier to Eriswell.	Godwine, thegn (sub King Edward)	Eudo the Steward	28.1b
	(Santon) Downham	Bury Abbey & 9 freemen (under it)	Bury Abbey (Frodo - & 9 free-men?)	14.21
	Elveden	Alsi, then Elgeric, 5.3; Bury Abbey, 14.20; Leofgeat, freeman (sub Wihtgar), 25.34; 1 freeman (sub Ely & Bury abbeys) – 26.3	Count Eustace of Boulogne – 5.3; Bury Abbey – 14.20; Richard son of Count Gilbert – 25.34; William of Warenne (Nicholas) – 26.3	5.3, 14.20, 25.34 & 26.3
	Eriswell	Godwine, thegn (sub King Edward)	Eudo the Steward	28.1a
	Freckenham	Orthi, thegn (sub Harold Godwine-son)	Bishop of Rochester	20.1
	Herringswell	Bury Abbey & 2 sokemen (sub Abbey)	Bury Abbey (2 sokemen)	14.18
	Icklingham – outlier to Milden-hall.	King Edward - gifted to Bury Abbey & held by Stigand	The King	1.115
	Lakenheath	Ely Abbey	Ely Abbey	21.6
	Mildenhall	King Edward – gifted to Bury Abbey & held by Stigand	The King	1.115
	Tuddenham	Canute, freeman (sub Earl Ælfgar)	Eudo the Steward	28.3
	Undley	Ely Abbey	Ely Abbey	21.7
	Wangford	Bury Abbey	Bury Abbey (Wulfweard)	14.19
	Worlington	Ordmær	Frodo, brother of Abbot of Bury	12.3
Risbridge	Badmondisfield	Earl Ælfgar	The King	1.121
	(Great & **Little**) **Bradley (rt)**	Ulf, thegn	Robert of Tosny	44.1
	Clare	Wihtgar (large estate gifted to church by father, Ælfric)	Richard, son of Count Gilbert	25.1

Place	TRE holder	TRW holder	Ref.
Cowlinge	Manni Swart, thegn	Count Alan of Brittany	3.1
Dalham	[1 sokeman – sub Wihtgar?]	Richard, son of Count Gilbert (William Peche)	25.6
Denham	[2 sokemen – sub Wihtgar?]	Richard, son of Count Gilbert (William Hurant)	25.7
Depden	Toki, thegn	William of Warenne (Frederic) – Hugh of Wanchy, sub-tenant	26.9
Desning	Wihtgar	Richard, son of Count Gilbert (Robert)	25.3
Haverhill	Clarenbold	Tihel of Helléan	42.2
Hawkedon	Ulf	Roger of Poitou	8.34
Hundon	Wihtgar	Richard, son of Count Gilbert	25.2
Kedington	Æthelgyth, freewoman, & 25 freemen	Ralph Baynard [25 freemen?]	33.1
Ousden	Leofric, thegn	Count Eustace of Boulogne	5.1
Poslingford	3 freemen (2 sub Æthelgyth & 1 sub Bury Abbey) – or 4 other freemen	Ralph Baynard (3 freemen, or 1 freeman, or 1 other freeman, or 2 freemen – all sub freewoman Richere)	33.2
Stansfield	Eadric Spud, or Wulfæd, or Crawa – all freemen [sic]	Richard, son of Count Gilbert (Gilbert, or Robert, or Roger)	25.78
Stoke (by Clare)	21 freemen	Richard, son of Count Gilbert (21 freemen)	25.97
Stradishall	16 freemen	Richard, son of Count Gilbert (16 freemen)	25.100
(Great & Little) Thurlow	Ealdgyth, freewoman 10 freemen	The King Richard, son of Count Gilbert (10 freemen)	1.90 25.93
Thurston	Eadmær, thegn (sub Earl Ælfgar)	Roger of Poitou	8.33
Wixoe	Godwine, thegn	Ralph Baynard	33.3

	Place			
	(Great & Little) Wratting	1 sokeman (sub Wulfmaer) – 25.10; Ailbern, freeman – 25.85	Richard, son of Count Gilbert (Wulfmaer & Ailbern)	25.10 & 85
Thedwestry				
	Ampton	22 freemen (sub Bury Abbey)	Bury Abbey (Robert & 22 freemen)	14.64
	(Great) Barton	Bury Abbey & 70 freemen (sub Abbey)	Bury Abbey (70 freemen)	14.48
	Bradfield (Combust, St. Clare & St. George)	Bury Abbey & 12 freemen (sub Abbey)	Bury Abbey (12 freemen)	14.52
	Drinkstone	Ely Abbey	Ely Abbey	21.3
	Felsham	34 freemen, inc. Adelund (sub Bury Abbey)	Bury Abbey (34 freemen, inc. Adelund)	14.58
	Fornham St. Genevieve – outlier to the Abbey	Bury Abbey & 6 freemen (sub Abbey)	Bury Abbey (freemen Peter & Ralph – also 6 other freemen)	14.53
	Fornham (St. Martin)	Bury Abbey & 11 freemen (sub Abbey)	Bury Abbey (11 freemen)	14.50
	Gedding	13 freemen (sub Bury Abbey)	Bury Abbey (13 freemen)	14.60
	Hessett	60 freemen (sub Bury Abbey)	Bury Abbey (60 freemen & Berard)	14.57
	(Great) Livermere	10 freemen (sub Bury Abbey), or 12 freemen (sub Frodo) or 1 freeman (sub Eadric of Laxfield) & his wife (sub Bury Abbey)	Bury Abbey (10 freemen), or Frodo (12 freemen), or Frodo (1 freeman) & Bury Abbey (that freeman's wife)	14.68
	Pakenham	Bury Abbey & 35 freemen (sub Abbey)	Bury Abbey (35 freemen)	14.49
	Rattlesden	Ely Abbey	Ely Abbey	21.1
	Rougham	Bury Abbey & 90 freemen (sub Abbey)	Bury Abbey (90 freemen)	14.51

	Stanningfield	11 freemen (sub Bury Abbey)	Bury Abbey (11 freemen & Warin)	14.66
	Thurston	Bury Abbey & 28 freemen (sub Abbey)	Bury Abbey (20 freemen & 8 under Richard)	14.54
	Timworth	29 freemen (sub Bury Abbey)	Bury Abbey (23 freemen & 6 sub John)	14.63
	Tostock	Bury Abbey & 17½ freemen (sub Abbey)	Bury Abbey (Frodo & 17½ freemen)	14.65
	(Great & Little) Welnetham (rt)*	41 freemen (sub Bury Abbey)	Bury Abbey (41 freemen, inc. Arnulf & Robert)	14.62
	Woolpit – outlier to the Abbey.	Bury Abbey & 40 freemen (sub Abbey)	Bury Abbey (40 freemen)	14.55
Thingoe	Barrow	King Edward	The King	1.120
	Brockley	3 freemen (sub Bury Abbey)	Bury Abbey (3 freemen sub Theobald the cleric & Robert)	14.14
	Chevington	Bury Abbey & 1 sokeman (sub Abbey)	Bury Abbey (1 sokeman)	14.5
	Flempton	10 sokemen (sub Bury Abbey)	Bury Abbey (10 sokemen under Wulfweard)	14.12
	Fornham (All Saints)	Bury Abbey & 3 sokemen & 2 freemen (sub Abbey)	Bury Abbey (3 sokemen & 2 freemen)	14.9
	Hargrave	Ælfgyth, freewoman (sub Bury Abbey)	William of Vatteville	54.2
	Hawstead	28 freemen (sub Bury Abbey)	Bury Abbey (? freemen, inc. Otto & Agenet, and clerics Albold & Peter)	14.13
	Hengrave (rt)	Bury Abbey & 8 sokemen (sub Abbey)	Bury Abbey (8 sokemen)	14.8

Horringer	Bury Abbey & 15 sokemen (sub Abbey)	Bury Abbey (15 sokemen)	14.2
Ickworth	Bury Abbey	Bury Abbey	14.10
Lackford	Bury Abbey & 1 sokeman (sub Abbey)	Bury Abbey (1 sokeman)	14.7
Nowton	Bury Abbey & 10 sokemen (sub Abbey)	Bury Abbey (10 sokemen)	14.4
Rede	7 freemen (sub Wihtgar)	Richard, son of Count Gilbert [7 freemen?]	25.32
Risby (rt)	Bury Abbey & 7 sokemen & 1 free-man (sub Abbey)	Bury Abbey (7 sokemen & 1 freeman sub Norman)	14.1
(Great & Little) Saxham (rt)	3 freemen (sub Bury Abbey)	Bury Abbey (3 freemen sub Albert & Fulcher)	14.11
Sudbury [located in Babergh]	Earl Morcar's mother	The King	1.97
Westley	11 freemen (sub Bury Abbey) – 14.17; 3 freemen (sub Wihtgar) – 25.27	Bury Abbey (10 freemen & 1 sub Peter) – 14.17; Richard, son of Count Gilbert (3 freemen) – 25.27	14.17 & 25.27
Whepstead	Bury Abbey & 1 sokeman & 6 free-men (sub Abbey)	Bury Abbey (1 sokeman, 6 free-men & Ralph)	14.3

Table details

- Communities shown in bold font, with **(rt)** appended, are those with round-tower churches. A single asterisk indicates existing buildings, a double one the ruins or remains of a round tower.

- Use of bold italic font shows communities where recorded churches had no endowment of land.

- The names in brackets in the third column indicate the patrons of land-owners (an adoption acceptable to both parties, by process of *commendation*) or exercisers of jurisdiction – in those cases where patronage or jurisdiction (or both, together) is stated or implied. Suffolk has far more detail recorded of such ties than Norfolk, but there are still a number of cases where the exact relationship is not made clear. Because of this element of uncertainty, no attempt has been made to identify patronage and jurisdiction specifically, but simply to record a bond which existed between both parties.

- The names in brackets in the fourth column are those of sub-tenants of the tenants-in-chief, in cases where this information is given.

- No distinction is made between freemen (*libi hoes*) and sokemen (*soc*) in the translation of the text, all such tenants being classed as the former. Necessary adjustment has been made in the table, as freemen usually held their land independently, whereas sokemen were tied to an estate by customary services of some kind. The latter were probably also unable to attach themselves to the patronage of a social superior by the process of *commendation* (see Roffe, p. 223).

- The church of St. John, Clare (Risbridge Hundred), had been endowed pre-1066 with a very large manor by the thegn Ælfric, supervisor of the vast estates of Emma of Normandy (mother of Edward the Confessor) in West Suffolk and North Essex. His son Wihtgar became involved with the Revolt of the Earls (1075) and was dispossessed of his landholdings by William I – a fact referred to in the final sections of *Domesday Book, Suffolk* (76.5), where annexations are listed. Lucy Marten, 'The Rebellion of 1075', in C. Harper-Bill (ed.), *Medieval East Anglia* (Woodbridge, 2005), pp. 176, 177, 178, 179 & 181, refers to him.

West Suffolk Summary (proportion of communities with churches)

- Babergh – 53% (1 early Christian foundation noted, in Sudbury; this town, recorded in Thingoe).

- Blackbourn & Bradmere – 80%. Later, known solely as Blackbourn Hundred.

- [Bury St. Edmunds] (1 early Christian foundation noted – attach to Thingoe).

- Cosford – 54%.

- Lackford – 94% (1 early Christian foundation noted).

- Risbridge 62%.

- Thedwestry – 90%.

- Thingoe – 94% (Bury Abbey, as above). Sudbury counted in Babergh.

- West Suffolk: 134 communities with churches, out of 187 in all = 72%.

- County as a whole: 357 communities with churches, out of a total number of 634 = 56%.

- Number of churches in county: 448+ (excluding Bury St. Edmunds & Ipswich).

Map details

- East Suffolk has the most complex layout of the two counties' hundreds, with a number of its sixteen jurisdictions having sectors physically removed from the main one. Only the largest and most topographically significant ones are shown (for Claydon, Loes, Parham and Plomesgate).

- Greater density of population prevailed in this sector of the county, with better soil-quality overall than in the western one able to sustain higher levels of settlement.

- Geological and topographical factors were key elements in the creation of boundaries, together with the influence of ancient estates. Ipswich is not included as a hundred, in its own right, and is not part of the data.

- Seven adjacent Norfolk hundreds (six in East Norfolk and one in West) are shown bracketed.

East Suffolk

Map 4. East Suffolk hundreds (overall percentages of communities with recorded churches)

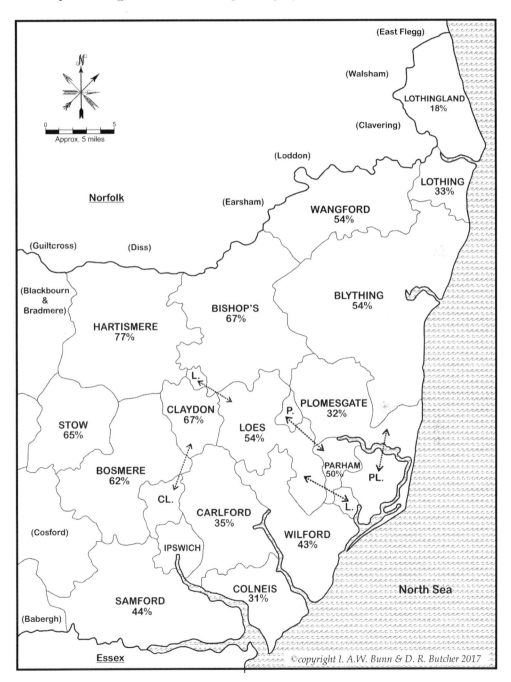

(East Flegg)

(Walsham)

LOTHINGLAND
18%

(Clavering)

(Loddon)

LOTHING
33%

Norfolk

(Earsham)

WANGFORD
54%

(Guiltcross)   (Diss)

(Blackbourn
&
Bradmere)

BISHOP'S
67%

BLYTHING
54%

HARTISMERE
77%

L.

CLAYDON
67%

PLOMESGATE
32%

P.

STOW
65%

LOES
54%

BOSMERE
62%

PARHAM
50%

PL.

CL.

CARLFORD
35%

L.

(Cosford)

WILFORD
43%

IPSWICH

North Sea

COLNEIS
31%

SAMFORD
44%

(Babergh)

Essex

©copyright l. A.W. Bunn & D. R. Butcher 2017

Approx. 5 miles
0   5

Table 9. Suffolk communities and churches (eastern half)

Hundred	Community	Church	Land (acres)	Reference
Bishop's	1. Badingham	1	60 & 1 plough	6.306
	2. Bedingfield – priest mentioned, under sub-patronage (6.319).	¼ & ¼ [1]	6 & 6	6.75 & 43.5
	3. Chickering	1	8	19.5
	4. Chippenhall	½ & ½ [1]	20 acres + 1 plough & 20	6.311 & 14.105
	5. Denham	1	12	7.4
	6. Dennington	1	40 (free) + ½ plough	6.303
	7. Horham – 1 freeman & 6 acres belonging to Judicael the Priest (75.3).	1	22	64.3
	8. Hoxne	1	120 (in Thrandeston & Yaxley)	18.1 & 6
	9. Kelsale [Located in Plomesgate]	1	30 + 1 plough	7.3
	10. Laxfield	1	43 + ½ plough	6.305
	11. Mendham – Ælfgar the Priest held 43 acres of church land under William of Noyers: Norfolk, Part 1, Earsham Hundred (10.32). [PW 133]	1 & ¹/₈; ¼; 1; ¹/₈ [3]	8 & 5; 10; 20; 40 + ½ plough	6.313, 8.37, 14.106 & 19.2
	12. (Monk) Soham	1	50	14.102
	13. Stradbroke	2	40 (combined) + ½ plough	6.308
	14. Syleham (rt)	1	16	44.2
	15. Tannington	1	30 + ½ plough	6.304
	16. Weybread (rt)	½ [1]	8 + ½ plough	6.312
	17. Wingfield	1	24	21.45
	18. Worlingworth	1	10 (free)	14.103

	(21)		
1. Aldringham [Located in Plomesgate]			
2. Bedfield			
3. Colston			
4. Fressingfield			
5. Instead			
6. Saxtead			
7. Whittingham			
8. Wilby			
9. Withersdale			
Blything			
1. *Alneterne* [near Dunwich?]	½ [1]	2	21.47
2. Blyford	1	12	13.2
3. ***Blythburgh*** – ref. to 2 churches *without land* (1.12) [PW 120]	1 / 2	240 / 0 & 0	1.12 / 1.12
4. **Bramfield (rt)**	1	28 (free) + ½ plough	3.3
5. Brampton	1	16	33.5
6. Chediston	⁵/₆ [1]	16	7.15
7. Cookley	½ [1]	1	9.3
8. Cratfield	1	6	33.10
9. Darsham – Ælfwine the Priest had held 30 acres as a manor (1.13) & Ansketel the Priest 120 acres & 7 freemen, pre-1066 (7.36) – Wulfric the Deacon was one of the sub-holders.	1	6	1.13
10. Dunwich – 1 church, pre-1066 [PW 127]	3	?	6.84

11. **Frostenden (rt)**	2	28 (combined) + 1 plough	33.6
12. Heveningham	¼ [1]	1½	7.27
13. *Hoppetuna/Oppituna*	½ [1]	4½	7.29
14. Huntingfield	1	14	6.80
15. Leiston [PW 134]	3	100 (combined, free) pre-1066	6.83
16. Middleton – Also, half-priest referred to. Leofric the Deacon, half-freeman, held 3 acres under the half-patronage of Toli the Sheriff (7.31).	1	15	26.13
17. Reydon	2	120 (combined)	33.4
18. Rumburgh [PW 133]	1	40 acres in South Elmham	3.105
19. Sibton	3	? & 18 (combined) & 3 meadow	6.90
20. Sotherton	1	5	48.1
21. Strickland – Ælfwine the Priest had held 180 acres as a manor, pre-1066 (1.14).	1	24 & 1 meadow	7.37
22. **Thorington (rt)**	1	8	32.19
23. Ubbeston	1	3	33.9
24. Uggeshall – ref. made to Æskell the Priest, pre-1066.	1	?	4.14
25. Walpole	1	16 & ½ meadow	3.4
26. Wenhaston	1	10 (free) & ½ meadow	3.5
27. Westleton – Brunmær the Priest had held 27½ acres, pre-1066 (66.12).	2	20 & 3	6.85 & 96

28. **Wissett** (**rt**) – <u>12 monks</u> in the church and 1 chapel in its control. [**PW 133**]	1	240 (free)	3.14
29. *Wrabetuna/UUrab(b)etuna*	1	6	7.28
30. Wrentham	2	40 & 8	26.12a
	(42)		
1. Bridge			
2. Bulcamp			
3. (South) Cove			
4. Covehithe			
5. Easton			
6. Fordley			
7. Halesworth – <u>Ulf the Priest</u> had held 40 acres as a manor, pre-1066.	?		4.13
8. Henham			
9. Henstead			
10. Hinton – 12 acres (King's alms) belonging to Blythburgh Church.			7.5
11. **Holton** (**rt**)			
12. Knodishall			
13. Linstead (Magna & Parva)			
14. Mells			
15. Minsmere			
16. Peasenhall			
17. *Riseburc*			
18. Southwold			
19. Stone Street			
20. Stoven			

21. **Theberton (rt)**			
22. Thorpe			
23. Wangford [PW 133]			
24. *Warle/UUarle*			
25. Yoxford			
Bosmere			
1. Ash(bocking)	½ & 1 [2]	16 & 3	1.73
2. Badley	1	14	25.53
3. Barking	2	83 (free) + 2 ploughs & 6	21.16 & 18
4. Battisford (nb. ¹/₁₂ of a church ref. in 2.11)	½ & ½ [1]	20 & 20	31.56 & 53.3
5. Baylham	½ & ½ [1]	12 & 12	7.58 & 76.15
6. (Great & Little) Blakenham	1	1	9.1
7. Bramford [PW 121]	2	80 (free) & 30 (fee)	1.2 & 119
8. (Great & Little) Bricett	1	54 & 15	34.8 (land ref. only) & 38.8
9. Coddenham – priest, Frideb[erht] held ½ acre "as alms" (74.16).	½,1 & 1; 2; a share of 3 churches & 1; ¼ [6]	2½ & 12½ & 8; 3 & 3; ? & 3; ¼ of land appertaining	7.67, 16.20, 34.9 & 38.5
10. Creeting (All Saints, St. Mary & St. Olave)	1	10	23.4
11. Hemingstone	½ & 1 [2]	15 & 3	8.59
12. Mickfield – Ælbald the Priest held 60 acres as a manor (14.39). Assessment in Ulverston (34.10).	1 & ½ [2]	8 + ½ plough & 2½	14.38 & 34.10
13. Nettlestead	2	8 & 70½	3.56
14. Offton	2	16 & 7½	7.60 & 62.1

15 "Olden" (Uledana)	1	7½	16.21
16. Ringshall (1/12 part of a church in Battisford – 2.11)	½ & ½ [1]	15 & 12	7.56 & 30.1
17. Somersham	¼ [1]	7½	7.59
18. (Earl & Little) Stonham – Judicael the Priest held 64.1 & 2; Ælbald the Priest also held 60 acres as a manor (14.39), while Ælwald the Priest, freeman, had jointly held 40 acres as 2 manors, pre–1066 (16.22).	⅓ & ⅓ & ⅓; 2 & 2; ¼; 2 [8]	5 & 4 & 5; 3 (combined) & 7½ & 2; 7½; 16 + ½ plough & 20	8.55, 16.15 & 22, 34.11, 64.1 & 2
19. Stonham (Aspal)	1	14	38.6
20. Willisham	1	32	8.56
1. Bricticesbaga	(39)		
2. Crowfield			
3. Darmsden			
4. Ella			
5. Facheduna			
6. Flowton – 15 acres held freely by a priest, pre–1066.	?		25.55
7. Horswold			
8. Lang(e)edana			
9. Pachetuna			
10. Pileberga			
11. Rigneseta			
12. Tunstall			
Carlford 1. Aluredestuna	1	12	39.12
2. (Great) Bealings – Anund the Priest was attached to an 84-acre estate, with 9 other freemen.	1	20	67.11

3. *Brightwell*	1	0	21.54
4. Burgh – Wulfwine the Priest had held 6 acres under Edric of Laxfield, pre-1066 (6.124).	1	8 ("Several have a share")	26.16
5. Clopton – Wulfwine the Priest held 6 acres (46.7) and Eadmund the Priest (Ely Abbey freeman) had held 142 acres, pre-1066 (47.2).	1	15 (from 4 lord-ships)	34.15
6. Culpho	1	10	8.5
7. Kesgrave	½ [1]	2	6.114
8. Martlesham	1	36	39.6
9. Newbourn	1	12	39.10
10. Otley – Walter the Deacon held 6 acres in lordship (41.19).	1	20	52.1
11. Playford	1	10	6.112
12. Rushmere (St. Andrew)	1	20	3.19
13. Tuddenham – Ælfric the Deacon held 12 acres as a manor (38.22).	1	15	6.120
	(13)		
1. Alnesbourn			
2. Barkestone			
3. Bixley			
4. "Derneford"			
5. *Eduluestuna*			
6. "Finesford"/"Finlesford" – Walter the Deacon held 26 freemen & 120 acres (41.18).			41.18
7. Foxhall			
8. *Grenewic*			
9. Grundisburgh			
10. **Hasketon (rt)**			
11. Haspley [Located in Colneis]			

12. *Hopestuna/Hobbestuna*				
13. *Ingoluestuna*				
14. Isleton				
15. Kingsland				
16. Kingston				
17. Little Bealings				
18. *Nec(c)bemara/Neckemara*				
19. Preston				
20. Seckford				
21. Thistleton				
22. Thorpe [Located in Loes]				
23. Waldringfield				
24. Witnesham				
Claydon				
1. Akenham – Godwine the Priest, freeman, had held 140 acres as a manor & Thorbern the Priest 30 acres as a manor, pre-1066 (38.11). Walter the Deacon held 4 freemen & 32 acres (41.16).	½ & 3 parts [1]	5 & 12	8.71 & 38.11	
2. **Ashfield (rt)*** – Snaring the Priest held 30 acres (16.34). Round-tower remnant.	1	4	67.4	
3. Barham	1	16	21.26	
4. Debenham – 2 churches, dedicated to St. Mary & St. Andrew.	½ & ¼; ¼ & ¾; ¼; ¼ [2]	20 & ¼ of the land; 10 & 1½; 10	6.18, 16.28 & 34.12	
5. Framsden	1	30 (free) + 1 plough (pre-1066)	4.1	

		¼, ¼ & ½ [1]	1½ free, ? free, & 3	
	6. Helmingham – 2.12 refers to 1 acre "belonging to the church".			16.26
	7. Henley – Walter the Deacon held 190 acres as a manor (41.14).	2	2 & 8	29.11 & 41.14
	8. Pettaugh	1	2½	67.3
	9. Swilland – Walter the Deacon was lord.	1	5	41.2
	10. Thorpe (Hall)	1	12	4.6
	11. Thurleston – church dedicated to St. Botolph. Ælfric the Priest held 3 freemen from Count Alan of Brittany (3.64). St. Peter's Church, Ipswich, held 91 acres (25.62). Ælfgar the Priest held 3 acres (8.75). Walter the Deacon held 1 freeman & 16 acres (41.3).	1 & ½ [1]	1 & 5	1.122e & 8.70
	12. Westerfield – Walter the Deacon held 1 freeman & 30 acres (41.4) & 3 freemen & 28 acres (41.6). Ælfric the Priest held 12 acres (74.14).	½ [1]	7½	8.73
	13. Whitton	1	10	74.13
	14. Winston	1	8	21.28
		(16)		
	1. Bermesdena			
	2. Bruntuna – Walter the Deacon held 160 acres as a manor.			41.15
	3. Claydon			
	4. Man(e)uuic/Manewic			
	5. Newton			
	6. Sharpstone – Walter the Deacon held 1 freeman with 2 acres.			21.35
	7. Ulverston – Ælfwine the Priest held 40 acres as a manor & Aelfric the Priest 30 acres as a manor.	?		16.30
Colneis	1. "Alston" (Alteinestuna)	1	5 (free)	7.96
	2. Bribtoluestuna	1	6	31.9
	3. Bucklesham	1	8	2.16

4. Burgh	1	12	7.80
5. Hemley	1	8	39.5
6. Kirton – Godric the Priest held 7 acres before and after 1066.	1	6	7.114
7. Levington	1	8	7.117
8. Stratton – Wulfmær the Priest, freeman, had held 120 acres as a manor, pre-1066 (6.110).	1	10	7.119
9. Trimley (St. Martin & St. Mary)	2	20 & 8	7.97
10. Walton [PW 135]	1	8	7.76
1. Burgate	(11)		
2. "Candlet" (Candelenta)			
3. Falkenham			
4. Grimston (Hall)			
5. Gulpher (Gulpelea)			
6. Guthestuna			
7. Isteuertona			
8. Kembroke			
9. Kul-Kyluerstuna/Culuerdestuna			
10. Langer (Langestuna)			
11. Leofstanestuna			
12. Maistana			
13. Morston – Ælfric the priest [see Samford Hundred below] held 1 freeman, Godric.			2.17
14. Mycelegata [Micklegate? – lost in Trimley]			
15. Nacton			

16. Norton – Godwine the Priest had held 50 acres as a manor under Harold, pre-1066.	?		7.122
17. *Oxelanda*			
18. "Plumgeard" (*Plűgeard*)			
19. *Struestuna/Struustuna*			
20. Thorpe			
21. *Turstanestuna*			
22. Wadgate			
Hartismere			
1. Aspall	$^2/_3$ & $^1/_3$ [1]	? & ?	6.206 & 34.18
2. Bacton – Walter the Deacon was lord.	1	24	41.7
3. Braiseworth	½ & ½ [1]	17 acres + ½ plough & 15 acres + ½ plough	6.225
4. **Brome (rt)**	½ [1]	14	7.75
5. Burgate	? churches & ¼ [3+]	29 + ½ plough & 1	35.5
6. Cotton – Walter the Deacon held 7 acres, once held by Fathir (25.24).	1	11	1.95
*Diss [Diss H., Norfolk – see Ch. 1, Table 3, p. 47]			1.8
7. Eye – church dedicated to St. Peter.	1	240 (free) + 4 ploughs, 3 meadow & a mill	6.191
8. Finningham	1	26	14.131
9. Mellis	1	8	6.195
10. Mendlesham	1	40 + 1 plough	1.76
11. Oakley	$^2/_3$ [1]	12	14.129

Place			
12. Occold	2	8 + ½ plough & 12	31.60
13. Palgrave	2	30 (combined) + ½ plough	14.45
14. Redgrave	1	30 (free) + ½ plough	14.42
15. Redlingfield	1	12	6.192
16. Rickinghall (Superior)	$\frac{1}{5}$ [1]	5	14.46
17. Rishangles	1	20 + 1 plough	6.222
18. Stoke (Ash)	1	15 + ½ plough	6.213
19. Stuston (rt)	1	24	14.137
20. Thorndon	1	50 (free) + 1 plough & 2 meadow	6.223
21. Thornham (Magna?) – same church as below?	¼ [1]	3½	62.5
22. Thornham Parva – same church as above?	¾ [1]	10 + ½ plough	6.218
23. Thrandeston	2	6 & 8	6.66 & 14.139
24. Wetheringsett	1	16 + ½ plough	21.39
25. Wickham (Skeith)	1	12	8.31
26. Wortham (rt)	2	40 (combined)	11.4
27. Wyverstone	1	16 + ½ plough	57.1
	(33+)		
1. Brockford			
2. Caldecota(n)-coton/Kaldecotes – Walter the Deacon held 19 acres belonging to Bacton manor.			41.8
3. Cranley			
4. Gislingham			

Hundred	Place	Churches	Acres / notes	References
	5. Hestley			
	6. *Tusemara*			
	7. Westthorpe			
	8. Yaxley			
Ipswich	1. Ipswich – churches dedicated to the Holy Trinity (Æthelwulf the Priest), St. Mary, St. Mary, St. Augustine (Leofstane the Priest) & St. Michael (Wulfstane the Priest) (1.122d); St. Laurence, St. Peter & St. Stephen (1.122f); St. Peter (25.52 & 62); St. George (38.3); St. Julian (74.9). Walter the Deacon held 5 houses & 3 empty dwellings, which had been held by Queen Edith (41.13). [PW 123]	5; 3; 1; 1; 1 [11]	26 (in alms), 26, 2, 11, & 8; 12, 1 & 1; St. Peter, 720 (as manor) & 91 in Thurleston; no land stated; 20.	1.122d; 1.122f; 25.52 & 62 (St. Peter's, land only in latter); 38.3; 74.9
	11 named churches (2 St. Mary & 2 St. Peter).			
	2. Stoke	1	40 (free)	21.15
		(12+?)		
Loes	1. Brandeston	1	12	47.3
	2. Charsfield	1	36 ("belonging to the church")	6.179
	3. Cretingham	2	18 & 8	4.18 & 52.5
	4. Dallinghoo	1	29 & 2 meadow	3.48
	5. Framlingham	1	60	4.42
	6. Hoo	1	8½	21.95
	7. Kenton [Located in Bishop's]	1	30	6.271
	8. Kettleburgh	1	16	3.34
	9. Letheringham	1	20	32.14
	10. Marlesford	1	16	1.94

11. Martley	1	12	3.52
12. Monewden	1	30 & 1½ meadow	8.22
13. Rendlesham [PW 115]	1	20	6.281
14. Staverton	1	10	6.260
15. Woodbridge [Located in Carlford]	1	19	6.287
	(16)		
1. Ash			
2. *Brodertuna*			
3. Butley [PW 114]			
4. Campsey (Ash)			
5. *Clacbestorp*			
6. Easton			
[Eyke – not recorded – PW 117]			
7. *Ethereg* [in Framlingham?]			
8. Gedgrave [Located in Plomesgate]			
9. Glevering			
10. Hacheston			
11. *Possefelda*			
12. Potsford			
13. (Earl) Soham			
Lothing			
1. Barnby	1	80	4.39
2. **Mutford (rt)**	2	43 (combined)	1.23

Hundred	Place	Churches	Acres	Reference
	3. Pakefield	½ [1]	16½	4.41
	4. **Rushmere (rt)**	¼ [1]	8	31.34
	1. *Beketuna/Bechetuna* [Absorbed by Pakefield]	(5)		
	2. Carlton (Colville)			
	3. **Gisleham (rt)**			
	4. *Hornes* [Absorbed by either Carlton or Rushmere]			
	5. Kessingland			
	6. Kirkley ["Church in a clearing"]	?		1.25 & 28, 31.33
	7. *Kislea* [Kirkley]			
	8. *Rodenhala* [Absorbed by Kessingland and Pakefield]			
	9. *Wimundhala* [Absorbed by Kirkley]			
Lothingland	1. **Burgh (Castle) (rt)** [PW 110]	1	10 & 1 meadow	69.1
	2. Flixton – church later became that of Oulton.	1	120 (in alms)	19.21
	3. **Somerleyton (rt)** – Wihtred the Priest held 40 acres as a manor. Church later became that of Blundeston.	1	20	1.52
	1. *Akethorpe* [Absorbed by Lowestoft] – Æthelmær the Priest held 80 acres as a manor.	(3)		
	2. **Belton (rt)**	?		1.56
	3. Browston [Absorbed by Belton, **Bradwell (rt)** & Hopton]			
	4. Caldecott [Absorbed by Belton & Fritton]			
	5. Corton			
	6. Dunston [Absorbed by Oulton]			

	7. Fritton (rt)			
	8. Gapton [Absorbed by **Bradwell (rt)**]			
	9. Gorleston			
	10. Herringfleet (rt)			
	11. Hopton			
	12. Lound (rt)			
	13. Lowestoft			
	14. Newton			
Parham	1. *Brutge*	¼ & ¼ [1]	6 & 6	6.28 & 67.5
	2. Parham [in *Niuetuna* lordship]	1	24 (free)	6.32
	3. Wantisden	½ & ¼; ¼ [1]	20 (free) & 10; 10	6.30 & 38; 7.137
		(3)		
	1. Beversham			
	2. Blaxhall			
	3. Tunstall			
Plomesgate	1. Aldeburgh	2	60 (combined)	6.130
	2. Boyton	2	30 (combined)	6.138
	3. Chillesford	1	5 (free)	3.93
	4. (Great) Glemham	½; 1; ½ [2]	10 + ½ plough; 10; 10	3.95, 6.49 & 28.6
	5. Rendham (outlier to *Chiletuna*)	1	24 + 1 plough	6.43

6. Saxmuundham	3	15, 24 (combined) + ½ plough	7.70 & 71
7. Snape	1	8	6.133
8. Sudbourne	2	16 & 8	6.143 & 21.38
9. Sweffling	1	15	6.46
	(15)		
1. *Becclinga*			
2. Benhall			
3. **Bruisyard (rt)**			
4. *Burch*			
5. *Burgesgata*			
6. Carlton			
7. *Cle'pham*			
8. Cransford – Godric the Priest had held 40 acres under Eadric of Laxfield pre-1066.	?		6.128
9. Dunningworth			
10. Farnham			
11. (Little) Glemham			
[Iken – not recorded – **PW 114**]			
12. *Ingoluestuna*			
13. *Keletuna/Cheletuna/Cbiletuna*			
14. *Nordberia* – Eadwine the Priest had held 30 acres as a manor, under Ely Abbey pre-1066.	?		8.81
15. *Prestetuna*			

16. Rushmere			
17. Sternfield			
18. Stratford (St. Andrew)			
19. Thorpe			
Samford — 1. Belstead	¼; 1; ¼ [2]	?; 34 (free); ?	32.5, 46.3 & 71.2
2. Boynton	¼ [1]	6	16.44
3. Burstall	1	26	16.18
4. Dodnash	1	30 acres (free, "belonging to church")	3.72
5. Freston	1	?	25.76
6. Gusford	⅓ [1]	8	46.5
7. Harkstead – outlier to Brightlingsea (1.96).	1 & 1 [2]	? & 46	1.96 & 46.4
8. **Higham (rt)**	⅕; 1; part [2]	4; 4; 2	5.6, 25.75 & 58.1
9. Hintlesham	1½ [2]	35 (free, combined)	1.118
10. Holton (St. Mary)	1	?	32.3
11. Pannington – Ælfric the Priest was lord. (3.76)	1	3 (free)	27.10
12. Raydon – Gilbert the Priest held 1 villan with 30 acres (32.4).	⅕; ⅕ & ⅕ [1]	5; 5 & 5	16.37 & 41
13. Shotley	2	62 (combined)	1.102
14. Stratford (St. Mary)	1	20 (free) + ½ plough	27.9
15. Stutton	⅓ & ½ [1]	15 & 15	32.6 & 36.2
16. Thorington	1	50 (free)	40.6

	Part; ¼; 1 [2]	?; 6; 20 (free) + ½ plough	3.67, 16.40 & 40.3
17. (Great & Little) Wenham			
18. Woolverstone – Ælfric the Priest held from Count Alan of Brittany.	1	10 ("belonging to the church")	3.74
1. *Afildestuna*	(24)		
2. *Belenei*			
3. Bentley – Ælfric the Priest was lord.	?		3.75
4. (East) Bergholt			
5. *Beria*			
6. Brantham			
7. *Canap(þ)etuna/Canepetuna*			
8. Chattisham			
9. Churchford			
10. *Eduinestuna*			
11. Erwarton			
12. Holbrook			
13. Kalweton – Ælfric the Priest was lord.	?		3.78
14. Kirkton			
15. *Manesfort*			
16. *Purtepyt*			
17. Shelley			
18. *Stanfelda*			
19. Tattingstone			
20. *Toft*			

21. *Torp*			
22. *Thurchetlestuna*			
23. Wherstead – Ælfric the Priest was lord.	?		3.77
Stow			
1. Buxhall – Munulf the Priest had held 80 acres under Ely Abbey, pre-1066 (26.5).	1	30 & ½ meadow	8.49
2. Combs	1	?	2.8
3. Creeting (St. Peter)	½ & 1; ½ [2]	10 & 10; 10 (free)	23.1 & 4 & 51.1
4. *Dagworth*	½; 1 & ½ [2]	25 (free); 0 & 30 + 1½ meadow	31.44 & 50
5. *Eruestuna*	1	10 (free)	31.46
6. (Great & Little) Finborough	1	30 (free) &1 meadow	29.1
7. Harleston	1	25 (free)	14.36
8. Haughley	1	31 (free) & ½ meadow	31.42
9. (Old) Newton	⅙ [1]	10 (free)	16.12
10. **Onehouse (rt)**	1	3 (free)	34.6
11. Stow(market) – church mentioned incidentally, in connection with Combs (Count of Mortain) and Onehouse (Ranulf Peverel).	1	?	2.8 & 34.6
12. Thorney	1 (+ 1 chapel)	120 (free), pre-1066	1.1
13. Wetherden	½ & ½ [1]	15 & 1 meadow; 15 (free) & 1 meadow	14.35 & 31.45
1. Chilton	(15)		

Place	Churches	Value	Reference
2. Rodebam			
3. Shelland			
4. Torpe			
5. Torstuna			
6. Ultuna			
7. Weledana			
Wangford			
1. Barsham (rt) – Leofstane the Priest had held 35 acres as a manor, from Earl Gyrth, pre-1066.	½ [1]	20	7.40
2. Beccles	1	24	14.120
3. Bungay (rt) [PW 132]	1; 1, 1 & 1; 1 [5]	5; 12, 8 & 30; 2 & 2 meadow	1.110; 1.111; 4.19
4. (South) Elmham (All Saints, St. Cross, St. James, St. Margaret, St. Michael, St. Nicholas & St. Peter) (rt) [PW 129]	1 & ½; 1; 1 & 3 [7]	8 & 6; 6; 40 (free) + ½ plough & 30 (combined)	13.6; 19.14; 19.16
5. Flixton	½ & ½ [1]	12 & 10	19.15 & 53.5
6. Homersfield	1 & 1 [2]	12 & 30	18.4 & 19.13
7. Ilketshall (St. Andrew, St. John, St. Lawrence & St. Margaret) (rt)	1	20	4.26
8. Mettingham (rt)	1	20	4.21
9. Ringsfield	1 & part of 1 [2]	15 & 20	1.16 & 20
10. Sotterley	1	7	4.30
11. Weston	1 & 1 [2]	20 & 20	1.21 & 113
12. Willingham	1	40	31.21
13. Worlingham (Parva) (rt)* – archaeological find (1980).	2 & ½ [3]	40 (combined) & 5	1.22 & 14.121

1. Catesfella	(28)		
2. "Croscroft"			
3. Ellough			1.38
*Gillingham [Clavering H., Norfolk]			
4. *Hatheburgfelda/Hetheburgafella* [in North Cove]			
5. *Itheburna*			
6. Linburne [in Homersfield]			
7. Redisham			
8. Shadingfield			
9. Shipmeadow			
10. *Thiccebrom*			
11. *Wicbedis*			
Wilford			
1. Alderton	1	24 & 1 meadow	6.159
2. Bawdsey	1	20	6.161
3. Boulge – Wulfwine the Priest referred to.	1	25	6.181
4. Boyton	1	8	6.172
5. Bredfield – Æthelwald the Priest had held 50 acres as a manor, under Ely Abbey, pre-1066 (3.31).	1 & 1 [2]	36 & 31 (free)	6.182 & 21.85
6. Bromeswell [PW 116]	1 & 1[2]	6 & 16	6.249 & 21.83
7. Capel (St. Andrew)	1	12	6.183
8. Debach	1	8	46.10
9. Harpole	1	?	*Inquisitio Eliensis* (p. 147)

10. Hollesley	1	14	6.148
11. Loudham	1	60	22.3
12. Shottisham	1	13	6.238
13. Sutton	1	22	6.170
	(15)		
1. Bing			
2. *Culeslea* [outlier to Hollesley]			
3. *Halgestou*			
4. Hoo			
5. *Hundestboft–tuf*			
6. *Laneburc–burb*			
7. Littlecross			
8. Melton			
9. Peyton			
10. **Ramsholt (rt)**			
11. Sogenhoe			
12. Stokerland			
13. *Tur–Tbor–Tbur–Torstanestuna*			
14. "Udeham"			
15. Ufford			
16. Wickham (Market)			
17. Wilford			

Table details

- A total of 299+ churches – excluding Ipswich (223 communities), plus 10 communities with the stated presence of a priest and one with "church" as a place-name element (Kirkley).

- Therefore, 11 other possibilities, on recorded presence of a priest and the place-name reference. P. Warner, 'Blything Hundred', p. 82, attributes 43 churches to that particular jurisdiction – presumably, taking Halesworth's priest as evidence of an established church.

- A total of 447 communities in all.

- There are 3 examples of churches recorded as being without an endowment of land (in Blything and Carlford) and a further 13 references (in Blything, Hartismere, Samford, Stow and Wilford) containing no mention of land whatsoever.

- East Suffolk has fewer references to freehold land than its western counterpart. Out of the 299+ recorded churches, 37 had such endowment (12%) and only two (neither freehold) – Holy Trinity, Ipswich, and St. Michael, Flixton, in Lothingland – had alms-gifted land. There is also a single, free-standing reference to Frideberht the Priest holding a half-acre in Coddenham, but without reference to a church.

- Freehold endowments vary widely per hundred, with Samford (7) and Stow (10) having most.

- There are 33 references to ploughing capacity (as opposed to 15 in West Suffolk), with Bishop's Hundred (9) and Hartismere (12) having the majority.

- Carlford, Loes, Lothing and Lothingland have no references to either freehold land or ploughs.

- 38 communities are shown as having 2 churches: Aldeburgh, Ashbocking, Barking, Belstead, Boyton (Plomesgate), Bramford, Bredfield, Bromeswell, Creeting St. Peter, Cretingham, Dagworth, Debenham, Frostenden, Great Glemham, Great & Little Wenham, Harkstead, Hemingstone, Henley, Higham, Hintlesham, Homersfield, Mickfield, Mutford, Nettlestead, Occold, Offton, Palgrave, Reydon, Ringsfield, Shotley, Stradbroke, Sudbourne, Thrandeston, Trimley, Westleton, Weston, Wortham & Wrentham. A further 12 had more: Blythburgh (3), Burgate (3), Dunwich (3), Leiston (3), Mendham (3), Saxmundham (3), Sibton (3), Worlingham (3), Bungay (5), Coddenham (6), South Elmham (7), and Earl & Little Stonham (8). Thus, 22% of "churched" settlements had more than one foundation.

- Communities in bold font, with **(rt)** appended, have round-tower churches. An asterisk indicates the remains or ruins of a round tower. Four "missing" parishes (Ashby, Blundeston, Bradwell and Gunton), all located in Lothingland and all with round towers, were post-Domesday settlements. So was Buxlow (absorbed by Knodishall), in Blything, which has the ruins of its tower still standing.

- Bold italic font shows communities where churches had no endowment of land (3 examples).

- Clergy presence is indicated by underlining. Communities thus noted (10 in number) might possibly have had churches. References to <u>deacons</u> might suggest pre-ordination to priesthood, but could also indicate men who were leaders of *tithing-groups*.

- Use of italic font in a recorded community's name indicates one which either disappeared during the period following the Survey or was subsumed in a neighbour and became part of it.

- The use of brackets in place-names show added elements which produce the names in use today.

- The bold font, square-bracketed initials PW, followed by a number, are page-references in P. Warner, *The Origins of Suffolk*, indicating early Christian sites of monastic or minster status (both definite and conjectured).

Table 10. Suffolk (eastern half) – tenancy details: communities with churches

Hundred	Community	Land-holder (1066)	Tenant-in-chief (1086)	Reference
Bishop's	Badingham	Eadric of Laxfield	Robert Malet	6.306
	Bedingfield	6 freemen (sub ?) – 6.75; Ælfric, freeman (sub Harold Godwineson) – 43.5	Robert Malet (6 freemen) – 6.75; Ralph of Limésy – 43.5	6.75 & 43.5
	Chickering	1 freeman (sub Bishop of Thetford)	Bishop of Thetford (1 freeman)	19.5
	Chippenhall	9 freemen (sub Bishop of Thetford & Eadric of Laxfield) – 6.311; Bury Abbey – 14.105	Robert Malet (9 freemen) – 6.311; Bury Abbey – 14.105	6.311 & 14.105
	Denham	Stigand	Roger Bigot (Aitard)	7.4
	Dennington	Eadric of Laxfield	Robert Malet	6.303
	Horham	Ælfgar, freeman (sub Stigand); 1 freeman (sub Bishop of Thetford); 1 freeman (sub Eadric of Laxfield)	Judicael the Priest	64.3
	Hoxne	Bishop of Thetford [personal]	Bishop of Thetford [personal]	18.1 & 6
	Kelsale [Located in Plomesgate]	Norman	Roger Bigot	7.3
	Laxfield	Eadric of Laxfield	Robert Malet	6.305
	Mendham	1 freeman (sub ?) – 6.313; Wulfric, thegn – 8.37; Bury Abbey & 6 sokemen & 1 freeman (sub Abbey) – 14.106; Ulf, thegn – 19.2	Robert Malet (Humphrey) – 6.313; Roger of Poitou – 8.37; Bury Abbey (Frodo, + 6 sokemen & 1 freeman) – 14.106; Bishop of Thetford – 19.2	6.313, 8.37, 14.106 & 19.2
	(Monk) Soham	Bury Abbey	Bury Abbey	14.102
	Stradbroke	Eadric of Laxfield	Robert Malet	6.308
	Syleham (rt)	Ulf, thegn, & 5 freemen (under him)	Robert of Tosny	44.2
	Tannington	Eadric of Laxfield	Robert Malet	6.304
	Weybread (rt)	1 freeman [sub Eadric of Laxfield?]	Robert Malet (Humphrey, son of Rodric)	6.312

Hundred	Place	1066 holder	1086 holder	Ref.
	Wingfield	1 freeman (sub Ely Abbey)	Ely Abbey (Roger Bigot – contested by the Abbey)	21.45
	Worlingworth	Bury Abbey & 1 sokeman (sub Abbey)	Bury Abbey (1 sokeman)	14.103
Blything	*Alneterne* [nr. Dunwich]			
	Blyford	Ely Abbey	Ely Abbey	21.47
	Blythburgh	Eadwine, freeman	Godric the Steward	13.2
	Bramfield (rt)	King Edward	The King	1.12
		Manni Swart, thegn	Count Alan of Brittany	3.3
	Brampton	11 freemen (sub ?) & 1 sokeman	Ralph Baynard (10 freemen & 1 sokeman)	33.5
	Chediston	Eadric, freeman (sub Eadric of Laxfield & Ely Abbey)	Roger Bigot (Robert of Vaux)	7.15
	Cookley	Wulfric, freeman	William of Ecouis (Huard of Vernon & Robert of Vaux)	9.3
	Cratfield	Thored	Ralph Baynard (William Baynard, nephew)	33.10
	Darsham	Ælfwine the priest	The King	1.13
	Dunwich	Eadric of Laxfield	Robert Malet	6.84
	Frostenden (rt)	Thored & 8 freemen	Ralph Baynard (Ranulf & 3 freemen)	33.6
	[Halesworth?]	Ælfric & Ulf the Priest	Earl Hugh of Cheshire (Bigot of Loges)	4.13
	Heveningham	Ulfketel, freeman (sub Ulf')	Roger Bigot	7.27
	Hoppetuna/ Oppituna	Bondi, freeman (sub Toli the Sheriff)	Roger Bigot [1freeman?]	7.29
	Huntingfield	Eadric of Laxfield	Robert Malet (Walter, son of Aubrey)	6.80

Place	Saxon holder	Norman holder	Ref.
Leiston	Eadric of Laxfield	Robert Malet	6.83
Middleton	Ælfric, freeman (sub Ranulf, nephew of Eadric of Laxfield)	William of Warenne	26.13
Reydon	Thored & 32 freemen under him	Ralph Baynard [32 freemen?]	33.4
Rumburgh	[Ref. here is to Rumburgh church land, held in South Elmham]	Count Alan of Brittany	3.105
Sibton	1 freeman & 7½ others (2 named as Eadric & Ælfric)	Robert Malet (Walter of Caen)	6.90
Sotherton	Rada, freeman (sub Harold Godwineson)	Drogo of Beuvrière	48.1
Strickland	1 freewoman [Ælfeva?] (sub Norman)	Roger Bigot (Hugh of Corbon)	7.37
Thorington (rt)	Haldane	Geoffrey de Mandeville (William of Bouville)	32.19
Ubbeston	Thored & 3 freemen under him	Ralph Baynard	33.9
Uggeshall	Æskell the Priest, freeman	Earl Hugh of Cheshire (Robert of Courson)	4.14
Walpole	7 freemen (sub ?)	Count Alan of Brittany (17 freemen)	3.4
Wenhaston	6 freemen (shared with Thorington)	Count Alan of Brittany (6 freemen)	3.5
Westleton	Aki, freeman (sub Eadric of Laxfield) – 6.85; 1 freeman [also sub Eadric?] – 6.96	Robert Malet (Gilbert Blunt) – 6.85; Robert Malet (1 freeman & Fulcred) – 6.96	6.85 & 96
Wissett (rt)	1 church (12 monks therein); Ralph the Constable held the manor – 3.10	Count Alan of Brittany	3.14
UUrabetuna [Wrabetuna]	Manson, freeman (sub Norman)	Roger Bigot [1 freeman?]	7.28
Wrentham	Eadric [of Laxfield?] & Wulfric, freeman	William of Warenne (Robert of Pierrepoint)	26.12a

Hundred	Place	Holder TRE	Holder 1086	Ref
Bosmere	Ash(bocking)	Æthelmær, freeman (sub Edeva the Fair)	The King (Æthelmær, freeman)	1.73
	Badley	Æskell	Richard, son of Count Gilbert (Robert)	25.53
	Barking	Ely Abbey	Ely Abbey (Roger Bigot held 21.18)	21.16 & 18
	Battisford – $\frac{1}{12}$ church ref, in 2.11	Ælfric, freeman (31.56); Cynric, freeman (53.3)	Hugh de Montfort (Roger of Candos) – 31.56; Eudo, son of Spirwic (Iarnagot) – 53.3	31.56 & 53.3
	Baylham	Mundling, freeman (sub Ely Abbey) – 7.58; Queen Edith – 76.15	Roger Bigot (William of Bourneville) – 7.58; the King, by annexation – 76.15	7.58 & 76.15
	(Great & Little) Blakenham	Ælfric, thegn	William of Écouis	9.1
	Bramford	King Edward – 1.2; Stigand – 1.119	The King	1.2 & 119
	(Great & Little) Bricett	Leofstane – 34.8; Godwine, freeman (sub the King & Earl of East Anglia) – 38.8	Ranulf Peverel (Ralph, son of Brian) – 34.8; Roger of Rames (Ansketel) – 38.8	34.8 & 38.8
	Coddenham	Wigulf, freeman (sub Toli the Sheriff) – 7.67; Æthelmær, Ælfric, Wihtric & Harold, freemen (all sub Ely Abbey) – 16.20; Leofric, freeman – 34.9; 3 freemen – 38.5	Roger Bigot (Warengar, freeman) – 7.67; Ely Abbey [same 4 freemen?] – 16.20; Ranulf Peverel (Humphrey, son of Aubrey) – 34.9; Roger of Rames – 38.5	7.67, 16.20, 34.9 & 38.5
	Creeting (All Saints, St. Mary & St. Olave)	24 freemen	Bernay Abbey (24 freemen)	23.4
	[Flowton?]	Godmane (sub Wihtgar, King & Earl of East Anglia) + a priest with 15 acres of free land (sub King & Earl of East Anglia)	Richard, son of Count Gilbert (Germund)	25.55
	Hemingstone	20 freemen	Roger of Poitou (20 freemen)	8.59

Mickfield	Æthelric, freeman, & wife (sub Bury Abbey) – 14.38; Saxi – 34.10 (assessment in Ulverston)	Bury Abbey, by gift of the King (Berengar) – 14.38; Ranulf Peverel (Ralph of Savenay) – 34.10	14.38 & 34.10
Nettlestead	Gauti, freeman, & 24 freemen (sub Ralph the Constable)	Count Alan of Brittany (Erland)	3.56
Offton	Leofcild, freeman (sub Stigand) – 7.60; & Siric, freeman – 62.1	Roger Bigot (Hugh of Houdain) – 7.60; Isaac – 62.1	7.60 & 62.1
"Olden" (*Uledana*)	8 freemen (4 sub Saxi)	Bishop of Bayeux (8 freemen)	16.21
Ringshall	Leofwine, freeman (sub Ely Abbey) – 7.56; & Godwy, freeman – 30.1	Roger Bigot (William of Bourneville) – 7.56; William of Auberville (Fulk) – 30.1	7.56 & 30.1
Somersham	Leofson, freeman (sub Leofric Hobbeson)	Roger Bigot (William of Bourneville)	7.59
(Earl & Little) Stonham	Wulfric, thegn; Wulfmær, thegn; & Ælfæd, freewoman (all sub Harold Godwineson) – 8.55; Leofwine, freeman (under Eadric of Laxfield) – 16.15; Wulfric, freeman (under Ely Abbey), Æthelwald the Priest & Godwy, freemen (sub Saxi) – 16.22; ¼ church only referred to – 34.11; Ælfric, freeman (sub Eadric of Laxfield) – 64.1; 9 other freemen – 64.2	Roger of Poitou – 8.55; Bishop of Bayeux (Roger Bigot) – 16.15; Bishop of Bayeux (?) – 16.22; Ranulf Peverel (Ralph of Savenay?) – 34.11; Judicael the Priest – 64.1 & 2	8.55, 16.15 & 22, 34.11, 64.1 & 2
Stonham (Aspal)	Æthelmær, freeman (sub Eadric of Laxfield)	Roger of Rames (Miles)	38.6
Willisham	Ælfæd, freewoman (sub Harold Godwineson)	Roger of Poitou (Albert)	8.56
Carlford *Alvresdestuna*	Durand, freeman (sub Eadric of Laxfield)	Ranulf, brother of Ilger (Ivo)	39.12

	(Great) Bealings	10 named freemen (9 sub Ely Abbey) or freeman Wulfmær (sub Haldane)	Hervey of Bourges	67.11
	Brightwell	Ely Abbey	Ely Abbey	21.54
	Burgh	Æthelric, freeman	William of Warenne (Robert of Glanville)	26.16
	Clopton	Eadric Grim (sub Ely Abbey & Eadric of Laxfield)	Ranulf Peverel (Thorold)	34.15
	Culpho	5 freemen (sub Ely Abbey)	Roger of Poitou [5 freemen?]	8.5
	Kesgrave	3 freemen (sub Godwine) or Oslac, freeman (sub Eadric of Laxfield)	Robert Malet [freemen, as in 1066?]	6.114
	Martlesham	Eadwald	Ranulf, brother of Ilger	39.6
	Newbourn	Norman	Ranulf, brother of Ilger	39.10
	Otley	Ælflæd, freewoman (sub Eadric of Laxfield), or Lustwine (sub Eadric of Laxfield), or 16½ freemen (sub Leofled)	Humphrey the Chamberlain	52.1
	Playford	Godwine, son of Ælfhere (sub Queen Edith)	Robert Malet (Unfrid, son of Robert)	6.112
	Rushmere (St. Andrew)	11 freemen (sub Gyrth Godwineson)	Count Alan of Brittany [11 freemen?]	3.19
	Tuddenham	1 freeman (sub Eadric of Laxfield)	Robert Malet [1 freeman?]	6.120
Claydon	Akenham	3 freemen – 8.71; Godwine the Priest, freeman – 38.11	Roger of Poitou (3 freemen) – 8.71; Roger of Rames (daughter) – 38.11	8.71 & 38.11
	Ashfield (rt)*	Godmane, freeman (sub Eadric of Laxfield)	Hervey of Bourges (Ranulf)	67.4
	Barham	Ely Abbey	Ely Abbey	21.26

Hundred	Place	1066 holders	1086 landholders	Reference
	Debenham	Eadric of Laxfield – 6.18 (ref. 6.11); Godwy, freeman (sub Saxi) – 16.28; Saxi – 34.12	Robert Malet – 6.18; Bishop of Bayeux – 16.28; Ranulf Peverel (Ralph of Savenay) – 34.12	6.18, 16.28 & 34.12
	Framsden	Æthelstan, thegn	Earl Hugh of Cheshire	4.1
	Helmingham	Godric, Leofstane & 11 other freemen (sub Eadric of Laxfield & Saxi)	Bishop of Bayeux	16.26
	Henley	Tepekin, freeman (sub Harold Godwineson) – 29.11; Wulfric, freeman – 41.14	Roger of Auberville (Eudo the Steward) – 29.11; Walter the Deacon (Roger) – 41.14	29.11 & 41.14
	Pettaugh	Brihtwald (sub Eadric of Laxfield) or 5 freemen (under him)	Hervey of Bourges	67.3
	Swilland	Queen Edith	Walter the Deacon	41.2
	Thorpe (Hall) – see also, Ashfield, 67.4	21 freemen (sub Earl Hugh's predecessor – Ely Abbey?)	Earl Hugh of Cheshire (Hugh, son of Norman)	4.6
	Thurleston	Godric – 1.122e; 18 freemen (sub Gosbert) – 8.70	The King (Godric) – 1.122e; Roger of Poitou (Gosbert) – 8.70	1.122e & 8.70
	[Ulverston?]	Ælfwine the Priest (sub Eadric of Laxfield & Saxi) & Ælfric the Priest (sub Ely Abbey)	Bishop of Bayeux (Roger Bigot, & Ralph of Savenay from him)	16.30
	Westerfield	? (½ church only referred to)	Roger of Poitou	8.73
	Whitton	Church referred to (+ 25 named freemen & 4 named freewomen)	The King (29 named vavassors, as specified for 1066)	74.13
	Winston	Ely Abbey	Ely Abbey	21.28
Colneis	"Alston" (*Alteinestuna*)	Thorbern & Wulfwine, freemen (sub Norman)	Roger Bigot (Thorbern & Wulfwine, sub Norman)	7.96
	Bribtoluestuna	18 freemen (sub Guthmund)	Hugh de Montfort [18 freemen?]	31.9
	Bucklesham	30 freemen (sub Harold Godwineson)	Robert, Count of Mortain (Eudo son of Nigel)	2.16

	Burgh	16 named freemen (sub Norman)	Roger Bigot [16 freemen, sub Norman?]	7.80
	Hemley	Brihtmær, or Wulfweard, or Hardwine, or Brihtric, freemen (sub varying patronage)	Ranulf, brother of Ilger (William of Bosc)	39.5
	Kirton	Godric the Priest, freeman (sub Eadric of Laxfield)	Roger Bigot (Wihtmer)	7.114
	Levington	10 named freemen (sub Norman)	Roger Bigot (10 freemen, sub William of Bourneville)	7.117
	[Norton?]	Godwine the Priest (under Harold Godwineson)	Roger Bigot (Thurstan, son of Guy)	7.122
	Stratton	Wihtric, freeman (sub Harold Godwineson), or Ulfketel, freeman (sub Norman), or Godmane, freeman (sub Norman)	Roger Bigot (William of Bourneville)	7.119
	Trimley (St. Martin & St. Mary)	Godric (sub Norman)	Roger Bigot (Thorold)	7.97
	Walton	Norman	Roger Bigot (Norman)	7.76
Hartismere	Aspall	1 freeman (sub ?) – 6.206; Saxi (as lord of Ulverston) – 34.18	Robert Malet – 6.206; Ranulf Peverel – 34.18	6.206 & 34.18
	Bacton	Leofwine, freeman (sub Harold Godwineson)	Walter the Deacon	41.7
	Braiseworth	Wulfeva, freewoman, & 16 freemen	Robert Malet	6.225
	Brome (rt)	Gode, freewoman (sub Stigand)	Roger Bigot (William Shield)	7.75
	Burgate	Wulfwine, freeman, & 9 sokemen	Aubrey de Vere (Adelelm)	35.5
	Cotton	3 freemen (sub Burgheard)	The King [3 freemen?]	1.95
	Eye	Eadric of Laxfield	Robert Malet	6.191
	Finningham	11 freemen (sub Bury Abbey)	Bury Abbey (11 freemen)	14.131

Mellis	Fulcard, freeman (half sub Eadric of Laxfield)	Robert Malet (Élise Malet, his mother)	6.195
Mendlesham	Burgheard	The King	1.76
Oakley	Goding the Reeve & 10 freemen under him (sub Bury Abbey)	Bury Abbey [same sub-tenancy as 1066?]	14.129
Occold	Guthmund, brother of the Abbot (sub Ely Abbey)	Hugh de Montfort (Roger of Candos)	31.60
Palgrave	Bury Abbey	Bury Abbey	14.45
Redgrave	Bury Abbey	Bury Abbey	14.42
Redlingfield	Ælfric, freeman (sub Eadric of Laxfield)	Robert Malet (William of Arques)	6.192
Rickinghall (Superior)	14 freemen (sub Bury Abbey)	Bury Abbey (14 freemen)	14.46
Rishangles	Wulfeva, freewoman (sub Stigand)	Robert Malet	6.222
Stoke (Ash)	Wulfeva, freewoman (sub Stigand)	Robert Malet	6.213
Stuston (rt)	5 freemen (sub Bury Abbey)	Bury Abbey (5 freemen)	14.137
Thorndon	Wulfeva (sub Stigand)	Robert Malet	6.223
Thornham (Magna)	Leofric (sub Brihtric, Bury Abbey reeve)	Isaac	62.5
Thornham Parva	8 freemen, or 2 freemen, or Siric, freeman (all sub Wulfeva)	Robert Malet	6.218
Thrandeston	Godmane (sub Eadric of Laxfield) – 6.66; [Anselm, sub Bury Abbey, as in 1086?] – 14.139	Robert Malet (William Goulafre) – 6.66; Bury Abbey (Anselm) – 14.139	6.66 & 14.139
Wetheringsett	Ely Abbey	Ely Abbey (Ranulf Peverel; ¼ share sub-let to Ralph of Savenay)	21.39
Wickham (Skeith)	Ælfæd, freewoman (sub Harold Godwineson)	Roger of Poitou	8.31

Place	1066	1086	Ref
Wortham (rt)	Modgæva or Godiva, freewomen (both sub Bury Abbey)	Ralph of Beaufour (Richard of Saint-Clair)	11.4
Wyverstone	Leofwine the Bald	Hubert of Mont-Canisy (Richard)	57.1
Ipswich (excl. town)			
Stoke	Ely Abbey	Ely Abbey	21.15
Loes			
Brandeston	Eadmund the Priest (sub Ely Abbey)	William of Arques	47.3
Charsfield	24 freemen (sub Eadric of Laxfield)	Robert Malet (Robert of Glanville – 24 freemen)	6.179
Cretingham	Eadric, freeman (sub Eadric of Laxfield & Æthelstan) – 4.18; Brictwald (sub Queen Edith) – 52.5	Earl Hugh of Cheshire – 4.18; Humphrey the Chamberlain (Amund) – 52.5	4.18 & 52.5
Dallinghoo	½ freeman (sub Anund)	Count Alan of Brittany [½ freeman?]	3.48
Framlingham	Æthelmær, thegn	Earl Hugh of Cheshire (Roger Bigot)	4.42
Hoo	Ely Abbey	Ely Abbey	21.95
Kenton [Located in Bishop's]	8 freemen, inc. Brictmær, Huna & Woodbrown (mainly sub Eadric of Laxfield)	Robert Malet (Élise Malet, his mother)	6.271
Kettleburgh	Eadric Grim (sub Ely Abbey & Eadric of Laxfield)	Count Alan of Brittany	3.34
Letheringham	Haldane (sub Harold Godwineson)	Geoffrey de Mandeville	32.14
Marlesford	[Thormod of Parham?]	The King	1.94
Martley	7 freemen (sub Eadric Grim)	Count Alan of Brittany [7 freemen?]	3.52
Monewden	14½ freemen (sub Wulfmær, Ely Abbey freeman)	Roger of Poitou (10 freemen, sub Wulfmær)	8.22
Rendlesham	1 freeman (sub Eadric of Laxfield)	Robert Malet (Gilbert of Wissant)	6.281

Staverton		Eadric of Laxfield	Robert Malet (Hubert)	6.260
	Woodbridge [in Carlford]	2 freemen & 1 sokeman (sub Eadric of Laxfield)	Robert Malet (Gilbert of Wissant)	6.287
Lothing	Barnby	5 freemen (sub Burgheard)	Earl Hugh of Cheshire (Hugh, son of Norman))	4.39
	[Kirkley?]	20 freemen – 1.25; 6 freemen – 1.28; 1 freeman (sub Burgheard & Wulfsi – 31.33	The King – 1.25 & 28 [freemen, as shown?]; Hugh de Montfort – 31.33 [freeman, as shown?]	1.25 & 28, 31.33
	Mutford (rt)	Wulfsi & 12 freemen (sub Gyrth Godwineson)	The King [freemen, as shown previously?]	1.23
	Pakefield	1 freeman (sub Gyrth Godwineson)	Earl Hugh of Cheshire [1 freeman?]	4.41
	Rushmere (rt)	1 freeman (sub Gyrth Godwineson)	Hugh de Montfort [1 freeman?]	31.34
Lothingland	[Akethorpe?]	Æthelmær the Priest	The King [Æthelmær the Priest?]	1.56
	Burgh (Castle) (rt)	Stigand	Ralph the Crossbowman	69.1
	Flixton	Stigand	Bishop of Thetford	19.21
	Somerleyton (rt) [now Blundeston]	Wihtred the Priest	The King [Wihtred the Priest?]	1.52
Parham	*Brutge*	Eadric of Laxfield – 6.28; Eadric (sub Eadric of Laxfield) – 67.5	Robert Malet (Walter de Risboil) – 6.28; Hervey of Bourges (Warner) – 67.5	6.28 & 67.5
	Parham (in *Nieutuna*)	Alnoth, freeman (sub Eadric of Laxfield)	Robert Malet (Walter, son of Aubrey)	6.32
	Wantisden	22 freemen [sub Eadric of Laxfield?] – 6.30, Ælfwine, freeman, & Ælfæd, freewoman (sub Eadric of Laxfield) – 6.38; 1 freeman (sub Norman) – 7.137	Robert Malet (Hubert, Gilbert, Gilbert of Wissant & William of Emalleville) – 6.30; Robert Malet – 6.38; Roger Bigot (Norman) – 7.137	6.30 & 38; 7.137

Hundred	Place	Holder	Tenant	Ref.
Plomesgate	Aldeburgh	Wulfric, freeman (sub Eadric of Laxfield)	Robert Malet	6.130
	Boyton	12 freemen (sub Eadric of Laxfield)	Robert Malet (William Goulafre)	6.138
	Chillesford	Ulf, freeman (sub Ely Abbey)	Count Alan of Brittany	3.93
	[Cransford?]	Godric the Priest (sub Eadric of Laxfield)	Robert Malet (Durand)	6.128
	(Great) Glemham	Sparrowhawk, freeman (sub Eadric of Laxfield) – 3.95; Wulfmær, freeman (sub Eadric of Laxfield) – 6.49; Wulfric (sub Ely Abbey & Eadric of Laxfield) – 28.6	Count Alan of Brittany – 3.95; Robert Malet – 6.49; Eudo the Steward (Pirot) – 28.6	3.95, 6.49 & 28.6
	[Nordberia?]	Eadwine the Priest (sub Ely Abbey)	Roger of Poitou	8.81
	Rendham (outlier to Chiletuna)	Eadric of Laxfield	Robert Malet (Robert)	6.43
	Saxmundham	Norman – 7.70; Ælfgar, thegn (sub King Edward) – 7.71	Roger Bigot (Norman) – 7.70; Roger Bigot (Ranulf) – 7.71	7.70 & 71
	Snape	21 freemen (sub Eadric of Laxfield)	Robert Malet (Gilbert Blunt)	6.133
	Sudbourne	12 freemen (sub Eadric of Laxfield) – 6.143; Ely Abbey – 21.38	Robert Malet (Gilbert of Wissant) Ely Abbey	6.143 21.38
	Swefling	11 freemen (sub Eadric of Laxfield)	Robert Malet (Robert – son of Fulcred?)	6.46
Samford	Belstead	Ulf, freeman (sub Æsgar) – 32.5; Ælfric of Weinhou – 46.3; Thuri – 71.2	Geoffrey de Mandeville (Ulf) – 32.5; Countess of Aumâle – 46.3; Robert of Stratford – 71.2	32.5, 46.3 & 71.2
	[Bentley?]	Thurstan	Count Alan of Brittany (Ælfric the Priest)	3.75
	Boynton	Godwine, freeman	Bishop of Bayeux [Freeman?]	16.44
	Burstall	Ailbern, freeman	Bishop of Bayeux [Freeman?]	16.18

Dodnash	Eadwine (sub Edeva – the Fair)	Count Alan of Brittany (unnamed tenants)	3.72
Freston	Robert, son of Wymarc	Richard, son of Count Gilbert (Robert of Abenon)	25.76
Gusford	Edeva [the Fair]	Countess of Aumâle	46.5
Harkstead (outlier to Brightlingsea, Essex 1.96)	Harold Godwineson – 1.96; Edeva the Fair – 46.4	The King – 1.96; Countess of Aumâle – 46.4	1.96 & 46.4
Higham (rt)	Leadmær, freeman – 5.6; Godric, freeman – 25.75; Æscman, freeman (sub Robert, son of Wymarc)	Count Eustace of Boulogne (Ralph of Marcy) – 5.6; Richard son of Count Gilbert (Osbern) – 25.75; Gundwin the Chamberlain – 58.1	5.6, 25.75 & 58.1
Hintlesham	Stigand	The King	1.118
Holton (St. Mary)	Æsgar	Geoffrey de Mandeville	32.3
[Kalweton?]	Thurstan	Count Alan of Brittany (Ælfric the Priest)	3.78
Pannington	Robert [son of Wymarc]	Sweyn of Essex (Ælfgar)	27.10
Raydon	Eadnoth, freeman – 16.37; Eadwy & Ælfwine, freemen – 16.41	Bishop of Bayeux (Roger Bigot) – 16.37; Bishop of Bayeux – 16.41	16.37 & 41
Shotley	Gyrth Godwineson & 210 sokemen (sub various patrons)	The King (119 sokemen)	1.102
Stratford (St. Mary)	Robert [son of Wymarc]	Sweyn of Essex (father: Robert, son of Wymarc)	27.9
Stutton	Fridebern, thegn (sub King Edward) – 32.6; Scalpi, thegn (sub Harold Godwineson) – 36.2	Geoffrey de Mandeville (Rainalm) – 32.6; Robert Gernon (William de Alno) – 36.2	32.6 & 36.2
Thorington	Ælfwine, freeman (sub Stigand)	Robert, son of Corbucion (Gifard)	40.6

	(Great & Little) Wenham	Ansgot (sub Edeva the Fair) – 3.67; Tuneman, thegn (sub Harold Godwineson) – 16.40; Auti, thegn – 40.3	Count Alan of Brittany (Ermengot) – 3.67; Bishop of Bayeux (Roger Bigot) – 16.40; Robert son of Corbucion – 40.3	3.67, 16.40 & 40.3
	[Wherstead?]	Thurstan (sub Edeva the Fair)	Count Alan of Brittany (Ælfric the Priest)	3.77
	Woolverstone	Thurstan (sub Edeva the Fair)	Count Alan of Brittany (Ælfric the Priest)	3.74
Stow	Buxhall	Leofwine Croc (Munulf the Priest noted in 26.5)	Roger of Poitou	8.49
	Combs	Wulfnoth, freeman (sub King Edward) – 2.6	Count Robert of Mortain (Nigel dec'd)	2.8
	Creeting (St. Peter)	[1 freeman?] – 23.1; Ælfric, freeman (sub Eadric of Laxfield) –51.1	Abbot of Bernay (1 freeman) – 23.1; Walter of St. Valéry – 51.1	23.1 & 51.1
	Dagworth	6 freemen (belonging to royal manor of Thorney) – 31.44; Bræme, freeman, killed at Hastings (sub King Edward) – 31.50	Hugh de Montfort (6 freemen belonging to royal manor of Thorney) – 31.44; Hugh de Montfort (William, son of Gross) – 31.50	31.44 & 50
	Eruestuna	10 freemen (sub Guthmund)	Hugh de Montfort [10 freemen?]	31.46
	(Gt. & Lt.) Finborough	Leofson, freeman (sub Guthmund)	Roger of Auberville [1 freeman?]	29.1
	Harleston	2 freemen (sub Bury Abbey)	Bury Abbey (Adelund & Peter)	14.36
	Haughley	Guthmund (sub King Edward)	Hugh de Montfort (Hervey, Ralph, Thorold, Pesserera, Robert & Richard)	31.42
	(Old) Newton	2 freemen (sub Alsi)	Bishop of Bayeux (Roger Bigot – Warengar sub him)	16.12
	Onehouse (rt)	Ketel, thegn (sub King Edward)	Ranulf Peverel	34.6

	Place	1066 holder	1086 holder	Reference
	Stow(market)	? [Church mentioned incidentally in connection with Combs – 2.8, and Onehouse – 34.6]	Count Robert of Mortain, Combs (Nigel dec'd) – 2.8; Ranulf Peverel, Onehouse – 34.6	2.8 & 34.6
	Thorney	King Edward	The King	1.1
	Wetherden	20 freemen (sub Bury Abbey) – 14.35; 17 freemen (sub Guthmund) – 31.45	Bury Abbey (Ralph & Arnulf) – 14.35; Hugh de Montfort [17 freemen?] – 31.45	14.35 & 31.45
Wangford	Barsham (rt)	Leofstane the Priest (sub Gyrth Godwineson)	Roger Bigot (Robert of Vaux)	7.40
	Beccles	Bury Abbey & 30 sokemen (sub Abbey)	Bury Abbey & 30 sokemen (under it)	14.120
	Bungay (rt)	Stigand – 1.110; Pat, freeman – 1.111; Ælfgar, freeman – 1.111; 15 freemen (sub Stigand) – 1.111; Ælfric, freeman – 4.19	The King (Wulfsi) & Wulfric (sub Earl of Cheshire) – 1.110; the King (Howard & Wulfsi) – 1.111; the King (Eadric) – 1.111; the King (15 freemen) – 1.111; Earl of Cheshire (William of Noyers) – 4.19	1.110 & 111 & 4.19
	(South) Elmham (All Saints, St. Cross, St. James, St. Margaret, St. Michael, St. Nicholas, St. Peter) **(rt)**	Godric, freeman (sub Ralph the Constable) – 13.6; 1 freeman (sub Bishop of Thetford) – 19.14; Ælfwine, freeman (sub Ingvar, thegn) & 25 freemen (sub Bishop of Thetford) – 19.16	Godric the Steward – 13.6; Bishop of Thetford (? tenants) – 19.14 & 16	13.6, 19.14 & 16
	Flixton	Æskell, freeman, or 8 other freemen (all sub Stigand) – 19.15; Offa, freeman (sub Stigand) – 53.5	Bishop of Thetford – 19.15; & Eudo, son of Spirwic (Geoffrey) – 53.5	19.15 & 53.5
	Homersfield	Bishop of Thetford (personal) – 18.4; 1 freeman (sub Bishop of Thetford) – 19.13	Bishop of Thetford (personal) – 18.4; Bishop of Thetford (diocesan) [1 freeman?] – 19.13	18.4 & 19.13
	Ilketshall (St. Andrew, St. John, St. Lawrence, **St. Margaret) (rt)**	1 freewoman (sub Burgheard)	Earl Hugh of Cheshire [1 freewoman?]	4.26

	Mettingham (rt)	Ælfric, freeman (sub Wulfsi)	Earl Hugh of Cheshire (Warin)	4.21
	Ringsfield	1 freeman (sub King Edward) – 1.16; royal share in a church referred to, with other parties – 1.20	The King [1 freeman?] – 1.16; part-share with others in a church – 1.20	1.16 & 20
	Sotterley	Burgheard, thegn	Earl Hugh of Cheshire (Mundred)	4.30
	Weston	[Unspecified freemen, sub King Edward] – 1.21; 2½ freemen (sub Stigand) – 1.113	The King (unnamed freemen) – 1.21; the King [2½ freemen?] – 1.113	1.21 & 113
	Willingham	15 freemen (sub Burgheard)	Hugh de Montfort [15 freemen?]	31.21
	Worlingham (Parva) (rt)*	[Royal freemen?] – 1.22; Bury Abbey – 14.121 (½ church only)	The King [Royal freemen?] & (Robert of Vaux) – 1.22; Bury Abbey – 14.121	1.22 & 14.121
Wilford	Alderton	31 freemen (sub Eadric of Laxfield)	Robert Malet (34 freemen)	6.159
	Bawdsey	12½ freemen (sub Eadric of Laxfield)	Robert Malet (Élise Malet, his mother)	6.161
	Boulge	[Wulfwine the Priest?]	Robert Malet (Robert of Glanville & Wulfwine under him)	6.181
	Boyton	Stanwine (sub Eadric of Laxfield)	Robert Malet (Humphrey, son of Rodric)	6.172
	Bredfield	? – 6.182; Eadric of Laxfield (sub Ely Abbey) – 21.85	Robert Malet – 6.182; Ely Abbey (Hervey of Berry) – 21.85	6.182 & 21.85
	Bromeswell	1 freeman (sub Eadric of Laxfield) – 6.249; Ely Abbey [2 freemen also?] – 21.83	Robert Malet (Hubert) – 6.249; Ely Abbey (2 freemen) – 21.83	6.249 & 21.83
	Capel (St. Andrew)	24 freemen (sub Eadric of Laxfield)	Robert Malet (24 freemen sub Walter, son of Aubrey)	6.183
	Debach	3 freemen (sub Eadric Grim)	Countess of Aumâle [3 freemen?]	46.10

Harpole	[Ely Abbey]	Ely Abbey	Inquisitio Eliensis
Hollesley	Eadric of Laxfield & 5 sokemen under him	Robert Malet [5 sokemen, as previously?]	6.148
Loudham	18 freemen (sub Thormod), 15 freemen (sub Eadric of Laxfield) & 1 freeman (sub Ely Abbey)	Bishop of Evreux [Freemen, as previously?]	22.3
Shottisham	Osmund, freeman (sub Eadric of Laxfield)	Robert Malet (Walter the Cross-bowman)	6.238
Sutton	2 freemen (sub Eadric of Laxfield)	Robert Malet (2 freemen sub Walter of Caen)	6.170

Table details

- Communities shown in bold font, with **(rt)** appended, are those with round-tower churches. An asterisk indicates the remains or ruins of a round tower. Four "missing" parishes (Ashby, Blundeston, Bradwell and Gunton), all located in Lothingland and all with round towers, were post-Domesday settlements. So was Buxlow (absorbed by Knodishall), in Blything, which has the ruins of its tower still standing.

- Use of bold italic font shows communities where recorded churches had no endowment of land.

- Communities which have a question mark appended within square brackets are those which have a priest referred to and which, therefore, might possibly have had a place of worship of some kind.

- Names in brackets in the third column indicate the patrons of land-holders (an adoption acceptable to both parties, by process of *commendation*) or exercisers of jurisdiction – in those cases where patronage or jurisdiction (or both, together) is stated or implied. Suffolk has far more detail recorded of such ties than Norfolk, but there are still a number of cases where the exact relationship is not made clear. Because of this element of uncertainty, no attempt has been made to identify patronage and jurisdiction specifically, but simply to record a bond which existed between both parties.

- No distinction is made between freemen (*libi hoes*) and sokemen (*soc*) in the translation of the text, all such tenants being classed as the former. Necessary adjustment has been made in the table, as freemen usually held their land independently, whereas sokemen were tied to an estate by customary services of some kind. The latter were probably also unable to attach themselves to the patronage of a social superior by the process of *commendation* (see Roffe, p. 223).

- Half-freemen were probably tenants commended to more than one lord (Welldon Finn, p. 125).

East Suffolk Summary (proportion of communities with churches)

Bishop's – 67% (2 early Christian foundations noted). Later, known as Hoxne Hundred.

Blything – 54% (5 early Christian foundations noted).

Bosmere – 62% (1 early Christian foundation noted). Later, absorbed part of Claydon.

Carlford – 35%.

Claydon – 67%. One-third of it later converted into Thredling Hundred; the remainder joined with Bosmere to form Bosmere & Claydon.

Colneis – 31% (1 early Christian foundation noted).

Hartismere – 77%.

[Ipswich – percentage not relevant/applicable.]

Loes – 54% (2 early Christian foundations noted).

Lothing – 33%.

Lothingland – 18% (1 early Christian foundation noted).

Parham – 50%. Later, incorporated in Plomesgate Hundred.

Plomesgate – 32% (1 early Christian foundation noted).

Samford – 44%.

Stow – 65%.

Wangford – 54% (2 early Christian foundations noted).

Wilford – 43%.

- No adjustments made for 4 communities (Boyton, Kelsale, Kenton & Woodbridge) geographically located in hundreds other than the ones in which they were assessed. Percentages would alter slightly for Carlford, Loes and Wilford, if applied.
- East Suffolk: 223 communities with churches, out of 447 in all = 50%.
- County as a whole: 357 communities with churches, out of a total number of 634 = 56%.
- Number of churches in county: 448+ (excluding Bury St. Edmunds & Ipswich).

Table 11. Suffolk primary title-holders and church location (whole county)

Tenant-in-chief (1086)	Land-holder (1066)	Community	Sector	Reference
The King	Earl Ælfgar	Badmondisfield	West	1.121 (m)
	King Edward	Barrow	West	1.120 (m)
	Earl Morcar's mother [Ælfeva]	*(Great & Little) Cornard*	West	1.98 (m)
	Bury Abbey (from King Edward)	Icklingham – outlier to Mildenhall	West	1.115 (o)
	Bury Abbey (from King Edward)	Mildenhall	West	1.115 (m)
	Ealdgyth, freewoman, or 34 sokemen	Norton	West	1.88 (u)
	Earl Morcar's mother [Ælfeva]	Sudbury	West	1.97 (m)
	Ealdgyth, freewoman	(Great & Little) Thurlow	West	1.90 (m)
	Æthelmær, freeman (sub Edeva the Fair)	Ash(bocking)	East	1.73 (2m)
	Æthelmær the Priest	[Akethorpe?]	East	1.56 (m)
(Annexation, from William of Bourneville)	Queen Edith	Baylham	East	76.15 (m)
	King Edward	*Blythburgh*	East	1.12 (m & 2u)
	King Edward – 1.2; Stigand – 1.119	Bramford	East	1.2 (m) & 1.119 (m)
	Stigand – 1.110; Pat, Ælfgar, & 15 other freemen (unnamed, sub Stigand) – 1.111	**Bungay (rt)**	East	1.110 (m) & 1.111 (2m & f)
	3 freemen (sub Burgheard)	Cotton	East	1.95 (f)
	Ælfwine the Priest	Darsham	East	1.13 (m)

	Harold Godwineson	Harkstead – outlier to Brightlingsea	East	1.96 (o)
	Stigand	Hintlesham	East	1.118 (2m)
	20 freemen – 1.25; 6 freemen – 1.28 (both lots unnamed)	[Kirkley?]	East	1.25 & 1.28 combined (f)
	[Thormod of Parham?]	Marlesford	East	1.94 (m)
	Burgheard	Mendlesham	East	1.76 (m)
	Wulfsi (sub Gyrth Godwineson) & 12 freemen (sub Gyrth)	Mutford (rt)	East	1.23 (m & f)
	1 freeman (sub King Edward) – 1.16; unnamed persons – 1.20	Ringsfield	East	1.16 (m) & 1.20 (u)
	Gyrth Godwineson & 210 sokemen (under him)	Shotley	East	1.102 (m & f)
	Wihtred the Priest	Somerleyton (rt) [now Blundeston]	East	1.52 (m)
	King Edward	Thorney	East	1.1 (m)
	Godric	Thurleston	East	1.122e (f – see also 8.70)
	Unspecified freemen (sub King Edward) – 1.21; 2½ freemen (sub Stigand) – 1.113	Weston	East	1.21 (f) & 1.113 (f)
	[Royal freemen?]	Worlingham (rt)*	East	1.22 (2u)
Count Robert of Mortain	Wulfnoth	Brettenham	West	2.13 (m)
	? [Church reference made in entry for Ringshall]	Battisford – 1/12 church ref.	East	2.11 (u) (not included)
	30 freemen (sub Harold Godwineson)	Bucklesham	East	2.16 (f)
	Wulfnoth, freeman (sub King Edward)	Combs	East	2.8 (u)

?			2.8 (u)
	Stowmarket [ref. made in connection with Combs]	East	
Count Alan of Brittany			
Manni Swart, thegn	Cowlinge	West	3.1 (m)
Thurstan	[Bentley?]	East	3.75 (m)
Manni Swart, thegn	**Bramfield (rt)**	East	3.3 (m)
Ulf, freeman (sub Ely Abbey)	Chillesford	East	3.93 (m)
Half-freeman (sub Anund)	Dallinghoo	East	3.48 (f)
Eadwine (sub Edeva the Fair)	Dodnash	East	3.72 (m)
Sparrowhawk (sub Eadric of Laxfield)	(Great) Glemham	East	3.95 (m)
Thurstan	[Kalweton?]	East	3.78 (m)
Eadric Grim (sub Ely Abbey & Eadric of Laxfield)	Kettleburgh	East	3.34 (m)
7 freemen (sub Eadric Grim)	Martley	East	3.52 (f)
Gauti, freeman, & 24 freemen (sub Ralph the Constable)	Nettlestead	East	3.56 (m & f)
? – reference to church land held in South Elmham	Rumburgh	East	3.105 (u)
11 freemen (sub Gyrth Godwineson)	Rushmere (St. Andrew)	East	3.19 (f)
7 freemen (sub ?)	Walpole	East	3.4 (f)
Ansgot (sub Edeva the Fair)	(Great & Little) Wenham	East	3.67 (m)
6 freemen (shared with Thorington)	Wenhaston	East	3.5 (f)
Thurstan (sub Edeva the Fair)	[Wherstead?]	East	3.77 (m)
[Ralph the Constable? – ref. 3.10]	**Wissett (rt)**	East	3.14 (m)
Thurstan (sub Edeva the Fair)	Woolverstone	East	3.74 (m)

Earl Hugh	5 freemen (sub Burgheard)	Barnby	East	4.39 (f)
	Ælfric, freeman	**Bungay (rt)**	East	4.19 (m)
	Eadric, freeman (sub Eadric of Laxfield & Æthelstan)	Cretingham	East	4.18 (m)
	Æthelmær, thegn	Framlingham	East	4.42 (m)
	Æthelstan, thegn	Framsden	East	4.1 (m)
	Ælfric & Ulf the Priest	[Halesworth?]	East	4.13 (m)
	1 freewoman (sub Burgheard)	**Ilketshall (rt)**	East	4.26 (m)
	Ælfric, freeman (sub Wulfsi)	**Mettingham (rt)**	East	4.21 (m)
	1 freeman (sub Ælfric, freeman of Gyrth Godwineson)	Pakefield	East	4.41 (f)
	Burgheard, thegn	Sotterley	East	4.30 (m)
	21 freemen, held with Ashfield – 67.4 (sub Earl Hugh's predecessor – Ely Abbey?)	Thorpe (Hall)	East	4.6 (f)
	Æskell the Priest, freeman	Uggeshall	East	4.14 (m)
Count Eustace of Boulogne	Alsi, later Engelric	Elveden	West	5.3 (m)
	Leofric, thegn	Ousden	West	5.1 (m)
	Leadmær, freeman	Higham (rt)	East	5.6 (m)
Robert Malet	Godwine, son of Ælfhere (sub King Edward)	Chilton	West	6.2 (m)
	Godwine, son of Ælfhere (sub King Edward)	Edwardstone	West	6.1 (m)
	1 freeman (sub Eadric of Laxfield & Bury Abbey)	Stanton	West	6.301 (f)
	Wulfric, freeman (sub Eadric of Laxfield)	Aldeburgh	East	6.130 (2m)
	31 freemen (sub Eadric of Laxfield)	Alderton	East	6.159 (f)
	1 freeman (sub ?)	Aspall	East	6.206 (m)

Place	Region	Ref.	Holder
Badingham	East	6.306 (m)	Eadric of Laxfield
Bawdsey	East	6.161 (f)	12½ freemen (sub Eadric of Laxfield)
Bedingfield	East	6.75 (f/m)	6 freemen (sub ?)
Boulge	East	6.181 (f)	[Wulfwine the Priest?]
Boyton (Plomesgate H.)	East	6.138 (2f)	12 freemen (sub Eadric of Laxfield)
Boyton (Wilford H.)	East	6.172 (m)	Stanwine (sub Eadric of Laxfield)
Braiseworth	East	6.225 (m)	Wulfeva, freewoman, & 16 freemen
Bredfield	East	6.182 (u)	?
Bromeswell	East	6.249 (f)	1 freeman (sub Eadric of Laxfield)
Brutge	East	6.28 (m)	Eadric of Laxfield
Capel (St. Andrew)	East	6.183 (f)	24 freemen (sub Eadric of Laxfield)
Charsfield	East	6.179 (f)	24 freemen (sub Eadric of Laxfield)
Chippenhall	East	6.311 (m)	9 freemen (sub Eadric of Laxfield & Bishop of Thetford)
[Cransford?]	East	6.128 (f)	Godric the Priest (sub Eadric of Laxfield)
Debenham	East	6.18 (2m)	Eadric of Laxfield – ref. 6.11
Dennington	East	6.303 (m)	Eadric of Laxfield
Dunwich	East	6.84 (3m)	Eadric of Laxfield
Eye	East	6.191 (m)	Eadric of Laxfield
(Great) Glemham	East	6.49 (m)	Wulfmær, freeman (sub Eadric of Laxfield)
Hollesley	East	6.148 (m)	Eadric of Laxfield (& 5 sokemen under him)
Huntingfield	East	6.80 (m)	Edric of Laxfield
Kenton	East	6.271 (u)	8 freemen, inc. Brictmær, Huna & Woodbrown (mainly sub Eadric of Laxfield)

	Holder	Place	Region	Reference
	3 freemen (sub Godwine) or Oslac, freeman (sub Eadric of Laxfield)	Kesgrave	East	6.114 (f)
	Eadric of Laxfield	Laxfield	East	6.305 (m)
	Eadric of Laxfield	Leiston	East	6.83 (3m)
	Fulcard, freeman (half sub Eadric of Laxfield)	Mellis	East	6.195 (f)
	1 freeman (sub ?)	Mendham	East	6.313 (2m)
	Alnoth, freeman (sub Eadric of Laxfield)	Parham (*Niue-tuna*)	East	6.32 (m)
	Godwine, son of Ælfhere (sub Queen Edith)	Playford	East	6.112 (m)
	Ælfric, freeman (sub Eadric of Laxfield)	Redlingfield	East	6.192 (m)
	Eadric of Laxfield	Rendham – outlier to *Chiletuna*	East	6.43 (o)
	1 freeman (sub Eadric of Laxfield)	Rendlesham	East	6.281 (m)
	Wulfeva, freewoman (sub Stigand)	Rishangles	East	6.222 (m)
	Osmund, freeman (sub Eadric of Laxfield)	Shottisham	East	6.238 (m)
	1 freeman & 7½ others (2 named as Eadric & Ælfric)	Sibton	East	6.90 (m & 2u)
	21 freemen (sub Eadric of Laxfield)	Snape	East	6.133 (f)
	Eadric of Laxfield	Staverton	East	6.260 (m)
	Wulfeva, freewoman (sub Stigand)	Stoke (Ash)	East	6.213 (m)
	Eadric of Laxfield	Stradbroke	East	6.308 (2m)
	12 freemen (sub Eadric of Laxfield)	Sudbourne	East	6.143 (m)
	2 freemen (sub Eadric of Laxfield)	Sutton	East	6.170 (f)
	11 freemen (sub Eadric of Laxfield)	Swefling	East	6.46 (f)
	Eadric of Laxfield	Tannington	East	6.304 (m)
	Wulfeva, freewoman (sub Stigand)	Thorndon	East	6.223 (m)

			East	
	11 freemen (sub Wulfeva – 1 of them shared with Eadric of Laxfield)	Thornham Parva	East	6.218 (f)
	Godmane (sub Eadric of Laxfield)	Thrandeston	East	6.66 (f)
	1 freeman (sub Eadric of Laxfield)	Tuddenham	East	6.120 (f)
	22 freemen [sub Eadric of Laxfield?] – 6.30; Ælfwine, freeman, and Ælfæd, freewoman (sub Eadric of Laxfield – 6.38)	Wantisden	East	6.30 & 6.38 combined (f)
	Aki, freeman (sub Eadric of Laxfield) – 6.85; 1 freeman [sub Eadric of Laxfield?] – 6.96	Westleton	East	6.85 (m) & 6.96 (m)
	1 freeman [sub – Eadric of Laxfield?]	**Weybread (rt)**	East	6.312 (m)
	2 freemen & 1 sokeman (sub Eadric of Laxfield?)	Woodbridge	East	6.287 (f)
Roger Bigot	Thorbern & Wulfwine, freemen (sub Norman)	"Alston" (*Alteinestuna*)	East	7.96 (f)
	Leofstan the Priest (sub Gyrth Godwineson)	**Barsham (rt)**	East	7.40 (m)
	Munding, freeman (sub Ely Abbey)	Baylham	East	7.58 (m)
	Gode, freewoman (sub Stigand)	**Brome (rt)**	East	7.75 (m)
	16 named freemen (sub Norman)	Burgh (Colneis)	East	7.80 (m)
	Eadric, freeman (sub Eadric of Laxfield & Ely Abbey)	Chediston	East	7.15 (m)
	Wigulf, freeman (sub Toli the Sheriff)	Coddenham (Bosmere)	East	7.67 (m & 2u)
	Stigand	Denham (Bishop's)	East	7.4 (m)
	Ulfketel, freeman (sub Ulf)	Heveningham	East	7.27 (f)
	Norman	Kelsale	East	7.3 (m)
	Godric the Priest (sub Eadric of Laxfield, & then Norman – after Eadric's outlawry)	Kirton	East	7.114 (f)
	10 named freemen (sub Norman)	Levington	East	7.117 (f)

	Godwine the Priest (sub Harold Godwineson)	[Norton?]	East	7.122 (m)
	Leofcild, freeman (sub Stigand)	Offton	East	7.60 (m)
	Bondi, freeman (subToli the Sheriff)	Opituna	East	7.29 (m)
	Leofwine, freeman (sub Ely Abbey)	Ringshall	East	7.56 (m)
	Norman – 7.70; Ælfgar, thegn (sub King Edward) – 7.71	Saxmundham	East	7.70 (m) & 7.71 (2m)
	Leofson, freeman (sub Leofric Hobbeson)	Somersham	East	7.59 (m)
	Wihtric, freeman (sub Harold Godwineson), or Ulfketel, freeman (sub Norman), or Godmane, freeman (sub Norman)	Stratton	East	7.119 (u)
	1 freewoman [Ælfeva?] (sub Norman)	Strickland	East	7.37 (f)
	Godric (sub Norman)	Trimley (St. Martin & St. Mary)	East	7.97 (2m)
	Norman	Walton	East	7.76 (m)
	1 freeman (sub Norman)	Wantisden	East	7.137 (f)
	Manson, freeman (sub Norman)	UU[W]rabetuna	East	7.28 (f)
Roger of Poitou	Ulf	Hawkedon	West	8.34 (m)
	1 freeman, with 7 added by Norman, son of Tancred – all un-named	Thorpe (Morieux)	West	8.35 (m)
	Eadmær, thegn (sub Earl Ælfgar)	Thurston (Risbridge)	West	8.33 (m)
	Wulfmær, thegn (sub Harold Godwineson)	(Great & Little) Waldingfield	West	8.48 (m)
	[3 freemen?]	Akenham	East	8.71 (f/m)
	Leofwine Croc	Buxhall	East	8.49 (m)
	5 freemen (sub Ely Abbey)	Culpho	East	8.5 (f)

Tenant	Holder	Place		Ref
	20 unnamed freemen – 1 of whom, sub Ely Abbey, had jurisdiction	Hemingstone	East	8.59 (2f)
	Wulfric, thegn	Mendham	East	8.37 (m)
	14½ freemen (sub Wulfmær, Ely Abbey freeman)	Monewden	East	8.22 (f)
	Eadwine the Priest, freeman (sub Ely Abbey)	[Nordberia?]	East	8.81 (m)
	Wulfric, thegn; Wulfmær, thegn; Ælfæd, freewoman (all sub Harold Godwineson)	(Earl & Little) Stonham	East	8.55 (m)
	[18 freemen – sub Gosbert?]	Thurleston	East	8.70 (f)
	? (½ church only referred to)	Westerfield	East	8.73 (u)
	Ælfæd, freewoman (sub Harold Godwineson)	Wickham (Skeith)	East	8.31 (m)
	Ælfæd, freewoman (sub Harold Godwineson)	Willisham	East	8.56 (m)
William of Écouis	Ælfric, freeman	(Market) Weston	West	9.2 (m)
	Ælfric, thegn	Blakenham	East	9.1 (m)
	Wulfric, freeman	Cookley	East	9.3 (m)
Ralph of Beaufour	Modgeva or Godiva, freewomen (both sub Bury Abbey)	**Wortham (rt)**	East	11.4 (2m)
Frodo	Acwulf, thegn, & 15 freemen under him	Thelnetham	West	12.1 (m)
	Ordmær	*Worlington*	West	12.3 (m)
Godric the Steward	Eadwine, freeman	Blyford	East	13.2 (m)
	Godric, freeman (sub Ralph the Constable)	**(South) Elmham (rt)**	East	13.6 (2m)

Bury Abbey		Aldham (rt)		
	6 freemen (sub Abbey)	Aldham (rt)	West	14.112 (f)
	22 freemen (sub Abbey)	Ampton	West	14.64 (f)
	21 freemen & 1 sokeman (sub Abbey)	(Great) Ashfield	West	14.93 (f)
	8 freemen (sub Abbey)	Bardwell	West	14.82 (f)
	3 freemen (sub Abbey)	Barnham	West	14.89 (f)
	19 freemen (sub Abbey)	Barningham	West	14.81 (f)
	Abbey & 70 freemen (sub Abbey)	(Great) Barton	West	14.48 (m)
	Abbey + 3 freemen & 9 freemen (sub Abbey)	Bradfield (Combust, St. Clare & St. George)	West	14.52 (m)
	3 freemen, sub Theobald the priest & Robert (sub Abbey)	Brockley	West	14.14 (f)
	Abbey	Chelsworth	West	14.109 (m)
	Abbey & 1 sokeman (sub Abbey)	Chevington	West	14.5 (m)
	Abbey & 12 sokemen (sub Abbey)	Coney Weston	West	14.76 (m)
	Abbey & 9 freemen (sub Abbey)	(Santon) Downham	West	14.21 (m)
	Abbey & 5 sokemen (sub Abbey)	Elmswell	West	14.73 (m)
	Abbey	Elveden	West	14.20 (m)
	33 freemen & Adelund (sub Abbey)	Felsham	West	14.58 (f)
	10 sokemen, subWulfweard (sub Abbey)	Flempton	West	14.12 (f)
	Abbey, + 3 sokemen & 2 freemen (sub Abbey)	Fornham (All Saints)	West	14.9 (m)
	Abbey & 6 freemen (sub Abbey)	Fornham (St. Genev.) – outlier to ?	West	14.53 (o)
	Abbey & 11 freemen (sub Abbey)	Fornham (St. Martin)	West	14.50 (m)

Holder	Place	Region	Reference
13 freemen (sub Abbey)	Gedding	West	14.60 (f)
28 freemen (sub Abbey) – 4 named	Hawstead	West	14.13 (f)
Abbey & 8 sokemen (sub Abbey)	Hengrave (rt)	West	14.8 (m)
20 freemen (sub Abbey)	Hepworth	West	14.78 (f)
Abbey & 2 sokemen (sub Abbey)	Herringswell	West	14.18 (m)
60 freemen (sub Abbey)	Hessett	West	14.57 (f)
Abbey & 7 sokemen (sub Abbey)	Hinderclay	West	14.74 (m)
16 freemen (sub Abbey)	Honington	West	14.85 (f)
23 freemen (sub Abbey)	Hopton	West	14.80 (f)
Abbey & 15 sokemen (sub Abbey)	Horringer	West	14.2 (m)
9 freemen (sub Abbey)	Hunston	West	14.95 (f)
Abbey	Ickworth	West	14.10 (m)
Wulfwy, Abbey man-at-arms, & 21 sokemen (sub Abbey)	Ingham	West	14.69 (m)
4 freemen, sub Fulcher (sub Abbey)	Knettishall	West	14.99 (f)
Abbey & 1 sokeman (sub Abbey)	Lackford	West	14.7 (m)
7 freemen (sub Abbey)	Langham	West	14.94 (f)
20 freemen (sub Abbey)	Lindsey	West	14.113 (f)
7 freemen (sub Abbey)	Little Livermere	West	14.87 (f)
22 freemen (sub Abbey) & 1 other (sub Eadric of Laxfield)	(Great) Livermere	West	14.68 (f)
Abbey & 2 sokemen (sub Abbey)	(Long) Melford	West	14.23 (m)
Abbey & 10 sokemen (sub Abbey)	Nowton	West	14.4 (m)
Abbey & 34 freemen (sub Abbey)	Pakenham	West	14.49 (m)
Arnulf & 3 sokemen (sub Abbey)	Preston	West	14.26 (f)
Abbey, + 22 sokemen & 2 freemen (sub Abbey)	Rickinghall (Inferior) (rt)	West	14.75 (m)

14.1 (m)	West	**Risby (rt)**	Abbey, + 7 sokemen & 1 freeman (sub Abbey)
14.51 (m)	West	Rougham	Abbey & 90 freemen (sub Abbey)
14.83 (f)	West	Sapiston	11 freemen (sub Abbey)
14.11 (f)	West	(Great & **Little**) **Saxham (rt)**	3 freemen, sub Albert & Fulcher (sub Abbey)
14.108 (m)	West	Semer	Abbey
14.66 (f)	West	Stanningfield	11 freemen (sub Abbey)
14.72 (m & f)	West	Stanton	Abbey, + 60 sokemen & 7 freemen (sub Abbey)
14.77 (m)	West	Stow(langtoft)	2 freemen & 14 others (sub Abbey)
14.71 (f)	West	(West) Stow	21 freemen & 1 other (sub Abbey)
14.54 (m)	West	Thurston (Thedwestry).	Abbey & 36 freemen (sub Abbey)
14.63 (f)	West	Timworth	29 freemen (sub Abbey)
14.65 (m)	West	Tostock	Abbey & 17½ freemen (sub Abbey)
14.19 (m)	West	Wangford	Abbey
14.79 (f)	West	Wattisfield	20 freemen (sub Abbey)
14.62 (2f)	West	(Great & **Little**) **Welnetham (rt)***	41 freemen (sub Abbey)
14.17 (f)	West	Westley	11 freemen (sub Abbey)
14.3 (m)	West	Whepstead	Abbey, + 1 sokeman & 6 freemen (sub Abbey)
14.55 (o)	West	Woolpit – outlier to ?	Abbey & 40 freemen (sub Abbey)
14.88 (f)	West	Wordwell	11 freemen (sub Abbey)
14.120 (m)	East	Beccles	Abbey & 30 sokemen (sub Abbey)
14.105 (m)	East	Chippenhall	Abbey
14.131 (f)	East	Finningham	11 freemen (sub Abbey)

	Description	Place	Region	Reference
	2 freemen (sub Abbey)	Harleston	East	14.36 (f)
	Abbey, + 6 sokemen & 1 freeman (sub Abbey)	Mendham	East	14.106 (m)
	Abbey, + Æthelric, freeman, & wife (sub Abbey)	Mickfield	East	14.38 (m)
	Goding the Reeve (sub Abbey) & 10 freemen (sub him)	Oakley	East	14.129 (m)
	Abbey	Palgrave	East	14.45 (2m)
	Abbey	Redgrave	East	14.42 (m)
	14 freemen (sub Abbey)	Rickinghall (Superior)	East	14.46 (f)
	Abbey	(Monk) Soham	East	14.102 (m)
	5 freemen (sub Abbey)	Stuston (rt)	East	14.137 (f)
	Anselm & 12½ freemen (sub Abbey)	Thrandeston	East	14.139 (m)
	20 freemen (sub Abbey)	Wetherden	East	14.35 (f)
	Half-church only referred to	Worlingham*(rt)	East	14.121 (u)
	Abbey & 1 sokeman (sub Abbey)	Worlingworth	East	14.103 (m)
Archbishop of Canterbury	Archbishop of Canterbury	(Brent & Monks) Eleigh	West	15.5 (m)
	Archbishop of Canterbury	Hadleigh	West	15.2 (m)
Odo, Bishop of Bayeux	Godwine, freeman	Boynton	East	16.44 (m)
	Ailbern, freeman	Burstall	East	16.18 (f)
	Æthelmær, Ælfric & Wihtric & Harold, freemen (all sub Ely Abbey)	Coddenham (Bosmere)	East	16.20 (2m)
	Godwy, freeman (sub Saxi)	Debenham	East	16.28 (2m)

	Godric, freeman (sub Eadric of Laxfield subordinate & Saxi); Leofstan, freeman (sub Eadric of Laxfield subordinate); 11 unnamed freemen (2½ sub Saxi & ½ sub Eadric of Laxfield subordinate)	Helmingham	East	16.26 (f)
	2 freemen (sub Alsi)	(Old) Newton	East	16.12 (f)
	8 freemen (4 sub Saxi)	"Olden" (*Uledana*)	East	16.21 (f)
	Eadnoth, freeman – 16.37; Edwy & Ælfwine, freemen – 16.41	Raydon	East	16.37 (m) & 16.41 (m) – combined
	Leofwine, freeman, (sub Eadric of Laxfield) – 16.15; Wulfric, freeman (sub Ely Abbey), Æthelwald the Priest & Godwy freemen (sub Saxi) – 16.22	(Earl & Little) Stonham	East	16.15 (2m) & 16.22 (2m)
	Ælfwine the Priest, freeman (sub Eadric of Laxfield and Saxi) & Ælfric the Priest, freeman (sub Ely Abbey)	[Ulverston?]	East	16.30 (m)
	Tuneman, thegn (sub Harold Godwineson)	(Great & Little) Wenham	East	16.40 (m)
Ramsey Abbey	Ramsey Abbey	Lawshall	West	17.1 (m)
Bishop of Thetford (diocesan)	Bishop Æthelmær	Homersfield	East	18.4 (m)
	Bishop Æthelmær	Hoxne	East	18.1 (m)
Bishop of Thetford (acquired)	1 freeman [sub Bishop?]	Chickering	East	19.5 (f)
	1 freeman (sub Æthelmær) – 19.14; Ælfwine, freeman (sub Ingvar, thegn) & 25 freemen (sub Æthelmær) – 19.16	**(South) Elmham (rt)**	East	19.14 (m) & 19.16 (m & 3f)

Tenant	Place		Reference
Bishop Stigand	Flixton (Lothingland)	East	19.21 (m)
Æskell, freeman, or 8 other freemen (all sub Bishop Stigand)	Flixton (Wangford)	East	19.15 (m)
1 freeman (Bishop Æthelmær)	Homersfield	East	19.13 (m)
Ulf, thegn (followed by Æthelmær)	Mendham	East	19.2 (m)
Bishop of Rochester			
Orthi, thegn (sub Harold Godwineson)	Freckenham	West	20.1 (m)
Ely Abbey			
Abbey	Brandon	West	21.5 (m)
Abbey	Drinkstone	West	21.3 (m)
Abbey	Glemsford	West	21.10 (m)
Abbey	Hartest	West	21.11 (m)
Abbey	Hitcham	West	21.42 (m)
Abbey	Lakenheath	West	21.6 (m)
Abbey	Nedging	West	21.43 (m)
Abbey	Rattlesden	West	21.1 (m)
Abbey	*Undley*	West	21.7 (m)
Abbey	*Alneterne*	East	21.47 (m)
Abbey	Barham	East	21.26 (m)
Abbey / Roger [Bigot?] (sub Abbey)	Barking	East	21.16 (m) / 21.18 (m)
Eadric of Laxfield (sub Abbey)	Bredfield	East	21.85 (u)
Abbey	*Brightwell*	East	21.54 (m)
Abbey	Bromeswell	East	21.83 (m)
Abbey	Hoo	East	21.95 (m)

		Place	Region	Ref
	Abbey	Stoke	East	21.15 (m)
	Abbey	Sudbourne	East	21.38 (m)
	Abbey	Wetheringsett	East	21.39 (m)
	1 freeman (sub Abbey)	Wingfield	East	21.45 (m)
	Abbey	Winston	East	21.28 (m)
Gilbert, Bishop of Evreux	18 freemen (sub Thormod), 15 freemen (sub Eadric of Laxfield) & 1 freeman (sub Ely Abbey)	Loudham	East	22.3 (f)
Bernay Abbey	1 freeman sub Hardwine	Creeting (St. Peter)	East	23.1 (f/m)
	24 freemen	Creeting (All Saints, St. Mary & St. Olave)	East	23.4 (f)
Chatteris Abbey [Benedictine nuns]	Abbey	Kersey	West	24.1 (m)
Richard, son of Count Gilbert of Brionne	22 freemen (sub Wihtgar)	Bures	West	25.42 (f)
	Wihtgar	Cavenham – outlier to Desning	West	25.35 (o)
	Wihtgar (father, Ælric, gifted large manor to St. John's Church)	Clare	West	25.1 (m)
(Annexation)	2 freemen (sub Ælfric Kemp)	(Great & Little) Cornard	West	76.4 (m)
	1 sokeman (sub?)	Dalham	West	25.6 (m)
	2 sokemen (sub ?)	Denham (Ris-bridge)	West	25.7 (m)

	Wihtgar	Desning	West	25.3 (2m)
	Leofgeat, freeman (sub Wihtgar)	Elveden	West	25.34 (m)
	Wihtgar	Hundon	West	25.2 (2m)
	7 freemen (sub Wihtgar)	Rede	West	25.32 (f)
	Eadric Spud, or Wulfæd, or Crawa (all termed freemen – but 1 freewoman)	Stansfield	West	25.78 (f)
	21 freemen	Stoke (by Clare)	West	25.97 (f)
	16 freemen	Stradishall	West	25.100 (f)
	10 freemen	(Great & Little) Thurlow	West	25.93 (f)
	3 freemen (sub Wihtgar)	(Great & Little) Waldingfield	West	25.46 (f)
	3 freemen (sub Wihtgar)	Westley	West	25.27 (f)
	1 sokeman (sub Wulfmær) – 25.10; Ailbern, freeman – 25.85	(Great & Little) Wratting	West	25.10 (m) & 25.85 (m)
	Æskell	Badley	East	25.53 (m)
	Godmane (under Wihtgar, King & Earl of East Anglia), + priest with 15 acres (sub King & Earl)	[Flowton?]	East	25.55 (f)
	Robert, son of Wymarc	Freston	East	25.76 (m)
	Godric, freeman	Higham (rt)	East	25.75 (m)
William of Warenne	Toki, thegn [later held by Frederic, de Warenne's brother-in-law]	Depden	West	26.9 (m)
	1 freeman (sub Ely & Bury abbeys)	Elveden	West	26.3 (m)
	Æthelric, freeman	Burgh (Carlford)	East	26.16 (f)
	Ælfric, freeman (sub Ranulf, nephew of Eadric of Laxfield)	Middleton	East	26.13 (m)
	Eadric [of Laxfield?], freeman, & Wulfric, freeman	Wrentham	East	26.12a (2m)

Tenant-in-chief	Holder	Place	Hundred	Reference
Sweyn of Essex	Robert (son of Wymarc)	Stoke (by Nayland)	West	27.3 (m)
	Robert (son of Wymarc)	Pannington	East	27.10 (m)
	Robert (son of Wymarc)	Stratford (St. Mary)	East	27.9 (m)
Eudo the Steward	Godwine, thegn (sub King Edward)	Chamberlain's Hall – outlier to Eriswell	West	28.1b (o)
	Godwine, thegn (sub King Edward)	Eriswell	West	28.1a (m)
	Ælfric Kemp	Layham	West	28.7 (m)
	Canute, freeman (sub Earl Ælfgar)	Tuddenham	West	28.3 (m)
	Wulfric (sub Ely Abbey & Eadric of Laxfield)	(Great) Glemham	East	28.6 (m)
Roger of Auberville	Tovi, thegn	Elmsett	West	29.12 (m)
	Leofson, freeman (sub Guthmund)	Finborough	East	29.1 (m)
	Tepekin, freeman (sub Harold Godwineson)	Henley	East	29.11 (m)
William, brother of Roger of Auberville	Godwy, freeman	Ringshall	East	30.1 (m)
Hugh de Montfort	Guthmund, thegn	Stanstead	West	31.41 (m)
	Ælfric, freeman	Battisford	East	31.56 (m)
	18 freemen (sub Guthmund)	*Bribtoluestuna*	East	31.9 (f)

Tenant-in-chief	Holder(s)	Place		Reference
	6 freemen (sub Guthmund, who was sub Thorney manor) – 31.44; Bræme, freeman (sub King Edward & killed at Hastings) – 31.50	*Dagworth*	East	31.44 (f) & 31.50 (m)
	10 freemen (sub Guthmund)	*Eruestuna*	East	31.46 (f)
	Guthmund (sub King Edward)	Haughley	East	31.42 (m)
	1 freeman (sub Burgheard & Wulfsi)	[Kirkley?]	East	31.33 (f)
	Guthmund (sub his brother, Wulfric, Abbot of Ely)	Occold	East	31.60 (m & f)
	1 freeman (sub Gyrth Godwineson)	**Rushmere (rt)**	East	31.34 (f)
	17 freemen (sub Guthmund)	Wetherden	East	31.45 (f)
	15 freemen (sub Burgheard)	Willingham	East	31.21 (f)
Geoffrey de Mandeville	Ulf, freeman (sub Æsgar)	Belstead	East	32.5 (m)
	Æsgar	Holton (St. Mary)	East	32.3 (m)
	Haldane (sub Harold Godwineson)	Letheringham	East	32.14 (m)
	Fridebern, thegn (sub King Edward)	Stutton	East	32.6 (m)
	Haldane	**Thorington (rt)** (Blything)	East	32.19 (m)
Ralph Baynard	Æthelgyth, freewoman, & 25 freemen	Kedington	West	33.1 (m)
	3 freemen (2 sub Æthylgyth & 1 sub Bury Abbey) or 4 other freemen	Poslingford	West	33.2 (f)
	Æthelgyth, freewoman (sub King Edward)	Shimpling	West	33.13 (m)
	Godwine, thegn	Wixoe	West	33.3 (m)
	11 freemen [sub Thored?] & 1 other	Brampton	East	33.5 (f)
	Thored	Cratfield	East	33.10 (m)

	Thored & 8 freemen	Frostenden	East	33.6 (2m)
	Thored & 32 freemen (under him)	Reydon	East	33.4 (2m)
	Thored & 3 freemen (under him)	Ubbeston	East	33.9 (m)
Ranulf Peverel	Siward of Maldon, thegn	Acton	West	34.2 (m)
	Siward of Maldon, thegn	Assington	West	34.3 (m)
	Saxi (as lord of Ulverston)	Aspall	East	34.18 (m)
	Leofstan	(Great & Little) Bricett – church land only referred to	East	34.8
	Eadric Grim (sub Ely Abbey & Eadric of Laxfield)	Clopton	East	34.15 (m)
	Leofric, freeman	Coddenham (Bosmere)	East	34.9 (m)
	Saxi	Debenham	East	34.12 (m)
	[Saxi]	Mickfield	East	34.10 (m)
	Ketel, thegn (sub King Edward)	Onehouse (rt)	East	34.6 (m)
	? (¼ part of a church referred to)	(Earl & Little) Stonham	East	34.11 (u)
Aubrey de Vere	Wulfwine, freeman	Aldham (rt)	West	35.6 (m)
	Wulfwine, freeman, & 9 sokemen	Burgate	East	35.5 (2m & f)
Robert Gernon	Scalpi, thegn (sub Harold Godwineson)	Stutton	East	36.2 (m)
Peter of Valognes	Alstane, thegn	(Great) Faken-ham	West	37.1 (2m)

Roger of Rames	Godwine the Priest, freeman	Akenham	East	38.11 (m/f)
	Godwine, freeman [sub King Edward & Earl Ælfgar?]	(Great & Little) Bricett	East	38.8 (m)
	3 freemen	Coddenham (Bosmere)	East	38.5 (m)
	Æthelmær, freeman (sub Eadric of Laxfield)	Stonham (Aspal)	East	38.6 (m)
Ranulf, brother of Ilger	Durand, freeman (sub Eadric of Laxfield)	Aluresdestuna	East	39.12 (m)
	Brihtmær, or Wulfweard, or Hardwine, or Brihtric, freemen (sub varying patronage)	Hemley	East	39.5 (f)
	Eadwald	Martlesham	East	39.6 (m)
	Norman	Newbourn	East	39.10 (f)
Robert, son of Corbucion	Ælfwine, freeman (sub Stigand)	Thorington (Samford)	East	40.6 (m)
	Auti, thegn	(Great & Little) Wenham	East	40.3 (m)
Walter the Deacon	Queen Edith	Bildeston	West	41.1 (m)
	Leofwine of Bacton, thegn (sub King Edward)	Milden	West	41.10 (m)
	Leofwine, freeman (sub Harold Godwineson)	Bacton	East	41.7 (m)
	Wulfric, freeman	Henley	East	41.14 (m)
	Queen Edith	Swilland	East	41.2 (m)

Tihel of Helléan (al. le Breton)	Clarenbold	Haverhill	West	42.2 (m)
Ralph of Limésy	Norman (sub King Edward)	Cavendish	West	43.2 (m)
	Norman (sub King Edward)	Coddenham – outlier to Cavendish	West	43.2 (o)
	Uhtred (sub Harold Godwineson)	Newton	West	43.3 (2m)
	Ælfric, freeman (sub Harold Godwineson)	Bedingfield	East	43.5 (m)
Robert of Tosny	Ulf, thegn	(Great & Little) Bradley (rt)	West	44.1 (m)
	Ulf & 5 freemen (under him)	Syleham (rt)	East	44.2 (m)
Countess of Aumâle	Wulfric, thegn (sub King Edward)	Shimpling	West	46.1 (m)
	Ælfic of Weinhou	Belstead	East	46.3 (m)
	3 freemen (sub Eadric Grim)	Debach	East	46.10 (f)
	Edeva the Fair	Gusford	East	46.5 (m)
	Edeva the Fair	Harkstead	East	46.4 (m)
William of Arques	Eadmund the Priest (sub Ely Abbey)	Brandeston	East	47.3 (m)
Drogo of Beuvrière	Rada, freeman (sub Harold Godwineson)	Sotherton	East	48.1 (m)
Walter of St. Valéry	Ælfric, freeman (sub Eadric of Laxfield)	Creeting (St. Peter)	East	51.1 (m/f)

Humphrey the Chamberlain	Brictwald (sub Queen Edith)	Cretingham	East	52.5 (m)
	Ælfflæd, freewoman (sub Eadric of Laxfield), or Lustwine (sub Eadric of Laxfield). or 16½ freemen (sub Leoflæd)	Otley	East	52.1 (m)
Eudo, son of Spirwic	Cynric, freeman	Battisford	East	53.3 (m)
	Offa, freeman (sub Stigand)	Flixton (Wangford)	East	53.5 (m)
William of Vatteville	Ælfgyth, freewoman (sub Bury Abbey)	Hargrave	West	54.2 (m)
Hubert of Mont-Canisy (al. Munchesny)	Leofwine the Bald	Wyverstone	East	57.1 (m)
Gundwin, the Chamberlain	Æscman, freeman (sub Robert, son of Wymarc)	**Higham (rt)**	East	58.1 (m)
Robert of Verly	Alsi, freeman	(Market) Weston	West	60.1 (m)
Isaac	Siric, freeman	Offton	West	62.1 (m)
	Leofric (sub Brihtric, Bury Abbey reeve)	Thornham (Magna)	East	62.5 (m)
Judicael the Priest	Ælfgar, freeman (sub Stigand), & 2 other freemen (1 each sub Bishop of Thetford & Eadric of Laxfield)	Horham	East	54.3 (m)

	Ælfric, freeman (sub Eadric of Laxfield) – 64.1; 9 freemen – 64.2	Stonham (Aspal)	East	64.1 (m) & 64.2 (f)
Robert Blunt	Aki or 14 freemen (under him); or Ketel, freeman; or 3 other freemen (sub ?)	(Great) Ashfield	West	66.3 (m)
	Aki, or 30 freemen (under him)	Ixworth	West	66.1 (m)
	Aki, or 23½ freemen (under him)	Walsham (le Willows)	West	66.2 (m)
Hervey of Bourges	Godmane (sub Robert Malet – should this be Eadric of Laxfield, his predecessor?)	**Ashfield (rt)***	East	67.4 (m)
	10 named freemen (9 sub Ely Abbey) & Wulfmær, freeman (sub Haldane)	(Great) Bealings	East	67.11 (m)
	Eadric (sub Eadric of Laxfield)	*Brutge*	East	67.5 (m)
	Brihtwald (sub Eadric of Laxfield) & 5 freemen (sub same patronage?)	Pettaugh	East	67.3 (m)
Ralph the Crossbowman	Stigand	**Burgh (Castle) (rt)**	East	69.1 (m)
Robert of Stratford	Thuri	Belstead	East	71.2 (m)
Vavassors (free men and women of varying status)	Church referred to, along with 25 named freemen & 4 named freewomen	Whitton	East	74.13 (f)

Table details

- Communities shown in bold font, with (rt) appended, are those with round-tower churches. An asterisk following indicates the ruins or remains of a round tower.

- Use of bold italic font shows communities where recorded churches had no endowment of land.

- The fifth and last column indicates, wherever possible (from the information given), the type of estate to which a church or churches was/were attached. The symbols used are as follows: (f) = freeholding, (m) = manor, (o) = outlier and (u) = uncertain. Uncertainty occurs mainly when the Domesday scribe places a church at the very end of a series of entries, making it difficult to attach it to any one of the preceding estates, large or small, when two or more of these are listed. Bury Abbey has by far the greatest number of such entries, the result of having many manors held directly and numerous holdings in the hands of subordinate freemen. Given the generally larger size of manors, relative to that of freemen's and sokemen's estates (across all tenancies in the county), it would seem that the church was mainly a manorial asset and this has therefore usually been the categorisation adopted – unless it seems clear that freemen held the church estate, or unless it is not possible to make an informed judgement as to tenure. There are a number of cases where a "best-fit" principle was applied because certainty of categorisation was not possible.

- With 24 churches having a shared interest in them, under different tenants-in-chief (22 with two, 1 with three and another with four), and with the consequent repetition of recording taken into account, the estate-type summary is as follows: 301 manor and 8 outlier (69%), 116 freeholding (26%), 3 manor and freeholding combined (0.7%) – Akenham, Bedingfield and Creeting St. Peter – and 21 uncertain (5%). A slight excess in the figures, over and above 100%, is caused by rounding-up.

- Ipswich is excluded because of its urban complexity and the large number of churches recorded (which may not be the total one) and Bury does not feature either. The estate figures are not exact to the last digit (unlike those for Norfolk) because of occasional seeming ambiguities in the recording process and because of the shared interest in some churches leading to proportions recorded which do not add up to a precise whole – thereby resulting in an "overplus" and leading to the possibility of another church being in existence.

- The largest number (38) and proportion (32%) of churches located on freehold estates is to be found in communities connected with Bury Abbey.

- The 24 Suffolk churches which had a shared interest in them (5% of the county total), under two or more different tenants-in-chief (compared with only 3 in Norfolk – 1%), were located in the following communities, shown underlined in the table above: Akenham, Aspall, Battisford, Baylham, Bedingfield, Belstead, *Brutge*, Chippenhall, Coddenham, Creeting St. Peter, Debenham, Elveden (4 landholders), Flixton (Wangford H.), Great Glemham, Higham, Mendham (3 landholders), Ringsfield, Ringshall, Stutton, Thurleston, Wantisden, Great & Little Wenham, Westley and Wetherden. In the case of tenant-in-chief Ranulf Peverel (entry no. 34.9), reference is made to this particular manor in Coddenham as having "part of 3 churches" – though there is no indication of which of the community's 6 foundations is being referred to.

- In addition to the 24 churches having a shared interest under two or more tenants-in-chief, there are a further 4 which had such interest in them under the same overlord: Dagworth, Helmingham, Raydon, and Earl & Little Stonham. This probably reflects earlier patterns of tenure, pre-dating the redistribution of land following the Conquest.

- Note, also, 11 possible other churches, based on 10 references to the presence of a priest and 1 place-name derivation (Kirkley). Priests are recorded in connection with the following communities: Akethorpe, Bentley, Cransford, Flowton, Halesworth, Kalweton, *Nordberia*, Norton, Ulverston and Wherstead (same priest in the 3 underlined vills). They are square-bracketed in the table. Deacons have been overlooked because of ambiguity (the word can mean *headborough*, as well as someone in holy orders). Darby, *Domesday England*, Fig. 17, p. 54, cites 2 "priest-only" cases for Suffolk.

Table 12. Complete and incomplete shared church interest (1086) – two or more references

Community	Hundred	Proportion	Reference
Elveden	Lackford	1 [1]	5.3, 14.20, 25.34 & 26.3
Westley	Thingoe	$\frac{1}{3}$ & 1 [1]	14.17 & 25.27
Chippenhall	Bishop's	½ & ½	6.311 & 14.105
Battisford	Bosmere	½ & ½	31.56 & 53.3

Baylham		½ & ½	7.58 & 76.15
Ringshall		½ & ½	7.56 & 30.1
(Earl & Little) Stonham		$1/_3$ & $1/_3$ & $1/_3$	8.55
Akenham	Claydon	½ & 3 parts [1]	8.71 & 38.11
Debenham		½ & ¼ & ¼ ¼ & ¾	6.18, 16.28 & 34.12 6.18 & 16.28
Helmingham		¼ & ¼ & ½	16.26
Thurleston		1 & ½ [1]	1.122e & 8.70
Aspall	Hartismere	$2/_3$ & $1/_3$	6.206 & 34.18
Wantisden	Parham	½ & ¼ & ¼	6.30 & 38; 7.137
(Great) Glemham	Plomesgate	½ & ½	3.95 & 6.49
Creeting (St. Peter)	Stow	½ & ½	23.1 & 51.1
Dagworth		½ & ½	31.44 & 50
Wetherden		½ & ½	14.35 & 31.45
Flixton	Wangford	½ & ½	19.15 & 53.5
Ringsfield		part & share by others [1]	1.20
Bedingfield	Bishop's	¼ & ¼	6.75 & 43.5
Mendham		$1/_8$ & ¼ & $1/_8$	6.313, 8.37 & 19.2
Coddenham	Bosmere	½ & ¼	7.67 & 38.5
Brutge	Parham	¼ & ¼	6.28 & 67.5
Belstead	Samford	¼ & ¼	32.5 & 71.2
Higham		$1/_5$ & part	5.6 & 58.1
Raydon		$1/_5$ & $1/_5$ & $1/_5$	16.37 & 41
Stutton		$1/_3$ & ½	32.6 & 36.2
(Great & Little) Wen-ham		part & ¼	3.67 & 16.40

Table details

- In five cases, regarding complete churches, the arithmetic is not neat (Akenham, Elveden, Ringsfield, Thurleston and Westley) and judgements have been applied in interpreting the data as relating to a single church only.

- Akenham appears to show a recording aberration of some kind regarding the respective endowment proportions of the church, leading to a simple one-quarter excess, rather than suggesting the presence of a second foundation. Elveden has four, repeated, identical statements of "a church and 15 acres of land", which would seem to apply to the same foundation, not to four individual ones. Ringsfield refers to the King having part of one church, with "others having a share there". Thurleston has specific reference made to St. Botolph's church in its first recorded entry, with mention of a half-church in the second one – the presumption being that the same building is referred to. And, finally, Westley (in having one-third and whole-unit descriptions applied) is adjudged to have had one church, not two, because the respective endowments of arable land (four acres and eight) add up very neatly to one-tenth of a carucate.

- The nine churches whose details add up to less than the whole (the last ones in the table) probably do not imply missing data, so much as the differing nature of the founding endowments. There is no possible means of knowing what these were, however, or even of working out a notional structure.

- It is just possible that both Higham's and Wenham's data might have produced a whole church, if the "part" referred to in each was a sufficiently substantial proportion.

Table 13. Incomplete church interest – single reference (1086)

Community	Hundred	Proportion	Reference
Newton	Babergh	½	43.3
(Great & Little) Walding-field		$^1/_3$	25.46
	Blackbourn & Bradmere		
Barnham		½	14.89
Hunston		½	14.95
Sapiston		2 parts [$^2/_3$?]	14.83
Stanton		¼	14.72
Walsham (le Willows)		½	66.2
Hawkedon	Risby	½	8.34
Thurston		½	8.33
(Great & Little) Saxham	Thingoe	2 parts [$^2/_3$?]	14.11
Weybread	Bishop's	½	6.312
Alneterne	Blything	½	21.47
Chediston		5 parts [$^5/_6$?]	7.15
Cookley		½	9.3
Heveningham		¼	7.27
Hoppetuna/Oppituna		½	7.29
Ash(bocking)	Bosmere	½	1.73

Hemingstone		½	8.59
Mickfield		½	34.10
Somersham		¼	7.59
(Earl & Little) Stonham		¼	34.11
Kesgrave	Carlford	½	6.114
Westerfield	Claydon	½	8.73
Brome	Hartismere	½	7.75
Burgate		¼	35.5
Oakley		2 parts [²/₃?]	14.129
Rickinghall (Superior)		$1/_5$	14.46
Thornham (Magna?)		¼	62.5
Thornham Parva		¾	6.218
Pakefield	Lothing	½	4.41
Rushmere		¼	31.34
Boynton	Samford	¼	16.44
Gusford		$1/_3$	46.5
Hintlesham		½	1.118
(Old) Newton	Stow	$1/_6$	16.12
Barsham	Wangford	½	7.40
(South) Elmham		$1/_5$	13.6
Worlingham		½	14.121

Table details

- The first word in the table's title may be misleading, since it is possible that there was no other party, or parties, with an interest in each church (given the level of detail present in Domesday, it is hard to believe that as many as thirty-eight foundations would have been inaccurately recorded in this respect). The different fractions given probably refer to the nature of the various founding endowments made, though there is no means of working out what these were.

Summative comments for the County of Suffolk

The number of churches recorded

Altogether, a total of 448+ churches has been arrived at, excluding the ones present in the major urban centre of Ipswich (11 recorded and named) – the plus being the result of Burgate (Hartismere) having at least three.[1] There are no churches recorded in Bury, though the abbey's presence is made manifest by reference to thirty priests, deacons and clerics and twenty-eight nuns and poor persons "who pray daily for the king and all Christian people". It is possible that the abbey was such a dominant presence that there were no lesser foundations in the town to rival its influence in any way, be that spiritual or pecuniary in nature. Fewer calculations have been made of the total number of churches in Suffolk than is the case for Norfolk, with even the county's *Historical Atlas* not devoting a section to it – unlike its Norfolk counterpart. Darby, in his *Domesday Geography of Eastern England*, p. 190, does not give a specific number, but says that churches are referred to in connection with 345 villages, as well as those of the urban communities of Ipswich, Dunwich, Bury (no churches recorded, as noted above), Beccles, Clare, Eye and Sudbury – making a total of 352 in all. The total arrived at in this book is 357, so the two figures are not far apart. However, Darby's implied total from his tally of communities is well short of the 448+ churches which are referred to in the Domesday Survey itself. Norman Scarfe's tally of 417 in *The Suffolk Landscape*, pp. 35 & 139, is far closer and given greater impact on pp. 34-5, when he says that "four out of every five of the Suffolk churches we look at today stand on sites where a church stood in 1066". Evocatively and cogently expressed!

Darby also says on p. 190 that Suffolk's churches were "therefore more numerous than those of Norfolk, but, even so, we cannot believe that the Domesday record included all the churches in the county". He then goes on to say that, in many hundreds, the number of villages with churches was well below the total number of settlements – almost implying that this should not have been the case and that there must, therefore, have been more churches than the ones recorded. Norman Scarfe's comment, quoted above, gives a far truer picture regarding Suffolk's churches in the Anglo-Norman period: that eighty per cent of the medieval buildings present in the twentieth and (now) twenty-first centuries were already on site at the time of Domesday – albeit in most cases (it has to be said), in a very different style of construction. The statement he made, early on in his formative work, was based on a calculation revealed much later (on p. 139), whereby he had worked out that 141 churches were built during [late] medieval times, thus leading to a grand total of 558. Of this number, nearly 500 had survived into the modern age, hence the "four out of every five" analogy.

Accuracy or inaccuracy?

The comment taken from *The Anglo-Saxon Chronicle* regarding the level of detail evident in the Domesday survey-process and in the data collected, used earlier in Chapter 1 (p. 95), does not require repeating. But if its premise of meticulous and exhaustive recording of demesne assets is accepted as fact, then the number of Suffolk churches logged need not be seen as deficient in any way. Minor anomalies exist, such as Harpole church (Wilford Hundred) being recorded in *Inquisitio Eliensis*, but not in Domesday, and Falkenham (Colneis Hundred) slipping through the net altogether.[2] However, these are probably best considered as lesser omissions, rather than treated as examples of a larger number of missing churches whose supposed existence is largely speculative and theoretical. The argument for Norfolk's total of churches being seriously deficient may be broadly summarised as a belief that a county so populous and wealthy just had to have had many more churches than the ones recorded – a notion that has, at least in part, been reinforced by a presumption that the system of parishes known so well today must have been fully developed by 1086. Suffolk, with 190 more churches recorded than its sister-county, can hardly be said to have been grossly under-represented!

A desire to have every Domesday community endowed with a church must be resisted – especially in the case of Suffolk. If Scarfe's figure of 141 medieval churches built in the later medieval period (taking the Anglo-Saxon age as its earlier counterpart) is accepted as broadly accurate, and if that programme of church construction was one building per parish, it would (if added to the 357 Domesday vills) produce a total of 498 parishes or communities with churches. The number of parishes in late medieval Suffolk amounted to about 500 in all, so there is little significant difference in the two totals – hopefully, thereby demonstrating that Domesday does not show under-recording, to any degree, of churches present in the county. Suffolk's lowest recorded percentage of churches per hundred is to be found in Lothingland (18%), in the extreme north-eastern corner. Chapter 3 will show how thirteen or fourteen foundations were added here in the century following Domesday and how Mutford Half-hundred, next door, doubled its own total from four communities with churches to eight. Thus, in one small part of Suffolk, seventeen or eighteen post-Domesday churches constituted 12-13% of Scarfe's 141 late medieval foundations.

Possible influences on the existence and location of Suffolk Churches

The two main points of reference for sites of organised Christianity – i.e. monasteries or minsters (both words deriving from *monasterium*) – are Norman Scarfe's formative work on the county's landscape, already much cited, and Peter Warner's *The Origins of Suffolk*. Both books mention centres of communal activity, three of which are to be found in the west of Suffolk: Brandon, Bury and Sudbury. Scarfe's point of focus is very much on the eastern sector of the county and only the mighty abbey at Bury (*Beodericsworth*) comes under his scrutiny, but Warner draws attention to the two other communities. Major discoveries at Brandon during the 1980s (information, therefore, which was not available to Scarfe) are perhaps suggestive of a mid-Saxon minster site (Warner, pp. 123-7), while an eighth-century minster was also known to have been present in Sudbury (Warner, p. 142).[3]

As in the previous chapter, an attempt will be made to assess the possible effect of such institutions in the areas where they were located and an identical layout will be adopted when presenting the information. Thus, each hundred will have the number of communities with churches recorded, together with the percentage this represents of the total number of settlements, followed by a broad summary of the tenancy pattern which manifests itself in 1086 and pre-1066. It is also worth saying that the seven hundreds which constituted the western sector of Suffolk formed the Liberty of St. Edmund, granted to the abbey of that name in Bury by Edward the Confessor, in 1044 – the area having once been part of the royal estate of his mother, Emma, widow of Ethelred the Unready, wife of Cnut and daughter of Richard I, Count of Normandy.[4] Often described as consisting of eight and a half hundreds, this figure is arrived at by dividing Blackbourn and Bradmere into separate jurisdictions and treating Bury as a hundred in its own right (it had probably been part of Thingoe originally). One apparent anomaly (an administrative one of some kind) to the reader of today is to see Sudbury included in Thingoe, whereas its geographical location was in Babergh.

One further comment which needs to be made concerns those communities (both with churches and without) indicated in Tables 7 and 9, which were placed for administrative purposes in hundreds other than the ones in which they were geographically located. With due adjustment made for this particular feature, Babergh Hundred's percentage of its vills with churches rises marginally to 54% (from 53%), while Carlford increases from 34% to 38%, Colneis to 33% from 31%, and Plomesgate to 35% from 32%. Bishop's decreases from 67% to 65% and Loes from 53% to 51%. Such small differences do not materially affect the overall picture of church location and distribution, but are worth recording nevertheless – if only to demonstrate the effect of departures made from the process of total locational gathering of data on the part of the Domesday commissioners.

WEST SUFFOLK

Babergh (20 – 53%) – Sudbury (possible minster) – **1086**, 15 tenants-in-chief: Ralph of Limésy x 3; Richard son of Count Gilbert x 3; Bury Abbey x 2; Ely Abbey x 2; Ranulf Peverel x 2; Robert Malet x 2; the King; Archbishop of Canterbury; Ramsey Abbey; Walter the Deacon; Ralph Baynard; Countess of Aumâle; Hugh de Montfort; Sweyn of Essex; Roger of Poitou. **Pre-1066**, King Edward x 7: Norman x 2, Godwine son of Ælfhere x 2, thegn Leofwine of Bacton, freewoman Æthelgyth, and thegn Wulfric (all under him); Ely Abbey x 2: both direct; Bury Abbey x 2: 1 direct (with 2 sokemen) and freeman Arnulf (under it); Siward of Maldon x 2; Wihtgar x 2: 22 freemen and 3 freemen (all under him); Harold Godwineson x 2: Uhtred and thegn Wulfmær (under him); Earl Morcar's mother (Ælfeva, or Ælfgifu); 2 freemen (sub Ælfric Kemp); Canterbury Cathedral; Ramsey Abbey; thegn Guthmund; Robert son of Wymarc.

Blackbourn & Bradmere (28 – 80%) – no early Christian centre identified, but Bury Abbey close by – **1086**, 8 tenants-in-chief: Bury Abbey x 23; Robert Blunt x 3; Peter of Valognes; the King; Robert Malet; Frodo brother of Abbot of Bury; William of Écouis; Robert of Verly. **Pre-1066**, Bury Abbey x 24: 4 direct with 12, 5, 7, 60 sokemen & 7 freemen also under it; then 21 freemen or 1 sokeman, 8 freemen, 3 freemen, 19 freemen, 20 freemen, 16 freemen, 23 freemen, 9 freemen, man-at-arms Wulfwy & 21 sokemen, 4 freemen, 7 freemen, 7 freemen, freewoman Ealdgyth or 34 sokemen, 22 sokemen & 2 freemen, 11 freemen, 1 freeman shared with Eadric of Laxfield; 22 freemen, 2 freemen + 14 others, 20 freemen, 11 freemen (all under it); Aki or Ketel, or 3 other freemen; Aki or 30 freemen (under him); 15 freemen (sub thegn Acwulf); Aki or 23½ freemen (under him); freemen Ælfric & Alsi.

Cosford (13 – 54%) – no early Christian centre indentified – **1086**, 10 tenants-in-chief: Bury Abbey x 4; Ely Abbey x 2; Chatteris Abbey; Archbishop of Canterbury; Aubrey de Vere; Count Robert of Mortain; Roger of Auberville; Walter the Deacon; Eudo the Steward; Roger of Poitou. **Pre-1066**, Bury Abbey x 4: 2 direct and 6 freemen and 20 freemen (under it); Ely Abbey x 2; Chatteris Abbey; Archbishop of Canterbury; Wulfwine; Queen Edith; Wulfnoth; thegn Tovi; Ælfric Kemp; 1 freeman (+ 7 added).

Lackford (15 – 94%) – Brandon (possible minster) – **1086**, 9 tenants-in-chief: Bury Abbey x 4; Ely Abbey x 4, Eudo the Steward x 3; Richard son of Count Gilbert x 2; the King x 2; Count Eustace of Boulogne, William of Warenne, Bishop of Rochester, Frodo brother of Abbot of Bury. **Pre-1066**, Bury Abbey x 5: 2 direct and 9 sub freemen, 2 sub sokemen and 1 sub freeman shared with Ely Abbey; Ely Abbey x 4: 3 direct and 1 sub freeman shared with Bury Abbey; King Edward x 2: both gifted to Bury Abbey and held by Stigand; thegn Godwine (sub King Edward) x 2; Wihtgar x 2: 1 direct and freeman Leofgeat under him; Alsi, then Elgeric; thegn Orthi (sub Harold Godwineson); freeman Canute (sub Earl Ælfgar); Ordmær.

Risbridge (21 – 62%) – no early Christian centre identified – **1086**, 9 tenants-in-chief: Richard son of Count Gilbert x 11; Ralph Baynard x 3; the King x 2; Roger of Poitou x 2; Count Alan of Brittany; William of Warenne; Tihel of Helléan; Count Eustace of Boulogne; Robert of Tosny. **Pre-1066**, Wihtgar x 3; thegn Ulf x 2; Earl Ælfgar x 2: 1 direct and thegn Eadmær under him; thegn Manni Swart; 1 sokeman ?; 2 sokemen ?; thegn Toki; Clarenbold; freewoman Æthelgyth & 25 freemen; thegn Leofric; 3 freemen (sub Æthelgyth & Bury Abbey); Eadric Spud, or Wulflæd, or Crawa – all freemen [*sic*]; 21 freemen; 16 freemen; freewoman Ealdgyth; 10 freemen; thegn Godwine; 1 sokeman (sub Wulfmær); freeman Ailbern.

Thedwestry (19 – 90%) – no early Christian centre identified, but Bury Abbey close by – **1086**, 2 tenants-in-chief: Bury Abbey x 18 (inc. 2 possibles); Ely Abbey x 2; Frodo x 2 (possibles). **Pre-1066**, Bury Abbey x 16: 9 cases of abbey in tandem with 70, 3, 6, 11, 34, 90, 28, 17½ and 40 subordinate freemen; then 7 cases of 22 freemen, 33-34 freemen, 13 freemen, 60 freemen, 11 freemen, 29 freemen and 41 freemen (all under it); 1 equivocal case of 10 freemen (sub Bury Abbey), or 12 freemen (sub Frodo), or 1 freeman (sub Eadric of Laxfield) with wife (sub Bury Abbey); Ely Abbey x 2.

Thingoe (18 – 94%) – Bury (Abbey of St. Edmund) – **1086**, 4 tenants-in-chief: Bury Abbey x 15; the King x 2; William of Vatteville; Richard son of Count Gilbert. **Pre-1066**, Bury Abbey x 16: 1 direct; 8 cases of abbey in tandem with 1 sokeman, 3 sokemen & 2 freemen, 8 sokemen, 15 sokemen, 1 sokeman, 10 sokemen, 7 sokemen & 1 freeman, 1 sokeman & 6 freemen (all under it); then 6 cases of 3 freemen, 10 sokemen, freewoman Ælfgyth [*sic*], 28 freemen, 3 freemen & 11 freemen (all under it); Wihtgar x 2: 7 freemen & 3 freemen (under him); Wihtgar x 2: 7 freemen and 3 freemen (under him; latter combined with 11 Bury Abbey) ; King Edward; Earl Morcar's mother (Ælfeva, or Ælgifu).

Undoubtedly, at first glance, the most noticeable feature of the summarised data regarding the different land-holders of the churches and their estates is the dominance of Bury Abbey in three of the four hundreds which had the highest percentages of endowed communities: Blackbourn & Bradmere, Thedwestry and Thingoe. Only Lackford, with its widely dispersed pattern of settlement, does not conform. Bury sat between Thedwestry (to the east) and Thingoe (to the west), with Blackbourn & Bradmere to the north of them. Lackford, in its own turn, was located to the west of Blackbourn & Bradmere – not far removed from Bury in terms of miles, but apparently far less influenced by it if control of the churches and their lands is taken as an indication. Is it possible, therefore, that the possible presence of a minster at Brandon was a factor in the founding of churches in that particular hundred (at least, in the earlier stages of the establishment of Christianity)?

Using the Domesday information available, it would appear that Lackford had what may be described as a mixed type of lordship, spread between ecclesiastical and secular agencies, both in 1086 and during the pre-Conquest period. There is no need to replicate the various names because they can be easily read and identified above. What does differ, however, is the type of secular patron of the various churches during the earlier era: the presence of elevated Anglo-Saxon freemen of thegnly status, some of them under the commendation of very powerful patrons, including Edward the Confessor himself and his successor, Harold Godwineson. Also, of notable importance were Ælfgar of Mercia, Earl of East Anglia during the 1050s, and Withgar who, with his son Ælfric, had custodianship of the personal estate of Edward the Confessor's mother, Emma – eventually to become the Liberty of St. Edmund in 1044.[5]

In the three hundreds where Bury Abbey was the overriding influence, the presence of subordinate freemen and sokemen is immediately apparent. The latter do not feature in Thedwestry, but are plain to see in Blackbourn & Bradmere and Thingoe, which may be residual evidence of an early (probably royal) estate, long pre-dating the establishment of Bury Abbey.[6] In presenting the summarised data, a distinction has had to be made between those entries which have the Abbey referred to first, followed by its freemen and/or sokemen, and the ones which place the freemen or sokemen first. This results from the way in which the information is recorded in Domesday, with either the Abbey named first as direct holder of the estate or with its subordinates taking documentary precedence. Whatever may be implied in this aspect of the recording process, one thing is clear: the apparent importance of freemen and sokemen in the matter of founding churches, probably under encouragement from their landlord and patron.

The three remaining hundreds suggest a lesser influence on the part of Bury Abbey. In Risbridge, the dominant presence in 1086 was that of Richard, son of Count Gilbert of Brionne, whose family assumed the title of de Clare from the Suffolk community of that name, which became its principal seat in the county.[7] Richard de Clare (as he may be called) was closely connected with William I, whose guardian his father had been during the Conqueror's minority. The family concentration of estates in West Suffolk and Essex became known as the Honour of Clare and its history has been well recorded.[8] It is noticeable, however, that his dominance seems to have been under some kind of royal scrutiny (if not control) because his fellow tenants-in-chief, though holding fewer estates, were men of considerable standing in the Norman hierarchy: Ralph Baynard (Sheriff of Essex), William of Warenne (Earl of Surrey), Count Alan of Britanny (lord of the Honour of Richmond), Roger of Poitou (son of the Earl of Shrewsbury), Count Eustace of Boulogne and Robert of Tosny (lord of Stafford). Only Tihel of Helléan (in Britanny) was of lesser significance and the King himself, of course, had a large estate in Badmondisfield.

Risbridge is also interesting for the holders of the recorded church estates prior to the Conquest. As well as the various subordinate freemen and sokemen recorded, there are also a number of thegns and higher-status freemen (those whose names are given) – the latter including the freewoman Æthelgyth. Also present are Earl Ælfgar, previously referred to, as well as father and son, Withgar and Ælfric – all of them members of the ruling Anglo-Saxon élite. Thus, the pattern of tenancy was a wide-ranging and mixed one, which had become far less so by the time of Domesday as Norman incomers took over the lands of men who had fallen at Hastings or who were dispossessed if they had survived or had not joined Harold's muster. If Table 8 is studied in detail, it can be seen that a number of lower-status freemen (those unnamed) remained in occupancy – especially on the estates of Richard de Clare, where even two named ones continued as tenants. But the terms of tenure were probably much more demanding than they had been in 1066!

Babergh Hundred (a double-sized jurisdiction) had the highest number of tenants-in-chief in West Suffolk – some fifteen in all. Four of them (Bury Abbey, Ely Abbey, Ramsey Abbey and the Archbishop of Canterbury) represent an ecclesiastical presence, but the rest were secular – and some important figures manifest themselves. Richard de Clare, Ralph Baynard and Roger of Poitou feature once again, as do Ralph of Limésy (nephew of William I), Robert Malet (lord of the Honour of Eye and greatest land-holder by far in East Suffolk), Hugh de Montfort (Constable of Dover Castle), the Countess of Aumâle (William I's sister) and Sweyn of Essex (lord of Rayleigh).[9] Prior to the Conquest, the pattern of tenancy reveals the ecclesiastical connection noted, but there is also the strongly detectable presence of thegns and named freemen (including the woman Aethelgyth again) under royal commendation – Edward the Confessor being referred to seven times and Harold Godwineson twice. Below the level of royalty, the Anglo-Saxon aristocracy is represented by Earl Morcar's mother (Ælfeva, or Ælgifu) and by Withgar, custodian of Emma of Normandy's dower, who held three unnamed freemen under patronage.

It remains only to discuss Cosford, with its ten principal land-holders. Again, the presence of three abbeys is seen (but with Chatteris representing

Cambridgeshire, instead of Ramsey), as is that of the Archbishop of Canterbury, and notable secular tenants-in-chief included Aubrey de Vere (lord of Hedingham), Count Robert of Mortain (William I's half-brother) and Eudo (the royal steward). Again, as with Babergh – perhaps not surprisingly, as they were adjacent hundreds – the pre-Conquest pattern of tenancy was broadly similar ecclesiastically, but the secular one was less elevated in terms of Anglo-Saxon royalty and aristocrats holding title and consisted mainly of thegns and high-status freemen. Although a smaller jurisdiction than Babergh in terms of size, and with fewer settlements, Cosford had an almost identical percentage of its communities endowed with churches. Together, the pair of them constituted the least churched part of West Suffolk – though comfortably on a par with much of the eastern sector of the county.

It is clear that Bury Abbey seems to have been a major influence of some kind on the founding of churches in Blackbourn & Bradmere, Thedwestry and Thingoe during the pre-Conquest period, but a lesser one in the other four jurisdictions – especially Risbridge. This particular hundred (along with Cosford) is seen to have had thegns and freemen as the apparent dominant presence, while in Babergh and Lackford it was also these levels of society which predominated – but with royal or aristocratic patronage a feature also. Collectively, the widely varying cross-section of Anglo-Saxon society (in social and economic terms) consisting of thegns, freemen and sokemen, under the patronage of Bury Abbey, other ecclesiastical agencies and elevated secular lords (including monarchy), seems to have been a key factor in the founding of churches in West Suffolk. The evidence seems to suggest that the first half of the eleventh century was a major time of new church building and perhaps of reconstruction also, as earlier timber structures were replaced with masonry.

And what of the twenty years between the defeat of Harold Godwineson and the Domesday Survey? Summative comments in the previous chapter considered the possibility of Norman overlords encouraging and perhaps even helping to fund the building of churches as a means of reinforcing the new order. Is there any possibility of this having been the case in West Suffolk? The most obvious candidate for such proposed influence is Richard de Clare, particularly in Risbridge Hundred, but it is then hard to find anyone who had such a dominant presence in any other locality. A number of the "new men", such as Ralph of Limésy, Ranulf Peverel, Robert Malet, Robert Blunt, Ralph Baynard and Roger of Poitou, might theoretically be offered as sponsors, but their estates were comparatively few in number compared with de Clare's and (except for Robert Malet) their main interests were concentrated elsewhere, beyond the county of Suffolk.

EAST SUFFOLK

Bishop's (18 – 67%) – Hoxne (diocesan estate) and Mendham (minster) – **1086**, 9 tenants-in-chief: Robert Malet x 9; Bury Abbey x 4; Bishop of Thetford x 2; Roger Bigot x 2; Ralph of Limésy; Judicael the Priest; Roger of Poitou; Robert of Tosny; Ely Abbey. **Pre-1066**, Eadric of Laxfield x 8: 5 direct and 3 with various freemen under him; Bury Abbey x 4: 2 direct and 2 with freemen & sokemen under it; Bishop of Thetford x 3: 1 direct and 2 with freemen under him ; Stigand x 2: 1 direct and freeman Ælfgar under him; thegn Ulf x 2: 1 direct and 5 freemen under him; 6 freemen (sub ?); freeman Ælfric (sub Harold Godwineson); 1 freeman; Norman; 1 freeman (sub ?); thegn Wulfric; 1 freeman (sub Ely Abbey).

Blything (30 – 54%) – Blythburgh (royal estate & minster), Dunwich (diocesan centre), Leiston (possible minster), Rumburgh-Wissett (possible minster) and Wangford (possible minster) – **1086**, 12 tenants-in-chief: Robert Malet x 6; Roger Bigot x 5; Ralph Baynard x 5; Count Alan of Brittany x 5; the King x 2; William of Warenne x 2; Ely Abbey; Godric the Steward; William of Écouis; Drogo of Beuvrière; Geoffrey de Mandeville; Earl Hugh of Cheshire. **Pre-1066**, Eadric of Laxfield x 5: 3 direct and freemen Eadric & Aki (under him); Thored x 4: 1 direct and 3 with 8 freemen, 32 freemen & 3 freemen (under him); Ely Abbey x 2: 1 direct and freeman Eadric (under it); Norman x 2: 1 freewoman [Ælfeva?] and freeman Manson (under him); freeman Eadwine; King Edward; thegn Manni Swart; 11 freemen (sub ?) and 1 other freeman; freeman Wulfric; Ælfwine the Priest; freeman Ulfketel (sub Ulf); freeman Bondi (sub Toli the Sheriff); freeman Ælfric (sub Ranulf, nephew of Eadric of Laxfield); 1 freeman and 7½ others; freeman Rada (sub Harold Godwineson); Haldane; Æskell the Priest; 7 freemen (sub ?); 6 freemen; Ralph the Constable; Eadric [of Laxfield?] and freeman Wulfric.

Bosmere (20 – 62%) – Bramford (royal estate) – **1086**, 17 tenants-in-chief: Roger Bigot x 5; Ranulf Peverel x 5; the King x 4; Bishop of Bayeux x 3; Roger of Poitou x 3; Roger of Rames x 3; Ely Abbey x 2; Richard de Clare x 2; Judicael the Priest x 2; Hugh de Montfort; Eudo, son of Spirwic; William of Écouis; Bernay Abbey; Bury Abbey; Count Alan of Britanny; Isaac; William of Auberville. **Pre-1066**, Ely Abbey x 5: 1 direct and freemen Mundling, Ælmer-Ælfric-Wihtric-Harold (4 together), Leofwine and Wulfric (under it); Eadric of Laxfield x 3: freemen Leofwine, Ælfric and Æthelmær (under him); Stigand x 2: 1 direct and freeman Leofcild (under him); Harold Godwineson x 2: thegns Wulfric & Wulfmær and freewoman Ælflæd x 2 (under him); King Edward x 3: 1 direct, Leofstane & freeman Godwine (under him & Earl Ælfgar), and freeman Godmane (under him, Wihtgar and Earl Ælfgar);

Saxi x 2: 4 freemen and Æthelwald the Priest & freeman Godwy; freeman Ælmer (sub Edeva the Fair); Æskell; freeman Ælfric & freeman Cynric; Queen Edith; thegn Ælfric; freeman Wigulf (sub Toli the Sheriff); freeman Leofric; 3 freemen; 24 freemen; 20 freemen; freeman Æthelric & wife (sub Bury Abbey); freeman Gauti; 24 freemen (sub Ralph the Constable); freeman Siric; 8 freeman (4 sub Saxi); freeman Godwy; freeman Leofson (sub Leofson Hobbeson); 9 freemen.[10]

Carlford (13 – 35%) – no early Christian centre identified – **1086**, 9 tenants-in-chief: Robert Malet x 3; Ranulf brother of Ilger x 3; Hervey of Bourges; Ely Abbey; William of Warenne; Ranulf Peverel; Roger of Poitou; Humphrey the Chamberlain; Count Alan of Brittany. **Pre-1066**, Eadric of Laxfield x 6: freemen Durand, Eadric Grim and Oslac, 1 other freeman, freewoman Ælflæd and Lustwine; Ely Abbey x 4: 1 direct, 9 named freemen, Eadric Grim and 5 freemen; Haldane x 2: Anund the priest and freeman Wulfmær (latter sharing with the 9 named Ely Abbey freemen); freeman Æthelric; 3 freemen (sub Godwine); Eadwald; Norman; 16½ freemen (sub Leoflæd); Godwine son of Ælhere (sub Queen Edith); 11 freemen (sub Gyrth Godwineson).

Claydon (14 – 67%) – no early Christian centre identified – **1086**, 11 tenants-in-chief: Roger of Poitou x 3; Hervey of Bourges x 2; Earl Hugh of Cheshire x 2; Ely Abbey x 2; Bishop of Bayeux x 2; Walter the Deacon x 2; the King x 2; Roger of Rames; Robert Malet; Ranulf Peverel; Roger of Auberville. **Pre-1066**, Eadric of Laxfield x 4: 1 direct, freeman Godmane, Godric-Leofstan-11 other freemen (combination of 3, shared with Saxi) and Brihtwald or 5 freemen (all under him); Saxi x 3: 1 direct, freeman Godwy (under him) and Godric-Leofstan-11 other freemen (shared with Eadric of Laxfield); Ely Abbey x 2; 3 freemen; Godwine the priest; thegn Æthelstan; freeman Tepekin (sub Harold Godwineson); freeman Wulfric; Queen Edith; 21 freemen (sub Ely Abbey?); Godric;18 freemen (sub Gosbert); 25 named freemen & 4 named freewomen (sub ?).

Colneis (10 – 31%) – Thorpe & Walton (ancient ecclesiastical jurisdiction) – **1086**, 4 tenants-in-chief: Roger Bigot x 7; Hugh de Montfort; Count Robert of Mortain; Ranulf brother of Ilger. **Pre-1066**, Norman x 8: 1 direct and freemen Thorbern & Wulfwine, 16 named freemen, freeman Hardwine (shared with Eadric of Laxfield), 10 named freemen, freeman Ulfketel, freeman Godmane and freeman Godric (all under him); Harold Godwineson x 2: 30 freemen and freeman Wihtric (under him); Eadric of Laxfield x 2: freeman Hardwine (shared with Norman) and Godric the priest; 18 freemen (sub Guthmund); freeman Wulfweard (sub Godric); freeman Brictmær (sub Britric and Ely Abbey); freeman Brictric (sub Brictmær & Stanmer).

Hartismere (27 – 77%) – no early Christian centre identified – **1086**, 13 tenants-in-chief: Robert Malet x 10; Bury Abbey x 7; the King x 2; Ranulf Peverel; Roger Bigot; Walter the Deacon; Aubrey de Vere; Hugh de Montfort; Isaac, Ely Abbey; Roger of Poitou; Ralph of Beaufour; Hubert of Mont-Canisy. **Pre-1066**, Bury Abbey x 9: 2 direct & 11 freemen, Goding (its reeve), 14 freemen, 5 freemen, Leofric, Anselm (?) and freewomen Modgeva & Godiva (all under it); Stigand x 4: freewoman Gode and freewoman Wulfeva x 3 (under him); Eadric of Laxfield x 4: 1 direct and freemen Fulcard, Ælfric and Godmane (under him); Harold Godwineson x 2: freeman Leofwine and freewoman Ælflæd (under him); Ely Abbey x 2: 1 direct and Guthmund, abbot's brother (under it); Wulfeva x 2: 1 direct & 8 freemen, or 2 freemen, or Siric (under her); Burgheard x 2: 1 direct and 3 freemen (under him); 1 freeman (sub ?); Saxi (as lord of Ulverston); freeman Wulfwine & 6 sokemen; Leofwine the Bald.

Ipswich (11 named churches recorded in **1086**) – probable minster – no further analysis of town. Stoke church held by Ely Abbey in **1066** & **1086**.

Loes (15 – 54%) – Rendlesham (royal estate, including Bromeswell) – **1086**, 9 tenants-in-chief: Robert Malet x 5; Count Alan of Britanny x 3; Earl Hugh of Cheshire x 2; William of Arques; Humphrey the Chamberlain; Ely Abbey; Geoffrey de Mandeville; the King; Roger of Poitou. **Pre-1066**, Eadric of Laxfield x 7: 1 direct and 24 freemen, freeman Eadric (shared with Æthelstan), 8 freemen named & unnamed (mainly his), Eadric Grim (shared with Ely Abbey), 1 freeman and 3 freemen (all under him); Ely Abbey x 4: 1 direct and Eadmund the Priest, Eadric Grim (shared with Eadric of Laxfield) and freeman Wulfmær with 14½ other freemen (under it); Eadric Grim x 2: himself commended to Ely Abbey and Eadric of Laxfield & 7 freemen (under him); Brictwald (sub Queen Edith); ½ freeman (sub Anund); thegn Æthelmær; Haldane (sub Harold Godwineson); [Thormod of Parham?].

Lothing (4 – 33%) – no early Christian centre identified – **1086**, 3 tenants-in-chief: Earl Hugh of Cheshire x 2; the King; Hugh de Montfort. **Pre-1066**: Gyrth Godwineson x 3: Wulfsi & 12 freemen, 1 freeman and 1 other (all under him); 5 freemen (sub Burgheard).

Lothingland (3 – 18%) – Burgh (monastery-minster) and Flixton (possible minster) – **1086**, 3 tenants-in-chief: Ralph the Crossbowman; Bishop of Thetford; the King. **Pre-1066**, Stigand x 2; Wihtred the Priest.

Parham (3 – 50%) – no early Christian centre identified – **1086**, 3 tenants-in-chief: Robert Malet x 4, Hervey of Bourges & Roger Bigot. **Pre-1066**, Eadric of Laxfield x 5: 1 direct and Eadric, freeman Alnoth, 22 freemen, freeman

Ælfwine & freewoman <u>Ælflæd</u> (under him); 1 freeman (sub Norman).

<u>Plomesgate</u> (9 – 32%) – *Icanho* (monastery) – **1086**, 6 tenants-in-chief: Robert Malet x 7; Count Alan of Brittany x 2; Roger Bigot x 2; Eudo the Steward; Roger of Poitou; Ely Abbey. **Pre-1066**, Eadric of Laxfield x 9: 1 direct and freeman Wulfric, 12 freemen, freeman Sparrowhawk, freeman Wulfmær, freeman Wulfric (shared with Ely Abbey), 21 freemen, 12 freemen and 11 freemen (under him); Ely Abbey x 4: 1 direct and freeman Ulf, freeman Wulfric (shared with Edric of Laxfield) and Eadwine the Priest (under it); Norman; thegn Ælfgar (sub King Edward).

<u>Samford</u> (18 – 44%) – no early Christian centre identified – **1086**, 12 tenants-in-chief: Bishop of Bayeux x 5; Geoffrey de Mandeville x 3; Countess of Aumâle x 3; Count Alan of Brittany x 3; the King x 3; Richard de Clare x 2; Swein of Essex x 2; Robert, son of Corbucion x 2; Robert of Stratford; Count Eustace of Boulogne; Gundwin the Chamberlain; Robert Gernon. **Pre-1066**, Edeva the Fair x 5: 2 direct and Eadwine, Ansgot and Thurstan (under her); Robert, son of Wymarc x 4: 3 direct and freeman Æscman (under him); Harold Godwineson x 3: 1 direct and thegns Scalpi and Tuneman (under him); Stigand x 2 : 1 direct and freeman Ælfwine (under him); freeman Ulf (sub Asgar); Ælfric of *Weinhou*; Thuri; freeman Godwine; freeman Ailbern; freeman Leadmær; freeman Godric; Asgar; freeman Eadnoth; freemen Eadwy & Ælfwine; Gyrth Godwineson & 210 sokemen (sub various patrons); thegn Fridebern (sub King Edward); thegn Auti.

<u>Stow</u> (13 – 65%) – no early Christian centre identified, but probable late minster church – **1086**, 10 tenants-in-chief: Hugh de Montfort x 5; Count Robert of Mortain x 2; Ranulf Peverel x 2; Bury Abbey x 2; Roger of Poitou; Bernay Abbey; Walter of St. Valéry; Roger of Auberville; Bishop of Bayeux; the King. **Pre-1066**, King Edward x 5: 1 direct and Wulfnoth, freeman Bræme, Guthmund and thegn Ketel (all under him); Guthmund x 4: 1 direct (sub King Edward) and 10 freemen, freeman Leofson and 17 freemen (under him); Bury Abbey x 2: 2 freemen and 20 freemen (under it); Leofwine Croc; 1 freeman?; freeman Ælfric (sub Eadric of Laxfield); 2 freemen (sub Alsi); 6 freemen (sub Thorney Manor – and, therefore, King Edward).

<u>Wangford</u> (13 – 54%) – Bungay (possible minster) and South Elmham (diocesan centre & minster) – **1086**, 8 tenants-in-chief: the King x 9; Bishop of Thetford x 6; Earl Hugh of Cheshire x 4; Bury Abbey x 2; Roger Bigot; Godric the Steward; Eudo, son of Spirwic; Hugh de Montfort. **Pre-1066**, Stigand x 5: 1 direct and 15 freemen, freeman Æskell or 8 other freemen, freeman Offa and 2½ freemen (all under him); King Edward x 4: 1 with other

unspecified parties, then 1 freeman, various unnamed freemen and others of the same standing (all under him); Bishop of Thetford x 4: 1 direct and 1 freeman, 25 freemen and 1 freeman (all under him); Burgheard x 3: 1 direct and 1 freewoman and 15 freemen (under him); Bury Abbey x 2: 1 direct with 30 sokemen and 1 where ½ church only is mentioned ; Leofstan the Priest (sub Gyrth Godwineson); freeman Pat; freeman Ælfgar; freeman Ælfric; freeman Godric (sub Ralph the Constable); freeman Ælfwine (sub thegn Ingvar).

Wilford (13 – 43%) – Bromeswell (part of Rendlesham royal estate) – **1086**, 4 tenants-in-chief: Robert Malet x 10; Ely Abbey x 3; Countess of Aumâle; Bishop of Evreux. **Pre-1066**, Eadric of Laxfield x 9: 1 direct and 31 freemen, 12½ freemen, Stanwine, 1 freeman, 24 freemen, 15 freemen, freeman Osmund, and 2 freemen (all under him); Ely Abbey x 3: 2 direct and 1 freeman (under it); Wulfwine the Priest?; 3 freemen (sub Eadric Grim); 18 freemen (sub Thormod).

Difficulty in making succinct comment on the tenancy pattern of East Suffolk is immediately apparent, because of its complexity in terms of the large number of freemen holding land in pre-Conquest times – either as independent operators or under the patronage of a social superior. Starting with Bishop's Hundred, the post-Conquest period saw the pre-eminence there of Robert Malet as a secular power (following on from his father, William) – lord of the so-called Honour of Eye and the most important tenant-in-chief in the whole of the county in terms of his extensive holdings. This may have been one reason why Roger Bigot, Sheriff of Norfolk and Suffolk, was the next most influential figure. A man of considerable talents, he was William I's main "enforcer" in East Anglia, and his holding of estates in the hundred may have been one way of shadowing Malet's activities – for good or bad. Prior to 1066, the main secular presence had been that of Eadric of Laxfield, a man whose interests and estates spread far and wide and provided the power-base for the Malet family when it acceded to them, following the Conquest.

The other detectable feature in Bishop's Hundred is the number of ecclesiastical references, with Bury Abbey and the Bishop of Thetford appearing in both 1086 and 1066 and with Ely Abbey also mentioned. The Anglo-Saxon cleric Stigand (Bishop of Elmham, 1043-47) is also to be noted pre-1066 – a presence, unfortunately, to be considered rather more for avarice than for religious zeal.[11] Given that the fact that the hundred had one of the higher percentages of its communities endowed with churches, the presence of a one-time minster at Mendham may have been a factor early on (though it is not possible to estimate to what degree) – to say nothing of the possible effect of the large personal estate in the Hoxne area, bequeathed to the Elmham diocese by Bishop Theodred of London during the mid-tenth century (a legacy which probably led to the jurisdiction bearing the name it did). References to the Bishop of Thetford are tied in with any earlier ones relating to Elmham, because it was changes in location of the diocesan centre which resulted in the changes of name.[12] Leaving that particular matter aside here, in the main text, the combination of religious bodies, thegns and freemen (both named and unnamed in the latter case) would seem, once again, to suggest that many of the churches recorded in Domesday may have been the product of the first half of the eleventh century.

Blything was by far the largest of the East Suffolk jurisdictions, constituting a "double hundred" and deriving from a Danish administrative unit which survived until hundreds were formed during the early tenth century (Scarfe, pp. 94-5). Its hub was Blythburgh, a royal estate originally in control of the ruling Wuffing family (Scarfe, p. 95 and Warner, pp. 120-1), with the strong likelihood of a minster attached to it (Scarfe, p. 94 and Warner, p. 121). The other major ecclesiastical presence was Dunwich (Scarfe, p. 118 and Warner, pp. 127-9), centre of the East Anglian diocese, which bore its name until the see was divided c. 670 and then continued in tandem with Elmham, until it ceased to exist in its own right in 870.[13] Leiston and Wangford have also been suggested as the sites of possible minsters (Warner, pp. 134-5 & p. 134), while Rumburgh-Wissett certainly had one – though of late establishment in 1064 (Warner, pp. 133 & 135).[14] Thus it can be seen that Blything, out of all the East Suffolk hundreds, not only had the biggest geographical area, but the largest number of potential influences for the establishment of churches.

Yet its percentage of communities so endowed saw it standing no higher than sixth in the East Suffolk "league table", equal with Wangford Hundred – which suggests that any influence its major ecclesiastical hubs may have had early on (Rumburgh-Wissett being ruled out as a late arrival) had been obliterated by the Danish invasion of 869-70. The record of 1086 shows one appearance by Ely Abbey as the sole ecclesiastical reference, all the others being secular. Some "big-hitters" (to use a current term) manifest themselves: Roger Bigot, Robert Malet, Ralph Baynard and Count Alan of Brittany featuring prominently, with Earl Hugh of Cheshire, William of Warenne and the King providing a presence also. Not surprisingly, perhaps, the monarch himself held Blythburgh (succeeding Edward the Confessor), thereby continuing a royal connection established as far back as the reign of King Anna (ob. 654). The information relating to 1066 replicates the one direct reference to Ely Abbey and shows Eadric of Laxfield as the foremost presence – though not overwhelmingly so. The pattern of tenancy is seen to be broadly a fabric of thegns and freemen, either as individuals or under commendation to a superior, with the patronage itself (where recorded) being exercised by six different people – including Eadric of Laxfield himself and Harold Godwineson.

Bosmere Hundred is noted as having one community, Bramford, identified as an early royal estate (Warner, pp. 120-3), though whether this had any material effect on its comparatively high percentage of communities with churches cannot be assessed. It might well be the case that comparative proximity to Ipswich, with at least eleven known foundations and its highly developed urban nature, is a factor to be taken in to account. The data for 1086 shows the largest number of tenants-in-chief per hundred for the whole of Suffolk, containing many of the usual names in the secular sphere (e.g. Roger Bigot, Ranulf Peverel, the King, Roger of Poitou, Richard de Clare, Hugh de Montfort and Count Alan of Brittany), but showing also three religious houses and a bishop. The abbeys at Bury and Ely are almost to be expected, but the one at Bernay, in Normandy, may appear surprising.[15] Not so, the appearance of Odo, Bishop of Bayeux (younger half-brother of William I) who, on being made Earl of Kent in 1067, reputedly became the largest land-holder in England after the King – as well as a byword for rapacity and vindictive behaviour.[16] In keeping with the large number of overlords in 1086, the record for twenty years earlier shows the most varied and complex of all Suffolk tenancy patterns, East or West. Ely Abbey represents the most noticeable ecclesiastical presence, but the overall picture (even more than in Bishop's and Blything) is one of thegns and freemen (and one freewoman) holding the land, with or without commendation. Where patronage is recorded, a royal connection is most definitely in evidence, with mention made of Queen Edith (wife of Edward the Confessor) and, more noticeably, of Harold Godwineson and his first spouse, Edeva the Fair – but no residual link with the Bramford *regia* is able to be established.[17]

Carlford was among the hundreds with a lower percentage of churches per community, forming a geographical trio with Colneis and Samford – and yet, all of them grouped around Ipswich. There was no single dominant presence in 1086, though Robert Malet and Ranulf, brother of Ilger, were each recorded three times. The remaining seven lords consisted of six regular, secular faces, with Ely Abbey representing religious establishment. Prior to 1066, the tenancy structure was one largely of freemen, with a couple of thegns (neither specifically named as such) – the latter including Norman, who was an important presence in neighbouring Colneis. With most of the land-holders having patrons, it is noticeable that Eadric of Laxfield was the dominant presence, with six commendations, while Ely Abbey had three and a further estate held in its own right (Brightwell).[18] Single appearances by Queen Edith and Gyrth Godwineson (Earl of East Anglia) represented the highest levels of the secular world – that of the royal court.

The smaller part of Claydon Hundred was situated immediately to the north of Ipswich – the jurisdiction being split into two geographical components. The larger portion lay further to the north, being separated from its companion by Bosmere and Carlford.[19] The jurisdiction, as a whole, had one of the higher church-community percentages, which may have been due in part to proximity with urban Ipswich (on the part of its smaller element) and with the hundreds of Bishop's, Bosmere and Hartismere where the larger one was concerned – all three of them being high-percentage areas also. The data for 1086 shows a selection of familiar tenants-in-chief, again mainly secular (repetition of names would seem to be superfluous) but with Ely Abbey and the Bishop of Bayeux also present, and that for 1066 once again observes the established model of freemen holding the churches and associated land. There is a degree of uncertainty present, in certain cases, as to the identity of patrons, but of the ones known Eadric of Laxfield features most, while the thegn Saxi is also present – as, at the very highest level of society, are Queen Edith and Harold Godwineson.[20] One interesting detail in the recording process itself is that the last church of all to be mentioned, alphabetically as well as in the Domesday sequence (Whitton), was in the hands of twenty-nine named, independent *freemen* – except that four of them (Gunvati, Eadith, Leofeva and Tovild) were women!

Also close to Ipswich, but occupying land to the east of the Orwell estuary, was Colneis –another of the Suffolk hundreds with a comparatively low percentage of its settlements having churches. Some kind of posssible early association with ecclesiastical organisation is evidenced by a medieval court located in the Thorpe-Walton area, which proved wills and sanctioned marriages at one time (Warner, p. 135), but whether or not this agency had any influence on the founding of churches cannot be assessed.[21] The pattern of overlordship in 1086 is a very interesting one, with seven of the ten church estates being held by Roger Bigot and one each in the hands of Hugh de Montfort, Count Robert of Mortain and Ranulf, brother of Ilger. Altogether, Bigot held forty-five properties in the hundred and one reason for his overriding presence could well have been that William I was entrusting him with the security of the Orwell estuary (and therefore of Ipswich also) – as well as that of the Deben. Prior to 1066, the dominant figure in Colneis had been the thegn Norman, Sheriff of Suffolk for a time and a man who, on the evidence of his name (deriving from "Northman"), had Danish antecedents.[22] Perhaps as a balance to his influence, Harold Godwineson had thirty freemen, collectively, and one other individual, under commendation, and Eadric of Laxfield was also present as full patron of Godric the Priest and with a half-interest in one of

Norman's vassals, Hardwine. It is worth adding, as a postscript, that Norman Scarfe produced a very interesting study of Colneis in *Suffolk Atlas*, pp. 42-3, focusing on the pattern of settlement and the presence of churches. It is well worth reading.

Although not having any known or recorded early centre of religious organisation, the hundred of Hartismere had the highest percentage of communities with churches in East Suffolk. This was probably the result of it being located nearest (along with Stow) to the most heavily churched part of the county as a whole, with Bury Abbey acting as an influence on the founding process. This proposition would seem to be borne out by the tenancy pattern, with the abbey acting as one of the two major presences in 1086 (Robert Malet being the other one), as well as in 1066. As a generalisation, secular overlordship at the time of Domesday can be seen as having more prominence than ecclesiastical tenancy-in-chief, but the opposite was true during pre-Conquest times. The exercise of patronage by religious bodies and persons is plain to see (Ely Abbey and Stigand, in addition to Bury), with a moderating secular presence perhaps exercised by Harold Godwineson.

Also of interest is the presence of freewomen among the tenantry: Wulfeva, Gode, Ælflæd (a name also encountered in Carlford), Modgeva and Godiva.[23] The first named is of particular interest, as she was the daughter of Ælfgar, Earl of Mercia, and mother of Earl Morcar of Northumbria. Other versions of her name are found as Ælfeva and Ulveva, and her main land-holdings in Suffolk were nucleated around Eye (Hartismere), Kelsale (Plomesgate-Bishop's) and Sudbury (Babergh-Thingoe). There is a good summary of her interests to be found in Warner, p. 200, where Figure 7.3 shows very clearly both her own estates and the freemen she held in commendation.[24] More than this, and in a wider context, the writer goes on to discuss the presence of women generally among the free tenantry recorded in Suffolk Domesday (having pertinently made reference, on p. 199, to their "invisibility" at the hands of most Domesday commentators up to the time of publication of his work).

The hundred of Loes, in the days before hundreds were formed, contained the important royal palace of Rendlesham (seat of the Wuffing family) and the associated burial-ground at Sutton Hoo. The discoveries made at the latter site in 1939 have long been internationally famous, but the true significance of the former will only become clear as the finds from archaeological investigation carried out between c. 2008 and 2016 are fully analysed and the necessary writing-up carried out and completed. There is an excellent explanation of the Rendlesham-Bromeswell-Eyke estate (the last-named place not recorded in Domesday) in Warner, pp. 115-18, but what effect it may have had on early church founding in the area is not able to be assessed. As things stand, Domesday shows Loes Hundred to have had half of its communities possessed of churches in 1086, with these and their associated holdings in the hands of well-known Norman overlords – Robert Malet being foremost among them. In 1066, Eadric of Laxfield had been the leading patron of the various freemen occupants, with Ely Abbey following and with the uppermost level of Anglo-Saxon society represented by Queen Edith and Harold Godwineson.

Lothing Hundred, in the far north-eastern sector of Suffolk (eventually to become known as Mutford Half-hundred, after the vill of that name where the main manor was located) had one of the highest percentages of freemen in Suffolk – c. 70%, compared with a county average of c. 40% – but was one of the lower-percentage jurisdictions in terms of communities with churches. This may have been partly the result of its geographical remoteness within the county – though Beccles, with its church and market, was within relatively easy reach to the west. In 1086, Earl Hugh of Cheshire held two of the four church estates, with the King and Hugh de Montfort tenants-in-chief of the other two. Twenty years or more, earlier, Gyrth Godwineson had held three of them, with the remaining one in the hands of the thegn, Burgheard. Whether or not this was the same man as "Burghard of Mendlesham" (Bishop's Hundred) must remain conjectural, given the distance between the two jurisdictions, and there is also the matter of indentical forenames shared by different people. Whoever he was, though, he was a leading figure in the hundred, with at least eleven estates held in his own right and another three shared with other individuals (Gyrth Godwineson, Eadric of Laxfield and the thegn, Wulfsi). Gyrth Godwineson himself held thirteen estates directly and shared one with Burgheard; he may well have used this man as his bailiff, or representative, in Lothing.[25]

Lothingland Hundred lay immediately to the north of its similarly named neighbour.[26] It was the least churched jurisdiction in the whole of Suffolk – and this in spite of its having had a monastery established c. 633 by the Irish missionary Fursa (or Fursey) within the old Roman shore-fort of *Gariannonum* (Warner, p. 112) – later to be known as *Cnobheresburh* and, ultimately, as Burgh Castle.[27] It is beyond the scope of this study to fully investigate a Celtic establishment in Suffolk's remotest corner, but Norman Scarfe considered it to be of sufficient threat to the Roman mission of Felix the Burgundian for that first bishop of East Anglia, from his base at Dunwich, to found a church at Flixton (and also across the River Yare, at Reedham, in Norfolk) in order to monitor its activities (Scarfe, p. 125). By the time of Domesday, the Flixton ecclesiastical estate with its 120 acres of arable land (one of the ten richest endowments in Suffolk) was in the hands of the Bishop of Thetford, with that at Burgh (Castle) – one twelfth of the size – held by Ralph the Crossbowman. One other church, at Somerleyton, was held by the King, and the freeman-priest Wihtred named in connection with it may also have been the occupant twenty years earlier. The presence of another priest, Æthelmær (al. Ælmer), at Akethorpe – an outlier, to the north and north-west of Lowestoft – when taken with certain local topographical features is suggestive of a church, but there is none recorded in Domesday.

During the pre-Conquest era, Bishop Stigand had held Burgh (*Cnobheresburh*) and Flixton, both estates having long been part of Elmham diocese's assets. The church present in each community may possibly have had its origins back in the seventh century, but this is not able to be proved, and Fursa's Celtic monastery was of comparatively short duration, in any case, perhaps coming to the end of its activities in 654.[28] Similarly, it is not possible to trace any evangelising effect from Flixton, which has been suggested as the site of a possible minster (Scarfe, p. 123). With fully four centuries interposing between the competing missions and ritual practice of Felix and Fursa and the reign of Edward the Confessor (together with all the political, religious, social and economic upheavals which took place), any kind of linkage is simply not able to be established. Thus, to adjudge Lothingland's low count of churches as evidence of the ineffectiveness of *Cnobheresburh* and Flixton is neither valid nor just, and the question of just why the hundred had so few churches at Domesday remains – especially as the freeman element of its population was a respectable 43% (county average, c. 40%). The most likely explanation lies in its being the remotest part of Suffolk, both in terms of geographical position and distance from established urban communities. It was also an island, being surrounded by water on all sides and with four fording-points as the only means of crossing into either Norfolk or neighbouring Mutford. Finally, its coastal location, with large areas of heath, led to a dispersed pattern of settlement, with fewer vills than in more favoured localities.

The half-hundred of Parham (later to be absorbed by Plomesgate) was the smallest of the Suffolk jurisdictions and arranged in two sectors, with a portion of Loes interposing. The data for 1086 shows Robert Malet as the main holder of its three church estates, with Hervey of Bourges having a quarter-share of the church at *Brutge* (Ely Abbey held the jurisdiction) and Roger Bigot having a similar interest at Wantisden. Prior to the Conquest, Eadric of Laxfield had been the main instrument of control, with a quarter of *Brutge* held directly and other endowments in the hands of dependent freemen and a freewoman named Ælflæd. The last-named held a quarter-share of the church at Wantisden with someone named Ælfwine and is herself classified as a freeman alongside him.[29] Lest it be thought that this shows gender-bias in favour of men (a temptation, perhaps, to the modern way of thinking), it might well have been the opposite: a view of women as their equals, with no discriminatory overtones of any kind.

Once the hundredal structure had fully developed, and the various jurisdictions been given their names, Plomesgate could be counted among those areas of jurisdiction which had had an early monastery. This had been founded by the East Anglian missionary Botwulf (Botolph) in c. 653, with the encouragement and support of King Anna, at a place called *Icanhoh*. This is generally agreed to have been at Iken, on the River Alde not far from Snape – a vill not featured in Domesday – and two of Suffolk's leading historians have written about it (Scarfe, *Suffolk in the Middle Ages*, pp. 39-40 and Warner, p. 114).[30] Once again, given that the focus of this work is on the Domesday record of churches, there will be no investigation of its possible influences in the area where it was located. It would seem, in any case, that the effects it may have had during its lifetime (which is said to have lasted over 200 years, until the Danish invasions of 869) were lost during the periods of disruption which must have dislocated Christian function and practice during the ninth and tenth centuries.

Domesday shows Plomesgate to have been one of Suffolk's lesser areas of church founding, with Robert Malet (yet again) the dominant presence in 1086, and with Roger Bigot and Count Alan of Brittany in lesser roles. Prior to 1066, Eadric of Laxfield had held one church estate in his own right and was the patron of various freemen, named and unnamed, in eight others (one of which was shared with Ely Abbey). The abbey, in its own turn, was sole patron in two other cases and also held a church endowment in Sudbourne, while the thegns Norman and Ælfgar (the latter under the commendation of Edward the Confessor) held one estate each. One factor in the comparatively low count of churches in Plomesgate may have resulted from its having an extensive area of coast in its total area, with large tracts of heath and dispersed human settlement. If the Suffolk coast is scrutinised in its entirety, it is seen that from Lothingland, in the far north, down as far as the Deben estuary, the vills were thinly spread – which would have acted on its own as a limiting factor in the number of churches present.

Though not as sparsely settled as the coastal heathland belt, Samford Hundred, bordering on the county of Essex to the south, was also among the number of jurisdictions having lower percentages of churches recorded – being on a par with Loes and Wilford.[31] There is no clear indication as to why this should have been, but the major physical barriers created by the Orwell and Stour estuaries might conceivably have played a part. In 1086, Odo, the Bishop of Bayeux, was the leading tenant-in-chief, with his half-brother, the King, and his half-sister, the Countess of Aumâle, joining him to form a noticeable family group. There was also a detectable Essex representation as well, with Geoffrey de Mandeville (Sheriff of London), Sweyn of Essex (lord of Rayleigh) and Robert Gernon (lord of Stansted) numbered among the controlling influences – perhaps in recognition of the strategic significance of the two river-systems and the potential vulnerability of Ipswich and Colchester to incursion from the sea. Richard de Clare featured also, perhaps to provide a Suffolk "heavyweight" presence of his own.[32]

There was a pronounced high-profile pattern of lordship evident in the pre-Conquest era also, which again may indicate the perceived importance of the area. Direct links with Essex are to be seen in the references to Robert, son of Wymarc (al. fitz Wymarc), father of Sweyn of Essex and sheriff of that county also. Of possible (even likely) Breton origins, he was related to both Edward the Confessor and William of Normandy and was therefore sufficiently well connected to function as a leading servant of the Crown. It will be seen in the summarised data above, relating to Samford, that more than half of the thegns and freemen are not recorded as being under commendation to a patron, but the rest were pledged to very influential people indeed: Edward the Confessor, Harold Godwineson and his wife, Edith (named, again, as Edeva the Fair and holding two church-estates in her own right), Gyrth Godwineson and Bishop Stigand. Perhaps the most singular feature in the whole hundred is to be found in Shotley, where two churches are recorded. Gyrth Godwineson held a substantial manor of 301 acres of arable land, while attached to it was a massive holding of 2,670 acres occupied by 210 sokemen under the jurisdiction of his older brother, Harold, and many other unnamed patrons. Even though this number had almost halved by 1086, there were still 119 of them working the same area of land.

Though it was among the smaller hundreds, in terms of size, Stow had one of Suffolk's higher percentages of churches per community. This may have been due in part to its proximity to the Blackbourn & Bradmere and Thedwestry jurisdictions in the western sector of the county – making it, therefore, open to the influence of Bury Abbey, as previously noted in Hartismere (with which it also shared a boundary). There is also the matter of a (probably) late minster foundation in Thorney possibly having had some influence, its presence being suggested in the description of a "mother church" (*mat æccle*) being located there in the Domesday record.[33] The leading tenant-in-chief in 1086 was Hugh de Montfort, in company with a number of other familiar names, and William I himself also features – significantly, perhaps, as holder of the valuable main manor of Thorney, which had been in the hands of Edward the Confessor before the Conquest. Bury Abbey is to be seen as a presence in both

1086 and 1066, though not dominantly so, and it was Edward the Confessor himself who was the leading figure in terms of influence, with four varying combinations of thegns and freemen under his commendation in addition to his direct tenure of Thorney.[34] A thegn named Guthmund is detectable also, with four references (one in his own right, under commendation to Edward the Confessor, and three as patron himself); he provides a possible ecclesiastical link in the hundred, being the brother of Abbot Wulfric of Ely.

Wangford, along with Bishop's and Hartismere hundreds, formed most of the demarcation with Norfolk – all of them being bounded on their northern limits by the River Waveney – and two early Christian sites have been identified in the jurisdiction. Bungay, with its five churches, has been suggested as a possible minster location (Warner, pp. 132-3 & p. 136), while South Elmham, with its seven foundations, has an established and proven ecclesiastical pedigree (Scarfe, pp. 116-28 and Warner, pp. 129-31). Along with Dunwich, it possibly became one of the two centres of the East Anglia diocese when the see was divided in c. 670 and remained as such for about three hundred years until the Elmham seat (as it had become known) was moved to North Elmham, in Norfolk. It also has the remains of a church building (long known as "The Minster" or "Moat Minster"), of seventh century design and layout but probably of early-mid eleventh century construction.

Whether or not the seven churches can trace their origins back to the seventh century must remain conjectural, but (together with the four parishes in neighbouring Ilketshall) they eventually came to form a group of villages which became known locally as "The Saints": South Elmham All Saints, St. Cross, St. James, St. Margaret, St. Michael, St. Nicholas and St. Peter; Ilketshall St. Andrew, St. John, St. Lawrence and St. Margaret. Even without the Ilketshalls, the seven churches of South Elmham (together with the ruined minster) are perhaps the best surviving evidence of an Anglo-Saxon minster and its satellites – particularly if the churches at nearby Flixton and Homersfield (and even that at Rumburgh-Wissett) are added to the list.

The king was the dominant presence in Wangford in 1086, followed by the Bishop of Thetford and Earl Hugh of Cheshire. Bury Abbey had a foothold in the jurisdiction (mainly by virtue of its tenure of Beccles, with its market), as did Roger Bigot, Godric the Steward, Eudo son of Spirwic and Hugh de Montfort. Prior to the Conquest, the usual pattern of thegn-freeman tenancy prevailed – mainly, but not exclusively, with the occupants under commendation to a superior. Prominent among the patrons were Edward the Confessor (four examples), Stigand (five examples) and the Bishop of Thetford (four examples), with the thegn Burgheard (the likely supervisor of adjoining Lothing Half-hundred) holding two commendations as well as one church-estate of his own. His associate Wulfsi, who probably acted as Gyrth Godwineson's surrogate in Lothingland, can also be detected in the role of patron in one instance – as can Godwineson himself.

Wilford Hundred is the last of the East Suffolk jurisdictions to be summarised. It has been noted as having one of its vills, Bromeswell, once constituting part of the Rendlesham royal estate (Warner, pp. 116-18) – though, yet again, any possible connection with the early period of Anglo-Saxon evangelisation and church founding cannot really be established with any degree of certainty for such a centre of influence. As with the other Suffolk coastal hundreds (Blything excepted), Wilford had one of the lower percentages of churches per community and by far its most dominant presence in 1086, in terms of the church-estates held, was Robert Malet. Ely Abbey also featured (as might be expected in a component of its liberty), as did the Countess of Aumâle and the Bishop of Evreux, in Normandy.[35] During pre-Conquest times the abbey's presence, predictably enough, is still to be seen, but the overwhelming one in terms of patronage of local freemen is Eadric of Laxfield. This should come as no surprise, as his was the dominant presence in East Suffolk, and it was his estates which formed most of what was to become the Malet family's mighty fiefdom after the Battle of Hastings and its aftermath had run their definitive course.

What, then, can be said by way of summing up, without too much repetition of earlier commentary? First of all, in the absence of relevant documentation, little can be said regarding the effect of what may be termed "first-phase" monasteries or minsters in the matter of founding churches in their various localities – and to assess any possible long-term effects they may have had is largely a matter of speculation. As things stand, East Suffolk had far less influence from Bury Abbey than its western counterpart (except in the case of Hartismere and Stow) – a direct, even expected, result of the county's geography – while Ely Abbey's influence in its own liberty does not seem to have been as marked as might perhaps have been assumed. However, definite clerical influence is to be seen in the presence of bishops of the Elmham-Thetford diocese, particularly in pre-Conquest times, and so is that of the ruling classes of Anglo-Saxon society – even up to the level of the Crown itself. And it was this combination of ecclesiastical and secular authorities which seems to have been the determining factor, often through the social mechanism of commendation, in encouraging the many individual thegns and freemen (and freewomen) to establish churches.[36]

There are a handful of examples where the number of places of worship may seem to be surprisingly large for the size of community, the best examples of this being Coddenham and Stonham (later, Earl Stonham and Little Stonham) in Bosmere Hundred. The former is recorded as having six churches and the latter eight! There is always the (theoretical) chance of "double counting" on the part of the commissioners, but this does not seem to have been the case. All fourteen churches would appear to have been individual ones on the evidence of the data and the way it is presented, because all of them with one exception (a quarter-church in Stonham) have different land-holders referred to and varying endowments of parent soil. The latter ranged from two and a half acres to twelve and a half in the case of Coddenham and from two acres to twenty in that of Stonham. The largest area in each case was very much the exception, with the majority of the holdings being a good deal smaller. Exactly why these two communities should have had such a large number of churches is not clear, but it may have been the result of particular devotion on the part of the local freeman population (one of the Stonham entries refers to its nine founders' endowment being made "for their souls") or even of rivalry between peers trying to match or outdo each other.

Given the paucity of relevant, earlier information, it would appear from the Domesday record that much of the founding of churches may have dated from the first half of the eleventh century, during the period of national political consolidation from 1016 onwards (Cnut to Edward the Confessor). When compiling William I's national record of taxable assets, his commissioners were drawing their information from oral evidence presented in the various hundred and shire courts by juries of local men. It would seem reasonable, therefore, to suppose that most of the information collected related to the recent past rather than to the historic one – and the names of the more elevated members of society who acted as patrons of the different thegns, freemen and freewomen very much reflect this, relating noticeably to the 1040s-60s. Additionally, as previously referred to in the section dealing with West Suffolk and with those in the previous chapter relating to both sectors of Norfolk, there is the matter of new, dominant, Norman overlords (and their sub-tenants) possibly encouraging the founding and construction of churches as a means of cementing the changed social order.

In the absence of substantial and reliable documentation, a major intention of this study is to encourage a re-appraisal of the ecclesiastical landscape at parish level and motivate people who are sufficiently interested to carry out investigations of their own in the areas where they live. An exercise of this nature will form the subject matter of the next chapter.

Notes

1 The overall figure is the same as that calculated (as a possible maximum total) during the early 1950s by V.B. Redstone. See H. Munro Cautley, *Suffolk Churches and their Treasures*, 3rd ed. (1954), p. 5.

2 Scarfe, *Suffolk Landscape*, p. 138, comments on Falkenham and points out that its dedication to St. Ethelbert (Æthelberht) – a King of East Anglia murdered in Herefordshire for dynastic reasons in the year 794 – is a significant one in terms of its local association and comparatively early date.

3 For further information on Brandon, see also K. Wade, 'Later Anglo-Saxon Suffolk', in *Suffolk Atlas*, p. 38.

4 See E. Martin, 'Hundreds and Liberties', in *Suffolk Atlas*, p. 18, and Scarfe, *Suffolk Landscape*, p. 39.

5 Ælfgar first became Earl of East Anglia in 1051, when the Godwine family was exiled and Harold forfeited the title. Reinstatement was granted by Edward the Confessor the following year and, when Earl Godwine died in 1053, Harold became Earl of Wessex in place of his father – allowing Ælfgar (son of Leofric of Mercia and his wife, Godiva) to regain his former status. His son, Morcar, was adopted as Earl of Northumbria in 1065 and his daughter Ealdgyth (Edith) became the second wife of Harold Godwineson early in 1066.

6 Williamson, *Norfolk*, pp. 100 & 117, makes this observation concerning sokemen in communities located in both sectors of that county.

7 Its other centre of power and influence was Tonbridge, in Kent.

8 See J.C. Ward, 'The Honour of Clare in Suffolk in the Early Middle Ages', *Proceedings of the Suffolk Institute of Archaeology & History*, xxx (part 1), 94-111 (1964).

9 The last-named tenant-in-chief was the son of Robert fitz Wymarc (or Wimarc), a man of Breton descent who was related to both Edward the Confessor and William I.

10 Bosmere is the most complex of all the Suffolk hundreds (West or East), in terms of the number of Domesday tenants-in-chief and also of the number of pre-1066 tenants and their allegiances. Coddenham (with its six churches) and Earl & Little Stonham (with eight) compound the level of complexity.

11 Following his time at Elmham, he became Bishop of Winchester (1047-52) and Archbishop of Canterbury (1052-70). He was deposed from the latter position in favour of Lanfranc.

12 With the East Anglian diocese having been originally centred on Dunwich in c. 630 and then apparently divided c. 670, with a new entity being established at South Elmham (Wangford Hundred), this latter administration was then moved to North Elmham (in Norfolk) during the mid-late tenth century. In 1074-5, Bishop Herfast (a former Chancellor of England) moved the centre of operations to Thetford – and there it remained until Herbert de Losinga translated it to Norwich in 1094-5 and renamed the diocese accordingly.

13 This was the year following the great Danish invasion of 869 and death of King Edmund, in battle.

14 Rumburgh Priory (as it became known) was founded by Æthelmær, Bishop of Elmham (1047-70), in Wissett parish. He was Stigand's brother.

15 Its church is said to be the earliest surviving Romanesque building, dating from c. 1010. An ongoing programme of construction continued until the late eleventh century and the grant of lands in Suffolk may have been intended to assist with this.

16 He was also the older brother of Robert, Count of Mortain, and had been appointed to Bayeux at

an early age, in 1049. He was more of a soldier than a clergyman and his prelacy must have been more of a sinecure than genuine ministry. He was also, of course, the person who commissioned the Bayeux Tapestry.

17 Edeva the Fair is also referred to elsewhere as Edeva the Rich, but perhaps her best known title beyond the references here is Edith Swan-neck – a description meant to convey her gracefulness and beauty.

18 Carlford, Colneis, Loes, Parham, Plomesgate and Wilford constituted the five and a half hundreds (Parham being the half) which formed the Liberty of St. Etheldreda (known sometimes as the Wicklaw) – a large royal estate formally gifted to Ely Abbey by King Edgar in 970 (following a long period of religious dislocation caused by major Danish incursion) in honour of the daughter of King Anna. It may have originally been an endowment made to the abbey by Etheldreda (al. Æthelthryth) herself, as foundress, round about the year 672.

19 The community of Sharpstone was a further, much smaller detachment in Carlford itself – perhaps as the result of some earlier jurisdictional arrangement, such as a local soke.

20 Saxi is sometimes found referred to as Saxi of Debenham (but not in Domesday) and was a prominent holder of lands in central Suffolk – around thirty individual estates in all.

21 Thorpe eventually had "le Soken" added to its name in recognition of the presence of this local jurisdiction or *soke*.

22 He also features as patron of tenants in Blything, as well as holding land in his own right in Carlford. The 1086 information shows him as having retained an interest in three of his former areas of influence ("Alston", Burgh and Walton).

23 The Latin version of Godiva, given in the Domesday text, is *Godgeva*. With the original Anglo-Saxon spelling of the name rendered as *Godgifu*, it is possible that *Modgeva* is a scribe's error and that the two names refer to the same woman – though the difference in the form of the starting capital letters is pronounced.

24 As has been previously referred to, both Kelsale and Sudbury were placed (probably, for administrative reasons not entirely clear to us today) in hundreds other than the ones in which they were physically located.

25 The settlement of Kirkley (on the evidence of the first element of its name) must have had a church at one time, but it is not recorded in Domesday and must, presumably, either have gone out of use or disappeared. It is also possible, given Kirkley's proximity to Pakefield and the fluidity of parish boundaries, that the latter's church might originally have belonged to Kirkley.

26 The name Lothing derives from OE *Hluding*, meaning "the descendants of Hluda". Hluda (literally, "the loud one") seems to have been an early Anglo-Saxon incomer, who established a settlement – *Hluda's toft* – on the northern edge of a coastal lagoon, which has long served as Lowestoft's inner harbour. Lowestoft itself is an example of Scandinavian influences (following the Danish invasions of either the late ninth century or the early eleventh) modifying earlier English ones and producing *Hloðver's toft* as the penultimate version of the final form of the place-name. The Latinised form of Lothingland in Domesday is *Ludingalanda* and, throughout much of the late medieval period, the area continued to be known as Ludingland.

27 This name resulted from the occupant of the time, Ralph the Crossbowman, building a small motte-and-bailey fortification in the south-western corner of the Roman fort.

28 This was the year in which King Anna of the East Angles was killed in battle at Bulcamp (near Blythburgh) against the pagan forces of Mercia, led by Penda.

29 The same administrative foible was noted earlier, on p. 226, with regard to Whitton church

(Claydon Hundred). The name Ælflæd is encountered elsewhere, but the woman here is almost certainly not the one who held substantial estates in Bosmere, Carlford and Hartismere.

30 Iken first appears in documentary sources, in 1212, as *Ykene* (*Red Book of the Exchequer* and *Liber Feodorum*). Norman Scarfe's comments are to be found in an essay entitled, 'St. Botolph, the Iken Cross, and the Coming of East Anglian Christianity', which serves as Chapter 3 in his book (pp. 39-51).

31 Essex itself had only seventeen churches recorded in Domesday, including that of St. Peter, Colchester (Darby, p. 249).

32 Roffe, p. 166, notes what may be termed "strategic" grants of land in various parts of the country.

33 Thorney features as the very first entry in Suffolk Domesday. Subsequent developments in the manor form the basis of discussion in N.R. Amor, 'Late Medieval Enclosure – a Study of Thorney, near Stowmarket, Suffolk', in *PSIA*, vol. XLI (2), 175-97 (2006).

34 One of them, Bræme by name, of Dagworth, is recorded as having been killed at Hastings.

35 This prelate, Gilbert, held three estates in England, all in Wilford – one of which, Loudham, had a church.

36 For area-specific comment on freemen founding churches, see P. Warner ,'Blything Hundred', pp. 92-6, and 'Shared Churchyards, Freemen Church Builders and the Development of Parishes in Eleventh-century East Anglia', in *Landscape History*, 8 (1986), pp. 39-52.

Post-Domesday Developments in Lothingland and Mutford

The primary aim of this chapter is to take the furthest north-eastern part of Suffolk and show how its Domesday communities underwent notable boundary changes in the century following the Survey – thereby demonstrating that it may be unsafe to regard parish boundaries as being in fixed and final form by the end of the Anglo-Saxon period. Accompanying this will be an account of an extensive programme of church-building which seems to have taken place at the same time, leading to the least churched area of the county having all of its parishes endowed with places of worship by about the year 1200. It is also hoped that the evidence presented may serve to act as a model for similar work to be attempted in other parts of Norfolk and Suffolk where the opportunity exists. The eastern sector of Suffolk particularly has many examples of communities either not able to be immediately or easily identifiable from the name recorded in Domesday or which did not survive as independent entities in the decades following the survey. Norfolk has far fewer, but it would be good to have a wider and clearer understanding of the process of change wherever it is possible to identify and describe it.

Lothingland (Ludingalanda)

Gorleston was the hub of the hundredal manor with 600 acres of arable land and a further associated holding of ninety acres. Three outliers were located in Belton (120 acres), Lound (240 acres) and Lowestoft (450 acres), their north-north-west/south-south-east diagonal alignment creating an element of control beyond the hub itself, and there was a final estate of ninety acres in Somerleyton. This added up to 1,590 acres in all, but the biggest individual community in terms of cultivated land (and population) was Flixton, with 1,085 acres and c. 300 inhabitants.[1] Immediately prior to 1066, the half-hundred had been under the overlordship of the Earl of East Anglia, Gyrth Godwineson, with the thegn Wulfsi as his local supervisor, but after the Conquest the area was very largely part of William I's vast royal estate and therefore under the scrutiny of Roger Bigot, Sheriff of Norfolk and Suffolk – or, rather, under that of a bailiff appointed by him.

Two significant departures from this pattern of control were the manor of Burgh [Castle], together with its church, and that of Caldecot (both held by Ralph the Crossbowman) and the church-estate of Flixton (part of the Bishop of Thetford's holdings). The only other place of worship recorded for the jurisdiction was to be found in Somerleyton, possibly attached to the forty-acre manor held by Wihtred the Priest. It had an endowment of twenty acres of arable land, which was larger than Burgh's eleven acres but much smaller than Flixton's 120. Neither Burgh nor Flixton had the presence of a priest recorded, but each must presumably have had one to exercise cure of souls.

Æthelmær (or Ælmer) the Priest, on his eighty-acre manor of Akethorpe, must also have carried out a Christian ministry of some kind, but no building is recorded in connection with him. Akethorpe was an outlier to Lowestoft, both in topographical and place-name terms, becoming integrated with its larger neighbour in the years following the Domesday Survey and remaining part of its parochial structure thereafter – though with the status of a separate estate within the manorial set-up. Eventually, of course, Lowestoft became the dominant community in Lothingland, but that is another story and no part of the narrative here.[2]

Map 5. Lothingland Half-hundred at Domesday

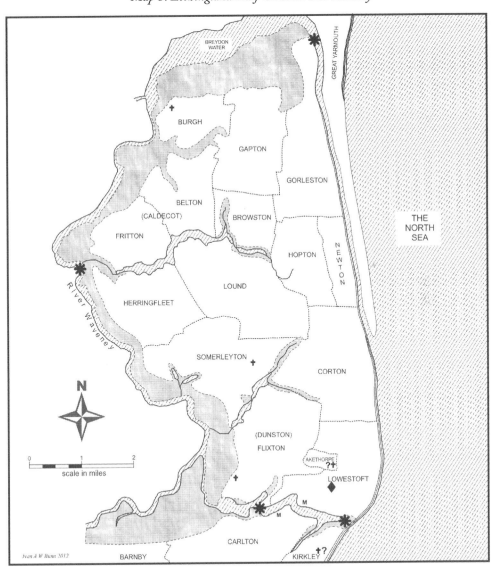

Map details

- Crosses at Burgh, Flixton and Somerleyton mark the location of churches referred to in 1086. Akethorpe, in having a priest, must have had some kind of Christian practice being exercised, though no building is referred to. A likely site for such observation is that of the later parish church of St. Margaret, Lowestoft (hence, the cross). Kirkley was located in Mutford Half-hundred and will be discussed in due course.

- All three Domesday churches had early dedications: Burgh (St. Peter & St. Paul), Flixton (St. Michael) and Somerleyton (St. Mary).

- Thickened asterisks show the four fording-places or crossing-points providing access to, and egress from, the Island of Lothingland (for such it was). The bridges eventually built across them were a much later feature.

- An upper-case M, either side of Lake Lothing, marks the location of two former, lost burial-mounds.

- The areas represented in light grey shading are the tidal mudflats alongside the River Waveney and the main inland stretches of marsh. Lakes, rivers and the sea are shown in diagonal lining.

- Approximate boundaries for the communities are defined by dotted lines. Caldecot and Dunston are shown in their respective locations, but are bracketed because of insufficient information regarding their limits.

- The sandbar on which Great Yarmouth was founded (the result of the fall in sea-levels during late Anglo-Saxon times and of longshore drift bringing eroded material from much further up the Norfolk coast) grew progressively southwards in spit form until well into the fourteenth century. During the Anglo-Saxon era, it gradually closed off the mouth of the estuary of Roman times and, by impeding the outflow of the rivers Yare, Bure and Waveney to the sea, made possible the gradual reclamation of the area known today as Halvergate Marshes. Its extent shown on the map is approximate only.

Focus must first be given to the boundary changes which occurred in the half-hundred during the twelfth century and which can be seen illustrated in Maps 5 and 6 (the evidence-base for these alterations consisting largely of Ordnance Survey and earlier maps, hundred roll and manorial records, and existing landscape features). Five of the Domesday vills (Akethorpe, Browston, Caldecot, Dunston and Gapton) ceased to exist in their own right, either becoming absorbed by neighbouring settlements or forming part of new ones which developed. Thus, Akethorpe was integrated with Lowestoft; Browston became part of Belton, of the newly created Bradwell and of Hopton; Caldecot was absorbed by Belton and Fritton, and Dunston by Oulton; and Gapton formed part of Bradwell. In the place of these five Domesday vills, six new parishes appeared. Two of them (Bradwell and Oulton) have been referred to with regard to their absorption of earlier settlements; the other four (Ashby, Blundeston, Gunton and Southtown) were formed by boundary changes and land-deals. Thus, Ashby was created from Herringfleet and Lound, Blundeston from Corton, Lound and Somerleyton, Gunton from Corton and Lowestoft, and Southtown from Gorleston. Significantly, perhaps, all six of these names appear in documentary sources at the end of the twelfth-beginning of the thirteenth century: Ashby and Gunton in 1198 (*Feet of Fines* material), Blundeston and Oulton in 1203 (*Curia Regis Rolls*), Bradwell in 1211 (*Feet of Fines*) and Southtown, under its alias *Little Yarmouth*, in 1219 (*Book of Fees*).[3] All of which suggests that they had established themselves in their own right as independent communities.

The five "lost" settlements are still remembered today by use of their ancient names in their localities, but in greatly changed circumstances. Browston is now a named area of the parish of Belton and the venue of a country hotel, restaurant and golf course (*Browston Hall*, after a one-time manor); Caldecot is also perpetuated as another country hotel and golf course (*Caldecot Hall*, the name of its sole manor); Gapton is the location of a large industrial and retail park (*Gapton Hall*, after one of its three medieval manors); and Akethorpe and Dunston bear the names of roads in modern housing developments of the 1980s (*Akethorpe Way* and *Dunston Drive*), where mercifully the developers felt able to use historical references rather than opt for the inane "themed" names which so often identify contemporary housing schemes! The six "replacement" communities, if they may be so termed, have four of their number deriving their titles from personal names (Scandinavian in three cases and Anglo-Saxon in one) and the other two are based on topographical associations. The three Scandinavian vills are Ashby (*Aski's býr*), Gunton (*Gunni's tun*) and Oulton (*Ali's tun*), and they speak of Danish connections at some point in the past, while the sole Anglo-Saxon example is Blundeston (*Blunt's tun*).[4] Presumably, all four families (or the patriarchs thereof) had built up sufficiently large estates in their respective areas of habitation for their patronyms to become used as a means of recognition in both parochial and occupancy contexts. Bradwell and Southtown – the latter having already been discussed in fn. 3 –

were both topographical in origin, the former (OE *brād wælle*) referring to the large stretch of tidal lagoon, long known as *Breydon Water* in which the flows of the Bure, the Waveney and the Yare mixed together (and still do) on their outward passage to the sea.

Map 6. Lothingland Half-hundred in the Thirteenth Century

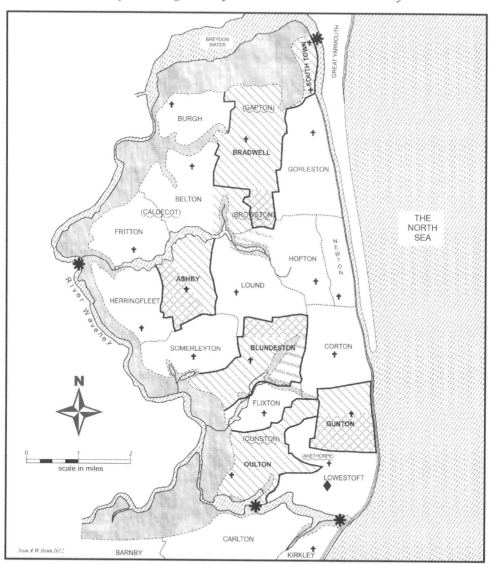

The second note below, relating to Map 6, refers to the Lothingland churches having increased in number from three in 1086 to eighteen a century or so later. Some idea of the founding-period may be gained from the granting of four of them (plus a chapel) to the recently established Augustinian priory of St. Bartholomew, West Smithfield, in London. This was done during the reign

Map details

- Crosses indicate parish churches (founding dates unknown) and, at the map's northern extremity, the chapel of Northville. The possible assembly-place for worship in Akethorpe had now become St. Margaret's Church, Lowestoft, situated half a mile or so due north of the settlement and occupying a high-point in the landscape.

- Church founding and building (three recorded at Domesday; eighteen in existence, a century or so later) needs to be seen not only as the spread of organised religion in terms of Christian faith, but also as a means of social and moral control of local populations. Personal elevation and influence in the community may also have been a motivating factor, in raising the buildings, on the part of the founders of churches, who were probably very largely drawn from those families which had become the dominant land-holders in the various communities.

- Crossing-places are indicated as in Map 5 – as are tidal mudflats, areas of inland marsh and stretches of water.

- Dotted lines indicate parish boundaries, as previously, and may still be best regarded as approximate in a number of cases.

- Six new parishes (Ashby, Blundeston, Bradwell, Gunton, Oulton and Southtown) have their boundaries shown by thickened lines and their names given in bold font. Contrasting types of shading indicate the land they developed from, formerly located in what then became adjoining communities. Part of Browston was taken to form Bradwell; two other sectors were incorporated, respectively, into Belton and Hopton.

- Akethorpe, Browston, Caldecot, Dunston and Gapton are bracketed and underlined in the locations they occupied within the parishes which had subsumed them. In the translated text of the Domesday Survey, Dunston is wrongly translated as Blundeston (3.54 & 7.54), which had not even come into existence at that time.

- The sand-spit formed by the combination of longshore drift and outward flow of the River Yare is shown as having reached further south, compared with Map 5 – this to reflect the passage of time during which the new parishes had formed (on documentary evidence, all of them seem to have been well established by c. 1200). The length and width of the spit is approximate only, owing to a lack of specific topographical data.

of Henry I (1100-35), who acted as a major sponsor of the new creation, which had been started in 1123 by a cleric named Rahere. The benefices of Belton, Gorleston, Little Yarmouth (or Southtown) and Lowestoft, together with the chapel of Northville, formed the gift made by Henry out of his Lothingland estate (a missing element was the outlier in Lound, which may indicate that the parish had not yet acquired a church).[5] Thus, all five foundations must have been established at some point between 1086 (Domesday) and 1135 – a fifty-year time-slot which probably saw profound changes in the local ecclesiastical landscape. As described in fn. 5 below, Northville's chapel is long gone, and so is the church of St, Nicholas, Southtown – later to become (during the late thirteenth century) part of a notable Augustinian priory located at the northern end of Gorleston.

However, three of the churches remain in use today: Belton All Saints, Gorleston St. Andrew and Lowestoft St. Margaret. The first-named has a round tower, almost certainly originally Norman in construction and style, but completely rebuilt from a ruinous state in the middle of the nineteenth century (the nave and chancel are basically of fourteenth century origins). Gorleston church, as seen today, is obviously the replacement of an earlier building also, its square tower dating from late thirteenth century with fourteenth and fifteenth century modifications added. The body of the church also reflects a variety of styles and the view of it from the east end, with north and south aisles flanking the chancel in a composite elevation and producing a triple-gable effect, is an imposing one. Lowestoft church is the third longest in Suffolk (at 182 feet), a mighty Perpendicular creation dating from c. 1450-80, with an

Plate 2. St. Margaret's parish church is located at the eastern extremity of the former Domesday manor of Akethorpe – just half a mile or so to the north of the Lowestoft township's original site somewhere within what is now the Normanston Cemetery. It stands in an elevated position, within its surrounding topography, and may well have been a place of assembly for local Christian worship under the aegis of Æthelmær (al. Ælmer), an Anglo-Saxon priest, who was lord of Akethorpe's eighty-acre holding. No building, as such, is mentioned – but, at some point, St. Margaret's Church (a much earlier edifice than that seen today) was constructed to serve Akethorpe's much larger neighbour.

early fourteenth century tower and crypt at either end speaking of a grand civic scheme begun before the Black Death disrupted proceedings and put everything on hold, until a long period of social and economic recovery allowed work to continue.[6] It, too, succeeded an earlier building on the same site – a place of worship of some kind associated, at Domesday, with an Anglo-Saxon priest called Æthelmær (but without a church specifically recorded).

What of the three churches which were specifically referred to in 1086? Burgh [Castle], which is dedicated to St. Peter and St. Paul, is still functioning on its site close to the old Roman shore fort of *Gariannonum*, once home to the monastery founded in the 630s by the Irish monk, Fursa (St. Fursey). The first element of the settlement's name, deriving from OE *burg* or *burh* and meaning "fortified place", is a direct reference to the late third century, coastal defensive facility, and its early Anglo-Saxon title was *Cnobheresburh* – presumably, after the name of its leading inhabitant. This first element was dropped at some stage, leaving the second one on its own to define the vill, and it only became Burgh Castle after the Conquest, when its new lord, Ralph

Plate 3. The church of St. Peter & St. Paul, Burgh Castle, is by far the most northerly of the Suffolk churches recorded in Domesday. Extensive restoration in recent years has greatly enhanced the appearance of the building, both inside and out, and it is well worth visiting. Its dedication to two of the key figures in the early consolidation and spread of the Christian Faith suggests ancient origins. Integration of the parish into the County of Norfolk (in 1974) has tended to blur its historical pedigree, but the church remains an important part of the religious development both of the Island of Lothingland and of the County of Suffolk.

the Crossbowman, built a motte-and-bailey fortification in the south-western corner of the former Roman cavalry-base as the centre of his own private, knight's-fee jurisdiction.[7] The church of St. Peter & St. Paul is another of Lothingland's nine round towers and, although generally classified as Norman, might just be (at least in part) an Anglo-Saxon structure – thereby giving it a direct link with the Domesday record.

This holds true of the church in Somerleyton, also referred to in 1086 – except that it is now the church of St. Mary, Blundeston, as a result of the previously described boundary changes which took place in Lothingland during the twelfth century. Its absorption into a new parish necessitated the building of a replacement church in Somerleyton (also St. Mary) – though the present square-tower structure is an updated successor to an earlier one and greatly affected by major reconstruction during the 1850s, when Samuel Morton Peto and his architect, John Thomas, were radically re-shaping the village. The round tower of what is now Blundeston St. Mary is markedly out of proportion with the main body of the church, which was extended southwards

Plate 4. St. Mary, Blundeston, stands as a reminder today of the major boundary changes which took place in Lothingland during the post-Conquest period – having at one time served as the church of neighbouring Somerleyton. The round tower, with its much later castellated top, is a notable local landmark and the church itself is perhaps best known for the literary character, David Copperfield, whom Charles Dickens describes as having been born "at Blunderstone, in Suffolk." The nearby rectory building is generally regarded as the model for The Rookery, where the young David lived.

during the fourteenth century, and it is the narrowest of all such East Anglian structures. The irregular construction of the lower part (as opposed to the coursed masonry further up), together with the internal arch's projecting horizontal stones at the springing-point, are possibly suggestive of Anglo-Saxon work (and certainly of stylistic influence). Topographically, in reference to its earlier association with Somerleyton, St. Mary's stands only 350 yards or so from the parish boundary and even now, in spite of all the modern building which has taken place, can be seen as not being closely connected with the core-area of Blundeston village. Equally, Somerleyton church also stands apart from the main area of settlement (as it has developed) and is much closer to the hall – this, either because the ruling Fitzosbert family must have had it placed there for personal convenience or because the centre of population has moved.

The third of the Domesday churches recorded for Lothingland, with its early dedication to St. Michael, now stands in Oulton rather than in Flixton – the result, once more, of boundary changes. Nothing remains of the

Plate 5. The church of St. Michael, Oulton, is yet another reminder of the Lothingland boundary changes, a predecessor having served the large and populous settlement of Flixton until the emergence and development of a new parish overwhelmed it. At the time of Domesday, Flixton St. Michael was one of the ten richest churches in Suffolk, forming part of the Bishop of Thetford's estates – but it had earlier been in the hands of Stigand, Bishop of Elmham, then of Winchester and of Canterbury. One noticeable feature of the building's structure is the length of the chancel (43% of the whole, excluding the tower-section) compared with that of the nave (57%) – as well as the higher pitch of its roof.

building referred to; what we see today is an impressive Norman tripartite replacement-structure, with square central tower and the transepts missing. The size and quality of build reflect both the church's level of wealth (it had an endowment at Domesday of 120 acres of arable land) and the fact that Flixton was the largest of all the Lothingland communities in terms of population and cultivated ground. Once Oulton had emerged and developed, however, it became a parish greatly reduced in size, with a small church dedicated to St. Andrew at what had been its northern end. This was very badly damaged in a hurricane of November 1703 and not replaced, the congregation transferring to Blundeston. The ruins of the building can still be traced, close to the site of the medieval hall (long known as *Hall Farm*) and herringbone brickwork visible in the walls of the nave clearly indicates construction of the Norman period. Regarding the church of St. Michael, Norman Scarfe in *Suffolk Landscape* (pp. 124-7) suggests that it was originally established during the 630s by St. Felix, the *Roman* bishop of East Anglia, to monitor the *Celtic* activities of Fursa at *Cnobheresburh* – the place-name's first element even being a variant of his own name.

So much for the churches of the Domesday record, but a further nine remain to be discussed. Earliest of these, in terms of architectural features, are the ones at Fritton (St. Edmund) and Herringfleet (St. Margaret), both of them displaying characteristics of what may be termed "the Saxo-Norman overlap", that period following on from the Conquest in which native Anglo-Saxon methods and styles of construction gradually gave way to those of the continental incomers.[8] Both buildings have round towers and are thatched, with certain distinctive features which would seem to suggest late eleventh century origins. Fritton has a rare, tunnel-vaulted, apsidal chancel, with fourteenth century wall paintings depicting the martyrdom of Edmund, while Herringfleet's tower has upper windows combining double Anglo-Saxon triangular heads set within a Romanesque surround (it also has billeted ornament on the chancel arch and a typical south doorway, with moulded chevron carving of the hood). The two churches are classic buildings of their type and sit comfortably within their long-established surrounds.[9]

The next church most obviously of Norman origins is St. Peter, Gunton, with round tower and typical north and south doorways embellished with simple chevron decoration on semi-circular hoods. It is one of nine buildings still in use in Lothingland (out of a total of fifteen) which has a round tower – a feature which probably shows an insufficiency of wealth (or the lack of a sufficiently wealthy and motivated individual) in those communities, to eventually upgrade the earlier type with a square one. Ashby, Bradwell and Lound have round towers also, all three of which would again appear to be of Norman date and type – with the last-named rebuilt at some stage. The first of them (another thatched building) is dedicated to St. Mary and is the most interesting of the trio, standing isolated in the middle of fields close to a former cross-ways, the upper two-thirds of the tower rebuilt at some stage in octagonal form (probably during the fifteenth century), with angles quoined in brick. Any landscape amenity once attaching to St. Nicholas, Bradwell has been completely lost in the spread of housing development constructed during the later part of the twentieth century – this, due more than a little to the pressure exerted by Great Yarmouth's outward growth and expansion. Lound, however, remains unarguably a village community and the church of St. John the Baptist appears at first sight to be all that it should, in terms of its restrained outlines and construction. Step inside, however, and the eye is overwhelmed by Ninian Comper's extravagant restoration (in 1914) of the chancel screen and rood-loft – an experience then reinforced by his own font cover and organ case, executed in similar style. "The golden church of Lound" was an expression once used to describe the work!

The last three parishes and churches remaining to be discussed are Corton, Hopton and Newton. Together, they form a trio of communities linked to each other by geographical proximity and by the effects of long-term coastal erosion. Corton and Newton had been losers of land (as had Gorleston, further to the north) for periods of time beyond recall, but Hopton only became directly involved after the Local Government Act of 1972. When this was implemented on 1 April 1974, the five northernmost parishes in Lothingland (Belton, Bradwell, Burgh Castle, Fritton and Hopton), along with the St. Olaves sector of Herringfleet, were annexed to Norfolk to form part of the new Great Yarmouth District Council. Gorleston had been incorporated with Yarmouth long before this (a process beginning electorally as early as the Reform Acts of 1832 and 1835), even though many of its inhabitants continued to regard it as still part of Suffolk. With coastal erosion having almost totally destroyed the small parish of Newton by the early-mid seventeenth century (the terminal stage of a long, on-going process), just a narrow cliff-top strip of it was left between the ocean and Hopton. This became, and remained, part of Corton up until April 1974, when it was given to Hopton, enabling it to become for the first time in its history Hopton-on-Sea. Over the course of the last 800-900 years, the Lothingland coastline has lost something like half a mile or more to the sea, both by direct attrition and cliff-collapse. It is a process which continues – though impeded in places by man-made defences.

The churches of these three parishes, so closely tied together, had square towers – all of them rebuilds, probably, of previous ones. That of St. Mary, Newton, of course, disappeared centuries ago, but an image of it is to be found on a late sixteenth century map of the local coastline, once in the possession of the Suffolk antiquarian, Thomas ("Honest Tom") Martin of Palgrave. This particular map is representational, rather than cartographical, and it shows a building with separate nave and chancel. It also shows it to have stood a good deal further from the sea than the church at Hopton, to the north, and on almost the same alignment as that of Corton, to the south – yet it has long gone and they both remain standing! The former building ("Old St Margaret's", as it is known) was destroyed by fire in February 1865 and never rebuilt.[10] In recent years, it has undergone preservation of the remaining fabric under the aegis of Great Yarmouth District Council, serving also as a conservation workshop to encourage and teach traditional building skills. Two Romanesque, grotesque, stone heads found incorporated in the fabric of the fourteenth century tower during 2015 show that an earlier, post-Conquest church had preceded it. St. Bartholomew, Corton (its dedication being a typically Norman-period one), may possibly have begun life as a private chapel of the de Corton family before becoming the parish church. A priest, Philip, is documented (as *le Clerk*) during the reign of Henry II (1154-89) and the building, as seen today, is a large and imposing one of the late fourteenth century – though with earlier, Norman work detectable in the south wall of the nave.[11]

Such, then, is a statement of parochial developments in Lothingland in terms of boundary changes and the founding and construction of new churches during the period following Domesday. It is now the turn of its smaller neighbour, Mutford to have its history similarly revealed.

Mutford/Lothing (Ludinga)

It is not possible to say when Lothing Hundred became known as Mutford – probably as a means of differentiating it from its near-neighbour, Lothingland. The change seems to have occurred during the reign of Henry II (1154-89), noting evidence to be found in the sale of the manorial title by the Crown to Baldric du Bosco, but it might conceivably have been even earlier. In theory, a hundred consisted of 100 hides of cultivated land (12,000 acres) – hence the name – but both Lothingland and Mutford were considerably smaller than than this (6,265 and 3,209 acres, respectively).[12] It can thus be seen that each jurisdiction fell far short of the required area, placing them in the half-hundred category – a title they bore right through the late Medieval and Early Modern periods. Mutford either took its name from its largest community or from the location of the local hundred court (perhaps the more likely origin of the two), which was shared by both jurisdictions from early on. It was held at the crossing-place over the junction of Lake Lothing and the stretch of water long known as Oulton Broad. This particular location is still called Mutford

Bridge or Mutford Lock, in reference to the bridge which eventually replaced the old earthern causeway or to the basin constructed as part of the failed Lowestoft-Norwich Navigation scheme of 1827-30.[13] The meeting-place itself was located on a rise of ground on the Lothingland side of the boundary, just into what is now Commodore Road and, by the Early Modern period, a building stood there to hold the what had become by then the six-monthly hundred court – on the site occupied today by *The Commodore* public house.[14]

Mutford, the settlement, was the largest vill in Lothing Hundred and its 420-acre estate formed the hub of the hundredal manor. Altogether, with the various other holdings in Mutford itself (600 acres) and in surrounding communities (423 acres) added on, the total cultivated area came to 1,443 acres.[15] Along with concentration of the majority of the manorial land, Mutford also had by far the largest population, with its twenty-six freemen, twenty villans, ten bordars and ten slaves producing over 330 inhabitants.[16] The manor had been held in 1066 by Gyrth Godwineson, with the thegn Wulfsi acting as his local supervisor. A majority of the other estates in the half-hundred, lesser manors and freeholdings, were in the control of the thegn Burgheard, who may also have shared the governing role with Wulfsi, while the ubiquitous Edric of Laxfield was patron of two separate freemen in Kessingland. In 1086, the ruling Anglo-Saxon presence had gone completely. The King held title to the main manor, while all the other estates were in the hands of Hugh d'Avranches, Earl of Cheshire, and of Hugh de Montfort, Constable of Dover Castle.

Five churches are recorded for the half-hundred in 1086: one in Barnby (eighty acres), two in Mutford (forty-three acres combined), one in Pakefield (sixteen and a half acres) and one in Rushmere (eight acres). On the wording of the Domesday document, it is not clear as to exactly which estate the two Mutford foundations were attached, but one feasible interpretation is to place one of them on the hub manor and the other on a large 360-acre holding worked by four resident and nine outside freemen. No priest is referred to in connection with any of the churches mentioned, but obviously clergy must have been present to exercise ministry and work the land attached to each building. Over the course of the centuries which followed, one of the Mutford churches disappeared, leaving its companion as the building seen today. It will be discussed in due course, along with the three other foundations recorded in the pages of Domesday.

Before that stage is reached, boundary changes occurring in the half-hundred during the century following the Survey must be discussed. These involved four of the jurisdiction's twelve vills, but unlike neighbouring Lothingland there was no accompanying emergence of new settlements or parishes. Beckton, Hornes, Rothenhall and Wimundhall were all simply absorbed by adjoining communities and became part of them – though with three of them remaining in existence for a while in people's names and the other one surviving in a local landscape reference. Beckton became part of Pakefield, as did half of Rothenhall – the other part becoming incorporated into Kessingland – while Wimundhall was taken into Kirkley. Hornes, in having two possible locations, either became part of Carlton (later, Carlton Colville) or of Rushmere. It was by far the smallest of the four settlements under discussion – being only a single, five-acre holding, worked by one freeman.

Map 7. Mutford Half-hundred at Domesday

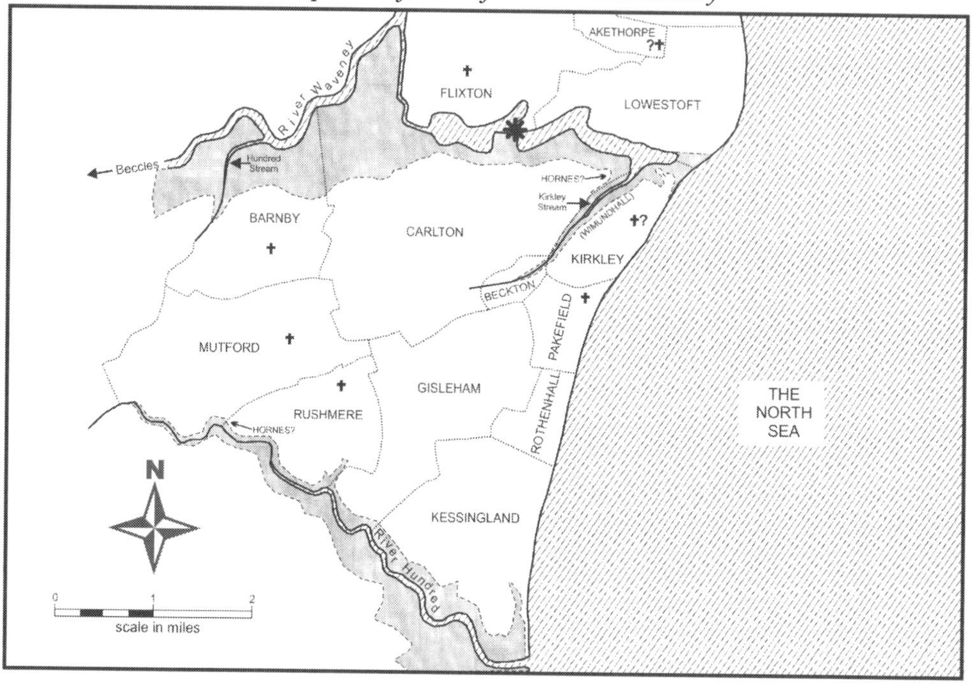

Map details

- Crosses at Barnby, Mutford, Pakefield and Rushmere represent churches referred to in the survey, in their geographical positions. A position for the second church in Mutford is not able to be shown with any certainty. Kirkley, on the evidence of its name, had had a church at some point, but none is recorded in Domesday – hence the question mark appended.

- The Domesday churches all have appropriate, early dedications: Barnby (St. John the Baptist), Mutford (St. Andrew), Pakefield (All Saints – what later became the southern mediety of the "two churches in one") and Rushmere (St. Michael). So, too, has Kirkley (St. Peter).

- The thickened asterisk shows the fording-place or crossing-point providing access to, and egress from, the Half-hundred of Lothingland at the point commonly known as Mutford Bridge.

- The areas represented in light grey shading are the tidal mudflats alongside the River Waveney and River Hundred and the main inland stretches of marsh. Lakes, rivers and the sea are shown in diagonal lining.

- Approximate boundaries for the communities are defined by dotted lines. Hornes and Wimundhall are shown in their respective locations, but without limits shown – the former in two possible areas (hence the question marks) and the latter bracketed within Kirkley in its general area of location.

Taking the three larger communities first, Beckton survived as a local surname (de Beckton) into the earlier part of the fourteenth century. So did Wimundhall, but usually in the form of Wymendhale – the family being lords of the manor of Kirkley. Rothenhall had a longer currency, lasting well into the fifteenth century, in Pakefield, as a means of family identification and for a good deal longer as the name of one of that community's two manors. It also served in this capacity for Kessingland, being one of the four manors located there (the others were Etchingham's, Kingston's and Stapleton's – the last-named being largest and most influential). Furthermore, an area of heathland shared by both Pakefield and Kessingland was known as *Rothinghall Heath* well into the seventeenth century and as *Runhill* into the early nineteenth. *Heath Farm*, at the northern end of Kessingland, acts as a reminder of this former topographical feature and helps to perpetuate it.

Map 8. Mutford Half-hundred in the Thirteenth Century

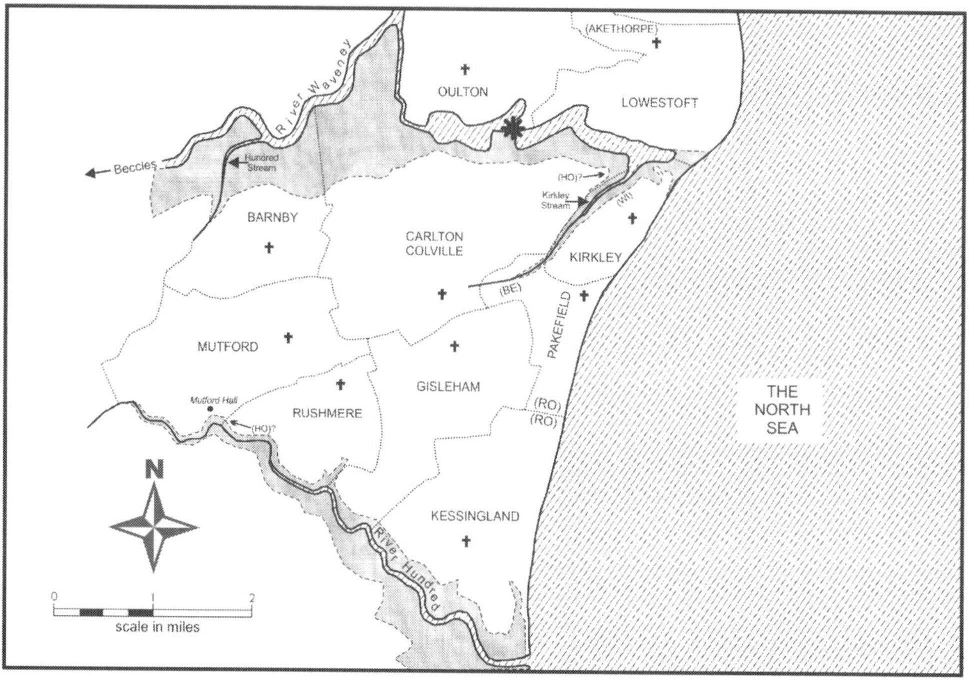

Map details

- Crosses indicate churches (as in the previous map), placed in their respective locations in the different communities As noted in the neighbouring half-hundred of Lothingland, the post-Conquest period saw the building of churches where there had previously been none.

- The Mutford Bridge crossing-place is indicated as in the Domesday map; so are tidal flats and marshland, and stretches of water.

- Dotted lines indicate parish boundaries, which (in places) may still not have reached final definition.

- The four Domesday vills absorbed into neighbouring communities are each shown in their former locations, with all of them having bracketed abbreviations representing the name: (Be) = Beckton, (Ho) = Hornes, (Ro) = Rothenhall and (Wi) = Wimundhall. Rothenhall is shown located either side of the Pakefield-Kessingland parish boundary and Hornes is shown in two possible positions, as previously.

- Carlton had the Colville added to its name, at some point during the 13th century, because of association with the family (de Coleville) which held the more important of the two manors located in the parish and perhaps also to distinguish it from the hamlet of that name in Bradwell, Lothingland.

- The location of the Mutford manor house is indicated by a bullet-pointed symbol (•), in the southern sector of the parish, on a spur of land, overlooking the River Hundred.

Little Hornes may have been small in extent, but there is a candidate for its location at opposite ends of the half-hundred. The "spit of land", as alluded to in the name, may have been a projection into Lake Lothing, close to the point where Kirkley Beck (or Stream) once entered the mere and where, at a much later date the Co-operative Canning Factory and its wharf stood (TM59 540926).[17] The name Horn Hill (applied to the main roadway in this area) is not provable as a descendant of the small estate's title (it was only five acres in area), but nevertheless remains as a possible link with the earlier name. Although it eventually became part of Carlton Colville's great East Heath, the soil might well have been workable because of proximity to water and its associated silt – and the area of land constituting the bluntly-shaped promontory is still approximately five acres in size. Another site which fits the topographical reference contained in the name is to be found in the extreme western "tip" of Rushmere parish, on a spit or spur of land known as Horns Hill, which projects towards the River Hundred at a point opposite a similar promontory on which Mutford Hall stands.[18] Both of these opposing spurs are defined by the 25-feet contour line and that in Rushmere is to be found at TM48 483875. There could easily have been a five-acre holding in this vicinity, and it is difficult to favour one location or the other because both of them satisfy the topographical element contained in the name Hornes. It does, however, have to be said that the soil in Rushmere was probably of better quality for agriculture than the land adjacent to Lake Lothing.

Of the four Domesday communities recorded with churches, Barnby is probably the most surprising, being unequivocally Scandinavian in origin (OD *Biarni's býr*) but with by far the largest endowment of land for its place of worship. The eighty acres constituted 39% of the parish total of 204 – an impressively large proportion – but there is no explanation or clue as to the reason. From the evidence in Domesday, it would seem that the church was attached to a forty-four acre holding worked by five freeman, who had one plough between them and may well have tilled the glebe-land as well.[19] The third estate in the parish was another eighty-acre one (part of the hundredal manor), worked by eight freemen and two ploughs – labour which might also have assisted with the church holding as well as its own, if extra input were needed. No priest is referred to in Domesday (this is also true of the other

Plate 6. St. John the Baptist, Barnby, stands on an eminence close to one set of the notorious "Barnby bends" on the A146 main road – detached now from the built-up area of the village. Its prominence in the landscape is diminished by the trees growing around it, but this late 13th–early 14th structure contains much of interest under its thatched roof. There is a notable series of restored paintings on the south wall of the nave, depicting the Annunciation, scenes from the Passion and the Seven Acts of Mercy, while excellent, painted, 20th century glass by Margaret Rope (focusing on the patronal saint and his cousin, Jesus) is to be found in certain of the windows. Finally, a banner-stave locker, with original oak door, is located just to the west of the blocked-up south door.

half-hundred communities with churches) and there is no surviving physical evidence of the building recorded in 1086. As seen today, St. John the Baptist is a simple late thirteenth church, with combined nave and chancel surmounted by a thatched roof and with a square tower. Inside, on the south wall of the nave, is an important series of wall paintings depicting the Annunciation, the Passion and Crucifixion, and the Seven Acts of Mercy.

Adjoining Barnby, on its southern boundary, is the parish of Mutford. It had two churches recorded in 1086, endowed with a combined total of forty-three acres. There is no clue as to the size of each individual holding and no comment is offered as to whether the land was freely held or granted "in alms". The information is placed towards the end of the vill's main Domesday entry and the churches could therefore have been attached either to the hub manor itself or to the large associated free-holding. As a convenient and equable means of apportionment within this analysis, one church will be given to each estate and the endowment(s) of land counted within the overall totals, not

Plate 7. The round tower of St. Andrew is the tallest one in East Anglia and the building's position, on a raised site beside the road, serves to accentuate this. It is the only example of a church with a west, "Galilee" porch appended to a round tower. Such additions were probably used for all kinds of parish business – including the gathering of penitents, prior to absolution – and the name itself may have originated from the geographical separation between Judæa and Galilee, with the church's altar representing the death of Christ in Jerusalem and the Galilee porch his home in Nazareth. Inside the building, the font-base carries an inscription commemorating Elizabeth de Hengrave (al. Hemgrave), lady of the manor during the late 14th century.

added on. At some point, one of the churches disappeared, leaving the building seen today (dedicated to St. Andrew), standing on a roadside eminence close to where most of the parish's houses were once located. However, the village saw a substantial amount of late twentieth century residential development in the *Mill Road* area, to the south – though still retaining the elements of an un-nucleated settlement, with its original framework of outlying farmsteads and cottages. St. Andrew's Church has the tallest of all the surviving round towers in Norfolk and Suffolk, with a later octagonal top, and is a very interesting building – its most distinctive feature probably being the Galilee porch appended to the tower. Norman work is detectable in the fabric as whole and the question is then raised as to which of the two Domesday churches this is.

There is no certain answer and a degree of topographical complexity manifests itself in trying to provide one. The later name of the half-hundred, superseding Lothing, has already been mentioned. It derived from OE *mōt* (meeting) and *ford* (shallow place in water) – this, in reference to the crossing-point between

Lake Lothing and the adjacent broad in Oulton. Does the vill of the same name and of (presumably) earlier pedigree fit the same topographical context? The answer is yes – albeit in a different location. The site of *Mutford Hall*, the likely one-time seat of the de Hemgrave medieval lords, is to be found nearly a mile south-west of the church, in a key location on a spur of land overlooking the River Hundred and the neighbouring Blything jurisdiction – as well as backing westwards towards that of Wangford (TM48 481875). As seen today, it is basically a mid-sixteenth/early seventeenth century structure, with later modifications, and there could easily have once been a church in this vicinity which dropped out of use at some point and of which no physical sign remains today. To add to the confusion, a dwelling named the *Manor House* stands close to the remaining church. Behind a plain, early nineteenth century façade is a much earlier core dating from the late thirteenth or early fourteenth century – but the building's location does not fit the place-name etymology. Might it, therefore, have been built at some stage as the residence of whoever controlled the large free-holding of 360 acres (or what remained

Plate 8. St. Michael, Rushmere – like Barnby church – is one of a number of the smaller rural structures throughout East Anglia which has the main body of the building run through in an unbroken line without any external distinction between nave and chancel. It stands quietly at a cross-ways, its presence a reminder of how churches define an earlier landscape and way of life. During the 1970s, it was derelict and facing an uncertain future, but the small, dispersed, local community managed to save it and keep it in use. Along with neighbouring Mutford and Gisleham, it is one of three round towers which act almost like sentinels in the landscape lying to the north of the River Hundred.

of it), as recorded in Domesday?

Fortunately, no such difficulties are to be found in relation to the church of St. Michael, Rushmere, which stands a mile to the south-east of Mutford church at a perfect, largely isolated, rural crossroads location. Domesday declares this to have been a quarter-church with an endowment of eight acres of arable land – attached to a sixteen-acre freeholding worked by one man. The question of whom the remaining three-quarters of the foundation belonged to, or by whom it was shared, cannot be answered, but presumably it was an interest held without any accompanying gift of land and probably related largely to the appointment of clergy. The building seen today is a simple, thatched one (both nave and chancel being of similar size), with round tower, probably mainly of Norman construction but with evidence of minor updating of around c. 1300 in the various Y-tracery windows. It is a gem of its kind, valued for its unobtrusiveness.

The final Domesday church in Lothing/Mutford half-hundred is to be found in the eastern sector of the jurisdiction (not the western one), on the coast at Pakefield – one of the smaller communities in terms of its physical area. The survey records a half-church with sixteen and a half acres of land – seemingly attached to one-man free-holding of fifteen acres, with half a plough-team (four oxen). There is little evidence today of any immediately detectable early work in the fabric, but surviving herringbone masonry in the north wall of the nave and some of the lower parts of the tower may be suggestive of the Saxo-Norman overlap. Basically speaking, the bulk of the building (dedicated to All Saints and St. Margaret) seems to be late fourteenth century, with fifteenth century modifications, and its main point of interest (historically speaking) is that it was once two churches in one, with adjoining naves and chancels separated by a wall and with a single square tower at the west end, attached to the southern part of the building. It was only with the appointment of the same priest to both medieties during the early fifteenth century that this feature was arcaded. During the later medieval period, the respective lords of the two Pakefield manors were responsible individually for the appointment of the two priests, and the fact of there being two separate entities may have had its roots in the Domesday reference to the half-church – it being entirely possible that the "missing" half was what later resulted in the parish having two separate areas of ministry.[20]

If, however, this portion simply related to the appointment of clergy (as was possibly the case at Rushmere – and indeed, in other places), other explanations for "the two churches in one" offer themselves. It was the lords of Rothenhall manor who appointed to the All Saints part of Pakefield church (the southern one) and those of the Pakefield Pyes estate who did the same for St. Margaret's (the northern one). Pakefield had no manor recorded at Domesday – just two free-holdings of thirty acres (six men) and fifteen acres (one man), the latter referred to in the previous paragraph. Was it these two estates which were blocked up, together with the land formerly belonging to Beckton, to form what became the manor of Pyes?[21] If so, that would make what became the St. Margaret's element of the dual church the earlier part, because the Domesday foundation was attached to the smaller fifteen-acre holding. With Rothenhall having derived from the sector of that former Domesday vill absorbed by Pakefield, the All Saints mediety would seem to be of later origins than its companion. Yet its dedication is earlier than the other one, St. Margaret being very much a feature of the Norman influence in the naming of churches. There is no satisfactory solution regarding these apparent contradictions. Pakefield church holds its secrets still.

Plate 9. The double gable-end of All Saints & St. Margaret, on the edge of the cliff, is a defining feature of the Pakefield landscape. The building once stood much further from the sea, but two rapid periods of erosion – the early 1900s and the late 1930s-early 1940s – nearly caused its destruction, before remedial coastal defence work (ending in 1950) made it safe. Another drastic threat occurred when enemy incendiary bombs landed on its thatched roof at about 10 p.m. on the evening of Monday, 21 April 1941, reducing it to a burned-out wreck. Restoration was undertaken in 1949 and the church re-consecrated in 1950. As if to remind us of the antiquity of many church sites, a large, glacial-erratic boulder of unknown proportions lies under the heating-chamber built against the western wall of the tower. Could it have once stood on site, vertically, in pre-Christian times?

So does nearby Kirkley, which stands less than a mile away, to the north. Again, Kirkley was a small parish (something over 500 acres before its integration into Lowestoft during the mid-late nineteenth century), even after its absorption of Wimundhall, and the place-name itself means "a church in a clearing". The first element derives from OE *cirice* or OScand *kirkia*, but no church is referred to in Domesday, suggesting that no building (whatever the reason) was present for the commissioners to record.[22] Kirkley's patronal figure has always, from late medieval times onwards, been St. Peter (an early dedication), with the parish only becoming that of St. Peter & St. John after the demolition of a large Victorian place of worship in the late 1970s and the merging of the two benefices. As seen today, the church is a largely, well-conceived, mid-late Victorian gothic creation, with rebuilt medieval square tower (distinguished by four corner-pinnacles) and with a most singular western baptistry as perhaps its defining interior feature. Given the proximity

Plate 10. Once dedicated to St. Peter only, Kirkley church now has the title of St. Peter & St. John, since the demolition of its neighbouring Victorian companion (c. threequarters of a mile away, north-by-east) in 1978 and amalgamation of the two parishes. It is completely surrounded by dense, late 19th century, terraced housing of both large and smaller-scale construction, reflecting the rapid growth of Lowestoft after the arrival of rail-links in 1847 (Norwich) and 1859 (Ipswich) boosted both the local fishing industry and seaside leisure activity. Mention was made, in text, of the church's fine baptistry, but there are also other things of interest to be seen: notably a fine Arts and Crafts wrought-iron chancel screen and a carved and painted reredos by Robert Anning Bell and Dacres Adam.

of both churches and the small size of the two parishes, it is not impossible that Kirkley and Pakefield shared a priest at Domesday and that the former community constituted the other half of the church recorded for the latter one. Such a proposition cannot, of course, be conclusively proved.

The three remaining Domesday vills which had no churches recorded, and which were too large physically to be absorbed by neighbours, were Carlton, Gisleham and Kessingland. The first and the last of these had large areas of cultivated land and substantial populations (540 acres and 200+ people; 735 acres and c. 280 people), but the middle one only had thirty-two and a half arable acres (some 2% of its surface-area) and about thirty inhabitants. Why should this have been? There are no clues in Domesday, but scrutiny of Map 7 provides a possible answer. It can be seen that Gisleham was directly accessible for seven of the half-hundred's twelve communities through sharing its boundaries with them. Barnby, Hornes, Kirkley and Wimundhall had no direct physical contact, but could have accessed it by movement across neighbours' territory. Was Gisleham, therefore, some kind of central resource for surrounding settlements and, if so, what was on offer? It is possible, given the nature of the local, light, glacial soils present in places, that a large area of heath was available (the tract at Rothenhall being an eastward continuation), which provided a range of materials for the use of nearby communities under the aegis of the half-hundred's governing structure. The church of Holy Trinity is one of the jurisdiction's three round-tower fabrics, with battlemented octagonal top of fifteenth century origins (as at Mutford), but the rest of the fabric is Norman, with its well-defined nave and chancel having fourteenth century fenestration. A well-built south porch of fifteenth century origins was probably an impressive addition of the time, but the building's roots are best defined by the surviving interior Norman tower arch.

Carlton Colville (as it later became known) drew its name from a family whose progenitor, Gilbert de Coleville, had fought at Hastings. It seems to have acquired the title of the Domesday manor (another one developed alongside it during the post-Conquest period) in the early thirteenth century, when Sir Robert de Colvile is named as lord in the year 1227.[23] Carlton, as it was originally called, was by far the largest community, in terms of area, in the half-hundred and the Domesday data shows that its two larger estates (including the manor) had been granted to Hugh d'Avranches, Earl of Chester, and its two lesser ones to Hugh de Montfort. St. Peter's Church, as seen today, is a much-restored structure (the work having been carried out between 1859 and 1872) of the thirteenth and fourteenth centuries, with square, embattled tower, nave and chancel. However, one small clue as to its origins is to be found in the north wall of the nave where a small, restored Norman window is to be seen, thus giving the observer, if not proof-positive, at least the suggestion of its much earlier provenance.

And so, finally, to Kessingland and the parish church of St. Edmund, largest of the Mutford Half-hundred's places of worship, with its fine fifteenth century tower and ruined fourteenth century south aisle – the latter providing evidence of a more substantial structure than the one seen today. Late seventeenth century reconstruction of the thatched nave has altered the appearance of original features and nothing can be detected of any work relating to the church's predecessor, which must have stood on the site. At Domesday, the main manor in the community (240 acres) was among the extensive holdings of the Earl of Cheshire and the first place of worship was probably built during his period of tenure – the advowson seen as being in the gift of the lord during the centuries which followed. Attached to the manor was a larger free-holding of 360 acres, worked by forty freemen, who might well have been the driving force behind the church's founding. Comment has already been made concerning Fritton church, in Lothingland, as to how its dedication to Edmund, king and martyr, might possibly have been a means of maintaining an Anglo-Saxon identity in the face of Norman dominance.[24] The same could also be true of Kessingland.

One further feature of the two half-hundreds worthy of comment is the male population-structure of each, at Domesday. Lothingland had 118 freemen, 42 villans, 98½ bordars (the half presumably relating to a man not fully tied to his manor) and 18 slaves, making a total of 277 family heads and a notional population of 1,316 people. Mutford (or Lothing, as it was in 1086) had 190 freemen, 28 villans, 35 bordars and 16 slaves, producing a total of 269 family heads and a notional population of 1,278 people – almost as many as its neighbour, but occupying a jurisdiction about half the size in terms of total area and available arable land. Against a county average of 40% freemen, as a proportion of recorded adult males (Warner, p. 196 and Darby, p. 379), Lothingland had 43% and Mutford 71% – an extraordinarily high figure. A further feature of interest is that nineteen of the Lothingland freemen had their names recorded, whereas in Mutford it was only three – suggesting that the former half-hundred had a greater number of tenants with status above the basic level of *ceorl*. Furthermore, there is evidence in a description of the Mutford Half-hundred manor, from the 1274 Hundred Rolls of Edward I, that there were three kinds of tenant belonging to the manor: free gersumary tenants (the *gersuma* being a customary payment made to the lord), sokemen, and those on fixed wages and services.[25] Thus, unless their status had been degraded during the 200 years following Domesday, not all of the Mutford freemen may have been fully unencumbered at the time the survey was made.

This account of post-Domesday developments in the half-hundreds of Lothingland and Mutford is now complete. The Survey of 1086 recorded three settlements with churches in the former jurisdiction and four in the latter. A hundred years or more later, Lothingland had eighteen places of worship and Mutford had eight. The figures have to stand as manifested; the interpretation of them offered is the writer's own.

Notes

1   A figure arrived at by treating its twenty-five freemen, 4 villans, thirty-four bordars and four slaves as family heads (which they may not all have been) and applying an approved demographic multiplier of 4.75 per head.

2   See D. Butcher, *Medieval Lowestoft: the Origins and Growth of a Suffolk Coastal Community* (Woodbridge, 2016).

3   If Map 6 is scrutinised, the reason for both names becomes clear. Southtown was indeed located to the south of the core settlement of Yarmouth in the Fuller's Hill area (not able to be shown because of the scale of the map) and was also in a sense a smaller version, on the Suffolk side of the River Yare, of its larger Norfolk neighbour.

4   The apostrophe s (though it was still centuries away, before its use became standard) is employed here for the purposes of clarity and simplicity. The freeman, Ali, is one of the two Dunston tenants named in Domesday.

5   Northville was located at the extreme northern end of Gorleston, becoming part of Little Yarmouth/ Southtown when that community had formed. Its chapel, dedicated to St. Mary, occupied a site on the west side of what is now Southtown Road, not far from where Southtown railway station once stood. Given the fact that it was relatively close to the crossing-place providing access to Yarmouth (probably a ferry), it might well have been a wayfarers's chapel. It was demolished in 1548, probably as a result of Edward VI's suppression of the chantries.

6   For a detailed account of the history of St. Margaret's church, see Butcher, *Medieval Lowestoft*, Chapter 6.

7   This work of construction eventually caused a collapse of the fort's perimeter wall, which has long been a feature of the place.

8   In all probability, this change-over would have lasted some considerable while (perhaps decades), until the fully recognisable Norman (Romanesque) architectural style had become universally adopted.

9   Their dedications are of particular interest within the local context, as Edmund was patron saint of both Suffolk and England. It is highly unlikely that there could have been any early connection between him and Fritton, so might the dedication of its church to him have been a way of local people maintaining their Anglo-Saxon identity in the face of a foreign take-over? Margaret of Antioch had five churches dedicated to her in north-east Suffolk (three of them in Lothingland) and nine in south-east Norfolk – all of them in communities associated one way or another with Roger Bigot, Sheriff of Norfolk and Suffolk, who may have adopted Margaret as his religious patron.

10 Its replacement of the following year was constructed slightly less than half a mile away to the west, on land given by the local ruling family (close to its seat). It is a wonderfully idiosyncratic building by Samuel Teulon, in Gothic style, with squat, octagonal, central tower and superb Burne Jones windows in the chancel.

11 There was a short-lived church of some kind in the hamlet of Thorpe, located in the south-western sector of the parish (not indicated on Map 6), but little is known of its existence other than its transitory presence.

12 There was possibly another ten acres in Lothingland to be added to its total, while Mutford had a further ten acres located in Ellough and an outlier of twenty-four acres in Willingham – both communities belonging to the adjacent Wangford Hundred.

13 This was constructed as a means of bypassing Great Yarmouth, but it did not succeed commercially.

14 This court was referred to as the *Tourn* – a long-established term used of the county sheriff's yearly visit to all the jurisdictions under his control. Two minute-books of its proceedings, for the years 1588-94 and 1595-1612, have survived for Lothingland transactions, but not for those of Mutford: Suffolk Record Office (Lowestoft) 192/4 & 194/C1/1. In 1763, both half-hundreds were combined into a single jurisdiction, Mutford & Lothingland, for the purposes of poor law administration.

15 Barnby, 80 acres; Beckton, 120 acres; Kirkley, 160 acres; Pakefield, 30 acres; and Rushmere, 33 acres.

16 Nine other freemen, who helped to work a 360-acre holding, are recorded as living in Rushmere (2), Gisleham (2), Pakefield (3) and Kirkley (2). Again, a multiplier of 4.75 has been applied (see fn. 1 above).

17 Beckton took its name from this water-course, which has survived in part down to the present day.

18 This waterway formed much of the boundary between the Lothing/Mutford and the Blything/Wangford jurisdictions – hence the name.

19 In theory at least, one team of eight oxen was supposed to be able to plough one hide of land (120 acres) in a calendar-year, which makes the combined acreage of church and free-holding able to be cultivated on the resources available.

20 The complex history of Pakefield and its church(es) cannot be recounted here, fascinating though it is. Recourse is recommended to B.P.W. Stather Hunt, *Flinten History*, 7th ed. (Lowestoft, 1953), written by the parish rector of 1927-53.

21 Pakefield's total area, following its absorption of Beckton and part-Rothenhall, was only 771 acres. It must have been far smaller at Domesday.

22 The Scandinavian element in Mutford Half-hundred place-names is not as evident as it is in Lothingland (Barnby being the most obvious example), but is present nevertheless. See Appendix 3.

23 W.A. Copinger, *The Manors of Suffolk*, vol. 5 (Manchester, 1909), p. 69. Gilbert de Coleville had what may be termed an earlier toe-hold in Suffolk as a sub-tenant of Robert Malet in the following Domesday communities: Clopton (Carlford), Rendlesham (Loes), Bromeswell (Wilford) and Stokerland (Wilford).

24 Interestingly, medieval dedications to Edmund are not common in East Anglian parishes. Altogether, there are six in Suffolk and twelve in Norfolk. See Appendix 6.

25 A. Suckling, *The History and Antiquities of the County of Suffolk*, vol. 1 (London, 1846), pp. 271-2. No reference is made to sokemen in the Domesday data.

Appendix 1

Individual Church Land Valuations (1086)

Table 14. Norfolk Churches (West and East) land values

	Community	Land etc.	Value	Reference
Brothercross	Colkirk	40 acres	2s (½d)	10.6 (m)
Clackclose	Barton (Bendish)	24 acres	2s (1d)	31.21 (m)
	Beechamwell	30 acres	2s 6d (1d)	9.233 (m)
	Bexwell (rt)	24 acres	16d (¾d)	66.9 (f)
	Boughton	20 acres	20d (1d)	31.25 (m)
	Shouldham (All Saints & St. Margaret) (2)	73 acres (combined)	6s 1d (1d)	31.22 (2m)
	Stoke (Ferry) (¼ & 1 = 2)	5 acres & 27 acres	5d (1d) & 27d (1d)	31.26 (2f)
	Stow (Bardolph)	53 acres	3s (¾d)	13.7 (m)
	(Shouldham) Thorpe (½)	16 acres	12d (¾d)	66.14 (f)
	Wallington	26 acres	16d (½d)	66.16 (f)
Docking	(Bircham) Newton	20 acres	12d (½d)	20.1 (m)
Freebridge	Appleton	12 acres	12d (1d)	9.7 (m)
	Congham	120 acres, + manorial assets & personnel	20s (2d)	8.27 (m)
	Flitcham	8 acres	8d (1d)	9.4 (f)
	Pentney	30 acres	2s 8d (1d)	9.2 (m)
	(West) Walton (½ & ½ = 1)	7 acres, free, & 15 acres	12d (2d) & 2s (1½d)	15.29n (u) & 66.21 (f)
Gallow	(Pudding) Norton	8 acres	6d (¾d)	1.16 (u)
North Greenhoe	Stiffkey	30 acres	2s (¾d)	21.25 (m)

Hundred	Place	Land	Value	Valuation
South Greenhoe	(East & West) Bradenham	15 acres	15d (1d)	31.34 (m)
	(Great) Cressingham (2)	20 acres & 15 acres	20d (1d) & 15d (1d)	10.1 (m) & 22.4 (o)
	(North & South) Pickenham (rt)	17 acres	17d (1d)	22.3 (o)
Grimshoe	Feltwell (rt) (2)	No info. (8.37) & 30 acres, free (15.29n)	4s. (1½d)	8.37 (f) & 15.29n (u)
	Northwold	12 acres, free	18d (1½d)	15.29n (u)
Guiltcross	(Blo) Norton	5 acres	10d (2d)	14.8 (m)
Launditch	(North) Elmham	60 acres & 1 plough	5s 4d (1d)	10.5 (m)
	(East & West) Lexham (rt)	30 acres	16d (½d)	20.8 (m)
	Swanton (Morley)	1½ acres	2d (1½d)	20.7 (m)
	Tittleshall	6 acres	5d (1d)	31.38 (m)
Shropham	Bridgham	12 acres, free	2s (2d)	15.29n (u)
	Wilby	10 acres	3s (3½d)	19.11 (m)
Wayland	Griston	24 acres	2s (1d)	49.4 (o)
	Watton (rt)	20 acres	20d (1d)	9.11 (m)
	West Carbrooke	20 acres	12d (½d)	49.5 (m)
33 communities	37 churches (22m, 3o, 7f, 5u)			
Blofield	Bradeston	10 acres	10d (1d)	10.76 (m)
	(North) Burlingham (2)	30 acres & 10 acres	2s 8d (1d) & 10d (1d)	10.68 (f) & 10.73 (f)
	South Burlingham (½)	15 acres	15d (1d)	10.74 (f)

Letha		5 acres	5d (1d)	10.72 (f)
	Postwick	20 acres	2s (1¼d)	24.6 (m)
Clavering	Aldeby	12 acres	2s (2d)	20.36 (m)
	Kirby (Cane) (rt)	20 acres, in alms	20d (1d)	14.41 (m)
	Thurketeliart	20 acres	40d (2d)	20.36 (m)
	Wheatacre (2)	60 acres, in alms (combined)	5s (1d)	31.17 (2m)
Depwade	Tharston	40 acres	3s (1d)	9.99 (m)
Diss	Bressingham	15 acres	2s (1½d)	14.24 (m)
	Dickleburgh	30 acres	3s (1¼d)	14.29 (m)
	Shelfhanger	16 acres	2s. 6d (2d)	14.32 (f)
	Shimpling (rt)	10 acres	12d (1d)	9.46 (m)
	Tivetshall (2)	40 acres (combined)	7s 6d (2¼d)	14.23 (2m)
Earsham	Pulham (2)	2 acres (combined)	3d (1½d)	15.29n (2u)
	Thorpe (Abbots) (rt)	12 acres	2s (2d)	14.18 (m)
North Erpingham	Sheringham	15 acres	4s (3¼d)	19.18 (m)
South Erpingham	Buxton	30 acres, in alms	3s (1¼d)	20.29 (m)
	Corpusty (¾)	9 acres	6d (¾d)	19.34 (u)
	Erpingham	6 acres	6d (1d)	30.6 (f)
	Oxnead	24 acres	2s (1d)	61.2 (m)
Eynsford	Helmingham (2)	10 acres (combined)	8d (¾d)	10.16 (2m)
	Hindolveston	26 acres	20d (¾d)	10.15 (m)
	(Wood) Norton (1/3)	2½ acres	4d (1¾d)	10.15 (o)

Hundred	Place			
East Flegg	Weston (Longville)	12 acres	4d (¼d)	19.32 (o)
	Scratby	36 acres	3s (1d)	10.43 (f)
	Stokesby	23 acres & 3 acres meadow	16d (¾d)	19.36 (m)
	Thrigby	5 acres	6d (1d)	19.37 (f)
	Yarmouth	? (no info.)	20s (?)	1.68 (u)
West Flegg	Billockby (2/3)	7 acres	5d (¾d)	10.90 (m)
	Hemsby	20 acres	16d (¾d)	10.30 (m)
	Martham	50 acres	50d (1d)	10.86 (f)
Forehoe	Dykebeck (¼)	5 acres	5d (1d)	31.42 (m)
Happing	Walcott	20 acres	20d (1d)	36.5 (m)
	Waxham (2)	20 acres & 18 acres	16d (¾d) & 18d (1d)	4.40 (f) & 4.42 (m)
Henstead	Bixley	24 acres	2s (2s)	9.32 (m)
	Bramerton	24 acres	24d (1d)	9.28 (f)
	Caistor (St. Edmund)	11 acres	16d (1½d)	14.15 (m)
	Framingham (Earl & Pigot) (rt)	30 acres	3s (1¼d)	9.30 (f)
	Howe (rt)	15 acres	2s (1½d)	14.16 (m)
	Kirby (Bedon)	10 acres	12d (1¼d)	9.29 (f)
	Poringland (rt)	12 acres	12d (1d)	9.37 (f)
	Rockland (St. Mary)	12 acres	8d (¾d)	9.27 (f)
	Saxlingham (Nethergate)	10 acres	16d (1½d)	49.7 (m)
	Shotesham (All Saints & St Mary) (½ & ¼ = 1 or 2?)	15 acres & ?	15d (1d) & ?	9.24 (m) & 14.16 (f)

Hundred	Place	Acres	Value	Reference
Holt	Whitlingham	10 acres	12d (1¼d)	9.31 (m)
	Yelverton	20 acres	20d (1d)	9.36 (f)
	Blakeney (al. Snitterley)	30 acres	16d (½d)	10.56 (m)
	Briningham	12 acres – 2 refs. (same church)	12d (1d)	10.57 & 10.59 (m)
	Langham (2)	16 acres (combined)	16d (1d)	10.22 (2m)
	Melton (Constable)	6 acres	5d (1d)	10.58 (f)
	Thornage	32 acres	32d (1d)	10.8 (m)
Humbleyard	Bracon Ash	20 acres	2s (1¼d)	45.1 (u)
	Earlham	14 acres & ½ acre meadow	15d (1d)	1.206 (f)
	Eaton	14 acres	14d (1d)	1.205 (f)
	Hethersett (2)	60 acres & 8 acres	5s (1d) & 8d (1d)	4.52 (2m)
	Markshall	6 acres	12d (2d)	20.35 (m)
	Mulbarton	15 acres	2s (1½d)	20.34 (m)
Loddon	Chedgrave	50 acres & 1 acre meadow	2 orae [32d] (¾d)	31.44 (m)
	Claxton	30 acres	3s (1¼d)	9.56 (m)
	Kirstead [or Langhale]	12 acres	16d (1¼d)	14.38 (f)
	Loddon	60 acres & 4 meadow	5s (1d)	14.35 (m)
	Seething (rt) (3)	18 acres; 16 acres (combined)	2s (1¼d) & 2s (1½d)	9.25 (m) & 9.51 (2m)
	Torp	12 acres, free, + ½ plough	18d (1½d)	15.29n (u)

	Woodton (rt)	12 acres	12d (1d)	9.54 (f)
Mitford	(East) Dereham	30 acres, free, + 1 plough	4s (1½d)	15.29n (u)
	Mattishall	20 acres	16d (¾d)	20.16 (f)
	Thurestuna	16 acres	16d (1d)	9.134 (f)
	(North) Tuddenham (2)	20 acres (combined)	16d (¾d)	20.15 (2m)
Norwich	Norwich (St. Simon & St. Jude) – excluded from overall calculations	¾ of a mill, ½ acre meadow & 1 dwelling-house	20s	1.61 (u)
Taverham	Attlebridge	6 acres	6d (1d)	10.37 (f)
	Drayton	8 acres	16d (2d)	20.26 (m)
Tunstead	Barton (Turf) (2)	33 acres (combined)	15d (½d)	17.50 (2f)
	Sloley	1 acre	2d (2d)	20.33 (f)
	Swafield	28 acres, 2 acres meadow & 1 smallholder	2s (1d)	10.18 (f)
Walsham	Beighton	7 acres	7d (1d)	10.25 (m)
	Panxworth	8 acres	12d (1½d)	19.25 (m)
	Reedham	40 acres	6s 8d (2d)	19.24 (m)
	Tunstall	8 acres	8d (1d)	24.5 (m)
80 communities	92 churches (54m, 2o, 28f, 8u)			
113 communities, in all	129 churches (76m, 5o, 35f, 13u)			

Table details

- In this table, and the following one, rental values shown are those which appear to relate solely to church-endowments. The bracketed letter following each entry's reference number indicates whether the church was manorial (m), attached to a freeholding (f) or of uncertain status (u). The symbol (o), used five times (this table only), stands for *outlier* – meaning a manorial connection also.

- Bracketed figures in the value column are rental sums per arable acre to the nearest quarter of a penny (meadow not included).

- The highest value recorded is 3½d (Wilby, Shropham H.), the lowest ¼d (Weston Longville, Eynsford H.). The general range is 1d-2d, with a pronounced leaning towards the former. Welldon Finn, p. 174, cites values of 1d-6d per acre for Norfolk churches.

- Different rental values may reflect varying soil conditions and possible services and obligations attaching to the land. They probably indicate land leased out, not worked directly by the priest(s).

- With regard to *freely held land*, slender evidence (five examples) suggests slightly higher average rental values per acre (1½d-2d) than those recorded for Suffolk.

- Norfolk has 50% of its 256/258 recorded churches (exclusive of those listed in Norwich and Thetford) with rental values attached to the endowments of land – nearly double the rate of Suffolk.

- Welldon Finn, p. 175, says that land values are given for 116 Norfolk churches, with 144 having no rental data attached. The investigation here produces figures of 129 and 127/129.

- The Norwich church of St. Simon & St. Jude does not feature in calculations relating to the county as a whole, but has been shown here because of its valuation.

- In this table, and in the one which follows, use of bold font and added **(rt)** in the second column indicates the current existence of round-tower churches in the named communities.

Table 15. Suffolk Churches (West and East) land values

Hundred	Community	Land etc.	Value	Reference
*Blackbourn & °Brad-mere	°Ixworth	80 acres, free, 1 plough & 1 acre meadow	5s (¾d)	66.1 (m)
	*°Walsham (le Willows) (½)	10 acres & 1 acre meadow	8d (¾d)	66.2 (m)
Cosford	Hadleigh	120 acres, free, 1 plough & 1 mill	12s (1d)	15.2 (m)
Risbridge	Dalham	40 acres & ½ plough	5s (1½d)	25.6 (m)
	Poslingford	40 acres, free	6s (1¾d)	33.2 (f)
	Stoke (by Clare)	60 acres	10s (2d)	25.97 (f)
	Stradishall	30 acres	5s (2d)	25.100 (f)
7 communities	7 churches (4m, 3f)			
Bishop's	Horham	22 acres	22d (1d)	64.3 (m)
	Syleham (rt)	16 acres	2s (1½d)	44.2 (m)
	Weybread (rt) (½)	8 acres & ½ plough	16d (2d)	6.312 (m)
	Wingfield	24 acres	4s (2d)	21.45 (m)
Blything	Bramfield (rt)	28 acres, free, & ½ plough	3s(1¼d)	3.3 (m)
	Brampton	16 acres	16d (1d)	33.5 (f)
	Cratfield	6 acres	6d (1d)	33.10 (m)
	Darsham	6 acres	12d (2d)	1.13 (m)
	Frostenden (rt) (2)	28 acres (combined) & 1 plough	2s (1d)	33.6 (2m)
	Huntingfield	14 acres	2s (1¾d)	6.80 (m)
	Middleton	15 acres	2s (1¾d)	26.13 (m)

Hundred	Place			
	Opituna	4 acres & ½ acre	3d (¾d)	7.29 (m)
	Reydon (2)	120 acres (combined)	10s (1d)	33.4 (2m)
	Ubbeston	3 acres	3d (1d)	33.9 (m)
	Walpole	16 acres & ½ meadow	12d (¾d)	3.4 (f)
	Westleton	20 acres	40d (2d)	6.85 (m)
Bosmere	Ash(bocking)	3 acres	6d (2d)	1.73 (m)
	Blakenham	1 acre	2d (2d)	9.1 (m)
	Coddenham (5)	12½ acres & 8 acres; 3 acres & 1 acre; 3 acres	25d & 16d; 6d & 2d; 6d (all 2d)	7.67(2u), 16.20 (2m) & 34.9 (m)
	Hemingstone (½ & 1 = 2)	15 acres & 3 acres	30d (2d) & 6d (2d)	8.59 (2f)
	Offton	16 acres	33d (2d)	7.60 (m)
	"Olden" (*Uledana*)	7½ acres	15d (2d)	16.21 (f)
	(Earl & Little) Stonham (1, 1 & ¼ = 3)	7½ acres, 2 acres & 7½ acres	15d, 4d & 15d (all 2d)	16.22 (2m) & 34.11 (u)
Carlford	*Aluresdetuna*	12 acres	12d (1d)	39.12 (m)
	(Great) Bealings	20 acres	40d (2d)	67.11 (m)
	Clopton	15 acres	2s (1¾d)	34.15 (m)
	Culpho	10 acres	20d (2d)	8.5 (f)
	Martlesham	36 acres	3s (1d)	39.6 (m)
	Newbourn	12 acres	16d (1¼d)	39.10 (f)
	Playford	10 acres	20d (2d)	6.112 (m)
	Rushmere (St. Andrew)	20 acres	40d (2d)	3.19 (f)
Colneis	"Alston" (*Alteinestuna*)	5 acres, free	16d (3d)	7.96 (f)

Hundred	Place	Land	Valuation	Reference
	Burgh	12 acres	2s (2d)	7.80 (m)
	Hemley	8 acres	2s (3d)	39.5 (f)
	Kirton	6 acres	12d (2d)	7.114 (f)
	Levington	8 acres	12d (1½d)	7.117 (f)
	Stratton	10 acres	2s (2½d)	7.119 (u)
	Trimley (2)	20 acres & 8 acres	40d (2d) & 8d (1d)	7.97 (2m)
	Walton	8 acres	16d (2d)	7.76 (m)
Hartismere	Bacton	24 acres	3s (2½d)	41.7 (m)
	Brome (rt)	14 acres	2s (1¾d)	7.75 (m)
	Cotton (½)	11 acres	2s (2¼d)	1.95 (f)
	Finningham	26 acres	4s (1¾d)	14.131 (f)
	Oakley (²/₃?)	12 acres	16d (1¼d)	14.129 (m)
	Stuston (rt)	24 acres & ½ acre meadow	4s (2d)	14.137 (f)
	Thrandeston (2)	6 acres & 8 acres	12d (2d) & 16d (2d)	6.66 (f) & 14.139 (m)
	Wickham (Skeith)	12 acres	2s (2s)	8.31 (m)
	Wortham (rt) (2)	40 acres (combined)	7s (2d)	11.4 (2m)
Ipswich	Ipswich (2 – St. Peter and St. Julian)	91 acres (in Thurleston) & 20 acres	15s (2d) & 40d (2d)	25.62 (u) & 74.9 (u)
Loes	Brandeston	12 acres	2s (2d)	47.3 (m)
	Charsfield	36 acres	3s (1d)	6.179 (f)
	Cretingham	18 acres & 8 acres	3s (2d) & 16d (2d)	4.18 (m) & 52.5 (m)
	Hoo	8½ acres	16d (2d)	21.95 (m)

	Kettleburgh	16 acres	3s (2¼d)	3.34 (m)
	Letheringham	20 acres	40d (2d)	32.14 (m)
	Marlesford	16 acres	2 ora(e) [32d] (2d)	1.94 (m)
	Martley	12 acres	2s (2d)	3.52 (f)
	Monewden	30 acres & 1½ acres meadow	5s (2d)	8.22 (f)
	Rendlesham	20 acres	40d (2d)	6.281 (m)
	Staverton	10 acres	20d (2d)	6.260 (m)
	Woodbridge	19 acres	2s (1¼d)	6.287 (f)
Lothing	Barnby	80 acres	2s (¼d)	4.39 (f)
	Rushmere (rt) (¼)	8 acres	16d (2d)	31.34 (f)
Lothingland	Flixton	120 acres (+manorial appurtenances)	20s (2d)	19.21 (m)
	Somerleyton (rt) [later became Blundeston]	20 acres	3s (1¼d)	1.52 (m)
Plomesgate	Boyton (2)	30 acres (combined)	5s (2d)	6.138 (2f)
	Snape	8 acres	16d (2d)	6.133 (f)
	Sudbourne	16 acres	2s (1½d)	6.143 (m)
Wangford	**Barsham (rt)** (½)	20 acres	3s (1¾d)	7.40 (m)
	Bungay (rt) (4)	12 acres, 8 acres & 30 acres; 2 acres & 2 acres meadow [meadow not included in the valuation]	2s (2d) 12d (1½d) & 3s (1¼d); 40d (20d)	1.111 (2m & f) & 4.19 (m)
	(South) Elmham (rt) ($1^{1}/_{5}$ + 3 = 5)	8 acres & 6 acres; 30 acres (combined)	12d comb. (1d) & 5s comb. (2d)	13.6 (2m) & 19.16 (3f)
	Flixton (½)	10 acres	16d (1½d)	53.5 (m)
	Ilketshall (rt)	20 acres	2s (1¼d)	4.26 (m)

	Land	Value	Reference
Mettingham (rt)	20 acres	3s (1¾d)	4.21 (m)
Ringsfield (2)	15 acres & 20 acres	2s 8d (2d) & 3s (1¾d)	1.16 (m) & 1.20 (u)
Weston (2)	20 acres & 20 acres	3s (1¾d) & 3s (1¾d)	1.21 (f) & 1.113 (f)
Willingham	40 acres	7s (2d)	31.21 (f)
Worlingham (3) – one (rt)	40 acres (combined) & 5 acres	6s (1¾d) & 12d (2½d)	1.22 (2u) & 14.121 (u)
Wilford			
Alderton	24 acres & 1 acre meadow	3s (1½d)	6.159 (f)
Bawdsey	20 acres	3s (1¾d)	6.161 (f)
Boyton	8 acres	12d (1½d)	6.172 (m)
Bredfield (2)	36 acres & 31 acres free + 2 acres meadow	3s (1d) & 5s (2d)	6.182 (u) & 21.85 (u)
Bromeswell (2)	6 acres & 16 acres	6d (1d) & 2s (1½d)	6.249 (f) & 21.83 (m)
Capel (St. Andrew)	12 acres	2s (2d)	6.183 (f)
Debach	8 acres	16d (2d)	46.10 (f)
Hollesley	14 acres	2s (1¾d)	6.148 (m)
Loudham	60 acres	5s (1d)	22.3 (f)
Shottisham	13 acres	32d (2½d)	6.238 (m)
88 communities			
116 churches (66m, 38f, 12u)			
95 communities, in all			
123 churches (70 m, 41f, 12u)			

Table details

- Bracketed figures in the value column are rental sums per acre to the nearest quarter of a penny.

- The highest value recorded is 20d (Bungay 4.19, Wangford H.), the lowest ¼d (Barnby, Lothing H.) – both being out-of-line extremes. A more realistic high of 3d ("Alston" and Hemley. Colneis H.) and a low of ¾d (Ixworth and Walsham le Willows, Blackbourn & Babergh H., and *Opituna* and Walpole, Blything H.) are best accepted. The general range is 1d-2d, with a loading towards the latter. Welldon Finn, p. 172, states that values of 1d-6d per acre were common in Suffolk.

- Different rental values may reflect varying soil conditions and possible services and obligations attaching to the land.

- With regard to *freely held land*, slender evidence (five examples) suggests slightly lower average rental values per acre than those for Norfolk, but a greater range of payments (¾d-3d).

- Suffolk has 27% of its 448+ recorded churches (exclusive of Bury and Ipswich) with rental values attached to the endowments of land – slightly more than half the proportion appertaining to Norfolk.

- The Ipswich churches of St. Peter and St. Julian do not feature in earlier calculations relating to the county as a whole, but have been shown here because of their valuations. The former also had a major manor of 720 acres, with appurtenances, valued at £15 (25.52).

- The church of St. Peter, Eye, with a 240-acre manor and valuation of 40s. (6.191), cannot have a rental of 2d per acre attached because 3 acres of meadow and a mill also formed part of the price.

- The pronounced disparity between West Suffolk and East (with regard to the number of churches having land-valuations) is probably due to the dominance of Bury Abbey in the former sector, with its church-estates under direct control of the foundation, not leased out to third parties.

- Somerleyton is indicated as having a round tower – though it later became the church of neighbouring Blundeston, after boundary changes, and remains as such today.

Table 16. Church land-values recorded in 1086 (ecclesiastical bodies & persons)

Agency/Personage	County	All churches	Land valued	Communities
Bishop of Thetford	Norfolk (West)	4	3	Colkirk (Brothercross) – d
				(Gt.) Cressingham (S. Greenhoe) – d
				(North) Elmham (Launditch) – d
	Norfolk (East)	22	20	*Bradeston (Blofield) – p
				(North) Burlingham (Blofield) – p
				South Burlingham (Blofield) – p
				Letha (Blofield) – p
				Helmingham (Eynsford) – d
				Hindolveston (Eynsford) – d
				(Wood) Norton (Eynsford) – d
				Scratby (East Flegg) – p
				(Gt.) Yarmouth (East Flegg) – p
				*Billockby (West Flegg) – p
				Hemsby (West Flegg) – p
				Martham (West Flegg) – p
				*Blakeney (Holt) – p
				*Briningham (Holt) – p
				*Langham (Holt) – p
				*Melton (Constable) (Holt) – p
				Thornage (Holt) – d
				*Attlebridge (Taverham) – p
				Swafield (Tunstead) – d

Abbey	Region			Church
				Beighton (Walsham) – p
	Suffolk (East)	2	8	Flixton (Lothingland) – p?
				(South) Elmham (Wangford) – d
Bury Abbey	Norfolk (West)	1	1	(Blo) Norton (Guiltcross)
	Norfolk (East)	11	14	Kirby (Cane) (Clavering)
				Bressingham (Diss)
				Dickleburgh (Diss)
				Shelfanger (Diss)
				Tivetshall (Diss)
				Thorpe (Abbots) (Earsham)
				Caistor (St. Edmund) (Henstead)
				*Howe (Henstead)
				*Shotesham (All Saints & St. Mary) (Henstead)
				Kirstead (Loddon)
	Suffolk (West)	0	63	Loddon (Loddon)
	Suffolk (East)	5	16 (17)	Finningham (Hartismere)
				Oakley (Hartismere)
				Stuston (Hartismere)
				Thrandeston (Hartismere)
				Worlingham (Wangford)
Ely Abbey	Norfolk (West)	4	5	(West) Walton (Freebridge)

	Place		County	
	Feltwell (Grimshoe)			
	Northwold (Grimshoe)			
	Bridgham (Shropham)			
	Pulham (St. Mary Magdalen & St. Mary the Virgin) (Earsham)	3	Norfolk (East)	3
	Torp (Loddon)			
	(East) Dereham (Mitford)	0	Suffolk (West)	9
	Wingfield (Bishop's)	4	Suffolk (East)	13 (24)
	Hoo (Loes)			
	Bredfield (Wilford)			
	Bromeswell (Wilford)			
St. Benet's Abbey	*Billockby (West Flegg)	3	Norfolk (East)	12
	*Waxham (Happing)			
	Barton (Turf) (Tunstead)			
Elmham Diocese	*Shimpling (Diss) – *p*	2	Norfolk (East)	2
	*Shotesham (All Saints & St. Mary) (Henstead) – *p*			
	*Brome (Hartismere) – *p*	3	Suffolk (East)	3
	Bungay (Wangford) – *p*			
	Weston (Wangford) – *p*			

	Suffolk (West)	Suffolk (East)	
Canterbury Cathedral	2	1	Hadleigh (Cosford) – *d*
Bishop of Bayeaux	11	3	*Coddenham (Bosmere) – *p*
			*"Olden" (Bosmere) – *p*
			*(Earl & Lt.) Stonham (Bosmere) – *p*
Bishop of Evreux	1	1	*Loudham (Wilford) – *p*

Table details

- Communities marked with an asterisk preceding their names are ones in which church estates changed hands between 1066 and 1086.

- Use of *d* and *p* in communities (mainly in East Norfolk) having church-estates under the influence of the Bishop of Thetford – previously Elmham – indicate which were diocesan assets (*d*) and which were part of his personal estate (*p*). Æthelmær, or Ælmer (1047-70) had acquired most of the properties during his episcopacy, preceded by his brother Stigand (1043-7). After his ejection, he was succeeded by Herfast (1070-84) and William de Beaufeu (1084-91). It seems to have been policy to lease most of the glebe-land held. The letters are also used for other clerics.

- Bracketed figures in the third column (for the abbeys at Bury and Ely) indicate the total number of churches held in 1066.

- Bury Abbey leased the great majority of its Norfolk church-estates, but seems to have had the whole of its numerous West Suffolk holdings worked by the priesthood (without or without associates) – perhaps because direct control was easier to impose in the area(s) closest to it. In East Suffolk, five of its six leased estates were located in Hartismere – one of the two hundreds in that part of the county (the other being Stow) nearest to the town of Bury. The abbey also had influence in Wortham prior to 1066, but by 1086 that estate was part of Ralph of Beaufour's fiefdom.

- Ely Abbey, like Bury, had none of its West Suffolk church-lands rented out and only four of its East Suffolk equivalents. After the Norman Conquest, it lost direct control of nearly half of the churches it held to other tenants-in-chief – perhaps as punishment for actual, or perceived, involvement in Hereward's rebellion (1070-2). Eight of them were located in settlements in hundreds which formed part of its liberty: Bealings, Clopton and Culpho (Carlford); Hemley (Colneis); Brandeston, Kettleburgh and Monewden (Loes); Loudham (Wilford). Three others were in Bosmere: Coddenham (2) and Stonham.

- St. Benet Holm was very much a local institution, with churches held only in its own part of East Norfolk, and with all of its estates (with or without churches) stated as being held for "provisions for the monks". Three-quarters of communities with glebe-land had it worked by the resident priests.

- Canterbury Cathedral had its two churched communities and three other West Suffolk estates used for the same purpose of supply.

- Odo of Bayeux had simply picked up three land-valued church estates as part of his substantial holding in Suffolk (mainly in the eastern sector), two of them having been previously under the influence of Ely Abbey.

- It seems, from evidence suggested in the table above, that Bury Abbey particularly favoured having glebe-land located close (or reasonably close) to it managed by the individual priests, but saw renting-out as a more convenient process in communities further removed. All of Ely's East Suffolk church-estates were, of course, a considerable distance from the mother-house!

In conclusion, Roffe, p. 76, suggests that a survey of churches belonging to the King's demesne (together with the ecclesiastical dues attaching thereto) was carried out in most English shires. In Norfolk, leaving Norwich and Thetford aside (where diocesan interests intervened), only 4 churches with land valuations feature as part of the royal estate in the county of Norfolk: Pudding Norton (Gallow), Yarmouth (East Flegg), and Earlham and Eaton (Humbleyard) – which leaves a further 9 or 10 foundations without values attached. In Suffolk, a further 14 glebe valuations are to be found in the county at large: Darsham (Blything), Ashbocking (Bosmere), Cotton (Hartismere), Marlesford (Loes), Somerleyton (Lothingland) and Bungay 3, Ringsfield 2, Weston 2 and Worlingham 2 (all Wangford). However, this does leave another 23 churches in both counties without assessments. Roffe, p. 237, further asserts that the only assets recorded in Domesday Book (including churches) were those which were liable for the payment of geld.

Appendix 2

Round-Tower Churches

Table 17. Domesday references to churched parishes, distinctive now for having round towers

Area	Community	Hundred	Ruined tower
West Norfolk	Barmer	Brothercross	
	Shereford		
	Beechamwell	Clackclose	
	Bexwell		
	Gayton Thorpe		
	Appleton	Freebridge	[Yes]
	Croxton	Gallow	
	Little Snoring		
	South Pickenham	South Greenhoe	
	Feltwell	Grimshoe	
	East Lexham	Launditch	
	Watton	Wayland	
	11		
East Norfolk	North Burlingham	Blofield	[Yes]
	Hales	Clavering	
	Heckingham		
	Kirby Cane		
	Raveningham		
	Stockton		
	Forncett St. Peter	Depwade	
	Fritton		
	Morningthorpe		
	Shimpling	Diss	
	Thorpe Abbots	Earsham	
	Aylmerton	North Erpingham	
	Thwaite	South Erpingham	
	Wolterton		[Yes]
	Haveringland	Eynsford	
	Framingham Earl	Henstead	
	Howe		
	Kirby Bedon		[Yes]
	Poringland		
	Whitlingham		[Yes]
	Intwood	Humbleyard	

	Swainsthorpe		
	Seething	Loddon	
	Woodton		
	Taverham	Taverham	
	Witton	Tunstead	
	22		
West Suffolk	Rickinghall Inferior	Blackbourn & Bradmere	
	Aldham	Cosford	
	Little Bradley	Risbridge	
	Little Welnetham	Thedwestry	[Yes]
	Hengrave	Thingoe	
	Risby		
	Little Saxham		
	6		
East Suffolk	Syleham	Bishop's	
	Weybread		
	Bramfield	Blything	
	Frostenden		
	Thorington		
	Wissett		
	Ashfield	Claydon	[Yes]
	Brome	Hartismere	
	Stuston		
	Wortham		
	Mutford	Lothing	
	Rushmere		
	Burgh Castle	Lothingland	
	Somerleyton [now Blundeston]		
	Higham	Samford	
	Onehouse	Stow	
	Barsham	Wangford	
	Bungay		
	South Elmham (All Saints)		
	Ilketshall (St. Andrew)		
	Mettingham		
	20		

Table details

- The total of 33 churches for Norfolk (11 West and 22 East) represents 26% of the current county total of 126 round-tower buildings. Ruined remains of towers are not included.

- The total of 26 churches for Suffolk (6 West and 20 East) represents 62% of the county total of 42 round-tower buildings – the latter including the Lothingland parishes of Belton, Bradwell, Burgh Castle and Fritton, which were annexed to Norfolk on 1 April 1974.

- The total number of round-tower churches cited for each county has been taken from the Round Tower Churches Society website, but there appears to be flexibility in the reckoning if other available calculations are taken into account. Stephen Hart, author of *The Round Tower Churches of England* (2003), gives figures of 127 for Norfolk and 43 for Suffolk, while William ("Bill") Goode, in his *East Anglian Round Towers and Their Churches* (1982), specifies 119 buildings for Norfolk (pp. 47-90) and 42 for Suffolk (pp. 93-109). The former total includes the surviving tower of St. Benedict, Norwich, but then a further 10 visible ruins of round towers are listed (pp. 91-2) to produce an overall total of 129. Suffolk is similarly increased by 3 ruins (pp. 109-10) to arrive at a figure of 45. Goode also refers to a further 17 Norfolk towers which have been recorded at one time or another, but are no longer in existence (p. 92), and to 6 such structures in Suffolk (p. 110).

- Stephen Heywood, 'Round-Towered Churches', in *Norfolk Atlas*, p. 60, subtracts the 4 Lothingland churches from the overall Suffolk number and adds them to Norfolk, giving those counties respective totals of 123 and 38, post-1974. He broadly agrees with Goode concerning ruined structures (giving 11 for Norfolk and 3 for Suffolk), but differs considerably as to those which have disappeared (10 for Norfolk and 2 for Suffolk).

- It is not known in detail what types of structure were present at Domesday (1086), but many (if not most) of the existing church round-towers are almost certainly of post-Conquest origins. A number of the earlier Anglo-Saxon churches would probably have been built of timber.

Appendix 3

Female Landholders (Norfolk)

Table 18. Freewomen (West Norfolk) landholders

Name	Community	Hundred	Tenant(s)	Size (acres)	Year	Reference
Æthelgyth	**Barton (Bendish)**	Clackclose	Herself 4 [free]men (eP & eJ) & 4 other [free]men (eJ)	240 1 plough	1066 1066	31.21 31.21
Æthelgyth	**Boughton**		Herself 7 sokemen (eJ)	120 30	1066 1066	31.25 31.25
(Anon)	Crimplesham		Herself 20 freemen (eP & eJ)	240 60	1066 1066	21.3 21.3
Æthelgyth	Fincham		Herself	120	1066	31.20
(Anon) [Æthelgyth?]	Fincham		Herself	240	1066	8.16
Æthelgyth	*Mildenhall [Lackford H., Suffolk]*		Herself	2 ploughs	1066	42.1
Æthelgyth	**Shouldham (All Saints & St. Margaret)** (Shouldham) Thorpe		Herself	4 ploughs	1066	31.22
Æthelgyth	(Shouldham) Thorpe		Herself 15 sokemen, attached	2 ploughs 23	1066 1066	31.22 31.22
Æthelgyth	(Shouldham) Thorpe & Tottenhill		Herself	110	1066	31.23
Æthelgyth	**Stoke (Ferry)**		13 freemen (eJ)	2 ploughs	1066	31.26
Æthelgyth	Wiggenhall		Herself	240	1066	31.24
Ælfgifu (Ælfeva)	Gayton	Freebridge	Herself 3½ freemen (attached?)	120 60	1066 1066	8.24 8.24
Ælfgifu (Ælfeva)	Grimston		Herself 7 freemen, attached	120 4	1066 1066	8.25 8.25
Wulfrun	Grimston		Herself 2 sokemen, attached 3 freemen, attached	120 3 4	1066 1066 1066	51.1 51.1 51.1

Name	Place	Hundred	Holder	Size	Date	Ref
Wulfrun	Hillington		Herself	255	1066	51.3
Ælfæd	Massingham		Herself	120	1066	8.29
Æthelgyth	(East and West) Bradenham	South Greenhoe	Herself 8 sokemen (eJ)	5 ploughs 1½ ploughs	1066 1066	31.34 31.34
Ælfgifu (Ælfeva)	Feltwell	Grimshoe	Herself	6 ploughs	1066	8.35
Olova	Sutton		Herself	240	1066	21.19
Ælfgifu (Ælfeva)	Wilton		Herself 8 sokemen, attached	8 ploughs 20 & ½ plough	1066 1066	8.34 8.34
(Anon)	Hunstanton	Smethdon	Herself	30	1066	1.209
(Anon)	Griston	Wayland	Herself	80	1066	1.138
Æthelgyth	Merton		Herself 29 sokemen (attached?)	390 240	1066 1066	31.35 31.35
Ældreda	Watton (rt)		Herself 15 sokemen, attached	600 82	1066 1066	9.11 9.11
Oia (classed as a freeman)	Burnham (Overy)		Herself	30	1086	1.147
Ealdgyth (Aldith) [Sole Norfolk female tenant-in-chief]	Wells (next- the-Sea)	North Greenhoe	Herself [Ketel, in 1066] 19 sokemen attached, living in Warham	240 240	1086 1086	60.1 60.1
Daughter of Payne (shared with Reynold the Priest)	Dunham	Launditch	Herself & Reynold (under her brother, Eadmund – tenant-in-chief)	480	1086	46.1

Table details

- Use of bold font indicates church presence, with an added **(rt)** identifying a round-tower.

- (eP) indicates the exercise of patronage by women.

- (eJ) indicates the exercise of jurisdiction by women.

- The attachment of freemen or sokemen to an estate probably meant that they were under the patronage and jurisdiction of the landholder.

- Areas of arable land described in terms of plough-numbers, rather than in acres, can generally (but not totally) be reckoned at 120 acres per plough – that being the amount of soil (the *carucate*) acknowledged as being what a team of eight oxen could cultivate in one year. *Caruca* = plough.

- The Ælfgifu (Ælfeva) referred to may have been the mother of Earl Morcar of Northumberland.

- Aethelgyth also features in West Suffolk (Babergh & Lackford hundreds).

- Ealdgyth's name is found as Aldith in the version of the Domesday text used for this study.

- Brothercross (42%) and Guiltcross (25%) are the only two hundreds (out of a total of thirteen) in West Norfolk with no recorded freewomen. Their respective percentages of communities with churches are shown in brackets.

All the references relate to the pre-Conquest period, with the exception of three individuals – one of them (in Dunham) being a case of family tenure continuing and the other two (in Burnham and Wells) showing named Anglo-Saxon women as occupants. If the four anonymous freewomen (possibly from the lowest echelon of the freeman level of society) are regarded as individual people, the total number of recorded female tenants overall comes to thirteen. Æthelgyth was obviously a woman of importance (a fact noted in Welldon Finn, p. 7) and a likely factor in the founding of churches in those communities indicated as having them (five of her estates in ten Norfolk vills were recorded with churches). She had a similar significance in West Suffolk (with three or four churches located on lands held by her). Her social status is not indicated, but it must have been of an elevated nature (see fn. 2, p. 324). If Ælfgifu (Ælfeva) was indeed the mother of Earl Morcar, hers definitely was. Finally, with Aldreda holding a 600-acre manor, she too must have been of elevated status – 600 acres of arable land being the size of estate deemed suitable for the support of a thegn and his household.

Table 19. Freewomen (East Norfolk) landholders

Name	Community	Hundred	Tenant(s)	Size (acres)	Year	Reference
Bishop of Thetford's wife	Blofield	Blofield	Herself – shared with husband prior to his appointment 43 sokemen, attached	240 / 360	1066 / 1066	10.28 / 10.28
Wife of Godwine	Plumstead		Herself, following husband's decease / Bishop of Thetford (annexed, as woman had remarried within a year of husband dying)	120 / 120	c.1066 / After 1066	10.67 / 10.67
Freeman's wife (half of 40-acre holding with husband)	Tivetshall	Diss	Herself (uP & uJ – Bury Abbey?)	20	1066	10.93
Beorhtflæd	Starston	Earsham	Herself (uP)	240	1066	14.21
Wife of Ralph the Constable	Easton	North Erpingham	Shared with husband & later gifted to St. Benet Holm	120	1066	17.24
Mærwynn	Burgh (next Aylsham)	South Erpingham	Herself (uJ)	360	1066	30.5
(Anon)	Wickmere		Herself (uP)	24	1066	8.8
(Anon)	Billingford	Eynsford	Herself (uJ)	120	1066	39.2
(Anon) x 2	Bastwick	West Flegg	Themselves (uP)	13	1066	9.21
(Anon)	Bramerton	Henstead	Herself (uP) 2½ freemen (eJ)	16 / 6	1066 / 1066	66.80 / 66.80
(Anon)	Newton		Herself (uP & uJ)	120	1066	1.123
Wulfæt	Whitlingham		Herself (uP & uJ) 13 sokemen & 3 half-sokemen (uP & uJ)	160 / 43	1066 / 1066	9.31 / 9.31
(Anon) – held with son	Mulbarton	Humbleyard	Herself (uP)	30	1066	9.196

Ælgifu (Ælfeva)	(Wood) Rising	Mitford	Herself 8 freemen (attached?)	120 360	1066 1066	8.87 8.87
Æthelgyth	Yaxham?		Herself	4 wood & 1 meadow	1066	21.20
Stigand's sister	Norwich	Norwich	Herself (uP & uJ)	32	1066	1.61
Æthelgyth	**Wilby**	Shropham	Herself	120	1066	31.37
(Anon)	Taverham	Taverham	Herself 3 sokemen (attached?)	60 13	1066 1066	10.36 10.36
Ælfæd	(South) Walsham Outlier – Moulton (St. Mary)	Walsham	Herself 22 sokemen (attached?) Herself 3 sokemen (attached?)	480 80 120 18	1066 1066 1066 1066	1.150 1.150 1.150 1.150
Tofa (classed as a freeman)	(South) Walsham		Herself (uP & uJ) 17 sokemen (attached?)	120 120	1066 1066	12.6 12.6
Heloise, Bishop Herfast of Thetford's niece	Witton	Blofield	Herself, held from Bishop William	13	1086	10.81
Modgifu	Shelfanger	Diss	Herself (uP) 1 sokeman (attached?)	240 4	1086 1086	4.50 4.50
(Anon)	Norton (Sub-course)	Loddon [Clavering]	Herself (uP & uJ)	8	1086	9.55
(Anon) – attached to Hellington	Norton (Sub-course)	[Clavering]	Herself	16	1086	12.21
A poor nun (contested by Isaac)	Seething		Herself (previously under Ralph Wader)	4	1086	47.7

Table details

- Use of bold font indicates church presence.

- The question mark against Yaxham indicates possible church presence because of priest being recorded there.

- (uP) indicates women being under patronage.

- (eJ) undicates the exercise of jurisdiction by women, (uJ) their being under it.

- The attachment of freemen or sokemen to an estate probably meant that they were under the patronage and jurisdiction of the landholder.

- The Ælfgifu (Ælfeva) referred to may well have been the mother of Earl Morcar of Northumbria.

- Aethylgyth is probably the same woman who features prominently in West Norfolk.

- Clavering (69%), Depwade (50%), East Flegg (40%), Forehoe (4%), Happing (35%), Holt (21%), and Tunstead (45%) are the hundreds in East Norfolk (of which there were twenty in all) with no recorded freewomen. Their percentages of communities with churches are shown in brackets. The inclusion of Clavering is technically incorrect, since Norton Subcourse was (and still is) one of its communities – though also included in Loddon data from time to time, as shown here.

There is far less correlation apparent in this table between women and the founding of churches. Five of the references relate to the post-Conquest period, with three of them seeming to show unnamed women of low free status (in Norton and Seething), one of higher degree (Modgifu, in Shelfhanger) and the last of socially superior level (in Witton – the Bishop of Thetford's niece). Again, as in the previous table, if the eleven anonymous freewomen are regarded as individual people, the total number of recorded female tenants adds up to twenty-five – five of them identified by relationship to a specific male. Æthelgyth is once again associated with a community possessed of a church and another vill in which she held an interest had a priest. Four of the women recorded were of obvious high status: the wife of Æthelmær, Bishop of Thetford (known as Elmham diocese in 1066); the niece of his successor, Herfast; the wife of Ralph the Constable (al. Ralph de Gaël or de Guader – sometimes found referred to as Ralph the Staller); and the sister of Stigand, Bishop of Winchester and Archbishop of Canterbury – and also Bishop of Elmham, prior to his elevation. Further social distinction may be seen in the named and unnamed freewomen, the former almost certainly being of higher status within that level of society than their humbler counterparts from the *ceorl* category. Similarly, the "poor nun" referred to may not have been of sufficient status to be regarded worthy of having her name recorded for posterity.

The references to the four elevated male members of society, recorded by their association with female family members who held land, provide an interesting mini-study in office-holding (especially of an ecclesiastical nature) during the late Anglo-Saxon/Norman Conquest period. Æthelmær (al. Aelmer) was the younger brother of Stigand, the latter having preceded his sibling as Bishop of Elmham before moving on to more important positions in the Church. Stigand had presided over Elmham from 1043-47 and Æthelmær from 1047 onwards – being ultimately deprived of his office by papal authority in April 1070. Most ironically, this removal from office coincided with Stigand being removed from Canterbury at exactly the same time – his replacement being one of the most notable holders of the post in its whole history, Lanfranc. Stigand and Æthelmær were members of an East Anglian family (with possible Danish antecedents, on the evidence of the former's name) and, on the strength of the sister's estate in Norwich, may even have resided locally.[1]

The Bishop of Thetford, Herfast, was the man responsible for Elmham diocese changing its name, when he moved the centre of the see from North Elmham to Thetford in 1072. He was a Norman clergyman, who was appointed as William I's chief scribe or secretary after Hastings and who served him as Lord Chancellor from 1068-70. Ralph the Constable (or the Staller – the names being synonymous) was of Breton origins, reputedly born in Norfolk, who served in a military capacity under Edward the Confessor. He died in 1068 and his son, Ralph Wader (al. Waher or de Guader), having fought on the Norman side at Hastings, succeeded him. After resisting and defeating an invading Viking force in Norfolk, in 1069, he was made Earl of East Anglia, but fell from royal favour in 1075 by becoming involved against William I in the so-called Revolt of the Earls. After the rising had been put down and his English estates confiscated, he withdrew to the family barony of Gaël, in Brittany – de Gaël being a title also used to identify members of the family.

In both tables, the far smaller number of female landholders in 1086, contrasted with that in 1066, reflects the dispossession of the native population by the Normans and the diminished role of women in the newly established social order. However, given the ambiguous wording of the text, in places, it is possible that some of the tenants referred to as being in occupancy in 1066 might still have held the land twenty years later.

Notes

1   Stigand gained a reputation for acquisitiveness – some of it generated by later, medieval commentators – but there is no doubt that he was as much a politician and leading member of the royal circle as he was dedicated churchman.

Appendix 4

Female Landholders (Suffolk)

Table 20. Freewomen (West Suffolk) landholders

Name	Community	Hundred	Tenant(s)	Size (acres)	Year	Reference
Æthelgyth	**Shimplimg**	Babergh	Herself (uP)	780	1066	33.13
(Anon)	Bardwell	Blackbourn	Herself (uP)	10	1066	76.12
Ealdgyth	Hunston		7 freemen (eP)	60	1066	1.89
Ealdgyth	**Norton**		Herself (leased for life)	480	1066	1.88
(Anon)	Stanton		Herself (uP)	30	1066	76.8
(Anon)	Ash (Street)	Cosford	Herself	180	1066	2.14
Leofeva	Toppesfield		Herself	240	1066	15.3
Godgifu (Godiva)	Barton (Mills)	Lackford	Herself (uP & uJ))	60	1066	25.33
Æthelgyth	Mildenhall		Herself	4 ploughs	1066	ENf5 Norfolk 42.1
Æthelgyth	**Kedington**	Risbridge	Herself 25 freemen (eP & eJ)	600 240	1066 1066	33.1 33.1
Wulfæd	**Stansfield**		Herself	120	1066	25.78
Ealdgyth	**(Great & Little) Thurlow**		Herself	840	1066	1.90
Gode (Goda)	Wratting		Herself	270	1066	25.81
Ælfæd	Stanningfield	Thedwestry	Herself (sub Bury Abbey) 3 freemen (eP)	120 30	1066 1066	33.12 33.12
Ælfgyth [Æthelgyth?]	**Hargrave**	Thingoe	Herself (uP)	480	1066	54.2
Richere [Æthelgyth, 1066?]	**Poslingford**	Risbridge	4 freeman estates	620	1086	33.2

Table details

- Use of bold font indicates church presence.

- (eP) indicates the exercise of patronage by women, (uP) their being under it.

- (eJ) indicates the exercise of jurisdiction by women, (uJ) their being under it.

- The attachment of freemen or sokemen to an estate probably meant that they were under the patronage and jurisdiction of the landholder.

- Wulflæd is classified as a freeman, which may suggest equality of status with male tenants rather than gender-bias against women.

- The sole reference to 4 ploughs (Mildenhall) translates as 480 acres.

All references, with one exception, relate to the pre-Conquest period – and the sole tenant of 1086, taking local geography into account, might well have been the successor of Æthylgyth.[1] If the three anonymous freewomen (probably of low status) are regarded as individual people, the total number of female tenants recorded in West Suffolk comes to twelve (eleven, if Ælfgyth is a variant of Æthelgyth). This is a low number compared with the eastern sector and may have been due in part to the effect of Bury Abbey exercising such pronounced influence on tenancy. Female presence, such as it is, is most noted in the Blackbourn half of Blackbourn & Bradmere Hundred and also in Risbridge – the latter being the jurisdiction showing least influence overall from the Abbey. Æthelgyth has been previously identified as an important figure in West Norfolk and the same holds true here – though to a lesser extent.[2] All named freewomen may be regarded as having been of higher status than unnamed ones, with Ealdgyth (noting the size of her two major holdings) obviously a person of some substance. The description of her simply as *liba fem* ("free woman") probably rules out her being of noble birth – otherwise, the wife of Edward the Confessor or of Harold Godwinson might have been suggested as the land-holder. Both Ealdgyth herself and Æthelgyth seem to have had some kind association with five of the six churches recorded, with Richere added on for good measure. The disparity in tenant numbers between 1066 and 1086 shows the dispossession of Anglo-Saxon tenants following Hastings.

Table 21. Freewomen (East Suffolk) landholders

Name	Community	Hundred	Tenant	Size (acres)	Year	Reference
(Anon)	Chickering	Bishop's	Herself (uP & uJ)	8	1066	19.9
Ælfgifu (Ælfeva)	Darsham	Blything	Herself (uP & uJ)	46	1066	7.36
Asmoth (inc. as 1 of 6 freemen)	Middleton		Herself (uP & uJ), with 5 freemen	50	1066	4.15
Ælfgifu (Ælfeva)	Middleton		Herself (uP & uJ)	16	1066	7.39
Wife of Blackman – she, named "Bishop Stigand's man"	Sibton		Herself & husband – both (uP & uJ)	50	1066	6.93
(Anon)	Strickland		Herself (uP & uJ)	20	1066	7.37
Ælfgifu (Ælfeva)	Thorington		Herself (uP & uJ)	30	1066	7.38
Asmoth	UUrabretuna		Herself (uP)	30	1066	6.91
(Anon) [Asmoth?]	Warabetuna		Herself (uP & uJ)	100	1066	7.11
Leofeva	Coddenham	Bosmere	Herself (uJ)	10	1066	16.20
Wife of Æthelric, freeman	Mickfield		Herself, solo (uJ), then with husband	60 & 2 meadow	1066	14.38
Ælfæd	(Earl & Little) Stonham		Herself (uP & uJ)	240	1066	8.55
Ælfæd	Willisham		Herself (uP & uJ)	240	1066	8.56
Wife of Lustwine	Hasketon	Carlford	Herself & husband – both (uP & uJ)	40	1066	6.118
(Anon)	"Finesford"		Herself	½	1066	29.14
(Anon)	Grundisburgh		Herself & husband – both (uP)	60	1066	4.16
Wife of Eadwold, freeman	Otley		Herself & husband – both (uP)	240	1066	8.11

Holder	Vill	Hundred	Tenure	Acres	Date	Ref
Ælfæd	**Otley**		Herself (uP & uJ)	180	1066	52.1
Leoflæd	Otley		16½ freemen (eP)	69	1066	52.1
Ealdgyth (Aldgyth)	Tuddenham		Herself (uP)	6	1066	67.15
Queneva (mother of Brihtmær)	Waldringfield Preston, Haspley & **Newbourn**		Herself (uP) / 28 freemen in the 3 vills (all eP)	180 / 400	1066 / 1066	14.117 / 39.8, 9 & 10
Leoflæd (classed as freeman)	*Leofstanestuna*	Colneis	Herself (uP), with 7 freemen	12	1066	7.111
Wulfgifu (Wulfeva)	Morston		Herself (uP)	10	1066	39.4
Gode (Goda) of *Struostuna* (classed as freeman)	Stratton		Herself (uP), with 10 freemen & with Modgifu	87½	1066	6.110
Modgifu/Modgeva of Colcarr (classed as freeman)	Stratton		Herself (uP), with 10 freemen & with Gode	87½	1066	6.110
Thorild	*Struestuna*		Herself (uP)	55	1066	7.103
Ælfgifu (Ælfeva)	Walton		Herself (uP)	16	1066	21.50
Leofæva	Aspall	Hartismere	Herself (uP)	20	1066	16.48
Gode (Goda)	**Brome (rt)**		Herself (uP)	240	1066	7.75
(Anon) x2	Cotton		Themselves (uP)	5	1066	1.84
Wife of Alsi	Gislingham		Herself and husband leased from Bury Abbey (uJ)	240	1066	68.5
Menlæva	Mellis		Herself (uP & uJ)	14 (gifted to Bury Abbey)	Pre-1066	35.7
Ælfgifu (Ælfeva) – classed as freeman	Occold		Herself (uP & uJ), with 5 freemen	46	1066	6.193

Name	Place		Holding	Value	Date	Ref
Brihtflæd	Rickinghall (Superior)		Herself (uP & uJ]	150	1066	6.62
Ælflæd (recorded as freeman)	Wickham (**Skeith**)		Herself (uP)	240	1066	8.31
Modgifu/Modgeva [Godiva?]	**Wortham (rt)**		Herself (uP & uJ])	180	1066	11.4
Godgifu/Godgeva (Godiva)	**Wortham (rt)**		Herself (uP & uJ]	80	1066	11.4
Wife of Ælfwine [Ælflæd]	Wyverstone		Husband held (both uP & uJ]	100	1066	6.57
Ælflæd	Wyverstone		Herself (uP)	3	1066	6.57
Ælflæd (recorded as a freeman)	Wyverstone		Herself (uP & uJ], with 3 freemen (inc. husband, Ælfwine)	67	1066	6.211
Leoflæd	**Ipswich**	Ipswich	Herself	12, with St. Laurence's Church	Pre-1066	1.122f
Wife of Eadmund the Priest	**Brandeston**	Loes	Herself – shared with husband & gifted to the Church	60	1066	47.3
(Anon)	*Brodertuna*		Herself (uP)	4	1066	6.278
Leofæva	Charsfield		Herself (uP)	30	1066	32.9
Ieva	Framlingham		Herself (uP)	80	1066	6.264
(Anon)	Kettleburgh		Herself (uP)	14	1066	8.21
Godgifu (Godiva)	Rendlesham		Herself (uP)	60	1066	67.29
Ælflæd (classed as freeman)	**Wantisden**	Parham	Herself (uP) – shared with husband Ælfwine	7	1066	6.38

Wulfgifu (Wulfeva) - called "freeman"	(Great) Glemham	Plomesgate	Herself (uP & uJ) – shared with Wacra	20	1066	3.102
Tela	Brantham	Samford	Herself (uP)	30	1066	36.11
Wulfwaru	Raydon		Herself (uJ)	12	Pre-1066	5.8
Ælfæd	Creeting (St. Peter)	Stow	5 freemen (eP), + 2 others (under the King)	30	1066	8.53
(Anon)		Wangford	Herself (uP)	20	1066	4.26
	Ilketshall (rt)					
(Anon)	Darsham	Blything	Herself (father's gift, on marriage)	6	1086	7.36
Botild	(Great & Little) Bricett	Bosmere	Herself (uP)	20	1086	76.14
Ealdgyth (Aldgyth)	Creeting (All Saints, St. Mary & St. Olave)		Herself	½	1086	74.6
Leofæva	"Finesford"	Carlford	Herself (uP)	40	1086	21.70
(Anon)	Isleton		Herself (uP)	30	1086	21.66
Lictæva	Otley		Herself (uJ?)	1	1086	52.7
Tovild, Gunvati, Ealdgyth & Leofeva (classed as freemen)	**Whitton**	Claydon	Themselves (uJ), with 25 freemen	147½	1086	74.13
Godiva (classed as a freeman)	Morston	Colneis	Herself (uP), with 2 freemen	50	1086	7.90
Mild	Burgate	Hartismere	Herself (uP & uJ), with Wulfwaru and 18 freemen from nearby communities	90	1086	35.7

Wulfwaru	Mellis		Herself (uP & uJ), with Mild and 18 freemen from near-by communities	90	1086	35.7
(Anon)	Gislingham		Herself (uP)	15	1086	31.38
Leofsidu	Oakley		Herself (uP & uJ)	30	1086	14.138
Tutflæd (recorded as a freeman)	Benhall	Plomesgate	Herself (uP & uJ), with 6 freemen	44	1086	3.101

Table details

- Use of bold font indicates church presence, with an added **(rt)** identifying a round tower.

- (eP) indicates the exercise of patronage by women, (uP) being under it.

- (eJ) indicates the exercise of jurisdiction by women, (uJ) being under it.

- The attachment of freemen or sokemen to an estate probably meant that they were under the patronage and jurisdiction of the landholder.

- With the original Latin entries for Wortham having the two female names recorded as Modgeva and Godgeva, it is possible that one of the starting letters is an error and that the same woman is being referred to. Equally, the entries might also refer to two individuals.

- The names Ælfgifu (Ælfeva) and Wulfgifu (Wulfeva), in the table above, refer to women of free status who are probably not to be confused with the mother of Morcar, Earl of Northumbria.

Altogether, there are sixty-seven references to freewomen land-holders of one kind or another, producing a raw total of seventy people. Twelve of them are anonymous and a further six identified by reference to husbands. Eleven of the names (Ælfgifu, Ælflæd, Asmoth, Ealdgyth, Gode, Godgifu (Godiva), Leofæva, Leoflæd, Lictæva, Modgæva, Wulfwaru and Wulfgifu) are used more than once, but it has been possible to estimate the number of women bearing them by a combination of geographical location, size of holding and year of reference (1066 or 1086). Thus, there seem to have been four Ælfgifus, three Ælflæds, one Asmoth, two Ealdgyths, two Godes, three Godgifus (Godivas), four Leofævas, three Leoflæds, one Lictæva, two Modgævas, two Wulfwarus and two Wulfgifus – adding up to twenty-nine individuals.[3] Thirteen further women, named once only, complete the record and make an overall total of sixty identifiable females. This is ten more than the combined total of fifty for West Norfolk (thirteen), East Norfolk (twenty-five) and West Suffolk (twelve).[4]

Thirteen of the references appertain to the year of Domesday (1086), with all the others relating to the pre-Conquest period – again demonstrating the displacement of native tenants after Hastings. Three entries in the former category show anonymous tenants, at the lower level of the freeman class, but the rest record higher-status Anglo-Saxon women holding land from Norman overlords – with the majority of the estates being in what may be described as a "middle range" of size: twenty to fifty acres. Two others are very small (half an acre and one acre, respectively), while another two show much larger areas shared by a considerable number of tenants. The pre-Conquest data is the same, but much more extensive. It shows female Anglo-Saxon tenants, from a humble social level up to a more elevated one, holding a wide range of estates of different size (from three acres all the way up to 240, with about three-quarters of them being twenty acres or more). Altogether, sixteen churches (seventeen, if St. Laurence, Ipswich, is included) are seen to have been present in communities on, or near, land held by freewomen – and it may well have been the case that these tenants themselves had a hand in their establishment.

Other matters for discussion are generated by the data, the first being why East Suffolk should have had so many more freewomen than the western sector of the county and the whole of Norfolk combined. Regarding Norfolk, the eastern half of the county had twice as many freewomen as the western one and this can be suggested as being the likely result of it having nearly twice as many hundreds as its counterpart. Such arithmetic not will suffice as an explanation in the case of Suffolk. Yes, there was roughly the same disparity in terms of jurisdictions (seven in the west and sixteen in the east), but there was between six and seven times the number of freewomen in East Suffolk as in West. One explanation may lie in the dominance of Bury Abbey as the major land-holder in the western half, with its obviously long-standing connection with large numbers of freemen and sokemen simply not allowing for a notable female presence. It would be unwise to interpret this as deliberately partial or prejudicial in any way to women; it was probably more a matter of the particular way that patterns of tenure had evolved.

East Suffolk, on the other hand, was less obviously under the influence of any predominant organisation or individual. Even the five and a half hundreds which constituted the Liberty of St. Etheldreda (Carlford, Colneis, Loes, Parham, Plomesgate and Wilford) showed far less of a presence on the part of Ely Abbey than that exhibited by the one at Bury in West Suffolk, and the diocesan presence in Bishop's Hundred was hardly an overwhelming one either. Eadric of Laxfield appears to have been the most important secular presence in East Suffolk, both in terms of lands held and people under commendation to him, but another feature plain to see is the number of thegns and socially elevated freemen (and women) who were people of substance within the local context of the area in which they lived. The diversity seen, in terms of land-holding and social gradation within the freeman class, suggests a system of tenure which had been long in the making – possibly, as a result of the Scandinavian invasions and subsequent integrations of population which took place in the decades following (summarised in Warner, p. 195).

One interesting local feature in the extreme north-eastern corner of East

Suffolk is that the two half-hundreds there (Lothing and Lothingland) had no freewomen of any kind recorded in Domesday and, yet, the former had 70% of its recorded population in the freeman category. They are joined by Wilford, much further down the coast, to the south, where a zero score is also in evidence. Other low entries in the Survey are Bishop's (1), Claydon (1 – although a composite of four individual women), Stow (1), Wangford (1) and Plomesgate (2). Hartismere is, by some way, the hundred recorded with the greatest number of freewomen (16), with Carlford in second place (11) and Blything in third (7).

At this particular point, more than halfway through the sequence of Tables 18-23, it may be helpful to consider all the data presented. In terms of raw aggregation, Norfolk has eight places of worship which may show female influence in their founding and Suffolk forty-nine. This translates to 3% and 11% of each county's total number of churches, which may seem very small. However, these overall percentages do not reflect the geographical concentration(s) in certain parts of each county, to the exclusion of most others. Nor are they able to show the considerable difference in numbers between freemen holding land (on which churches were located) and their female counterparts. If it were possible to arrive at an accurate total of the former – which the writer, because of various inbuilt complications, has not managed to do – then the disparity in numbers would make any possible female founding-influence appear, proportionately, a little more significant.

Table 22. Aristocratic female landholders (whole county)

Name	Community	Hundred	Tenant	Size (acres)	Year	Reference
Abbess of Chatteris	**Kersey**	Costford	Her institution (eJ?)	420	1066 1086	24.1
Ælfgifu (Ælfeva), Earl Morcar's mother	Brandeston	Babergh	Herself (eJ?) 3 freemen (eP & eJ)	360 24	1066 1066	16.10 16.10
	(Great & Little) Cornard		Herself (eJ?)	360	1066	1.98
	Sudbury	Thingoe	Herself (eJ?)	360	1066	1.97
Wulfgifu (Wulfeva) [Ælfeva]	Kelsale	Bishop's	Herself (eJ?)	240	1066	7.3
	Bedingfield	Hartismere	1 freeman (eP)	½	1066	6.232
	Braiseworth		Herself (eJ)	60	1066	6.225
	Braiseworth		Alstan, freeman (eP)	30	1066	6.228
	Finningham		15 freemen (eP) – patronage shared with Leofric	180	1066	6.209
	Gislingham		3 freemen (2eP) 2 freemen (1eP) Sorcbes, freeman (eP)	7 26 (6) 6	1066 1066 1066	6.216 6.216 6.216
	Mellis		3 freemen (eP)	15	1066	6.227
	Occold		7 freemen (eP)	50	1066	6.224
	Rishangles		Herself (uP & eJ) 4 freemen (eP)	220 40	1066 1066	6.222 6.222
	Stoke (Ash)		Herself (uP & eJ) 5 freemen (eP & eJ)	160 32	1066 1066	6.213 6.213

Owner	Hundred	Place	Tenant	Value	Date	Ref
		Thorndon	Herself (uP & eJ)	400	1066	6.223
			Thorkell, freeman (eP)	30	1066	6.223
		Thornham (Magna)	24 freemen (eP)	132	1066	6.214
		Thornham (Magna)	Brihtmær (eP)	26	1066	6.215
			4 freemen (2½ eP)	108	1066	6.215
		Thornham Parva	8 freemen (eP)	28	1066	6.218
			2 freemen (1 eP)	15	1066	6.218
			Siric, freeman (eP)	14	1066	6.218
		Wickham (Skeith)	2 freemen (eP)	16	1066	6.230
		Yaxley	Hagris (eP)	15	1066	6.229
Adelaide, Countess of Aumâle	Babergh	Chadacre	Herself (eJ?)	120	1086	46.2
		Shimpling	Herself (eP & eJ)	600	1086	46.1
	Carlford	Burgh	2 freemen (eP?)	36	1086	46.8
		Clopton	Herself	140	1086	46.7
			Wulfwine the Priest	6	1086	46.7
		Clopton	12½ freemen (eP?)	92	1086	46.9
	Colneis	Hemley	1 villan (belonging in Clopton)	9	1086	46.6
	Loes	Charsfield & Monewden	(Sub-tenants?)	3 & 5	1086	46.12
	Samford	**Belstead**	Herself (eJ?)	400	1086	46.3
		Gusford	Herself (eJ?)	240	1086	46.5
		Harkstead	Herself (eJ?)	840	1086	46.4
	Wilford	Boulge	1 freeman	½	1086	46.11
		Debach	3 freemen (uP?)	20	1086	46.10
			1 church	8	1086	46.10

Robert Malet's mother [Élise]	Bedingfield	Bishop's	3 freemen (eP?)	44	1086	6.76
	Bedingfield		2 freemen (eP?)	26	1086	6.77
	Bedingfield		1 freeman (eP?)	½	1086	6.232
(In dispute with Odo, Bishop of Bayeux)	Bedingfield		2 freemen? (Cynric & Brihtheah, 1066)	40	1086	77.3
	Chippenhall		3 freemen (eJ)	80	1086	6.311
	Debenham (outlier to Kenton)	Claydon	Herself (from son)	120	1086	6.11
	Ulverston		Herself	8	1086	34.13
	Aspall	Hartismere	1 freeman (eP)?	30	1086	6.201
(In dispute with Odo, Bishop of Bayeux)	Aspall		4 freemen? (1066 holders named)	86	1086	77.4
	Eye		Herself (from son)	100	1086	6.191
	Finningham		Herself, from son –18 freemen (eP?)	180	1086	6.209
	Gislingham		2 freemen?	30 acres	1086	6.194
	Gislingham		21 freemen?	130 (10 holdings)	1086	6.216
	Harpole		Herself 10 freemen & 4 in Wickham Mkt (eP?)	100 / 29	1086 / 1086	6.251 / 6.251
	Harpole		1 freeman?	15	1086	6.253
	Mellis		1 freeman?	27	1086	6.195
	Occold		5 freemen?	46	1086	6.193
(In dispute with Odo, Bishop of Bayeux)	Occold		Herself (freeman Brihtheah in 1066)	20 (given by Stigand)	1086	77.1

(In dispute with Odo, Bishop of Bayeux)	Occold		1 freeman (Cynric in 1066)	20	1086	77.2
	Thornham Magna		1 freeman?	4	1086	6.200
	Thornham Parva		2 freemen?	7	1086	6.199
	Wickham (Skeith)		2 freemen?	16	1086	6.230
	Yaxley		1 freeman?	15	1086	6.229
	Kenton	Loes	Herself (from son)	82	1086	6.271
			2 freemen (eP?)	30	1086	6.271
			3 freemen (eP?)	4	1086	6.271
	Bawdsey	Wilford	12½ freemen?	72	1086	6.161
	Culeslea (outlier to Hollesley)		Herself (from son)	200	1086	6.156
	Halgestou		Herself	140	1086	6.176
Daughter of Roger of Rames	Langhedana	Bosmere	1 freeman (eJ?)	9	1086	38.9

Table Details

- Use of bold font indicates church presence.

- (eP) indicates the exercise of patronage by women, (uP) their being under it.

- (eJ) indicates the exercise of jurisdiction by women, (uJ) their being under it.

- The attachment of freemen or sokemen to an estate probably meant that they were under the patronage and jurisdiction of the landholder.

- Earl Morcar's mother, Ælfeva, is sometimes referred to by another version of her name, Wulfeva – with variant Anglo-Saxon forms existing as Ælfgifu and Wulfgifu. The larger estates (particularly manors) were held directly by her, the smaller ones being in the hands of freemen under patronage.

- The Countess of Aumâle was the sister of William I.

- Though it is not directly stated, the freemen occupying lands held by Élise Malet were probably under her patronage. In a minority of cases, she is described as holding particular estates from her son.

The women listed above were of higher social status than the ones recorded in Table 21 and have been classified "aristocratic", for convenience. Five of them feature in Domesday, with two in the pre-1066 time-frame and four in that of 1086 (one of which, the Abbess of Chatteris, is a repetition). In the earlier period, Ælfeva (al. Ælgifu), mother of Earl Morcar of Northumbria, was the dominant presence, with just a single reference to the Abbess – this latter, an institutional rather than a personal one. Ælfeva and sundry variants of her name have been effectively summarised elsewhere (Warner, p. 200) and the fact of seven churches existing on estates held by her may suggest that she acted in some capacity as either founder or encourager of others in their establishment. In some ways, to describe her as "Earl Morcar's mother" (as Domesday does) is less than she deserves. She was the wife of Ælfgar, Earl of Mercia (son of Leofric and Godiva), and for a brief time after the marriage of her daughter Ealdgyth, in January 1066, the mother-in-law of Harold Godwineson.[5]

With the destruction and disappearance of the old Anglo-Saxon order, another mother is seen to have been a dominant female presence in 1086 – this time entirely in the eastern half of Suffolk. Élise Malet is seen as a sub-tenant (mainly in the hundred of Hartismere) of her son, Robert, who was the largest Norman holder of land in the county at Domesday by right of accession to his father's estates. William Malet was of Anglo-Norman stock (his mother being English) and the brother of Ælfeva, thus providing a strong family connection with regard to certain of the estates held. He had fought at Hastings with William, becoming Sheriff of York in 1068, followed by similar service in Suffolk. Following his death in c. 1071 (possibly, caused by his involvement in suppressing the rebellion of Hereward the Wake), his son Robert succeeded him, becoming lord of the Honour of Eye and the largest holder of lands in Suffolk – much of his fiefdom having previously been in the control of Eadric of Laxfield. Élise Malet's overall holding was obviously not without its problems and in four cases she was in contention with Odo, Bishop of Bayeux (and Earl of Kent), half-brother of William I and the man who had commissioned the famous tapestry – a person well known for his acquisitiveness and vindictive nature. Her number of entries in Domesday tends to completely overshadow the single one of the daughter of Roger of Rames, a man who held a middling number of estates in South Suffolk and North Essex.

The remaining female presence to be discussed is that of Adelaide of Normandy, Countess of Aumâle and sister of William I. At Domesday, she held two estates in West Suffolk and another eleven in the Eastern sector. A majority of the holdings were substantial (even large) in size and five of them (including the four biggest) had churches attached – foundations that were definitely in existence prior to the Conquest: Shimpling in the hands of Æthelgyth, Belstead held by Ælfric of Weinhou, Gusford and Harkstead by Edeva the Fair, and Debach by three freemen commended to Eadric Grim. Whether or not Adelaide ever visited her English estates is not known, but with all three of her husbands being French, and with the family interests lying mainly on the other side of the English Channel, it is probably doubtful that she did.

Table 23. Royal female tenants-in-chief (whole county)

Name	Community	Hundred	Tenant	Size (acres)	Year	Reference
Queen Edith	(Ixworth) Thorpe	Bradmere	Sparrowhawk, freeman (eP)	30	1066	37.2
	Bildeston	Cosford	Herself (eJ?)	720	1066	41.1
Edeva	Thurlow	Risbridge	2 sokemen (eP & eJ)	25	1066	25.104
Edeva the Rich	Beyton	Thedwestry	1 freeman (eP)	40	1066	31.54
	Tostock		36 freemen (eP)	120	1066	1.61
	Saxham	Thingoe	6 freemen (eP)	120	1066	1.63
Queen Edith	Chediston	Blything	Wulfsi, freeman (½eP)	13	1066	7.15
			Ulf, freeman (eP)	13	1066	7.15
			Stanhard & Lædman, freemen (eP)	30	1066	7.15
	Baylham	Bosmere	½ church	12	1066	76.15
	(Gt. & Lt.) Bricett		Bondi; freeman (eP)	120	1066	25.56
	Otley	Carlford	Brihtwald, freeman (eP)	30	1066	52.1
	Playford		Godwine, son of Ælfhere (eP & eJ)	360	1066	6.112
	Swilland		Herself (eJ)	280	1066	41.2
	Helmingham (outlier to Otley)	Claydon	Grimwulf, freeman (eP)	120	1066	52.9
	Ipswich	Ipswich	Herself (eJ)	2/3 of half-hundred & borough	1066	1.122a
			Herself (eJ)	480 - a grange	1066	1.122b
	Belstead	Samford	Godwine, son of Alsi, thegn (eP)	240	1066	6.26
Edeva the Fair	**Ash(bocking)**	Bosmere	Æthelmær, freeman (eP & eJ)	93	1066	1.73
	Badley		2 freemen (eP & eJ)	30 & 20	1066	1.70

Landholder	Place	Hundred	Holder	Acres	Date	Value
	Blakenham		5 freemen (eP & eJ)	60	1066	1.67
	Darmsden		1 freeman (eP & eJ)	60	1066	1.71
	Offton		2 freemen (eP & eJ)	50	1066	1.69
	Langhedena		3 freemen (eP & eJ)	72	1066	1.68
	Sharpstone		1 freeman (eP & eJ)	2	1066	1.72
Countess Edeva	Burgh	Carlford	1 freeman (eP)	5	1066	4.17
Edeva	Bentley	Samford	Eadmund, freeman (eJ)	40	1066	3.71
			Thurstane (eP & eJ)	40	1066	3.75
	Beria		Herself (eJ)	240	1066	3.69
	Boynton		Wulfstane, freeman (eP)	50	1066	3.81
	Brantham		Eadwine (eP & eJ)	120	1066	3.73
	Dodnash		Eadwine (eP & eJ)	120	1066	3.72
Edeva the Fair	**Gusford**		Herself (eJ)	240	1066	46.5
	Harkstead		Herself (eJ?)	840	1066	46.4
	(Great & Little) Wenham		Ansgot (eP & eJ)	120	1066	3.67
			Ansgot (eP & eJ)	15	1066	3.84
Edeva	Holbrook		Godmane (eP)	120	1066	3.68
	[Kalweton?]		Thurstane (eP & eJ)	40	1066	3.78
	Pannington		Thurstane (eP & eJ)	60	1066	3.76
	[Wherstead?]		Thurstane (eP & eJ)	40	1066	3.77
	Woolverstone		Thurstane (eP & eJ)	120	1066	3.74
	Finborough	Stow	2 freemen (eP)	25	1066	1.64

Table details

- Use of bold font indicates church presence, or priest only (?).

- (eP) and (eJ) indicate the exercise of patronage and jurisdiction by the women over their tenants.

- The attachment of freemen or sokemen to an estate probably meant that they were under the patronage and jurisdiction of the landholder.

- Queen Edith was wife of Edward the Confessor. Her name has retained its common, modern form rather than the OE *Ealdgyth*, as it is the one familiar to most people.

- Edeva [Edith], as variously described, was the wife of Harold Godwineson and is sometimes found referred to in historical works as "Edith Swan-neck".

- According to one particular source, the wife of Ralph the Constable was also known as Eadgifu (Edeva) the Fair.[6] However, there is practically no correlation between the Suffolk communities which he and the Edeva identified here had a connection with. Only Bentley (Samford H.) – 1.101 and 3.71 – provides a possible connection by association with the same place, and certainly not one which is sufficient to make any positive link between husband and wife.

The final table shows the presence of two queens of England: Edith (Ealdgyth), sister of Harold Godwineson and wife of Edward the Confessor, and Edith (Ealdgyth or Eadgifu), first wife of the said Harold. All references to the former are framed as "Queen Edith", whereas those of the latter vary. She was renowned for her beauty – a personal feature reflected by the descriptions of her in Suffolk Domesday as "Edeva the Fair" (*Edua/Edeue faira/faire* etc.).[7] Edeva the Rich (*Ediue diuitis*) is another title accorded her and, in a single instance, "Countess Edeva" (*Ædgeua comitissa*), while eleven others simply use her forename.[8] Queen Edith is shown to have had a connection with fourteen Suffolk estates altogether (two in the West and twelve in the East), while Edeva had double that number at twenty-nine (four in the West and twenty-five in the East – fifteen of them in Samford). It would seem, therefore, that as with women of lesser degree, Bury Abbey might have acted as a restraining influence on the female holding of land even in the uppermost levels of society.

Regarding Edeva, she had probably acquired her Suffolk estates during the mid-late 1040s, when her husband Harold Godwineson was Earl of East Anglia. One feature which is also apparent in the data is the incidence of churches located on certain of the lands held by the two women: four in East Suffolk for Queen Edith (three in Carlford and one in Bosmere) and seven in the same sector for Edeva (five in Samford and two in Bosmere). This might well imply royal influence on the part of Queen Edith, either directly on her own part or by personal encouragement of the tenants in establishing places of worship. Edeva was still some way from her brief reign as queen when her husband was Earl of East Anglia, but as with her future sister-in-law, she also seems to have been a possible factor in the founding of churches.

Altogether, taking the figures for 1066 as shown in Tables 20-23, forty churches can be seen as possibly owing their existence to female patrons of varying social levels. This represents only 9% of the county total of 448+, but applies solely to women who are detectable as land-holders of one kind or another.[9] It does not (and cannot) take in to account the influence that the many wives of freemen and thegns across the whole of the county may have had in influencing or supporting their husbands in the building and endowing of places of worship. If the tables are assessed individually, different and more revealing statistics are produced. Table 20 shows that freewomen held estates in sixteen West Suffolk communities, seven of which had churches (44%), while Table 21 has them holding properties in fifty-two East Suffolk ones with fifteen associated churches (26%). In Table 22, the more socially elevated Ælfgifu (Ælfeva), mother of Earl Morcar, held properties in seventeen communities in the county as a whole (mainly in the East) with seven churches located on them (41%) and in Table 23 both of the Ediths had estates in thirty-six vills, county-wide (again, largely in the East), with eleven churches present (30%).[10] Thus, women become visible as a positive factor in the founding of churches, if not to the same extent as their male counterparts. Finally, another matter suggested by the data is that the first half of the eleventh century seems to have been a period of pronounced activity in the construction of Suffolk parish churches, with female involvement as part of a widespread, general pattern in which they probably played more than a minor role.

One final aspect of the presence of freewomen, of varying status, in the Domesday record remains to be discussed – and it is almost certainly a suggestion that will not necessarily be accepted by everyone. It concerns the disparity between the number of churches recorded for Norfolk (256/258) and that produced for Suffolk (448+) – a figure approaching the 200 mark. Sticking purely to the data given for pre-Conquest times, the former county has 29-30 women noted (Æthelgyth being referred to in each half of the county) and the latter 55-56 (Æthelgyth also features in West Suffolk). No claim is about to be made that Suffolk, in having nearly double the number of freewomen recorded than its neighbouring county therefore has 78% more churches! That would be unjustified both in terms of mathematics and logic. But may it not be that the notably greater presence of freewomen in Suffolk served as *one* of the factors in explaining why that particular county had many more places of worship than Norfolk?

Notes

1 Kedington and Poslingford are close to each other, near Haverhill, and Richere (a Norman woman, on the evidence of her French name) had obviously succeeded an earlier Anglo-Saxon occupant. Significantly, perhaps, her son Gilbert held the manor of Mildenhall – also previously in the hands of Æthelgyth – while another son, Walter, is detectable over in East Suffolk as sub-tenant of a thirty-acre manor in Darsham.

2 Norman Scarfe, 'The Naming of Alpheton', in *Suffolk in the Middle Ages*, p. 75, identifies her as the wife of Thurstan, great-grandson of Ealdorman Brihtnoth, leader of the defeated Anglo-Saxon army at the Battle of Maldon in 991 A.D. She had acquired her properties by the terms of her husband's will, c. 1043-5 and might merit inclusion in Table 22 rather than here.

3 Scarfe, 'Naming Alpheton', in *Suffolk in the Middle Ages*, p. 73, identifies the Ælflæd of Stanningfield (Thedwestry H.) as likely to have been the same person as the woman connected with Stonham and Willisham (Bosmere H.). Alpheton developed from Shimpling (Babergh H.) and is recorded as a community in its own right in 1204. If Ekwall, *English Place-Names*, p. 7, is to be believed, the name means "Ælflæd's tun".

4 Æthelgyth is recorded in both West and East Norfolk, thereby reducing the raw combined total (37) by one.

5 In addition to his hereditary title, Ælfgar had been Earl of East Anglia during the 1050s and it would have been at this time that his wife acquired her three centres of influence based on Sudbury, Eye and Kelsale. Morcar had been elected Earl of Northumberland in 1065 by the northern thegns, as a protest against the tyrannical behaviour of Tostig Godwineson. His period of office was a brief one, effectively ending with the Norman victory at Hastings.

6 C.L. Celebi, 'Conquest, Colonization and Cultural Change in Eastern Suffolk' (unpublished M.A. thesis, Bilkent University, Ankara, 2002), p. 52. Available on the Internet as a pdf at thesis.bilkent. edu.tr/0002133.pdf. This is a very interesting piece of work, which looks at what may be termed the cosmopolitan nature of the upper levels of society in Western Europe at the time, but with particular focus on the tenants-in-chief of six East Suffolk hundreds (Bishop's, Blything, Loes, Parham, Plomesgate and Wilford), using Domesday as an evidence-base.

7 Although sometimes referred to as Harold's mistress, she had become his wife c. 1045-6 – not by Christian ritual, but by the old Danish custom of "hand-fasting", which had legal recognition as a valid ceremony. Later on, in 1066, Harold also married the widow of Gruffydd ap Llewelyn, ruler of Wales – the woman formerly known as Ealdgyth (Edith) of Mercia.

8 The title of Countess presumably derives from Harold Godwineson's time as Earl of East Anglia.

9 The thirty-seven churches were located on an amalgamated total of 120 communities, which gives a 31% proportion – set against the county-wide average of 56% of settlements with churches.

10 If Edeva were placed in Table 22, as Countess of East Anglia rather than as Harold Godwineson's queen, she and Ælfgifu (Ælfeva) held estates in a total of forty-three vills with fourteen churches situated thereon (32% of the overall number).

Appendix 5

Place-name Derivation: Lothingland and Mutford

This list of place-names and their derivations is intended to provide details of "the roots" of the different communities making up the two half-hundreds, combining the essential elements of personal names and topographical features. Explanation then follows regarding both these features and relating them to the all the various communities, past and present.

1. Lothingland

Akethorpe (*Aketorp*): OE āc = "oak"; OE Þorp/ Þrop = "farm" or "hamlet", or OD Þorp = "farm" or "outlier". OD *Aki* (a personal name) is also a possibility for the first element.

Ashby: ON *Aski*, personal name (or ON *ask* = "ash tree"); ON *býr* = "village", "homestead".

Belton (*Beletuna*): ON/ODan *bil* = "interspace"; OE *tūn* = "enclosure", "homestead", "village".

Blundeston: OE *Blunt*, personal name; OE *tūn*, as above.

Bradwell: OE *bræd* = "broad"; OE *well* = "stream".

Browston (*Brockestuna*): OE *brocc* = "badger", possibly used as a personal name; OE *tūn*, as above.

Burgh [Castle] (*Burch*): OE *burg/burh* = "fort". Formerly called *Cnobheresburh*, after an earlier influential inhabitant, but still with reference to the Roman stronghold.

Caldecot (*Caldecotan*): OE *calde* = "cold"; OE *cot* = "hut", "cottage".

Corton (*Karetuna*): ON/ODan *Kari*, personal name; OE *tūn*, as above.

Dunston (*Dunestuna*): OE *dūn* = "hill", or OE *Dunn*, personal name; OE *tūn*, as above.

Flixton (*Flixtuna*): ODan *Flic*, personal name; OE *tūn*, as above. Norman Scarfe, in *Suffolk Landscape* (pp. 123-7) argues persuasively for both of the Suffolk Flixtons (Wangford and Lothingland) to be regarded as variants of *Felix*, the name of East Anglia's first evangelising bishop – the Lothingland connection resulting from the church founded by him in the vill, as a means of monitoring the Celtic mission of the Irishman, Fursa (Fursey), further to the north at *Cnobheresburh*.

Fritton (*Fridetuna*): OE *friÞ* = "enclosure"; OE *tūn*, as above.

Gapton (*Gabbatuna*): OE *Gabba*, personal name; OE *tūn*, as above.

Gorleston (*Gorlestuna*): OE *gyrele*, meaning "child" or "young person"; OE *tūn*, as above.

Gunton: ODan *Gunni*, personal name; OE *tūn*, as above.

Herringfleet (*Herlingaflet*): ODan *Herela* + OE *-ing*, personal name; OE *flēot* = "tidal stream".

Hopton (*Ho.tuna*): OE *hop* = "small enclosed valley" or "enclosed land in the midst of fens"; OE *tūn*, as above.

Little Yarmouth: a settlement to the north of Northtown and perhaps encompassing it. Yarmouth derives from OE *Gariannos*, the name of a specific river, later called the Yare, and OE *mūÞa* = "mouth" – which fits the local topographical situation of an estuarine location. The first element is from the OE *lytel* = "small". The settlement is first recorded in 1219, as *Parva Gernemuta*, in H.C. Maxwell Lyte (gen. ed.), *The Book of Fees*, vol. 1 (London, 1920), p. 282.

Lound (*Lunda*): ON *lundr* = "grove".

Lowestoft (*Lothu Wistoft*): ON *Hloðvér*, personal name; ON *topt* or OE *toft* = "house-site", "homestead". It is a Scandinavian form of an earlier Anglo-Saxon name (see fn. 26, p. 236).

Newton (*Neutuna*): OE *nēowe* = "new"; OE *tūn*, as above.

Northtown (al. Northville): OE *norÞ* = "north"; OE *tūn*, as above.

Oulton: ODan *Ali*, personal name; OE *tūn*, as above.

Somerleyton (*Sumerledetuna*): ON *Sumarliði*, generic name (meaning "summer raider"); OE *tūn*, as above.

Southtown: OE *sūÞ* = "south" and *tūn*, as above (a later, alternative name for *Little Yarmouth*). It does not feature in the 1274 *Hundred Roll* under this name.

- Domesday communities have the name used in the Survey italicised in brackets.
- Eleven of the twenty-four communities (Little Yarmouth and Southown being one and the same) have Scandinavian or part-Scandinavian names.

Landscape associations in place-names (identifiable/notional)

Akethorpe. In generalised, Scandinavian, linguistic terms, a *thorp* was subsidiary to a *toft*. Hence, Akethorpe was an outlier to Lowestoft, whose "core" lay half a mile or so due south, on lower ground. The higher land is heavier in nature (clay), which would have suited oak trees. A possible place-of-worship at Akethorpe (not necessarily a building) became Lowestoft's by adoption and the site of St. Margaret's church. It stands on rising ground near the 100-feet contour line (TM59 541942), as opposed to the original settlement of Lowestoft, which was sited closer to 50 feet above sea level. Relocation of the town to a clifftop site during the first half of the fourteenth century, together with its continuous expansion from the mid-nineteenth century onwards, has made the earlier topographical elements less obvious to see than was once the case. Nevertheless, they remain discernible. The dedication of the church may be a naming of the immediate post-Conquest period, St. Margaret seeming to have a connection with parishes associated with Roger Bigot (Sheriff of Norfolk and Suffolk), who acted as overseer of the royal estate in both counties (see Appendix 6). If a wholly Old English origin is attached to the place-name, Akethorpe can be viewed as an independent small settlement located near a larger neighbour. A further possibility regarding the vill's first element is that it derives from a Danish personal name, Aki.

Belton. The "interspace" implied in the first element may well have referred to the spur of land projecting into what is now marshland lying to the north, south and west of the old village, which formed itself along roadways constituting three sides of a square (the easterly road had little development) loosely centred on TG40 482030. At the time of Domesday, the marshes probably still formed part of the Yare-Waveney estuary, but by the time of the 1274 Hundred Roll (if Gorleston is indicative) drainage and reclamation had already converted mudflat areas into grazing-land. The three roads dictating the village's linear pattern follow the 25-feet contour line, though the old layout is now partially obscured by the village's outward expansion of house-building during the 1970s and 80s.

Bradwell. The "broad stream" probably referred to what has long been called Breydon Water – formerly a larger estuarine area, into which the rivers Bure, Yare and Waveney flowed. The original key settlement may well have been on the 25-feet contour line, above the estuary, in the area occupied by *Bradwell Hall* (TG50 503056), and the earliest recorded reference to the new parish is to be found in the *Feet of Fines*, 13 John (1211-12), p. 16. The main village itself developed a mile or so to the south of the hall (the church of St. Nicholas is located at TG50 503039) and is still detectable within its late twentieth century outgrowth. The development of Bradwell parish during the medieval period led to the decline of Gapton, which eventually shrank to the status of mere farmstead, with the former Domesday manorial structure remembered in name only by the amalgamation of one of its estates with land located in Belton.

Browston. If the first element does refer to badgers (either directly, or by association with a person), the original area of settlement, somewhere to the north of where Fritton Decoy and Lound Lakes join, might well have been sufficiently wooded for badgers to thrive (TG40 498013). That the settlement had woodland is attested by the Domesday assessment. The 25-feet contour line may be of topographical importance in indicating usable land, which stood above the lower marshy areas to the south and east. Although no longer a community in its own right, Browston retains its name to this day, existing as a sector of Belton parish. The settlement pattern is an interesting one, consisting of small, scattered farmsteads and smallholdings, with newer houses interpolated where plots have had development allowed.

Burgh (Castle). The late third century Roman shore-fort, situated on the cliff above the Yare-Bure-Waveney estuary, is the determining feature (TG40 475047). Again, the 25-feet contour line seems to be of significance as an indicator of land suitable for settlement and use. Burgh Castle, as it has long been called, makes reference to a Norman motte and bailey fortress built (presumably) by Ralph the Crossbowman in the south-western corner of the Roman site, close to the curtain wall. The village is of dual layout, the older part having the houses located along two parallel roads to the east of the parish church (TG40 476050), with later linear development to the south along Butt Lane (approximate mid-point TG40 481041). Up until now, the community has largely escaped the large-scale, modern, housing development that has so radically altered the appearance of both Belton and Bradwell. Although the community had no free tenancy recorded in Domesday, independent free tenements had developed at some stage afterwards as evidenced in E.J. Gallagher (ed.), *The Civil Pleas of the Suffolk Eyre of 1240* (Woodbridge, 2009), pp. 54 (306), 56 (311), 69 (363), 70 (364), 71 (368), 73 (376) and 239 (1150).

Caldecot. A "cold" or exposed position on the sandy soils in the vicinity of *Caldecott Hall* country hotel (TG40 474015), overlooking the Yare-Waveney estuary and standing about 50 feet above sea level, is imaginable. Belton lay to the north-north-east and Fritton to the south-south-west – the latter being wooded and more sheltered. *Caldecott Hall* itself (a late Georgian building replacing an earlier manor house) now functions as a country hotel, with adjacent land serving as a golf course.

Dunston. The siting was somewhere at the top of what is now the Gorleston Road, Oulton Village, probably not far from the junction with Hall Lane and Somerleyton Road, above the 50-feet contour line (TM59 524947). The Oulton *High House* area (TM59 525949) may also have been associated. See further under **Personal element in place-names**, below. The name has been perpetuated in the naming of a local road (Dunston Drive), whose houses were built during the 1980s.

Fritton. The "enclosure" referred to in the first element of the name may well have been in the vicinity of the site of St. Edmund's parish church (TG40 473001), on the 25-feet contour line, on a south-facing slope above Fritton Decoy, or Lake (a former medieval peat-digging). There is an earthwork close to the church (whose apsidal chancel perhaps suggests late eleventh century origins) and the area at one time was probably well wooded. *Fritton House* hotel (TG40 480006) was once the hall or manor house, but *Fritton Old Hall* (TG40 476001) probably has a good claim to have been its predecessor.

Herringfleet. The second element of the name ("tidal stream") probably referred to what is now the River Waveney, its estuarine/tidal nature at the time (ninth or tenth centuries) being far more obvious than it is today. The likely area of settlement is just above the 50-feet contour line, close to St. Margaret's Church (TM49 477978), on an elevated site above the Waveney marshes. The church has a fine Saxo-Norman round tower, which suggests a building of the early post-Conquest period, and the dedication may have a connection with Roger Bigod (Sheriff of Norfolk and Suffolk and the administrator of royal lands in his area of jurisdiction), who seems to have had an affinity for the saint – this, on the evidence of identical dedications in other parishes with which he had a connection.

Hopton. The "small enclosed valley" possibly suggested by the first element can be interpreted as the shallow depression (still discernible today) created by a pre-glacial outflow channel and accommodating the lake at *Hopton House* – as well as Lound Lakes and Fritton Decoy further to the west. In the present-day village of Hopton, this lies below the 25-feet contour line and is largely occupied by Station Road (mid-point TG50 527000). If, however, the first element implies "enclosed land in the midst of fens", that might relate to the pre-glacial outflow channel itself and the marshy area adjacent to it. The lake in the grounds of *Hopton House* is located at TM59 520998. Hopton is a greatly expanded village, as a result of late twentieth century housing development (and more recent, continuing construction), and since 1974 it has been known as Hopton-on-Sea. This resulted from boundary changes, emanating from the local Government Act of 1972, which gave Hopton a narrow coastal strip of land formerly belonging to Corton. This ran as far as Gorleston's southern limit and constituted what remained of the "lost" parish of Newton.

Little Yarmouth. It was probably situated just above flood-level and nearest to the crossing-point of the river into Great Yarmouth itself, being an earlier term used for what eventually became known as Southtown (TG50 521071). Both names indicate a position relative to the earliest settled part of Gt. Yarmouth and reflect that town's increase in wealth and importance. Southtown was added to the borough of Yarmouth in 1681. As early as the reign of Henry I (1100-35), the church of St. Nicholas, Little Yarmouth (along with the chapel of *Northville*) had been granted to the Priory of St. Bartholomew, Smithfield. In Lord John Hervey, *The Hundred Rolls and Extracts Therefrom* (Ipswich, 1902), pp. 72 & 73, reference is made to encroachment onto the royal market-place by the inhabitants of Little Yarmouth (suggesting a location at the northern end of Gorleston). This was probably the Half-hundred market, granted by King John in 1211 to the men of Lothingland, in return for the gift of a palfrey (*Patent Rolls*, 13 John, p. 7). It was originally held on a Sunday, but switched to Thursday after sea erosion (which suggests a siting on land adjacent to the river) had forced a change of venue (*Curia Regis Rolls*, xiii, pp. 108-11). The changes occurred at some point between 1212 and 1226, while William Longespée, Earl of Salisbury, was Lord of the Half-hundred. No information was forthcoming re the settlement's free tenements, but there are references to one of these holdings and to two half-messuages in E. J. Gallagher (ed.) *Suffolk Eyre of 1240*, pp. 48 (274), 229 (1099) and 238 (1149).

Lound. The "grove" derivation of the name would seem to have a connection with the considerable amount of woodland evidenced by the Domesday data. Given its Scandinavian origin, it might also possibly refer to a sacred oak-grove, where Nordic deities were once worshipped. If the core settlement were situated in the vicinity of today's church (TM59 506990) and village, it occupied land lying between the 25 and 50-feet contour lines. The remaining part of *Lound Great Wood* (TM59 513985) may have significance regarding the settlement's naming and its later medieval economy. If the church's dedication to St. John the Baptist has any significance, it might possibly be as an example of the "recycling" of a pagan site of worship, with John being seen (and used) as a symbol of rebirth and renewal. There is no priest or church recorded in the Domesday data.

Newton. In being a "new" settlement, the community may have been of more recent origins than its three neighbours: Corton, Hopton and Gorleston. Prolonged sea erosion, from the sixteenth to the nineteenth century, effectively destroyed the parish, leaving a narrow coastal strip that became incorporated into Corton and later made part of Hopton (April, 1974). One tiny vestige occupies the edge of the cliff on the eastern perimeter of *Potter's Resort*.

Northtown. References in the *Hundred Rolls* show that the settlement was clearly regarded as part of Gorleston and was indeed situated in its northern sector (TG50 522071). Because of the small geographical distances and areas involved, there has tended to be a blurring of distinctions between this settlement and Little Yarmouth-Southtown. As early as the reign of Henry I (1100-35), the chapel of *Northville* (along with the church of St. Nicholas, Little Yarmouth-Southtown) had been granted to the Priory of St. Bartholomew, Smithfield.

Southtown. A late, alternative name for the community otherwise known as Little Yarmouth. The varying terminology for the settlement immediately north of Gorleston probably reflects the dominance of Great Yarmouth, both in topographical and economic terms.

Personal element in place-names (Lothingland Half-hundred)

Ashby (ON *Aski*). A landscape association is theoretically possible if the first element derives from ON *ask* ("ash tree"), but this is not as likely as a place-name derivation – especially when combined with the classic Scandinavian suffix –*by*, deriving from *býr* and indicating a homestead or village (nor would the light soils of the parish have been a particularly favourable environment for *Fraxinus excelsior*). An early documented use of the settlement's name occurs in the *Feet of Fines*, 4 John (1202-3), p. 10, with reference made to a William de Askeby. In terms of the settlement's origins, *Aski* was presumably the man who (either personally or via other members of the family-group) built up an estate sufficiently significant to give his name to a new parish made up of land formerly belonging to Herringfleet and Lound. His origins may possibly have been as one of the unnamed freemen recorded in Lound at the time of Domesday. There is no village core as such and the parish consists of scattered farms and cottages. The church stands evocatively, adjacent to and above, a cross-ways of what are now farm-tracks (TM49 490990).

Blundeston (OE *Blunt*). The earliest documented use of the name is to be found in the *Curia Regis Rolls*, in 1203. The Anglo-Saxon *Blunt*, whoever he was, must have consolidated a sufficient amount of land to give his name to a new parish formed from parts of Corton, Lound and Somerleyton (especially the last-named). The location of the church (TM59 513972) a mere quarter of a mile from the parish boundary with Somerleyton, rather than its occupying a site further to the north-east in the main part of the village (much expanded by late twentieth century housing development), reinforces the sense of its having once been the church in Somerleyton referred to in the Domesday Survey.

Corton (ON/ODan *Kari*). The Scandinavian personal name may be literally translated as "the curly-haired one". It is a likely example of an incomer giving his name to an existing Anglo-Saxon vill and is probably of tenth or eleventh century derivation. The church is located half a mile to the north of the present-day village (increased in size during the 1970s and 80s by residential development on a former railway line and allotment land), at TM59 538981, and its dedication to St. Bartholomew is one that has Norman associations – as well as maritime ones. However, Anglo-Saxon pottery has been found on nearby fields, which may be indicative of the vill's approximate early location. A Scandinavian connection is also implied in the finding of a high-status, Nordic, belt-accoutrement whetstone, found on Corton beach during the autumn of 2011.

Dunston (possibly, OE *Dunn*). Map references are given above, in **Landscape associations in place-names**. A landscape connection in the first element of the name is more likely than a patronym, though the latter remains a possibility. The settlement's Domesday references have been mistakenly interpreted as appertaining to Blundeston.

Flixton (ODan *Flic*). The parish church of St. Michael, Oulton (TM59 510936), and the ruined nave of St. Andrew, Flixton (TM59 517955), mark the former extent of what was the half-hundred's largest Domesday community in terms of cultivated land and population. Progressive reduction in size, as Oulton developed, resulted in a greatly diminished parish. As with Corton, another Domesday vill, the name Flixton is possibly an example of a Scandinavian incomer taking over an existing Anglo-Saxon settlement and re-naming it. However, it has also been suggested that the name derives from that of Felix the Burgundian, who came to evangelize the Eastern Angles in 631 A.D. and who may have placed a church at Flixton to monitor the rival, Celtic activities of the Irish monk, Fursa (or Fursey), who had established a small monastery within the walls of the old Roman shore-fort at *Cnobheresburh* (later Burgh Castle) at about the same time (Scarfe, *Suffolk Landscape*, pp. 124-7). This is an elegant and appealing idea, and the church itself – for centuries now, the parish church of Oulton – certainly occupies a strategic position: built on a cliff-edge above former tidal reaches of the River Waveney (now marshes) and looking across to its counterpart on the Norfolk side at Burgh St. Peter. There may well have been a Roman fording-point between the two church-sites, so the location has an ancient pedigree.

Gapton (OE *Gabba*). A notional location for two of the recorded Domesday estates may be made, using *Gapton Hall* (TG50 511058) and *Bradwell Hall* (TG50 503056). The name is currently kept alive in the form of the Gapton Hall industrial and retail estate, a large commercial development on the western perimeter of Great Yarmouth, close to the A47 trunk road (formerly the A12) and with an imposing view northwards across Breydon Water and the Halvergate marshes. The former Domesday settlement has long been incorporated in its successor, Bradwell.

Gorleston (OE *gyrele*). The core-area of settlement may well have been on the higher ground near St. Andrew's parish church (TG50 524044). In progressively becoming a suburb of Great Yarmouth during the later nineteenth century and being incorporated into the borough by the Local Government Act of 1894, Gorleston lost a good deal of its historical integrity. It is an older settlement than its larger neighbour and its location on a cliff above the River Yare is still impressive when viewed from the lower level. Two ancient rhymes demonstrate the former feeling of Gorlestonians towards the people of Yarmouth: "Gorleston was Gorleston ere Yarmouth begun and will be Gorleston when Yarmouth be gone"; "Gorleston great one day will be, Yarmouth buried in the sea." Global warming and rising sea-levels may possibly see the latter prediction at least partially fulfilled!

Gunton (ODan *Gunni*). The earliest recorded use of the name is to be found in the *Feet of Fines*, 10 Richard I (1198-9), p. 5. The parish was never a very large or impressive one, being formed mainly from coastal heath located in the parishes of Corton and Lowestoft. Again, as with Ashby and Blundeston, the patronymic element in the name probably derives from one dominant, local land-holder (possibly one of the unnamed Domesday freemen in Corton). The parish church of St. Peter probably occupies a key site in the landscape (TM59 542958), on the former dividing-line between Lowestoft and Corton. Much of the parish has long been incorporated into the outward growth of North Lowestoft.

Herringfleet (ODan *Herela* + OE. *–ing*). See also above, in **Landscape associations in place-names**. The Scandinavian name of the "founding father" may date from either the ninth or tenth centuries, with his place of settlement being easily accessible from the River Waveney. The site of the manor house (TM49 479977) is not far removed from that of the parish church and the building itself is distinguished by a multi-cusped gable of the mid-seventeenth century. Close by, and fronting the road, stands a very fine barn of the same period built in characteristic, local, brick-and-flint bond. _

Lowestoft (ON *Hloðvér*). The original area of settlement was probably in the vicinity of the present-day meeting-point of Normanston Drive, Rotterdam Road and St. Peter's Street (TM59 541936), a half-mile to the south of the church of its outlier, Akethorpe. Although the name is Scandinavian, in both elements, it is possible that it represents a re-naming rather than original settlement by a Northman. There is a good chance that the early Anglo-Saxon incomer, *Hlūd(a)*, who gave his name to Lothingland itself (and also to the adjoining half-hundred, before it changed its name to Mutford), had it altered in form by later incomers. Thus, Lowestoft could well be the primary Anglo-Saxon settlement in the area. The location (as outlined above) was certainly a favourable one: a south-facing slope consisting mainly of light, well-drained topsoils; adjacent areas of heath for rough grazing and other amenities; and a large expanse of nearby fresh water (what later became known as Lake Lothing), with access to the sea over a low shingle bank. During the first half of the fourteenth century (for a combination of reasons unable to be discussed here), the town relocated to a cliff-top site (mid-point TM59 551938).

Oulton (ODan *Ali*). The earliest documented use of the name (*Aleton*) is to be found in the *Curia Regis Rolls*, in 1203. In being one of six, previously unrecorded, post-Domesday communities in Lothingland, it is interesting to note the third example of a man of possible Scandinavian origins giving his (or his family's) name to a new parish. It may be significant that one of the two freeman tenants named in Dunston (a vill absorbed by Oulton) in 1086 was called Ali. His tenure related to the pre-Conquest era, but it is obviously the same family-group being referred to. As with Gunton, much of the parish has been absorbed by the residential spread of Lowestoft, with its southern sector being amalgamated with the northern part of Carlton Colville in 1904 to form the new civil and ecclesiastical parish of Oulton Broad.

Somerleyton (ON *Sumarliði*). If the Old Norse element *sumarliði* is translated as "summer warrior", an insight is provided into Nordic expeditions of the past, with the Anglo-Saxon *tun* element of the name suggesting yet again Scandinavian re-naming of an established vill. As with the great majority of Lothingland settlements, Somerleyton was easily reached by water – in this case, by the tidal stretches of the River Waveney, which would have posed no problems at all for shallow-draught vessels such as longships (especially at high tide). The village is distinctive for having escaped large-scale housing development and for its mid-nineteenth century, mock-Tudor cottages grouped around an artificially created green – this, the creation of Samuel Morton Peto, with the help of architect, John Thomas.

As outlined above in the comments on Lowestoft, the name Lothingland itself may may be a Scandinavian form of the OE *Hlūdinga(s)* or *Ludinga(s)* and OE (also, ON) *land*: "the land/area of the people/descendants of Hlūd, or Luda". In turn, either of these names may have originally have derived from the OE *hlūd*, meaning "loud" – perhaps reflecting a personal characteristic of the original "name-giver". The area of primary settlement is a matter for speculation, but a good case can be made for Lowestoft.

2. Mutford

Barnby (*Barnebei/Barneby*): OScand *Biarni*, a personal name; and ON *býr*, meaning "village", "homestead".

Beckton *(Bechetuna, Beketuna)*: OE *bece* – cf. ODan *bæk* & ON *bekkr* – meaning "stream"; and *tūn*, meaning "enclosure", "homestead", "village". The second bracketed spelling, in use of the letter k, may reflect the Scandinavian form of an existing Anglo-Saxon word.

Carlton *(Karletuna/Carletuna)*: OScand *Karla*, a personal name; or a Scandinavian form of OE *ceorl*, meaning "freeman"; and OE *tūn*, as above.

Gisleham (*Gisleha.*): OE *Gysela*, a personal name; and OE *hām*, meaning "homestead", "village".

Hornes (*Hornes*): OE *horn*, meaning "spit, or tongue of land".

Kessingland (*Kessinglanda*): OE *Cussa/Cyssi*, a personal name, and *-ing*, meaning "descendants of"; and OE (or ON) *land*, meaning "estate"; or ON *lundr*, meaning "grove".

Kirkley (*Kirkelea*): OE *cirice* or OScand *kirkia*, meaning "church"; and OE *lēah*, meaning "glade" or "clearing".

Mutford (*Mutforda*): OE *mōt*, meaning "meeting"; and OE *ford*, meaning "shallow place in water".

Pakefield (*Paggefella*): OE *Pacca*, or ON *Pacci*, a personal name, and OE *feld*, meaning "open country".

Rothenhall (*Rodenhala*): poss. OE *rod* or *roÞ(u)*, meaning "clearing", or OE *HroÞ*, a personal name (+ *-ing*); and OE *halh*, meaning "secluded place" or "nook".

Rushmere (*Riscemara/Ryscemara*): OE *risc*, meaning "rush" (the aquatic plant); and OE *mere*, meaning "lake" or "stretch of water".

Wimundhall (*Wimundhala*): poss. OE *Wigmund*, a personal name; and OE *halh*, as above.

- Domesday communities have the name used in the Survey italicised in brackets.

- Six of the names above are unequivocally English in origin (Gisleham, Hornes, Mutford, Rothenhall, Rushmere and Wimundhall), one is Scandinavian (Barnby) and four show, or may show, Scandinavian influence (Carlton, Kessingland, Kirkley and Pakefield).

- Of the latter five, Carlton may be a *Grimston hybrid*, showing a combination of Scandinavian personal name and the Anglo-Saxon *tun*; Kirkley is either Scandinavian in the first element of the name or an example of a Scandinavian-influenced English form, using the "harder" letter k in place of c (probably the latter); Kessingland seems to be a combination of an Old English personal name and an Old English or Old Norse tenure term; and Pakefield has a personal name first-element that may be either Old English or Old Norse. The possibility of the *land* element in Kessingland being a variant of Old Norse *lundr* (meaning "a grove") has been considered, but Domesday records no woodland in the parish.

- Beckton is slightly problematical in the two forms of the name given in the Latin text: *Bechetuna* and *Beketuna*. The former spelling would seem to suggest OE *bece* as the first element's origin, the latter either ODan *bæk* or ON *bekkr*. Thus, it is possible that the name may show Scandinavian influence affecting an existing Anglo-Saxon word, or the variance might be the result of clerical foible in representing it.

- OE = Old English; ODan = Old Danish; ON = Old Norse; OScand = Old Scandinavian; OSw = Old Swedish.

Landscape associations in place-names (identifiable and/or notional)

Beckton. The watercourse in question was probably what is known as Kirkley Stream or Kirkley Beck. It rises in Carlton Colville, lying between the 25-feet contour lines and once running into the Lowestoft inner harbour to the east of Riverside Road (TM59 541925). A possible "core" location for the settlement itself is *Grove Farm*, Pakefield, at the junction of Bloodmoor Lane and Stradbroke Road (TM59 525905). The site is a long-established one, with the present house dating from the late sixteenth century. Although a great deal of twentieth century housing development is in evidence in this particular location (to say nothing of a relatively new industrial estate and relief-road system), there are still a sufficient number of basic geomorphological features left to form an impression of a much earlier landscape. Creation of the Lowestoft southern relief road has revealed the presence of the watercourse (through following its alignment for part of the way) to a greater number of people than has probably been the case for a considerable number of years. A local family bearing the name of Beckton (usually rendered as de Beketon) is detectable in public documentation of the early 14th century, with one of them (named Hugh) listed as a Pakefield tax-payer in the 1327 Subsidy.

Hornes. There are two possible locations for this estate, at either end of the half-hundred. The "spit of land" referred to in the name may have been a projection into Lake Lothing, in the vicinity of Kirkley Ham (TM59 540927) – close to the point where the stream referred to above entered the mere and where, at a much later date, the Co-operative food-processing factory and wharf were located. The name *Horn Hill* (applied to the main roadway in this area) is not provable as a descendant of the settlement's title but nevertheless remains as a possible link with the earlier name. The size of this holding (5 acres) was small, but probably viable as an agricultural unit for the one freemen who worked it – though, having no team of his own, he would have had to negotiate the ploughing of his soil with other local men. The area of land constituting the bluntly-shaped promontory was (and still is) approximately 5 acres in size. An alternative site that fits the topographical reference contained in the name equally well is to be found in the extreme western "tip" of Rushmere parish, on a "spit" or "spur" of land known as Horns Hill, which projects towards the River Hundred at a point opposite a similar promontory on which *Mutford Hall* stands. Both of these opposing spurs are defined by the 25-feet contour line and the Rushmere one's extremity is to be found at TM48 483875. There could easily have been a five-acre holding in this vicinity, and it is difficult to favour one site or the other because both of them satisfy the topographical element inherent in the name Hornes. However, it has to be said that the soil in the Rushmere location was probably of better quality for agriculture than the land adjacent to Lake Lothing and nearer to a source of available labour for the task of ploughing.

Kirkley. Kirkley parish church (both elements of the place-name seeming to make a defining statement) stands on the 50-feet contour line (TM59 540916) – possibly on the site of a building not listed in Domesday (the dedication to St. Peter, one of the founding fathers of the Western Church, may suggest a relatively early foundation). The "glade" or "clearing" (second element) suggests a woodland environment of some kind at some stage, though Domesday itself records no woodland in the community. Equally, an early clearing might have referred to removal of an area of coastal heath. In spite of the heavily built-up nature of its present-day surrounds (the community effectively becoming "South Lowestoft" following Samuel Morton Peto's seaside developments of the 1850s), the church's prominent position on its high-point still has a pronounced visual impact in landscape terms and is able to communicate something of significance regarding its location – particularly when its distinctive and much rebuilt, 14th century tower is seen from a distance. The Scandinavian influence in the name may reflect a Danish incomer of either the 9th or 10th centuries taking over an existing Anglo-Saxon vill. Since the merging of the parish (some years ago) with a much later, Victorian one, the church has been known as St. Peter and St. John.

Mutford. The village's approximate centre-point is located at TM48 486884. A number of small watercourses converge in the vicinity, before running down into the River Hundred. The 25-feet contour line is another defining feature, "framing" the course of both river and feeder-streams. The "meeting-place" itself may well have been an early point of assembly for half-hundred business (before being superseded by the one at Mutford Bridge) and was likely to have been located where the original manor house stood. As seen today, *Mutford Hall* incorporates work of the late sixteenth, late seventeenth and nineteenth centuries and stands on the 25-feet contour line, half a mile south-west-by-south of the village, in a key position above floodplain level, where the three feeder-streams referred to above join the River Hundred (TM48 481875) – a siting which may well have been at a crossing-point, in earlier times, into the adjoining parish of Henstead and the hundred of Blything. The parish church of St. Andrew, occupying an edge-of-village position (TM48 486886) is almost certainly on the site of one of the churches mentioned in Domesday, but no evidence of its companion's location has survived in recorded form. The building, as seen today, is a composite of medieval styles and features, but there is sufficient evidence in the round tower (the tallest one of all) and the north wall of the nave to identify Norman replacement of an earlier church.

Pakefield. The "clearing" or "open space" implied in the second element of the name is almost impossible to imagine today, because so much of the parish has been absorbed into the Lowestoft built-up area. The church of All Saints and St. Margaret stands close to the 25-feet contour line, near the edge of the cliff (TM59 538905) – but only because of coastal erosion; it was once situated a good deal further from the sea. About 200 yards width of land was lost during the early years of the twentieth century and another incursion of the 1930s almost reached the church itself. The building probably occupies the site of the "half-church" referred to in Domesday, with the northern aisle (dedicated to St. Margaret) possibly representing that particular foundation and with the southern part of the building (All Saints) having its origin either as a later foundation associated with the manor of Rothenhall or perhaps constituting the other half of the Domesday church. The St. Margaret element of the dedication may be a re-naming of the post-Conquest period, as the mythical female saint (who reputedly lived in Antioch during the late 3rd/early 4th centuries) was known as a personal patron among the Norman military elite.

Rothenhall. The first element's possible reference to a "clearing" cannot lead to a specific location in terms of the topography of today. Any "secluded place" or "nook" referred to in the second element of the name was probably located in the southern part of Pakefield, in the neighbourhood of *Pakefield Hall* (TM48 532889) – Suffolk's most easterly moated, domestic site. The land is higher here, being largely situated between the 25 and 50-feet contour lines. The northern part of Kessingland parish, in the neighbourhood of *Heath Farm* (TM48 531881) and *Oaklands Terrace* (TM48 529878) must also be included in this community's former area. It is possible (given the exposed nature of the landscape hereabouts) that the "secluded" reference might be to a coastal inlet of some kind or even a gulley-way in the cliffs – such as the nearby, and well-known, *Crazy Mary's Hole* (TM48 537888).

Rushmere. The "reeds" and the "stretch of water" referred to most likely derived from proximity to the River Hundred, which would have been of estuarine nature in the Anglo-Saxon era. St. Michael's Church (the reference to the Archangel reflecting his importance as the symbolic soldier-saint of the early church) is situated about three-quarters of a mile to the north, on the 25-feet contour line (TM48 495880), at a four-way crossroads – probably on the site of the "quarter-church" noted in Domesday. Its round tower and nave walls suggest Norman replacement of the building recorded, with later modifications also in evidence both internally and externally. *Rushmere Hall*, a late sixteenth century manor house (with eighteenth and nineteenth century additions), stands half a mile away to the south-south-west, above floodplain level and also close to the 25-feet contour line (TM48 493873) – probably on the same site as its predecessor.

Wimundhall. With Kirkley having long formed part of the Lowestoft urban area, the "secluded place" or "nook" implied in the second element cannot now be accurately placed. However, it may once have existed to the west or north-west of the church of St. Peter and St. John (a modern dedication in part, the second name representing a former Victorian parish and church which have disappeared), on the lower ground towards Kirkley Stream. The present-day Carlton Road, Kirkley Street, Enstone Road area offers a possible location, centring roughly on TM59 538919. It is still possible, even today, in spite of all the nineteenth and twentieth century housing development which has taken place, to envisage a "de-urbanised" environment and see something of basic land-forms that determined earlier settlement-patterns. The community was of sufficient note in its time to give its name to a local family, the de Wymundhales, which held the manor of Brampton (as well as that of Kirkley) during the later part of the thirteenth century.

Personal element in place-names (actual or possible)

Barnby (OScand *Biarni*). "The homestead of Biarni" may have stood in the vicinity of St. John the Baptist's parish church (TM48 481899), close to the 50-feet contour line, on higher ground above the nearby marshes (estuarine flats in Anglo-Danish times) and now well removed from the built-up area of the village. The building, with square tower and integrated, thatched nave and chancel, dates mainly from the 14th and 15th centuries, but probably stands on the site of its Domesday predecessor and is a prominent feature in the local landscape. Its dedication, to the cousin and fore-runner of Jesus, may be taken as a relatively early one and could even be original. Local landforms close to the building have resulted in the main road (A146) having to adopt a sinuous alignment across the sloping ground, thereby creating what have become known as the *Barnby Bends*. An alternative site for early settlement is *White House Farm* (TM49 491908), which has interesting crop-marks in the field immediately to the east of it, clearly visible on aerial photographs. The main, built-up area of the village lies to the west and south-west of the church, having coalesced with its neighbour, North Cove, but a strong sense of earlier landscape features remains.

Carlton (OScand *Karla* or a Scandinavian form of OE *ceorl*). Whether the settlement was that of a Scandinavian incomer or a ninth/tenth century renaming of an existing Anglo-Saxon vill, St. Peter's parish church (TM59 510901), situated as it is on rising ground between the 25-feet and 50-feet contour lines, is probably a significant site – especially when taken, in tandem, with the presence of a former manor house, *Carlton Hall*, close by to the north-north-west (TM59 509903). Its position in the local landscape is further enhanced by its occupying an eminence close to crossways, with open farmland to the south. The building is a much-restored version of what appears to have been a fourteenth century one, but there is a discernible trace of Norman origins in a reconstructed window on the north side of the nave. Concerning a much earlier phase of Carlton's development, a nationally important settlement-site of c. 500-700 A.D., located on Bloodmoor Hill (TM48 520897), was excavated by the Cambridge Archaeological Unit in 1998-2001. A late 7th Century cemetery was found, with burials showing an east-west alignment and with grave-goods also exhibiting signs of Christian belief intermingling with established pagan traditions. Since the 1960s, much of the parish has seen a large amount of residential development to provide homes as part of Lowestoft's expansion, but it is still possible to ascertain the earlier layout of the community within the urban spread.

Gisleham (OE *Gysela*). Holy Trinity parish church (TM48 514886) is located close to the 50-feet contour line, at a cross-ways. Its round tower and north doorway speak of Norman origins, but later re-modifications are in evidence too. The double-moated site of the medieval manor house lies half a mile away, south-by-west, at *Manor Farm*, and is probably of some antiquity (TM48 514879). It remains an impressive local landscape feature, both in terms of scale and visual impact – the outer ditch being outlined by trees. There would appear to be no strategic reason for its dual construction, so it was probably the result of the lord of the manor of the mid-fourteenth century (possibly, Sir John de Ulveston) wanting it to be a status symbol.

Kessingland (OE *Cussa/Cyssi*). The parish church of St. Edmund (TM48 528862), with its imposing mid-fifteenth century tower, stands close to the 50-feet contour line, with a former manor-house site located immediately alongside, west of the churchyard (*Manor Farm*). The proximity suggests an early association – probably with Stapleton's manor. The church's dedication is an interesting one, being to the patron saint of both East Anglia and England – an Anglo-Saxon king killed by the Danes in 869 A.D. Kessingland became a greatly expanded community during the second half of the twentieth century, with large areas of housing development infilling the existing village layout to the north of Church Road, but earlier elements of its physical structure are still traceable and the landscape south of the church remains relatively open and uncluttered, with a fine declivity running down to the River Hundred. An excellent map, showing Kessingland's late 18th century landscape (with noticeable remaining medieval features) may be found in Warner, p. 211.

Pakefield (OE *Pacca*/ON *Pacci*). See the comments made in the previous section. The personal name element is equivocal, with two possible linguistic origins – both of them reflecting waves of settlement into the local area from the 6th century onwards.

Rothenhall (OE *HroÞa-ing*?). If the early settlement was indeed that of *HroÞa* (Hrotha) and his descendants, it was located in southern Pakefield/ northern Kessingland, as previously described (roughly centred, in today's topographical situation, at TM48 531885).

Wimundhall (OE *Wigmund*?). A siting to the west or north-west of Kirkley parish church, has been previously identified and is based on the second element of the name.

- All six-figure grid references are "best fit", using OS First Series 1:25000 maps.

Appendix 6

Dedications to Margaret of Antioch & King Edmund of East Anglia

Table 24. Medieval Churches in Norfolk and Suffolk (St. Margaret)

Hundred	Community	Bigot connection	Comments
Brothercross	Burnham Norton (rt)	Tenant-in-chief	9.84 & 136
	Pudding Norton (D)	Crown agent	1.16 & 18
	West Raynham	Tenant-in-chief & Crown agent	9.139 & 1.88
Clackclose	Wallington (D)	Tenant-in-chief	9.230
	Wereham		Parish now in Ely Diocese, not Norwich. (Tenant-in-chief in West Dereham)
Freebridge	Lynn		Crown agent in North Wootton.
Gallow	Saxlingham (D)		Tenant-in-chief in Field Dalling – also, Crown agent there and in Sharrington.
South Greenhoe	Hilborough		Ruins of a wayside chapel founded in 1207.
Launditch	Little Dunham	Crown agent	1.212
	Stanfield		Tenant-in-chief in Whissonsett & Crown agent in Mileham.
	Worthing		[Post-Domesday community.]
Thetford	Thetford (D)	Tenant-in-chief & Crowb agent	9.1 & 1.69 & 210 [St. Margaret's Church no longer in existence.]
Wayland	Breccles (rt)	Tenant-in-chief & Crown agent	9.123 & 1.5,7,9, 10 & 137
	13		
Blofield	Cantley	Crown agent	1.94
	Witton	Crown agent	1.101
Clavering	Hales (D) (rt)	Tenant-in-chief	9.104
	Toft Monks	Crown agent	1.230 & 238

Hundred	Place	Status	Reference
Depwade	Hapton (D)	Tenant-in-chief	9.218
	Hardwick (rt)	Tenant-in-chief	9.98
	Hempnall (D)	Tenant-in-chief	9.101
Diss	Tivetshall (D)	Crown agent	1.173
Earsham	Starston (D)	Tenant-in-chief & Crown agent	9.167; 1.130 & 223
North Erpingham	Antingham	Tenant-in-chief	9.149 & 150; ruined church.
	Felbrigg	Tenant-in-chief	9.146
	Suffield	Tenant-in-chief	9.149
	Thorpe Market (D)		Tenant-in-chief in **Roughton (rt)**.
South Erpingham	Calthorpe (D)	Tenant-in-chief	9.87
	Stratton Strawless	Crown agent	1.57
	Wolterton (D)		Tenant-in-chief in Calthorpe; Crown agent in **Wickmere (rt)** & Mannington.
Eynsford	Lyng		[Four miles from Swannington.]
	Morton on the Hill		[Post-Domesday community.]
	Swannington		Crown agent in **Brandiston (rt)** & Witchingham.
East Flegg	Ormesby St. Margaret	Tenant-in-chief & Crown agent	9.16 & 1.59
West Flegg	Burgh St. Margaret	Tenant-in-chief & Crown agent	9.18 & 157; 1.165
Happing	Sea Palling	Tenant-in-chief & Crown agent	9.182 & 1.200
Henstead	Rockland St. Mary (D)	Tenant-in-chief & Crown agent	9.27. Scant remains of St. Margaret's church very close to parish church of St. Mary.
Holt	Cley	Crown agent	1.19

Hundred	Place	Role	Notes
Loddon	Hardley		Tenant-in-chief in **Heckingham (rt)**.
	Kirstead (D)		Tenant-in-chief in Seething & Crown agent in Mundham.
	Seething (D) (rt)	Tenant-in-chief & Crown agent	9.25 & 51; 1.230 – joint dedication to St. Margaret & St. Remigius (al. Remi).
	Topcroft		Tenant-in-chief in Fritton. Hempnall & **Woodton (rt)** – also, Crown agent in last named.
Mitford	Garveston (D)		Tenant-in-chief in Yaxham & Crown agent in Runhall.
Norwich	Norwich (D)	Crown agent for the city	Based in Norwich Castle.
Taverham	**Catton (rt)**		Close to Norwich; Crown agent in Sprowston.
	Drayton (D)		Close to Norwich; Crown agent, **Taverham vill (rt)**.
	Felthorpe	Crown agent	1.56
	Sprowston	Crown agent	1.188 & 234
Tunstead	Paston (D)		[Two miles from Witton.]
	Witton (D) (rt)	Crown agent	1.196
Walsham	Upton	Crown agent	1.154
	37		
Blackbourn & Bradmere	Wattisfield (D)		[Three-four miles from Westhorpe.]
Cosford	Whatfield	Tenant-in-chief	7.2
Risbridge	Cowlinge (D)		[Two miles from Stradishall.]
	Stradishall (D)		[Two miles from Cowlinge.]
	4		
Bishop's (Hoxne)	Southolt		[Post-Domesday community.]
Blything	Heveningham (D)	Tenant-in-chief	7.13 (chaplain, Ansketel, a sub-tenant) & 7.27

Hundred	Place	Status	Notes
	Leiston (D)		Tenant-in-chief in Knodishall.
	Linstead Parva		Tenant-in-chief in Chediston.
	Reydon (D)		Crown agent in Covehithe.
	Stoven (rt)	Tenant-in-chief	7.22
Hartismere	Rishangles (D)		Crown agent in Stoke Ash & Wetheringsett.
	Thrandeston (D)		Tenant-in-chief (& Crown agent) in Brome.
	Westhorpe		Crown agent in Cotton, Gislingham & Wyverstone.
Ipswich	Ipswich (D)	Crown agent in the borough	1.116, 122a-d & 122f-g
Lothing (Mutford)	Pakefield (D)	Crown agent	1.27; church of All Saints & St. Margaret, once two separate entities.
Lothingland	Herringfleet (rt)	Crown agent	1.60
	Hopton	Crown agent	1.51
	Lowestoft	Crown agent	1.33
Samford	Chattisham	Crown agent	1.106; church of All Saints & St. Margaret.
Wangford	Ilketshall (rt) (D)		Crown agent in **Bungay (rt)**.
	Sotterley (D)		Tenant-in-chief (& Crown agent) in Shadingfield,
	South Elmham St. Margaret (D)		Crown agent in Bungay.
Wilford	Shottisham (D)		[Held by Walter the Crossbowman, under Robert Malet.]
	19		

Table details

- In the fourth column, the first digit in reference numbers cited indicates estates held by Roger Bigot, as tenant-in-chief, in Norfolk (9) and Suffolk (7). The number 1 identifies Crown estates – William I being principal land-holder in the country, from whom all land was held by vassals of varying degree.

- The use of bold font and added **(rt)** indicates round-tower churches, as previously. There is one church recorded in Domesday for the Wangford community of Ilketshall (later to be defined as four separate settlements), and it is more likely to have been that of St. Andrew rather than St. Margaret. Both churches have round towers.

- South Elmham, with its seven communities and seven unnamed Domesday churches, is even more complex in structure. It has one round-tower church – that of All Saints.

- The symbol (D) following 34 place-names above indicates that the community had a church (or churches) recorded in Domesday. There is no way of knowing what the dedications were.

- Suffolk, with 14 out of 23 "St. Margaret" communities (61%) having a place of worship in 1086, has a higher rate of church presence at that time than Norfolk with its 20 out of 50 (40%) – a fact reflected in the respective overall number of churches recorded for each county in the Domesday Survey itself.

- Norwich and Ipswich each had a number of named churches referred to in Domesday (seven and eleven, respectively), but St. Margaret is not to be found among them.

- There is, however, a reference to a church of St. Margaret in Thetford at Domesday – one of four named foundations attached to what was seemingly the minster-church of St. Mary (1.69). Given Roger Bigod's connection with the Benedictine monastery of St. George (1.70), also located in Thetford (as a cell to Bury), it is not beyond the bounds of possibility that the dedication might have been the result of his influence.

- According to the Internet site, *Church of England Saint Dedications*, there are 235 churches in England which are dedicated to St. Margaret. Norfolk and Suffolk, taken together, therefore account for 30% of the total (at 20% and 10%, respectively). Lincolnshire and Essex also have noticeable numbers of the same dedication at around 20 and 15 respectively. Thus, the overall total of 105 or so for the four counties shows a concentration in Eastern England.

- Roger Bigot (ob. 1107) may have fought at Hastings as a young man. As Sheriff of Norfolk and Suffolk, he held extensive estates in both counties (especially the former), with a pronounced presence in the eastern half of Norfolk and the north-eastern sector of Suffolk.

- As overlord of his own estates and supervisor of those of the Crown, he may have influenced the founding and naming of churches in 30 out of 48 Norfolk communities (63%) and in 9 out of 23 Suffolk ones (39%). Hilborough is not included in the Norfolk figures, as the St. Margaret dedication related to a chapel founded in 1207.

- Further influence on his part is theoretically possibly in communities not directly under his supervision but which were located close to vills with which he had a connection, either in the same hundred or in adjacent ones. These have been indicated in the final column, together with information as to whether he held land or acted on behalf of the Crown. There are 13 such places listed for Norfolk and 9 for Suffolk, and if adjustments are made to suggest this presence as a potential founding/naming influence, overall figures for the two counties increase to 90% and 78%. No means exist of determining his pattern of visiting the estates under his charge, or of attending hundred- or shire-court sessions. Nor, for that matter, of the use he must have made of surrogates in order to exercise effective scrutiny and control of the many, many holdings under his jurisdiction.

- "Concentration" is probably too strong a word to use, suggesting as it may considerable numbers, but both Norfolk and Suffolk have areas in which the incidence of St. Margaret dedications is more pronounced than in other parts. The diagonally aligned hundreds of North Erpingham, South Erpingham and Eynsford have 10 of the eastern sector of the county's total of 36, while Blofield and Taverham (near Norwich – Roger Bigot's power-base) have 6 and Clavering, Loddon and Depwade a further 9 – adding up to 25 in all. In the western half, Launditch (next to Eynsford) has 3 of that sector's total of 13, as does Brothercross (next to Launditch). In Suffolk, the north-eastern part of the county (nearest to Norwich and consisting of the hundreds of Lothingland, Lothing, Wangford and Blything) has 12 altogether, which needs to be reduced to 11 following the omission of Leiston from the reckoning, because it lies so much further to the south in the last-named jurisdiction and is therefore very much "out of area". Thus, the remotest corner (to coin a phrase) has more than half of East Suffolk's total of 19, of which 3 more are to be found in Hartismere. West Suffolk, at 4, has few churches dedicated to Margaret and, of these, 2 are located in Risbridge.

- The correlation of St. Margaret dedications with communities connected with Bigot is sufficiently pronounced to suggest at least a possible influence on his part in their origins and naming.

- There were probably few dedications to St. Margaret at the time of Domesday. Therefore, most of the thirty-one churches recorded then are likely to have been re-named at some point after the survey had taken place – a change possibly accompanying reconstruction of the buildings.

- Carole Hill, 'Leave my Virginity Alone – The Cult of St. Margaret of Antioch in Norwich: In Pursuit of a Pragmatic Piety', in C. Harper-Bill (ed.), *Medieval East Anglia* (Woodbridge, 2005), pp. 225-45, gives a most interesting account of the saint's function as a talisman for women in the matter of sexual behaviour, pregnancy and childbirth, during the late medieval period. She also cites (on p. 239) a total of 48 parish churches or ruins dedicated to St. Margaret in Norwich Diocese, using the Diocesan Board of Finance's *Directory* for the year 2000 as source. The writer of this book suggests an overall number of 51, omitting Hilborough wayside chapel and Wereham (Ely Diocese) and including Lothingland Deanery's Herringfleet, Hopton-on-Sea, Lowestoft and Pakefield – the extreme north-eastern corner of Suffolk not forming part of the Diocese of St. Edmundsbury & Ipswich.

Table 25. Medieval Churches in Norfolk and Suffolk (St. Edmund)

Hundred	Community	Comments
Clackclose	Downham Market	Mainly freemen, under different lords (1086).
Freebridge	Emneth	Post-Domesday community (Pipe Rolls, 1170).
	(North) Lynn	Various freemen under different lords (1066 & 1086).
North Greenhoe	Egmere	Ruined church; diocesan manor of 360 acres (1066 & 1086).
South Greenhoe	Foulden	Ruined remains; 24 freemen held 720 acres (1066 & 1086).
Launditch	Horningtoft	Largely freemen, under control of Godric the Steward (1086).
Thetford	Thetford (D)	Comparative proximity to Bury and its abbey.
	7	
Blofield	South Burlingham (D)	Royal freemen under sub-tenancy of William of Noyers (1086).
	Southwood	Ruined remains; freemen, under control of Drogo of Beuvrières (1086).

East Flegg	(West) Caister	Tower ruins; royal freemen and St. Benet's Abbey manor (1066 & 1086).
West Flegg	Thurne	Freemen, mainly under control of St. Benet's Abbey (1066 & 1086).
Forehoe	Costessey	Substantial manor; tenant-in-chief, Count Alan of Brittany (1086).
Henstead	Caistor St. Edmund (D)	Bury Abbey manor (1066 & 1086).
Holt	Swanton Novers	Thetford Diocese estate; outlier to Hindolveston (1066 &1086).
Humbleyard	Markshall (D)	Now part of Caistor St. Edmund; freeman manor (240 acres) in 1066.
Norwich	Norwich (D)	Redundant church, currently serving as a pregnancy counselling and advice centre.
Taverham	**Taverham (rt)** (D)	Mixed types of holding under different lords – some freemen (1086).
Walsham	**Acle (rt)**	Royal manor of 600 acres + 4-man freeholding (1086).
	11	
Babergh	Assington (D)	960-acre manor, with thegn Siward of Maldon as lord (1066).
Thingoe	Hargrave (D)	480-acre manor, held by freewoman Aethelgyth (1066).
	2	
Blything	Southwold	Bury Abbey manor of 120 acres (1066 & 1086).
Lothing (Mutford)	Kessingland	240-acre manor & 360-acre holding held by 40 freemen (1066 & 1086).
Lothingland	**Fritton (rt)**	6 royal freemen, of varying status and holdings (1066 & 1086).
Wilford	Bromeswell (D)	Numerous freemen under Robert Malet (1086) & Ely Abbey (1066 & 86).
	4	

Table details

- The use of bold font and added **(rt)** indicates round-tower churches, as previously.

- The symbol (D) indicates that a church (or churches) was recorded in Domesday – dedication probably to Edmund then, but not known for certain.

- The matter of why there were comparatively few churches dedicated to Edmund, in his former realm, may lead to speculation – as might the fact that Norfolk had three times as many as Suffolk. Major Danish incursions of the mid-late 9th century (Edmund was slain in battle by Hingwar's forces in the year 869), and the establishment thereafter of the Danelaw, must have had a long and disruptive effect on the established Christian Church of the day. Not only would existing individual churches have disappeared, but few (if any) new ones been founded. By the time of full religious revival, from the later 10th century onwards, Edmund's memory may well have receded in people's minds and other, more fashionable dedications been available for adoption.

- His cult was firmly centred on the great abbey at Bury (Bædericeswyrð/ Beodericsworth) – both it and the town being named in honour of him.

- An earlier, canonized king of East Anglia, Ethelbert (Æthelberht) – murdered in Herefordshire in 794, for dynastic reasons, on the orders of Offa of Mercia – had twelve dedications: eight in Norfolk (Alby, Burnham Ulph, East Wretham, Herringby, Larling, Mundham, Norwich and Thurton) and four in Suffolk (Herringswell, Hessett, Falkenham and Tannington). Again, the Norfolk superiority in numbers is noticeable.

Select Bibliography

Text-related and relevant further reading

Amor, N.R., 'Late Medieval Enclosure: a Study of Thorney, near Stowmarket, Suffolk', in *Proceedings of the Suffolk Institute of Archaeology and History*, XLI (2) (2006), 175-97.

Ashwin, T., and Davison, A. (eds.), *An Historical Atlas of Norfolk*, 3rd ed. (Chichester, 2005).

Barringer, C., 'Norfolk Hundreds', in *Historical Atlas of Norfolk*, 3rd ed., 96-7.

Batcock, N., 'Medieval Churches in Use and in Ruins', in *Historical Atlas of Norfolk*, 3rd ed., 58-9.

Bede, The Venerable, *A History of the English Church and People* – translated by L. Shirley-Price & revised by R.E. Latham – Penguin Classics series (London, 1968).

Blair, J., *The Church in Anglo-Saxon Society* (Oxford, 2005).

Briggs, K., *Anglo-Saxon Dithematic Names* (Online resource, 2013).

Brown, P. (ed.), *Domesday Book: Norfolk*, vols. 1 & 2 (Chichester, 1984).

Butcher, D., *The Island of Lothingland: a Domesday & Hundred Roll Handbook* (Lowestoft, 2012).

The Half-hundred of Mutford: Domesday Analysis & Medieval Exploration (Lowestoft, 2013).

Medieval Lowestoft: the Origins and Growth of a Suffolk Coastal Town (Woodbridge, 2016).

Cautley, H.M., *Norfolk Churches* (Ipswich, 1949).

Suffolk Churches and Their Treasures, 3rd ed. (Ipswich, 1954).

Celebi, C.L., 'Conquest, Colonization and Cultural Change in Eastern

Suffolk' (unpub. M.A. thesis, Bilkent University, Ankara, 2002) – pdf available online.

Copinger, W.A. (ed.), *The Manors of Suffolk*, vol. 5 (Manchester, 1909).

Cox, the Revd. J., 'Ecclesiastical History', in W. Page (ed.), *The Victoria County History of Suffolk*, vol. 2 (London, 1907), 1-52.

Darby, H.C., *The Domesday Geography of Eastern England*, 3rd ed. (Cambridge 1971).

Domesday England (Cambridge, 1977).

Dymond, D., *The Norfolk Landscape* (London, 1985).

Dymond, D., and Martin, E. (eds.), *An Historical Atlas of Suffolk*, 2nd ed. (Ipswich, 1989).

Ekwall, E., *The Oxford Dictionary of English Place-Names*, 4th ed. (Oxford, 1960).

Ellis, Sir H., *A General Introduction to Domesday Book* (London, 1833).

Fellows-Jensen, G., 'Scandinavian Settlement Names in East Anglia: Some Problems', in *Nomina*, 22 (1999), 45-59.

Finn, R.W., *Domesday Studies: the Eastern Counties* (London, 1967).

Fryde, E.B., Greenway, D.E., Porter, S. & Roy. I. (eds.), *Handbook of British Chronology*, 3rd ed. (London, 1986).

Gallagher, E.J., *The Civil Pleas of the Suffolk Eyre of 1240*, Suffolk Records Society, vol. LII (Woodbridge, 2009).

Gittos, H., *Liturgy, Architecture and Sacred Places in Anglo-Saxon England* (Oxford, 2013).

Godfrey, M., 'The Churches, Settlements and Archaeology of Early Medieval Norfolk' (unpub. PhD thesis, University of Leicester, 2007) – pdf available online.

Goode, W.J., *East Anglian Round Towers and Their Churches* (Lowestoft, 1982).

Hart, S., *The Round Tower Churches of England* (Thorndon, 2003).

Hervey, J.W.N. (ed.), *The Hundred Rolls and Extracts Therefrom: Made by Authority, Second Edward I, County of Suffolk, Lothingland* (Ipswich, 1902).

Heywood, S.,   'The Round Towers of East Anglia', in J. Blair (ed.), *Minsters and Parish Churches: the Local Church in Transition* (Oxford, 1988), 169-77.

'Round-Towered Churches', in *Historical Atlas of Norfolk*, 3rd ed., 60-1.

Hill, C.,   'Leave my Virginity Alone – the Cult of St. Margaret of Antioch in Norwich: in Pursuit of a Pragmatic Piety', in C. Harper-Bill (ed.), *Medieval East Anglia* (Woodbridge, 2005), 225-45.

Hoggett, R.,   'Changing Beliefs: the Archaeology of the East Anglian Conversion' (unpub. PhD thesis, University of East Anglia, 2007) – pdf available online.

'The Early Christian Landscape of East Anglia', in N.J. Higham & M.J. Ryan (eds.), *The Landscape Archaeology of Anglo–Saxon East Anglia* (Woodbridge, 2010), 193-210 – pdf available online.

The Archaeology of the East Anglian Conversion (Woodbridge, 2010).

Hollis, S.,   *Anglo–Saxon Women and the Church: Sharing a Common Fate* (Woodbridge, 1992).

Hunt, J.,   *The Oxford History of the Laws of England*, vol. II (Oxford, 2012).

Keats-Rohan, K.S.B., *Domesday People: a Prosopography of Persons Occurring in English Documents, 1066-1166*, vol. 1 (Woodbridge, 1999).

Knott, S.,   Norfolk Churches (Internet resource: www.norfolkchurches. co.uk).

Suffolk Churches (Internet resource: www.suffolkchurches. co.uk).

Lees, B.A.,   'Introduction to the Suffolk Domesday', in W. Page (ed.), *The Victoria County History of Suffolk*, vol. 1 (London, 1911), 357-

582.

Marten, L.   'The Rebellion of 1075', in C. Harper-Bill (ed.), *Medieval East Anglia* (Woodbridge, 2005), 168-82.

Martin, E.,   'Hundreds and Liberties', in *Historical Atlas of Suffolk*, 2nd ed., 18-9.

Maxwell Lyte, H.S. (ed.), *Liber Feodorum*, vol. 1 (London, 1920).

Molyneaux, G., *The Formation of the English Kingdom in the Tenth Century* (Oxford, 2015).

Moorman, J.R.H., *A History of the Church in England*, 3rd ed. (London, 1973).

Mortlock, D.P., and Roberts, C.V., *The Popular Guide to Norfolk Churches*, vols. 1, 2 & 3 (Cambridge, 1985).

Mortlock, D.P., *The Popular Guide to Suffolk Churches*, vols. 1, 2 & 3 (Cambridge, 1988).

Norwich Diocesan Board of Finance, *Diocesan Directory* (Norwich, 2000).

Pestell, T.,   *Landscapes of Monastic Foundation: the Establishment of Religious houses in East Anglia, c. 650-1200* (Woodbridge, 2004).

    'Monasteries', in *Historical Atlas of Norfolk*, 3rd ed., 66-7.

Pevsner, N. (ed.), *The Buildings of England: North-West and South Norfolk*, 2nd reprint (London, 1973).

    The Buildings of England: North-East Norfolk and Norwich, 2nd reprint (London, 1973).

    The Buildings of England: Suffolk, 2nd ed. (London, 1974).

Roffe, D.,   *Decoding Domesday* (Woodbridge, 2007).

Rumble, A. (ed.), *Domesday Book: Suffolk*, vols. 1 & 2 (Chichester, 1986).

Rye, W. (ed.). *A Calendar of the Feet of Fines for Suffolk* (Ipswich, 1900).

Scarfe, N.,   *The Suffolk Landscape* (London, 1972).

    Suffolk in the Middle Ages (Woodbridge, 1986).

'Domesday Settlements and Churches: the Example of Colneis Hundred', in *Historical Atlas of Suffolk*, 2nd ed., 42-3.

Stamp, A.E. (ed.), *Calendar of Close Rolls, Henry III*, vol. 9 (London, 1931).

Stather Hunt, B.P.W., *Flinten History*, 7th ed. (Lowestoft, 1953).

Stenton, F.M, *Anglo-Saxon England*, 3rd ed. (Oxford, 1971).

Suckling, A.,   *The History and Antiquities of the County of Suffolk*, vol. 1 (London, 1846).

Wade, K.,   'Later Anglo-Saxon Suffolk', in *Historical Atlas of Suffolk*, 2nd ed., 38-9.

Ward, J.C.,   'The Honour of Clare in Suffolk in the Early Middle Ages', in *Proceedings of the Suffolk Institute of Archaeology and History*, XXX (1) (1964), 94-111.

Wareham, A.,   *Lords and Communities in Early Medieval East Anglia* (Woodbridge, 2005).

Warner, P.,   'Blything Hundred: a Study in the Development of Settlement, AD 400-1400' (unpub. PhD thesis, University of Leicester, 1982) – pdf available online.

'Shared Churchyards, Freemen Church Builders and the Development of Parishes in Eleventh Century East Anglia', in *Landscape History*, 8 (1986), 39-52.

The Origins of Suffolk (Manchester, 1996).

Williamson, T., *The Origins of Norfolk* (Manchester, 1993).

Index

Norfolk

Settlements with churches

Settlements with priest only

Suffolk

Settlements with churches

Settlements with priest only

Hundreds (West)

Hundreds (East)

Lothing Half-hundred (main references)

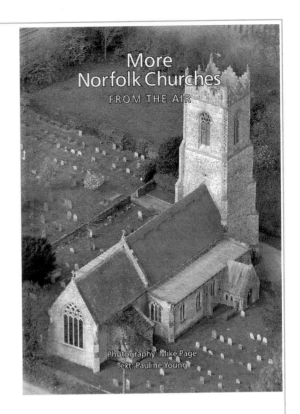
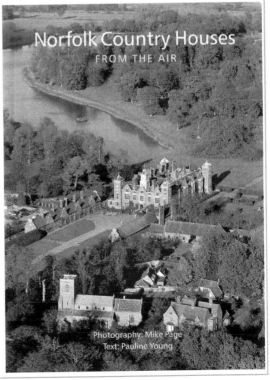

38728347R00208

Printed in Poland
by Amazon Fulfillment
Poland Sp. z o.o., Wrocław